The Firstborn Son in Ancient Judaism and Early Christianity

Biblical Interpretation Series

VOLUME 171

The titles published in this series are listed at *brill.com/bins*

The Firstborn Son in Ancient Judaism and Early Christianity

A Study of Primogeniture and Christology

By

Kyu Seop Kim

BRILL

LEIDEN | BOSTON

The Library of Congress Cataloging-in-Publication Data is available online at http://catalog.loc.gov

Typeface for the Latin, Greek, and Cyrillic scripts: "Brill". See and download: brill.com/brill-typeface.

ISSN 0928-0731
ISBN 978-90-04-39492-6 (hardback)
ISBN 978-90-04-39494-0 (e-book)

This book is printed on acid-free paper and produced in a sustainable manner.

Contents

Acknowledgements

This monograph is a revised version of my doctoral thesis, submitted to the University of Aberdeen in 2015. First of all, special thanks go to Dr. Andrew D. Clarke, my *Doktorvater*, whose careful reading and insightful guidance helped me to avoid many errors and inconsistencies which would otherwise have entered the work. Working with him was such a pleasure to me, as he gave me liberty to explore my ideas, while he also thoroughly read my thesis, and gave me insightful advice throughout my Ph.D. study.

I must also record thanks to my examiners of the original thesis, Dr. Jutta Leonhardt-Balzer (Aberdeen) and Dr. David M. Moffitt (St. Andrews), whose criticisms and suggestions were constructive. I also learned a number of things from their excellent monographs and articles on Philo and Hebrews in writing my doctoral thesis. Dialogues with Prof. Steve Mason and Dr. Tomas Bokedal have been always helpful for my work, and I would also like to express my gratitude to them. Remaining deficiencies are of course my own.

I am deeply grateful to Prof. Paul N. Anderson, NT Editor in Chief, and to an anonymous reviewer for accepting my work for the Brill Biblical Interpretation Series and for their encouraging and insightful comments. I would also like to express my gratitude to Ms. Liesbeth Hugenholtz, Brill acquisitions editor, for her kind help. My gratitude also goes to Prof. David Bossman and Prof. Zeba Crook, editors of the journal, *Biblical Theology Bulletin*. I cannot forget their warm encouragement and kind help shown during publishing my first ever academic article in their journal.

I wish to express my thanks to my Korean teachers who taught me at Chongshin Theological Seminary: Prof. Sang-Hoon Kim, Prof. Han-Soo Lee, Prof. Ezra Sang-Beob Shim, Prof. Cheon-Seol Han, Prof. Hyeon Woo Shin, Prof. Hyung Dae Park, Prof. Chang-Wook Chung and Prof. Sangil Lee. In particular, Prof. Sang Hoon Kim and Prof. Ezra Sang-Beob Shim's scholarship and lives have been models for my study and faith. This work could not be completed without their warm encouragement and advice.

My special thanks are also due to my Calvin teachers: Prof. Jeffrey A.D. Weima, Prof. Arie Leder and Prof. Mariano Avila; and also to my Aberdeen doctoral colleagues: Dr. Erlend Macgilivray, Dr. Bernard Leung, Dr. Andrew Keuer, Dr. Chun-Goo Kang, Dr. Kendall Cleveland, Dr. Jung-Jin Kim and Dr. Sang-Hoon Lee. Drs. Cleveland and Lee read a part of this work and gave me very helpful comments. My thanks also go to Prof. Kyoung-Shik Kim, Prof. Yoon-Man Park, Prof. Jaecheon Cho, and Prof. B. Hoon Woo. I must also thank Prof. Ju Hur and Prof. Sungkook Jung for showing wonderful models in teaching and scholarship. Other individuals to whom I am indebted are Rev. Jung-Ho Choi, Dr. Scott J. Hodges, Mrs. Ji-Sun Han, Mrs. Myonghwa Yu, and Rev. David Chang. Rev. Jung-Ho Choi always gave me warm encouragement to finish my doctoral course. Dr. Scott Hodges also generously gave me a great help in my time of need. Mrs. Ji-Sun Han was my student when I had my first ever teaching career at Daeshin University, and she gave me some useful advice and warm encouragement about my teaching. I also owe a debt of gratitude to Mrs. Myonghwa Yu and Rev. David Chang for their gracious advice and encouragement. I am also thankful to all of my students whom I met at Chongshin University, Daeshin University, Torch Trinity Theological University and Asia United Theological University.

I was supported in this endeavour by a number of communities. I am very grateful for the financial assistance from Sung-yak Church (Rev. Gil-Woong Yeon), Yullin church (Rev. Nam Joon Kim), my parents-in-law (Mr. Sung-Gwa Jung and Mrs. Myung-Sook Kim), my aunt-in-law (Mrs. Young-Sook Kim) and my mother (Mrs. Young-Shin Park). This monograph is dedicated to my children, Hayoon and Yeji for the love they showed to me as we laboured through this project. Εὐχαριστῶ τῷ θεῷ μου ἐπὶ πάσῃ τῇ μνείᾳ ὑμῶν. This book is also dedicated to my wife, Han-Na Jung, and I wish to express my loving appreciation to her. I would not have finished this work if it had not been for her sincere sacrifice and love. Finally, I give thanks to God.

Οὐ μόνον δέ, ἀλλὰ καὶ καυχώμεθα ἐν ταῖς θλίψεσιν, εἰδότες ὅτι ἡ θλῖψις ὑπομονὴν κατεργάζεται, ἡ δὲ ὑπομονὴ δοκιμήν, ἡ δὲ δοκιμὴ ἐλπίδα (Rom 5:3–4).

Kyu Seop Kim
October 2018
Yangpyeong, South Korea

Abbreviations

This work follows the abbreviations set out in Patrick H. Alexander, John F. Kutsko, James D. Ernest and Shirley A. Decker-Lucke, eds., *The SBL Handbook of Style: For Ancient Near Eastern, Biblical, and Early Christian Studies* (Peabody: Hendrickson, 1999). Some abbreviations which are not covered by the above include the following:

AGRL	Aspects of Greek and Roman Life Series
AYBRL	Anchor Yale Reference Library
BECNT	Baker Exegetical Commentary on the New Testament
BibInt	Biblical Interpretation Series
BS	Biblical Seminar
BU	Biblische Untersuchungen
CCS	Cambridge Classical Studies
CH	Collectanea Hellenistica
CollBibComm	Collegeville Bible Commentary
CSPESPT	Cambridge Studies in Population, Economy and Society in Past Time
ECC	Early Christianity in Context
ECCSeries	Eerdmans Critical Commentary Series
ECDCC	Eerdmans Commentaries on the Dead Sea Scrolls
EGRA	Enzyklopädie der griechisch-römischen Antike
EuroHoch	Europäische Hochschulschriften
FJTC	Flavius Josephus: Translation and Commentary Series
GAP	Guides to the Apocrypha and Pseudepigrapha
GeiLeb	*Geist und Leben*
HCOT	Historical Commentary on the Old Testament
HCS	Hellenistic Culture and Society Series
Hesperia	*Hesperia: The Journal of the American School of Classical Studies at Athens*
Historia	*Historia: Zeitschrift für Alte Geschichte*
HThKAT	Herders theologischer Kommentar zum Alten Testament
JAR	*Journal of Anthropological Research*
JBS	Jerusalem Biblical Studies
JBTR	*Journal of Biblical Text Research*
JCC	Jewish Culture and Contexts
JFH	*Journal of Family History*
JSJSup	Supplements to Journal for the Study of Judaism
KI	Routledge Key Ideas Series

LNTS	Library of New Testament Studies
LSTS	Library of Second Temple Studies
MnemosyneSup	Supplements to Mnemosyne: A Journal of Classical Studies
NCCS	New Covenant Commentary Series
PA	Philosophia Antiqua
Paideia	Paideia Commentaries on the New Testament
PBM	Paternoster Biblical Monograph Series
PNTC	Pillar New Testament Commentary
PTMSeries	Princeton Theological Monograph Series
SAPERE	Scripta Antiquitatis Posterioris ad Ethicam Religionemque pertinentia
SPA	Studies in Philo of Alexandria
SPhiloM	Studia Philonica Monographs
StBibTh	*Studia Biblica et Theologica*
TLJS	Taubman Lectures in Jewish Studies
USFISFCJ	University of South Florida International Studies in Formative Christianity and Judaism

CHAPTER 1

Introduction

1.1 Status Quaestionis

This study aims to investigate the meaning and the origin of the term πρωτότοκος in ancient Judaism and early Christianity. The title of πρωτότοκος in the NT was a *crux interpretum* and a constant source of headache to the early church. Arius of Alexandria understood "the firstborn son of every creature" in Col 1:15 as "the first created being,"[1] and his interpretation triggered one of the most contentious debates surrounding the person of Christ in the early Christian church.

As Harold Attridge states, it is still unclear where the designation of Christ as the firstborn son originated.[2] Despite its potential significance, the concept of the firstborn son has not as yet been a major research focus of NT Christology

1 E.g., Arius of Alexandria states, "Εἰ πρωτότοκός ἐστι πάσης κτίσεως, δῆλον ὅτι καὶ αὐτὸς εἷς ἐστιν τῆς κτίσεως" in Athanasius, *Orationes*, 2.63. The Arius-Athanasius debates are also deeply related to the Fourth Gospel. For the Arius-Athanasius debates surrounding the Gospel of John, see Paul N. Anderson, *The Christology of the Fourth Gospel: Its Unity and Disunity in the Light of John 6* (WUNT II/78; Mohr Siebeck: Tübingen, 1996), 1–2. Basil of Caesarea interprets the firstborn son of all creation (Col 1:15) and the firstborn son among many brothers (Rom 8:29) in terms of Matt 12:48–50: "the Lord gives the designation 'his own mother and brothers' to those who come into affinity with him by the works of virtue" (*Agains Eunomius*, 2.23; the translation taken from Mark Delcogliano and Andrew Radde-Gallwitz, tran., *St. Basil of Caesarea: Against Eunomius* (Washington: The Catholic University of America Press, 2011), 165). John Chrysostom states that Paul's designation of Christ as the firstborn son in Rom 8:29 implies the incarnation of Christ, while "the firstborn son among many brothers" in Rom 8:29 is linked with the motif of resurrection and new birth by Gregory of Nyssa ("the firstborn son of those spiritually born again"); John Chrysostom, *Homilies on Romans*, 15.453; Grecory of Nyssa, *Against Eunomius*, 2.8. Origen views "the firstborn son among many brothers" in Rom 8:29 as the pre-eminent status among those who are conformed to the image of the son of God (Origen, *Commentary on Romans*, 7.6). Cyril of Alexandria interprets Heb 1:6 that "the only-begotten became the firstborn when he appeared as a man like us," while "the firstborn son from the dead" in Col 1:18 refers to the first resurrected one (*The Twelve Chapters*, 12.31). See Norman Russell, trans., *Cyril of Alexandria* (London: Routledge, 2000), 186; Cyril of Alexandria, *The Twelve Chapters*, 8.23. Irenaeus of Lyons reads "the firstborn son of the dead" in Rev 1:5 as "the first place over those who are under the earth." Irenaeus of Lyons, *Against Heresies*, 20.2. Thus, there was no agreement on the meaning of πρωτότοκος in the early church.

2 Harold W. Attridge, *The Epistle to the Hebrews: A Commentary on the Epistle to the Hebrews* (Hermeneia, Philadelphia: Fortress, 1989), 56.

 | DOI:10.1163/9789004394940_002

in current scholarship.[3] Why did the early Christians confess that Christ is πρωτότοκος? What did the title of πρωτότοκος mean in ancient Judaism and early Christianity? This study will begin with a brief review of recent interpretations on the firstborn son in the NT.

1.1.1 *Review of Literature*

1.1.1.1 Πρωτότοκον ἐν πολλοῖς ἀδελφοῖς in Rom 8:29

Contemporary scholarly research has principally interpreted the term πρωτότοκος in Rom 8:29 using the following two perspectives: 1) the eldest brother as a *Vorbild*; and 2) the Davidic Messiah.[4] The latter view interprets πρωτότοκος in terms of a Davidic ruler who is designated as the firstborn son in Ps 89:27. The former view presupposes that πρωτότοκος in Rom 8:29 symbolises the first member of the family of God or the one who should be imitated as

---

3 Among major Christological researches, the studies which do not draw specific attention to the concept of the firstborn son include Frank Matera, *New Testament Christology* (Louisville: WJK, 1999); Richard N. Longenecker, *The Christology of Early Jewish Christianity* (London: SCM, 1970); Raymond E. Brown, *An Introduction to New Testament Christology* (New York: Paulist, 1994); Christopher M. Tuckett, *Christology and the New Testament* (Louisville: WJK, 2001); C.F.D. Moule, *The Origin of Christology* (Cambridge: Cambridge University Press, 1977); Scott Gambrill Sinclair, *Jesus Christ according to Paul: The Christologies of Paul's Undisputed Epistles and The Christology of Paul* (Berkeley: Bibal, 1988); Joseph A. Fitzmyer, "The Christology of the Epistle to the Romans," in *The Future of Christology: Essays in Honor of Leander E. Keck* (eds. A. Malherbe and W. Meeks; Minneapolis: Fortress, 1993), 81–90; Ferdinand Hahn, *The Titles of Jesus in Christology: Their History in Early Christianity* (trans. H. Knight and G. Ogg; London: Lutterworth, 1969); Maurice Casey, *From Jewish Prophet to Gentile God: The Origins and Development of New Testament Christology* (Cambridge: James Clark & Co, 1991); Paula Fredriksen, *From Jesus to Christ: The Origins of the New Testament Images of Jesus* (New Haven: Yale University Press, 1988); Jerome H. Neyrey, *Christ is Community: The Christologies of the New Testament* (Wilmington: Michael Glazier, 1985); Hans-Joachim Eckstein, *Kyrios Jesus: Perspektiven einer christologischen Theologie* (Neukirchen-Vluyn: Neukirchener Verlag, 2011); Martin Karrer, *Jesus Christus im Neuen Testament* (NTD 11; Göttingen: Vandenhoeck & Ruprecht, 1998); Riemer Roukema, *Jesus, Gnosis and Dogma* (London: T&T Clark, 2010); I. Howard Marshall, *The Origins of New Testament Christology* (Leicester: IVP, 1976); Werner Kramer, *Christos Kyrios Gottessohn* (AbThANT 44; Zürich: Zwingli, 1963).

4 Exceptionally, Thomas Schreiner argues that the firstborn son in Romans 8:29 alludes not merely to the Davidic king, but to Israel's position as the firstborn son. However, he does not provide any more proofs or arguments on its meaning and functions. See Thomas Schreiner, *Romans* (BECNT; Grand Rapids: Baker, 1998), 453–54. Keesmaat considers allusions to Exodus in Romans 8, and views the title of the firstborn son in Rom 8:29 as the Adam motif (the second Adam) and as the title of Israel which originated in Exod 4:22. However, she does not specifically explore the meaning of the firstborn son as the title of Israel. See Sylvia C. Keesmaat, *Paul and His Story: (Re)Interpreting the Exodus Tradition* (JSNTSup 181; Sheffield: Sheffield Academic Press, 1999), 123–24.

πρεσβύτατος (the eldest) by his younger brothers.[5] The two views are sometimes lumped together as Davidic messiah and simultaneously the eldest brother of the believers.

In his monograph, Aasgaard researches sibling relations in the Greco-Roman culture, and investigates the rhetorical functions of and their implications for Paul's sibling language in light of the Greco-Roman familial practices. Aasgaard argues that Christ as the son of God refers to the adopted Messiah as the son of God (i.e., the future-eschatological ruler),[6] and simultaneously he understands the firstborn son in Rom 8:29 in terms of brotherhood in the Greco-Roman family.[7] According to Aasgaard, the firstborn son is a Greco-Roman kinship metaphor.[8] In evidence, the eldest brother exhorts his younger siblings to imitate himself in *4 Macc* 9:23. In *4 Macc* 12:16, the eldest brother also says, "I do not deserve the excellent example of my brothers."[9] In this respect, Aasgaard insists that the firstborn son in Rom 8:29 signifies a model for younger brothers to imitate.[10]

In her monograph, Caroline Hodge attempts to understand Paul's kinship language in terms of the concept of ethnicity, to trace Paul's strategies to construct the Gentile believers' identity through his kinship language, and to consider the Gentile believers' new identity in terms of the concept of a mixed or hybrid ethnic identity. She also writes that the firstborn son in Rom 8:29 should be understood in terms of a kinship structure highlighted in Rom 8. After observing the usage of the firstborn son in the OT and Philonic literature, she concludes that the metaphor of the firstborn son in Rom 8:29 connotes the

5 E.g., Trevor Burke, "The Characteristics of Paul's Adoptive-Sonship (Huiothesia) Motif," *IBS* 17 (1995): 72; Reidar Aasgaard, *"My Beloved Brothers and Sisters": Christian Siblingship in Paul* (ECC; JSNTSup 265; London: T&T Clark, 2004), 144. Daniel von Allmen concludes that the firstborn son in Rom 8:29 refers to the first member of the family of God (i.e., the church) and postulates that the believers became a part of God's family as Christ's siblings. See Daniel von Allmen, *La famille de Dieu: la symbolique familiale dans le paulinisme* (OBO 41; Göttingen: Vandenhoeck & Ruprecht, 1981), 292–93. Byrne also argues that the firstborn title does not denote messianic dignity and "the Israelite 'firstborn' title" cannot be applied to Christ. Rather, the firstborn son refers to the eldest of many brothers, and believers will enjoy what Christ the eldest son hold as the son of God. See Brendan Byrne, *Sons of God—Seed of Abraham* (AnBib 83; Rome: Biblical Institute Press, 1979), 118.

6 Aasgaard, *My Beloved Brothers and Sisters*, 143.

7 Aasgaard, *My Beloved Brothers and Sisters*, 144.

8 Aasgaard, *My Beloved Brothers and Sisters*, 139, 144–45.

9 Aasgaard, *My Beloved Brothers and Sisters*, 76.

10 Aasgaard, *My Beloved Brothers and Sisters*, 145.

kinship relationship between Christ and Gentile Christians.[11] The new descendants, therefore, are conformed to the pattern of the firstborn son.[12]

Klaus Schäfer conducts extensive research on Paul's sibling metaphors in light of Jewish and Greco-Roman concepts of brotherhood, and concludes that Paul's community should be understood in terms of a *Bruderschaft*, not merely familial relations.[13] He also maintains that Christ and his believers in Romans are in a brotherly relationship as illustrated in Heb 2:10–18. In this vein, the firstborn son refers to the eldest brother as a prototype or a leader of his younger brothers. Accordingly, the believers as Christ's siblings participate in the suffering, glorification and sovereignty of Christ.[14]

However, we should note that Paul employs πρωτότοκος (the firstborn son) in Rom 8:29, not πρωτόγονος nor πρεσβύτατος (the eldest one). Πρεσβύτατος (ἀδελφός) is generally used in the sense of the eldest brother in Greco-Roman usage.[15] When the term πρωτότοκος is utilised in Greek literature, it is used as birth language, and is employed in relation to the parents.[16] For example, in *Theaetetus* 151c, Plato writes, "Do not be angry like women as they are deprived of their first offspring (πρωτοτόκοι)." In this citation, πρωτοτόκοι is used in relation to his mother, not to his brothers. In P.Lips. 28 lines 15–16 (= Chr.Mitt. 363; CE 381), some adoptee is addressed as a legitimate and firstborn son (πρωτότοκος), as if he was begotten to the adoptive father as his biological son (ὡς ἐξ ἰδίου αἵματος γεννηθέντα σοι). The term πρωτότοκος in P.Lips. 28 is used in relation to his (adoptive) father, not to his brothers. Accordingly, while πρωτότοκος can refer to the eldest son in a kinship concept, the term πρωτότοκος should not only be considered as the eldest brother, but also as birth language in relation to his parents. Further, contrary to Aasgaard's argument,[17] *4 Macc* 9:23 is not prescriptive for the readers. *4 Macc* 9:23 merely describes what the eldest brother exhorts his younger brothers to do in a specific situation, and does not convey a general principle relating to the role and responsibility as the eldest brother.

11 Caroline J. Hodge, *If Sons, Then Heirs: A Study of Kinship and Ethnicity in the Letters of Paul* (Oxford: Oxford University Press, 2007), 115.

12 Hodge, *If Sons, Then Heirs*, 116.

13 Klaus Schäfer, *Gemeinde als 'Bruderschaft': ein Beitrag zum Kirchenverständnis des Paulus* (EuroHoch 23; Frankfurt am Main: Peter Lang, 1989), 11.

14 Schäfer, *Gemeinde als 'Bruderschaft'*, 63–66.

15 See section 1.2.4.

16 The term πρωτότοκος is also employed as a translation of בכר as a birth language in the LXX (see section 1.2.4).

17 Aasgaard, *My Beloved Brothers and Sisters*, 76.

Moreover, we need to consider that Paul employs a final clause (in order that (εἰς τὸ εἶναι) he may be the firstborn son …), not a causal clause (because he is the firstborn son …). This point is significant, since some exegetes are confused with the function of Rom 8:29b and understand the firstborn son in Rom 8:29 as a prototype.[18] For instance, James G. Samra states,[19] "God's purpose is to conform all believers to the image of Christ … Christ [in Rom 8:29] is the prototype for all who become sons of God after him …" However, the goal in Rom 8:29 is not to be conformed to the image of son of God, but that Christ will be the firstborn son among many brothers. The believers in 8:29 are not conformed to the image because Christ is the firstborn son. Rather, they are conformed to the image *in order that* Christ may be the firstborn son among his brothers. If Paul utilised a causal clause (because he is …), Rom 8:29b could mean that the firstborn son refers to a model to imitate or a pattern to which to conform (συμμόρφους), because Rom 8:29b is the reason for συμμόρφους (8:29a). In other words, the believers would be conformed to the image of the son of God, *because* Christ was the model for his brothers. Yet, we should note the logical sequence in Rom 8:29: "predestined to be conformed to the image of his Son, in order that he may be the firstborn son …" That is, "to be conformed to the image of the son" temporally precedes Christ becoming the firstborn son among many brothers (not the converse).[20] Accordingly, when the believers are conformed to the image of God, Christ will, *then*, be the firstborn son among many brothers in the family of God. Conformity to the image is not the final goal in Rom 8:29. Rather, the final goal is that Christ becomes the firstborn son among many brothers. Therefore, Rom 8:29 does not mean that the believers are conformed to the image of God 'according to the pattern of the eldest brother,' and the grammatical arrangement in Rom 8:29 does not lead the reader to conclude that πρωτότοκος refers to a model or pattern.

18 E.g., Jewett states, "Given the purpose clause at the end of v. 29 … the mission will also serve to fulfill Christ's destiny to restore the image of God to a fallen human race," in Jewett, *Romans*, 529–30. However, what is fulfilled as the purpose in Rom 8:29 is not the restoration of the image of God, but Christ's being the firstborn son among many brothers. For similar cases, see Schäfer, *Gemeinde als 'Bruderschaft'*, 63–66; Schmidt, *Römer*, 152; de Jonge, *Christology in Context*, 120.

19 James G. Samra, *Being Conformed to Christ in Community* (JSNTSup 320; London: T&T Clark, 2007), 98.

20 Rather, the purpose of the predestination is substantialised in Rom 8:29a. See Schreiner, *Romans*, 453.

J.D.G. Dunn also claims that the firstborn son in Rom 8:29 should be read as Christ's Adamic role,[21] and he observes:[22]

> [A]gain the thought is of the resurrected Christ as the pattern of the new humanity of the last age, the firstborn (of the dead) of a new race of eschatological people in whom God's design from the beginning of creation is at last fulfilled … Paul was also probably mindful of the fact that Israel was also called God's 'firstborn' … Here again it is the Adam motif which predominates (beginning a new family of humankind) rather than the thought of Christ's continuity and identity with the divine (as in Wisdom).

Dunn also writes that Christ is "the firstborn of the eschatological family of God,"[23] and "the eldest of a new large family of God."[24] Hans Wilhelm Schmidt also allows for the firstborn son in the sense of Christ's Adamic role (or *Urbild*): "Der Mensch kommt dadurch, daß er dem Urbild des Gottessohnes gleichgestaltet wird, zu seiner Gottesbildlichkeit."[25] Friedrich Gulf postulates that the firstborn son in Rom 8:29 symbolises the chosen as first before the beginning of time and the representative for many (ersten erwählt, vor Beginn der Zeiten,

21 Dunn notes, "Christ's Adamic role as eldest brother in a new family of men begins with his birth from the dead where a share in the lost Adamic glory is finally attained by transformation of our lowly body to be like Christ's resurrection body." See J.D.G. Dunn, *Christology in the making* (SCM: London, 1989), 108. Seyoon Kim states that πρωτότοκος in Rom 8:29 refers to a *Stammvater* of saved humankind in the context of Adam Christology. See Seyoon Kim, *The Origin of Paul's Gospel* (WUNT II/4; Tübingen: Mohr Siebeck, 1981), 264.

22 J.D.G. Dunn, *Romans 1–8* (WBC; Waco: Word, 1988), 484–85.

23 Dunn, *Christology in the making*, 44.

24 Dunn, *Christology in the making*, 37. However, in his commentary on Colossians, he focuses on the relationship between Wisdom and the firstborn son. See J.D.G. Dunn, *The Epistles to the Colossians and to Philemon: A Commentary on the Greek Text* (NIGTC; Grand Rapids: Eerdmans, 1996), 90. "… again the antecedent for use of the word πρωτότοκος ('firstborn') in relation to creation is most obviously Wisdom …" and "The use of πρωτότοκος of the Davidic king in Ps 89:27 (LXX 88:28) or elsewhere of Israel … is less relevant here."

25 Hans Wilhelm Schmidt, *Der Brief des Paulus an die Römer* (THKNT; Berlin: Evangelische Verlagsanstalt Berlin, 1972), 152. For the similar interpretation, see Marinus de Jonge, *Christology in Context* (Philadelphia, Westminster, 1988), 120; Ulrich Wilckens, *Der Brief an die Römer, vol. 2* (EKKNT; Zürich: Benziger, 1980), 164–65; Michael Theobald, *Römerbrief: Kapitel 1–11* (SKKNT 6/1; Stuttgart: Katholisches Bibelwerk, 1992), 247; Ulrich Luz, *Das Geschichtsverständnis des Paulus* (BEvT 49; München: Kaiser, 1968), 251; Jacob Jervell, *Imago Dei: Gen. 1.26f im Spätjudentum, in der Gnosis und in den paulinischen Briefen* (FRLANT 58; Göttingen: Vandenhoeck & Ruprecht, 1960), 275; Ernst Käsemann, *An die Römer* (HNT 8a; Tübingen: Mohr Siebeck, 1973), 234.

stellvertretend für die vielen).[26] However, in the extant Jewish literature, Adam is not addressed as the firstborn son.[27] Further, in Rom 5:14, Adam is τύπος τοῦ μέλλοντος (a type or a pattern prefiguring the one who was to come).[28] As shown above, we have already clarified that the firstborn son in Rom 8:29b does not refer to a model or pattern in terms of the grammatical construction between 8:29a and 8:29b. So, the concept of Adam does not fit well with the context of Rom 8:29.

In support of a messianic view, Gordon Fee argues that πρωτότοκος in Rom 8:29 should be understood as holding the status of a messianic king in Ps 89:27.[29] According to Fee, "the firstborn son" in Ps 89:27–28 refers to the son of God who holds a unique status as an heir and as a ruler.[30] Some interpreters argue that πρωτότοκος in Rom 8:29 is related to the concept of messianic adoption in ancient Judaism. James M. Scott also finds an allusion to Ps 89:27 in Rom 8:29: "It seems, there πρωτότοκος in Rom 8:29c alludes to God's promise that the Davidic Messiah would be adopted as son to rule as chief among other rulers of the world (Ps 89:28)."[31] Mark Forman and Michael Peppard also espouse Scott's view,[32] and link the notion of the firstborn son in Rom 8:29 with the heavenly messiah at the right hand of God in Rom 8:34 (cf. Ps 110:1). Yet, if we presume that the firstborn son in Rom 8:29 is a messianic title, it makes it difficult to understand the relationship between "the firstborn son" and "among many brothers" in Rom 8:29b. We are not aware of a Jewish concept which directly indicates that a messianic figure is the eldest son (or brother) of the people of God.[33] In Rom 8:29, "among many brothers" modifies "the

26 Friedrich Gulf, "'Der Erstgeborene unter vielen Brüdern' (Rom 8,29)," *GeiLeb* 43 (1970): 469.

27 For various portraits of Adam in Jewish literature, see John R. Levison, *Portraits of Adam in Early Judaism: From Sirach to 2 Baruch* (JSPSup 1; Sheffield: Sheffield Academic Press, 1988).

28 C.E.B. Cranfield, *The Epistle to the Romans, vol. 1* (ICC; Edinburge: T&T Clark, 1977), 283.

29 Gordon D. Fee, *Pauline Christology: An Exegetical-Theological Study* (Peabody: Henrickson, 2007), 250; Heinrich Schlier also takes the firstborn son to be a messianic name and "Geliebtester." See Heinrich Schlier, *Der Römerbrief* (HTKNT; Freiburg: Herder, 1977), 125.

30 Fee, *Pauline Christology*, 315. For similar opinions, see Peter Stuhlmacher, *Der Brief an die Römer* (NTD 6; Göttingen: Vandenhoeck & Ruprecht 1998), 125; Peter O'Brien, *Colossians and Philemon* (WBC; Waco: Word, 1981), 44; Michael Peppard, *The Son of God in the Roman World: Divine Sonship in its Social and Political Context* (Oxford: Oxford University Press, 2011), 139.

31 James M. Scott, *Adoption as Sons of God: An Exegetical Investigation into the Background of YIOTHESIA in the Pauline Corpus* (WUNT II/48; Tübingen: Mohr Siebeck, 1992), 254–55.

32 Mark Forman, *The Politics of Inheritance in Romans* (SNTSMS 148; Cambridge: Cambridge University Press, 2011), 119. Michael Peppard, *The Son of God in the Roman World: Divine Sonship in its Social and Political Context* (Oxford: Oxford University Press, 2011), 139–40.

33 Cf. LXX Ps 44:8 and Heb 1:9. However, μετόχοι does not indicate a brotherly relationship.

firstborn son" and it implies that the term "firstborn son" is a kinship concept. Scott and Peppard maintain that the notion of the firstborn son in Rom 8:29 reflects the concept of 'messianic adoption (i.e., Christ is the adopted son of God),' but it is doubtful that this view is evidenced in the context of Rom 8 and Jewish literature. We have specific critiques on the concept of messianic adoption in section 4.1.3. While the interpretation for 'messianic adoption' is sceptical, it is still plausible that the title of the firstborn son has a double force as a kinship concept and a messianic title, and so, this study will consider its messianic implications in section 4.1.3.

1.1.1.2 Πρωτότοκος πάσης κτίσεως in Col 1:15

In current scholarship, there is no consensus on the meaning of the firstborn son in Col 1:15, and scholarly interpretations fall into two categories: 1) a title of Wisdom (a majority view); and 2) a messianic title (a minority view). Yet, Hockel's *Christus der Erstgeborene* (1965) offers an exception. Hockel argues that early Gnosticism was the principal background of the Colossian hymn.[34] In this perspective, the firstborn son of every creature should be understood within the gnostic hierarchy in relation to the son's supremacy. However, the gnostic origin of the Colossians hymn is rarely accepted by current interpreters, since the dating of the Gnostic sources makes this reading problematic.[35]

34 Alfred Hockel, *Christus der Erstgeborene: Zur Geschichte der Exegese von Kol 1,15* (Düsseldorf: Patmos, 1965), 47. See also Martin Dibelius and D. Heinrich Greeven, *An die Kolosser, Epheser, an Philemon* (HNT 12; Tübingen: Mohr Siebeck, 1953), 18.

35 Käsemann, Wilckens and Lohmeyer also read the Colossian hymn in terms of the Gnostic myth of the *Urmensch-Erlöser*. See Ernst Käsemann, "A Primitive Christian Baptismal Liturgy," in *Essays on New Testament Themes* (trans. W.J. Montague; Philadelphia: Fortress, 1964), 154–59; E. Lohmeyer, *Die Briefe an die Philipper, an die Kolosser und an Philemon* (Meyer 9; Göttingen: Vandenhoeck & Ruprecht, 1930), 46–47; Ulrich Wilckens, *Weisheit und Torheit* (BHT 26; Tübingen: Mohr, 1959), 200. However, as Fossum agrees, "evidence for the existence of a Gnostic *Urmensch-Erlöser* is lacking until Mani's time." See Jarl Fossum, "Colossians 1. 15–18a. in the Light of Jewish Mysticism and Gnosticism," *NTS* 35 (1989): 183. The existence of pre-Christian Gnosticism is also denied by Edwin M. Yamauchi, *Pre-Christian Gnosticism: A Survey of the Proposed Evidences* (London: Tyndale, 1973), 186: "the evidences which have been adduced to prove the priority of Gnosticism over Christianity have been … found wanting." For a similar view, see Carsten Colpe, *Die Religionsgeschichtlicheschule: Darstellung und Kritik ihres Bildes vom gnostischen Erlösermythus* (FRLANT 78; Göttingen: Vandenhoeck & Ruprecht, 1961). For the critique of Käsemann's reading, see Deichgräber, *Gotteshymnus*, 153–54. The Gnostic Interpretation of the Colossian hymn is also rejected by P.D. Overfield, "Pleroma: A Study in Content and Context," *NTS* 25 (1979): 384–96. On the other hand, it is probable that the opponents' teaching may contain some syncretic feature including proto-Gnosticism. For this view, see Günter Bornkamm, "The Heresy of Colossians," in *Conflict at Colossae* (eds. F.O. Francis and W.A. Meeks; SBLSBS 4; Missoula: Scholars, 1973), 123–45; F.F. Bruce, "The Colossian

Burney argues that ראשית (beginning or origin) is a key concept in the Christ hymn. He maintains that the notion of בראשית in Gen 1:1 underlies ἐν αὐτῷ, δι᾽αὐτοῦ and εἰς αὐτόν in the Christ hymn, and writes that πρὸ πάντων and τὰ πάντα ἐν αὐτῷ συνέστηκεν in Col 1:17 should be read in terms of creation.[36] In Prov 8:22, Wisdom is the first creature of God: "The Lord possessed me at the beginning (ראשית) of his work, the first of his acts of long ago." Burney maintains that πρωτότοκος πάσης κτίσεως in Col 1:15 is a direct allusion to Prov 8:22, and that Col 1:16–18 develops the notion of πρωτότοκος πάσης κτίσεως.[37] So, according to Burney, Christ fulfils the meaning of ראשית.[38]

However, we do not find any direct linguistic link between πρωτότοκος in Col 1:15 and Prov 8:22 (MT and LXX): "יהוה קנני ראשית דרכו קדם מפעליו מאז"/ "κύριος ἔκτισέν με ἀρχὴν ὁδῶν αὐτοῦ εἰς ἔργα αὐτοῦ." In contrast to Burney's view, we have no reason to interpret קנה (buy or acquire) in Prov 8:22 in the sense of 'beget.'[39] As de Savignac observes, the verb קנה is used in order to designate a production which is not of the same status (même ordre) as the creator in the OT.[40] In this context, de Savignac translates Prov 8:22a into "The Lord produced me according to his idea in the beginning."[41] So, it seems that birth language (πρωτότοκος) in Col 1:15 is not related to the creation of Wisdom in Prov 8:22a. Moreover, Prov 8:22 can only be a poetic figure of speech which is based on Prov 3:19–20, thus it appears that Prov 8:22 does not illustrate the hypostasis of Wisdom. Moreover, πρωτότοκος is the Greek equivalent of בכר

Heresy," *BibSac* 141 (1984): 195–208; Clinton Arnold, *The Colossian Syncretism*, 95–100. For further critiques on gnostic interpretations of the Colossian hymn, see Christian Stettler, *Der Kolosserhymnus: Untersuchungen zu Form, traditionsgeschichtlichem Hintergrund und Aussage von Kol 1,15–20* (WUNT II/131; Tübingen: Mohr Siebeck, 2000), 75–103. Moule notes, "… the Christian experience of redemption … cannot be accounted for in terms of a Redeemer who is included among created things." See C.F.D. Moule, *The Epistles to the Colossians and to Philemon* (The Cambridge Greek Testament Commentary; Cambridge: Cambridge University Press, 1958), 64.

36 C.F. Burney, "Christ as the APXH of Creation (Prov. viii 22, Col I 15–18, Rev. iii 14.)," *JTS* 27 (1926): 176.

37 Burney, "Christ as the APXH of Creation," 173–74.

38 Burney, "Christ as the APXH of Creation," 175. This view is followed by W.D. Davies, *Paul and Rabbinic Judaism: Some Rabbinic Elements in Pauline Theology* (4th ed.; Philadelphia: Fortress, 1980), 151; Jarl E. Fossum, *The Name of God and the Angel of the Lord: Samaritan and Jewish Concepts of Intermediation and the Origin of Gnosticism* (WUNT 36; Tübingen: Mohr Siebeck, 1985), 316.

39 *HALOT* does not include "beget" as the meaning of קָנָה. *HALOT* defines קָנָה in the sense of 'buy,' 'acquire' and 'create.' See Ludwig Koehler and Walter Baumgartner, *The Hebrew and Aramaic Lexicon of the Old Testament, vol. 2* (Leiden: Brill, 2001), 1111–13. LXX Prov 8:22 translates קָנָה into "create."

40 Jean de Savignac, "Note sur le sens du verset VIII 22 des Proverbes," *VT* 4 (1954): 430.

41 See de Savignac, "Note sur le sens du verset VIII 22 des Proverbes," 431.

in the LXX, but Burney does not observe Jewish usage of πρωτότοκος and בכר. Further, Burney's theory cannot explain that πρωτότοκος in Rom 8:29, Col 1:15, 18 and Heb 1:6 is referenced in the context of inheritance. Therefore, we conclude that πρωτότοκος in Col 1:15 is not directly related to Wisdom created by God in Prov 8:22 (cf. *Sir* 1:4; 24:9).

Some interpreters argue that the firstborn son in Col 1:15 originated in Hellenistic Jewish speculation about Wisdom. Eduard Schweizer maintains that πρωτο implies the meaning of "earlier than" or "before all," and that this phrase, the firstborn son of all creatures, refers to the pre-temporal being.[42] That is, Christ is the firstborn of all creation, because all things were created in, through and for Christ who is considered as Wisdom/Logos within the context of the Hellenistic Jewish background.[43] In a similar vein, Eduard Lohse also states that πρωτότοκος should be interpreted in terms of Hellenistic Jewish speculation about Wisdom, and that, using this perspective, the title of the firstborn son is associated with the pre-existence of Christ.[44] In addition, he argues that πρωτότοκος should not be interpreted as being created first, but as emphasising the uniqueness of Christ. That is, this phrase does not denote the temporal priority of Christ over all creatures, but his priority in status "as the agent of creation who is before creation."[45] Matthew Gordley notes the similarity of Christology in Col 1:15–17 with the notion of the intermediary figure such as Wisdom in terms of a mediating role in Hellenistic-Jewish literature,[46] and understands the firstborn son as "the first place, a place of prominence or supremacy, which in a family is the place of the πρωτότοκος."[47] The firstborn son is juxtaposed with the image of God (εἰκὼν τοῦ θεοῦ) in Col 1:15. In this vein, Martin Hengel argues that Christ is presented as "the heavenly, eschatological Adam, who as a 'life-giving spirit' overcomes death" through the expressions εἰκών and πρωτότοκος in Col 1:15. Hengel also postulates that the designation of Christ as εἰκών and πρωτότοκος was adopted from Hellenistic Wisdom tradition which calls Wisdom the firstborn son (πρωτόγονος).[48]

---

42 Eduard Schweizer, *Colossians* (trans. Andrew Chester; London: SPCK, 1982), 67.

43 Schweizer, *Colossians*, 74.

44 Eduard Lohse, *Colossians and Philemon* (trans. Robert J. Karris; Hermeneia; Minneapolis: Fortress, 1972), 48.

45 Lohse, *Colossians and Philemon*, 49.

46 Matthew Gordley, *Colossian Hymn in Context: A Study in Light of Jewish and Greco-Roman Hymnic and Epistolary Conventions* (WUNT II/228; Tübingen: Mohr Siebeck, 2007), 218–19.

47 Gordley, *Colossian Hymn in Context*, 217.

48 Martin Hengel, "Der Gottes Sohn," in *Studien zur Christologie, Kleine Schriften IV* (WUNT 201; Tübingen: Mohr Siebeck, 2006), 132 (= *Der Sohn Gottes: Die Entstehung der Christologie und die jüdisch-hellenistische Religionsgeschichte* (Tübingen: Mohr Siebeck, 1975)). See

J.D.G. Dunn concurs that the image of God and the firstborn son in Col 1:15 were derived from Hellenistic Jewish speculation about Wisdom.[49] However, contrary to Hengel's view, Dunn argues that Christ is not pre-existent Wisdom, but "the exhaustive embodiment of divine Wisdom" or the embodiment of God's wise activity.[50] Dunn focuses on the relationship between personified Wisdom (or Logos) and the firstborn son: "... again the antecedent for use of the word πρωτότοκος ('firstborn') in relation to creation is most obviously Wisdom ... The use of πρωτότοκος of the Davidic king in Ps 89:27 (LXX Ps 88:28) or elsewhere of Israel ... is less relevant here."[51] He argues that Wisdom is a created being as depicted in Prov 8:22 and *Sir* 1:4; 24:9,[52] and in this vein, he asserts that Logos was designated as πρωτόγονος (firstborn son) in Philo (*Agr* 51; *Conf* 146; *Somn* 1.215),[53] and that the status of Christ as πρωτότοκος originated in the status of Logos as πρωτόγονος.[54]

Yet, if we consider πρωτότοκος in Col 1:15 as the title of Wisdom, it is unclear how to understand the relationship between the Wisdom tradition and resurrection in Col 1:18 ("the firstborn son from the dead"). In several cases, while some scholars interpret the firstborn son in Col 1:15 as an allusion to the Wisdom tradition, they do not read the firstborn son in 1:18 as the title of Wisdom.[55] As Markus Barth and Helmut Blanke write, "It is unlikely that the same title is used within the hymn in a different sense."[56]

Scholars in support of this view refer to the usage in Philonic literature. Yet, the context where the term πρωτόγονος is used in Philo's writing are often neglected by scholars. The term πρωτόγονος is used as the title of Israel in *Prayer of Joseph* A, 3, and some similarities are found between *PrJos* and *Conf* 146, and the title of πρωτόγονος is linked with the status of Israel in *Conf* 146. Few scholars, however, investigate the tradition background of the term πρωτόγονος in Philo. With regard to Philo's uses of the concept of the firstborn

also Schweizer, *Colossians*, 67; Lohse, *Colossians and Philemon*, 48; Gordley, *Colossian Hymn in Context*, 218–19.

49 J.D.G. Dunn, *Christology in the Making: A New Testament Inquiry into the Origins of the Doctrine of the Incarnation* (London: SCM, 2010), 189.

50 Dunn, *Christology in the Making*, 195–96.

51 Dunn, *Colossians and Philemon*, 90.

52 Dunn, *Colossians and Philemon*, 90.

53 Dunn, *Colossians and Philemon*, 90.

54 Dunn, *Christology in the Making*, 189–90.

55 E.g., Douglas J. Moo, *The Letters to the Colossians and to Philemon* (PNTC; Grand Rapids: Eerdmans, 2008), 129; Peter T. O'Brien, *Colossians, Philemon* (WBC; Waco: Word, 1982), 50–51; Dunn, *Colossians and Philemon*, 98; Stettler, *Der Kolosserhymnus*, 242–43. Cf. Gordley, *Colossian Hymn in Context*, 23.

56 Barth and Blanke, *Colossians*, 207.

(πρωτότοκος, πρωτόγονος and πρεσβύτατος), focused research will be presented in section 3.14 (and 4.2.3).

Second, some scholars interpret the firstborn son in Col 1:15 in terms of a messianic title.[57] Gordon Fee does not connect Christology in the Colossian hymn to Hellenistic Jewish speculation about Wisdom. He argues that πρωτότοκος means "the privileged position of 'firstborn'—both heir and sovereign with regard to creation … derived from Ps 89:27," without incorporating notions of Wisdom.[58] N.T. Wright follows Burney's interpretation of the Christ hymn, but his analysis diverges in certain respects. The climax of Gen 1 is the creation of a human being. In Prov 8, *Sirach*, and *Wisdom of Solomon*, Wisdom is designated as a vice-regent of God over God's creation (cf. Gen 2:15–20). Israel was also the particular location where Wisdom dwelt, and was elected in order to accomplish true humanity. Solomon, David's son, is the model of a messianic figure and a wise man, and divine Wisdom also dwelt in him. The messianic ruler was designated as the firstborn son of God in Ps 89:27.[59] Christian Stettler argues that the firstborn son in Col 1:15 originated from the messianic title in LXX Ps 88:28.[60] Stettler writes that the firstborn son in Col 1:15 alludes to Hellenistic Jewish speculation about Wisdom, but is simultaneously associated with the messianic title in Ps 89:27.[61] Yet, while some scholars who reads the firstborn son in Col 1:15 as the title of Wisdom also affirm that it is also a messianic title,[62] few considers how the firstborn son can be a messianic title and simultaneously the title of Wisdom.

Donald Juel writes that the scriptural interpretations by early Christians were Christological, and that the foci and the directions of the interpretations were intended to confess that Jesus is the Messiah. He also states, "There is no

57 Kehl argues that πρωτότοκος was used as the equal sense with μονογενής in Zech 12:10, *Sir* 36:11, and *PsSol* 18:4. He also notes that πρωτότοκος can be understood in the sense of Messiah in LXX Ps 88:28. Kehl observes that the firstborn son in Col 1:15 is referenced in relation to all creatures, not to his father, and concludes that the notion of the firstborn son means the supremacy over all creatures. Nikolaus Kehl, *Der Christushymnus im Kolosserbrief: Eine motivgeschichtliche Untersuchung zu Kol 1,12–20* (SBM 1; Stuttgart: Katholisches Bibelwerk, 1967), 84–85.

58 Fee, *Pauline Christology*, 297. Cf. Peter T. O'Brien, *Colossians and Philemon* (WBC; Waco: Word, 1981), 44.

59 N.T. Wright, *The Climax of the Covenant: Christ and the Law in Pauline Theology* (Minneapolis: Fortress, 1993), 112–13.

60 Stettler, *Der Kolosserhymnus*, 150.

61 Stettler, *Der Kolosserhymnus*, 151.

62 E.g, Dunn, *Christology in the Making*, 189–90; Moo, *Colossians and Philemon*, 129; Gordley, *Colossian Hymn in Context*, 218–19; Stettler, *Der Kolosserhymnus*, 151; Wright, *The Climax of the Covenant*, 117; O'Brien, *Colossians, Philemon*, 44.

evidence from extant literature that Psalm 89 was interpreted as a messianic psalm prior to the Christian era.[63] However, he asserts, "There are … several instances of such exegesis in midrashic literature." Yet, Juel was not able to provide evidence that the firstborn son was actually used as a messianic title in midrashic literature.[64] No verse in midrashic literature presented by Juel indicates that the firstborn son was a messianic title. Juel, Lightfoot and Fee maintain that Ps 89:27 is messianically understood in *Exod. R.* 19:7 (see also *Exod. R.* 13:1).[65] Ostensibly, in *Exod. R.* 19:7, Rabbi Nathan mentions the firstborn son as the title of the Messiah: "God said, as I made Jacob a firstborn, so also will I make king Messiah a firstborn." However, "a firstborn" in *Exod. R.* 19:7 cannot be understood as a messianic title, and rather, *Exod. R.* 19:7a indicates that the term "a firstborn son" was originally the title of Jacob. That is, in *Exod. R.* 19:7, the title of Jacob is ascribed to a royal messianic figure, and the royal messianic figure receives blessings given to Jacob the firstborn son. So, in *Exod. R.* 19:7, "a firstborn son" does not refer to a messianic title which originated in Ps 89:27.[66]

Whilst many interpreters place their foci upon the firstborn son in Col 1:15, the title of the firstborn son in Col 1:18 has not received specific attention. Some scholars do not interpret the meaning of the firstborn son in Col 1:15 in terms of temporal priority over all creation, since they consider that Col 1:15 does not indicate that Christ belongs to all creation. However, they simultaneously assert that the firstborn son in Col 1:18 signifies temporal priority in terms of resurrection.[67] For example, as seen above, Lohse maintains that the firstborn son in Col 1:15 does not refer to temporal priority over all creation, but to the uniqueness of Christ. Yet, Lohse writes that the firstborn son in

63 Donald Juel, *Messianic Exegesis: Christological Interpretation of the Old Testament in Early Christianity* (Philadelphia: Fortress, 1988), 105.

64 Juel, *Messianic Exegesis*, 105–7.

65 Lightfoot also finds a link between Messiah and the firstborn son in *Exod. R.* 19:7. See J.B. Lightfoot, *Saint Paul's Epistles to the Colossians and to Philemon* (Grand Rapids: Zondervan, 1959), 146. This view is endorsed by Fee without any doubt. See Fee, *Pauline Christology*, 301. For examples of the similar mistake, see G.K. Beale, *The Book of Revelation* (NIGTC; Grand Rapids: Eerdmans, 1999), 191; Fossum, *The Name of God*, 318; Arnold Goldberg, *Erlösung durch Leiden: Drei rabbinische Homilien über die Trauernden Zions und den leidenden Messias Efraim (PesR 34, 36, 37)* (FJS 4; Frankfurt: Gesellschaft zur Förderung Judaistischer Studien, 1978), 114; Otfried Hofius, *Der Christushymnus Philipper 2, 6–11: Untersuchungen zu Gestalt und Aussage eines urchristlichen Psalms* (WUNT 17; Tübingen: Mohr Siebeck, 1991), 91.

66 Also see *T.Ong. Gen* 49:3; *T.Ps.-J. Gen* 49:3; *T.Ong. Exod* 24:5; *Gen.R.* 63.13, 84.8; *Num.R.* 4.

67 E.g., Charles H. Talbert, *Ephesians and Colossians* (Paideia; Grand Rapids: Baker, 2007), 187, 190.

Col 1:18 signifies temporal priority in terms of resurrection: "the first one who has arisen from those who have fallen asleep."[68] O'Brien writes, "the title [the firstborn son in Col 1:15] cannot refer to him [Christ] as the first of all created beings," but "the firstborn son from the dead" in a temporal sense.[69] Moo also states that the firstborn son in Col 1:15 "refers to Jesus' supreme rank over all the created world," but for the firstborn son in Col 1:18, "clearly the focus is now on temporal priority."[70] Fee writes that the term "the firstborn son" in Col 1:15 was derived from the title of the Davidic scion in Ps 89:27.[71] He, however, does not link the title of the firstborn son in Col 1:18 with that of the Davidic king, and he concludes that the notion of the firstborn son in Col 1:18 refers to the beginning of the new creation.[72] This lack of consistency justifies our attempts to re-define the meaning of the firstborn son in Col 1:15 and 1:18.

1.1.1.3 Τὸν πρωτότοκον in Heb 1:6

In general, scholars interpret the meaning of the firstborn son in Heb 1:6 in the following two ways: 1) the eldest brother as a model or prototype; or 2) a messianic title. The first option places a focus upon the temporal priority (πρωτο-) as a prototype or the role of the oldest brother. For example, Erich Grässer argues that the title of the firstborn son expresses the priority (*Vorsprung*) of Christ over his human brothers.[73] He does not regard this title as an eschatological title with regard to Christ's second coming as the son of man, the judge of the world and saviour. Instead, the title of the firstborn son is linked with the heir of all things in Heb 1:2 and understood as a precursor in Heb 6:20, and is to be interpreted in terms of his relationship with his brothers in Heb 2:10. Therefore, this title should be considered in the sense of a founder or a leader (Heb 2:10; 12:2 ἀρχηγός), the order of Melchizedek in Heb 6:20 and the great shepherd of the sheep in Heb 13:20.[74]

---

68 Lohse, *Colossians and Philemon*, 48, 56.

69 O'Brien, *Colossians, Philemon*, 44, 50.

70 Douglas J. Moo, *The Letters to the Colossians and to Philemon* (PNTC; Grand Rapids: Eerdmans, 2008), 129.

71 Fee, *Pauline Christology*, 301.

72 Fee, *Pauline Christology*, 306.

73 Erich Grässer, *An Die Hebräer (Heb 1–6)* (EKKNT; Zürich: Benziger, 1990), 78.

74 Similarly, O'Brien also writes that the firstborn son in Heb 1:6 refers to Christ's supremacy and priority of rank, and that it depicts the special relationship with his father. On the other hand, he maintains that at the same time, Christ as the firstborn is the founder of new humanity. See Peter T. O'Brien, *The Letter to the Hebrews* (PNTC; Grand Rapids: Eerdmans, 2010), 70. See also L.T. Johnson, *Hebrews: A Commentary* (NTL; Louisville: WJK, 2006), 79. Also see Ernst Käsemann, *The Wandering People of God: An Investigation of*

Patrick Gray argues that the firstborn son in Heb 1:6 refers to the older brother among brothers in terms of his role as a mediator or as a guardian.[75] According to Gray, in the Greco-Roman legal context, older brothers had a responsibility as guardians to take care of their younger brothers' inheritance. In effect, Christ as the firstborn son is presented as the mediator of the new covenant in terms of the role as a guardian in Greco-Roman society.[76]

Yet, the firstborn son in Heb 1:6 cannot refer to Christ's role as a guardian or mediator for his Christian siblings as the following demonstrates. In Heb 2:10, the one who brings the firstborn son (or many sons) into the heavenly realm (or glory) is not the firstborn son, but God himself. So, in Heb 2:10, God leads "many children" to glory. Christ is called ἀρχηγός τῆς σωτηρίας, but ἀρχηγός in Heb 2:10 can be read as a pioneer or an initiator of salvation. The one who made ἀρχηγός τῆς σωτηρίας perfect is also God himself. Furthermore, there is no direct reference to πρωτότοκος in Heb 2:10. What is stressed in Heb 1 is not the leadership nor the mediatorship of Christ, but the supremacy of Christ. The concept of the firstborn son in Heb 1:6 should be understood in the context of Christ's supremacy.

The notion of πρωτότοκος as a guardian of inheritance or divine blessing is unfamiliar in the OT and ancient Jewish literature. The guardianship (*tutela*) of the eldest brother in Greco-Roman societal practices[77] cannot be applied to the kinship metaphor in Heb 1:6, since there were generally two circumstances where the eldest brothers assumed guardianship. The first circumstance was the death of the father. If the father was alive, guardianship was unnecessary. The eldest brother could serve as guardian of his younger brothers in Greco-Roman families when *pater familias* was not alive.[78] However, it is

---

the Letter to the Hebrews (trans. Roy A. Harrisville and Irving L. Sandberg; Minneapolis: Augsburg, 1984), 119.

75 Patrick Gray, "Brotherly Love and the High Priest Christology of Hebrews," *JBL* 122 (2003): 338. Franz Laub also contends that the firstborn son in 1:6 is not simply to be understood as only a Christological title, but to be soteriologically considered with reference to the continuation of the theme in 1:5–15 and 2:5–18, particularly in relation to his brothers. See Franz Laub, *Bekenntnis und Auslegung: Die paränetische Funktion der Christologie im Hebräerbrief* (BU 15; Regensburg: Pustet, 1980), 59.

76 Gray, "Brotherly Love," 340–3, 349. Rhee also states that Christ as the firstborn son is "the representative of the family who brings the believers to glory (2:10)." See Victor Rhee, "The Role of Chiasm for Understanding Christology in Hebrews 1:1–14," *JBL* 131 (2012): 356.

77 Cf. Gaius, *Inst.* 1.156; *Digest* 27.3.9.1.

78 E.g., in P.Yadin 12, 14 and 15, guardians were appointed to support an heir of the father's property due to absence (death) of the father. In P.Ryl. 2.153 (CE 169), it is described that a son was appointed as an heir of the father although the father was alive. However, in this case, the father was absent in the town Smyrna where the son stayed since he already

clear that the author of Hebrews did not envisage the death of God the father in Hebrews. Secondly, the eldest brother did not assume his role as a guardian for his other brothers without compensation. A guardian in Greco-Roman society usually demanded some financial recompense for his role as guardian, and was allowed to "enrich himself from his brother's share of the inheritance while he held it in trust."[79] For example, in P.Ryl. 2.120 (CE 167), a guardian is appointed on the condition of receiving 9.5 obols for five years. So, Greco-Roman guardianship in which the guardian was financially remunerated does not fit with Christ's gracious sacrifice in Hebrews. Thirdly, someone other than the eldest brother could serve as a guardian for the inheritance by the father's designation.[80] Accordingly, it is unlikely that the firstborn son in Heb 1:6 refers to the eldest brother as a guardian for his younger brothers in terms of a Greco-Roman societal concept.

Scott Hahn considers the notion of the firstborn son in Heb 1:6 in terms of the divine promise.[81] However, he also sets out to interpret the notion of the firstborn son in Heb 1:6 in the context of royal priesthood in Exod 19:6.[82] He claims that the firstborn son in the OT can be interpreted as a priest. Firstly, Hahn finds two texts in the Targums which connect the concept of the firstborn son to priesthood and royalty.[83] Secondly, he contends that the notion of the firstborn is related to the sacred status of the firstborn in the OT. Hahn reaches his conclusion on the meaning of the firstborn son in Exod as follows: "As the bearer of divine blessing, Israel stands as the firstborn son within the family of nations, for the purpose of mediating the divine blessing of Abraham to all the nations."[84] Likewise, he also associates the notion of the firstborn son in Heb 1:6 with "the royal priestly primogeniture of Christ."[85]

However, Hahn's interpretation of the firstborn son in Heb 1:6 is not persuasive. Hahn argues that the firstborn son is linked to the notion of a priestly mediator in the OT, but this link is not explicitly found in the OT and Second Temple literature.[86] There is no evidence in Second Temple literature that

moved to Hermopolis. So, P.Ryl. 2.153 depicts the appointment of an heir at the absence of his father.

79 Bannon, *The Brothers of Romulus*, 47.

80 *Inst.* 1.13.5.

81 Scott Hahn, *Kinship by Covenant: A Canonical Approach to the Fulfillment of God's Saving Promises* (AYBRL; New Haven: Yale University Press, 2009), 284.

82 Hanh, *Kinship by Covenant*, 279, 468 n. 6.

83 Hahn, *Kinship by Covenant*, 137–38.

84 Hahn, *Kinship by Covenant*, 141.

85 Hahn, *Kinship by Covenant*, 284.

86 Hahn also concedes that Martin Buber's argument on Exod is an "interesting conjecture," in Hahn, *Kinship by Covenant*, 141.

the concept of the firstborn son was linked to Israel's intermediary role.[87] Hahn attempts to interpret the role of a priest in Exod 19 as a mediator, but the priesthood in Exod 19 can be explained in the sense of 'closeness to God' in Exod 19:22a.[88] As Hahn concedes, the motif of the firstborn son provides a significant hermeneutical key to the Exodus event.[89] In Exod 4, the concept of the firstborn son primarily presages Israel's superior position over Egypt, not Israel's intermediary role on behalf of the nations. Furthermore, Hahn does not investigate the other uses of firstborn son in Heb 11:28, 12:16 or 12:23. Therefore, his interpretation of the firstborn son in Heb 1 in terms of the royal priesthood is not compelling.[90]

---

87 Hahn relies on John Davies, when he interprets the kingdom of priests in Exod 19:6 in terms of royal priesthood, in Hahn, *Kinship by Covenant*, 426 n. 140, 468 n. 6. Yet, John Davies does not interpret the priesthood in Exod 19:6 in the sense of a mediating position, but of the privilege to draw near to God, contrary to Hahn. See John A. Davies, *A Royal Priesthood: Literary and Intertextual Perspectives on an Image of Israel in Exodus 19.6* (JSOTSup 395; Sheffield: Sheffield Academic Press, 2004), 76–102. Furthermore, it is doubtful that the kingdom of priests in Exod 19:6 should be read as royal priesthood. This interpretation would mean that Israel has not only a priestly but also kingly function among other nations. However, it is doubtful that ממלכת (kingdom) can contain the meaning of royalty in Exod 19:6, because it is semantically located in the same field as גוי (nation), and they are a common word pair in the Old Testament (e.g., Ps 46:7; 79:6; 102:23; 105:13; 2 Chr 16:20; 1 Kgs 18:10; Isa 60:12; Neh 9:22). Furthermore, Hahn's interpretation of Exod 19:6 misses the parallel between ממלכת כהנים (the kingdom of priests) and גוי קדוש (a holy nation) in Exod 19:6. As Fohrer notes, כהנים (the modifier) corresponds with קדוש (the modifier), and ממלכה (the modified) with גוי (the modified). See Georg Fohrer, "Priesterliches Königtum (Ex 19,6)," in *Studien zur alttestamentlichen Theologie und Geschichte (1949–1966)* (BZAW 115; Berlin: Walter de Gruyter, 1969), 151. So, it is most natural to say that ממלכה (kingdom) and גוי (nation) have the same nominal function as the modified in terms of the fact that ממלכה and גוי are a common word pair in the OT. Therefore, interpreting ממלכת כהנים (the kingdom of priests) as an attributive genitive is the view most suitable to the context. As גוי is qualified by קדוש (holy), so ממלכת is qualified by כהנים (priests; a plural of abstraction). This appears to be the simplest understanding of the grammatical construct. Accordingly, reading ממלכת כהנים as "royal priesthood" is not convincing. Instead, Scott argues that ממלכת כהנים means "a kingdom set apart like a priest." See R.B.Y. Scott, "A Kingdom of Priests (Exodus xix 6)," *OTS* 8 (1950): 213; Cornelis Houtman, *Exodus II, 7:14–19:25* (HCOT; trans. Sierd Woudstra; Kampen: Kok, 1996), 445. Kyu Seop Kim argues that it means "the kingdom near to God." See Kyu Seop Kim, "The Meaning of 'מַמְלֶכֶת כֹּהֲנִים' in Exodus 19:6 Revisited," *JBTR* 35 (2014): 249–67.

88 Steins argues that Israel is the priestly kingdom in that it is near to God and hears his voice, in Georg Steins, "Priesterherrschaft, Volk von Priestern oder was sonst? Zur Interpretation von Ex 19, 6," *BZ* 49 (2001): 28–32.

89 Hahn, *Kinship by Covenant*, 139.

90 I have more critiques on Scott Hahn's view on Hebrews. Hahn argues, "[D]istribution of the estate while the testator(s) was still living (Lat., *donatio inter vivos*) was quite widespread in the Hellenistic world." See Hahn, *Kinship by Covenant*, 309. In this vein, Hahn

Alternatively, some scholars view the term "the firstborn son" as a messianic title employed in Ps 89:27. Otfried Hofius argues that Christ in Heb 1:6 is designated as the firstborn son having dominion over the world (Weltherrschaft) as presented in Ps 89, and is synonymous with the heir of everything in Heb 1:2.[91] On the other hand, August Strobel claims that the firstborn son probably (wahrscheinlich) implies the election of Christ before time and the re-inauguration of Christ through the worship of all the angels in the world.[92] John Meier argues that the title of the firstborn son is related to a theme of Davidic enthronement.[93] The firstborn son in Heb 1:6 also indicates the temporal priority over the saints concerning the resurrection, and the firstborn son in Heb 1:6 is not related to the firstborn son in Luke 2:7 and Col 1:15, but to the firstborn from the dead in Col 1:18 and Rev 1:5.[94] Yet, generally, scholars assert

---

reads διαθήκη in Heb 9:16–17 as the Sinai covenant, not 'testament.' Yet, as Willy Clarysse and D.J. Thompson note, in Roman-Egyptian tax receipts and census returns, there is only one case in which the patrinomy was transferred during the life time of the testators. See *Willy Clarysse and D.J. Thompson, Counting the People in Hellenistic Egypt: I. Population Registers* (Cambridge: Cambridge University Press, 2006), 296. Thus, distribution of the testators' properties during the life time of the testators was not widespread, but something of a rarity in the Roman period. Furthermore, Hahn misses the significance of the concept of inheritance in Hebrews. The concept of διαθήκη is clearly linked with inheritance (τῆς αἰωνίου κληρονομίας) in 9:15. Ancient Mediterranean wills were a sort of inheritance contract, and the author of Hebrews may have understood the concept of διαθήκη in terms of the use of the land. For the concept of ancient διαθήκη, see Adrian Schenker, "Le contrat successoral en droit gréco–égyptien et la διαθήκη dans la Septante," *ZAR* 6 (2000) 175–85. As shown in section 1.2.2, Israelites perceived themselves as the heir of the promise, and they expected to receive the promised land from God according to the promise. The exodus (or eisodus) story of Israel is embedded in Hebrews, and this indicates the pilgrimage of the people of God who enters the promised land. Thus, Hahn does not consider that the concept of the firstborn son is the title of Israel and refers to a special heir of God.

91 Otfried Hofius, *Der Christushymnus Philipper 2, 6–11: Untersuchungen zu Gestalt und Aussage eines urchristlichen Psalms* (WUNT 17; Tübingen: Mohr Siebeck, 1991), 91–92. Similarly, Paul Ellingworth, *The Epistle to the Hebrews: A Commentary on the Greek Text* (NIGTC; Grand Rapids: Eerdmans, 1993), 118; Susan E. Docherty, *The Use of the Old Testament in Hebrews: A Case Study in Early Jewish Bible Interpretation* (WUNT II/260; Tübingen: Mohr Siebeck), 158.

92 August Strobel, *Der Brief an die Hebräer* (NTD; Vandenhoeck & Ruprecht: Göttingen, 1991), 23.

93 John Meier, "Symmetry and Theology in the Old Testament Citations of Heb 1:5–14," *Bib* 66 (1985): 510.

94 Meier, "Symmetry and Theology," 509. Hans-Friedrich Weiss also understands the firstborn son in Heb 1:6 as having the meaning of Davidic royal messiah. Weiss states that the firstborn son could refer to Israel, but he does not specifically discuss the meaning of the firstborn son with regard to Israel. See Hans-Friedrich Weiss, *Der Brief an die Hebräer* (KEK 13; Göttingen: Vandenhoeck & Ruprecht, 1991), 163.

the meaning of the firstborn son in Heb 1:6 without specific researches on the tradition-historical background of πρωτότοκος. Moreover, the uses of the firstborn son in Heb 11:28 and 12:23 (cf. 12:16) have not been the focus of extensive research. These texts (Heb 11:28 and 12:23) will prove vital in understanding the title of the firstborn son as referring to Christ and the believers in chapter 4.3. Therefore, there is no consensus on the origin of the firstborn son Christology in Hebrews.

1.1.2 *Problems*

In the previous sections, we have observed interpretative disagreements on the meaning and the origin of the firstborn son in the NT, which represent the following three viewpoints: 1) the eldest brother of Christians; 2) a messianic title; and 3) a title of Wisdom (particularly, Col 1:15). In this work, we will answer the following questions. Why did early Christians confess Christ as the firstborn son? Does the firstborn son in the NT refer to 'the first created being'? Otherwise, does the firstborn son in the NT symbolise a messianic king in Ps 89:27? Was the term "the firstborn son" related to divine election in ancient Judaism and early Christianity? These questions still remain unresolved, and there is no scholarly consensus on the meaning and origin of the firstborn son in the NT.

In spite of its potential significance, recent NT scholarship has given surprisingly less attention to the concept of the firstborn son in the NT than one would expect. In terms of existing research, no monograph-length works have been published, and moreover, few full-range historical study have been undertaken.[95] The review of previous published research indicates that a new work on the firstborn son Christology in Romans, Colossians and Hebrews may provide fresh insight into NT Christology and add to the existing body of knowledge. Furthermore, despite scholars' ongoing historical and sociological investigations into the ancient family, the right and the status of the firstborn son have been rarely explored by NT scholars, and this topic has not attracted the careful attention that it deserves. Several scholars maintain that the concept of the firstborn son refers to the privileged position rather than primogeniture.[96] Following this assumption, current scholars tend not to link

95 One exception is found in L.R. Helyer, "The Prototokos Title in the New Testament" (Ph.D. diss., Fuller Theologolical Seminary, 1979). However, his focus is limited to the issue on the pre-existence of Christ. The specific historical background of the term remains unexplored.

96 E.g, Scott, *Adoption as Sons of God*, 252; Peppard, *The Son of God in the Roman World*, 139; Frederick E. Greenspahn, *When Brothers Dwell Together: The Preeminence of Younger Siblings in the Hebrew Bible* (Oxford: Oxford University Press, 1994), 27. Michaelis

the title of the firstborn son in the NT with the concept of inheritance, as discussed in section 1.1.1. The specific discussion on primogeniture will be made in chapter 2.1 and 2.2 of this work.

1.2 Clarification of Terminology

1.2.1 *Israel*

In this section, we will clarify two significant concepts before using them in this work: Israel and Israel's inheritance. As Leonhardt-Balzer observed, the notion of Israel in the Second Temple period was not monolithic. So, Israel was "the name of the Jews as the people of God," and "was rarely used to describe the contemporary political entity."[97] The concept of Israel in the Second Temple era can be categorised at least in the following four views. Firstly, Israel referred to an ethnic term to define Abraham's offspring (e.g., 1QSa I 1–3).[98] In Acts 9:15, "the children of Israel" refers to the ethnic Jews who are distinct from the Gentiles. In Rom 9:3–4 and 1 Cor 10:18, Israel is defined "according to the flesh," i.e., in an ethnic sense. Secondly, the concept of Israel was also understood in a geographic sense. In 4Q171 3 10 (4QpPsa (Psalms Pesher)), "the high mountain of Israel" refers to the land of Palestine. Thirdly, the notion of Israel was redefined by each group in ancient Judaism, and the range of Israel was often confined to 'the chosen one amongst ethnic Israel (i.e., the remnant of Israel)' or 'members of certain sects (or communities).' "The blessed" in 1Q34+1Q34bis 1–3 i 7 and "a people" in line 5 do not seem to refer to the whole of ethnic Israel, but to the chosen few or the Qumran members. In CD A VI 5, the community members are identified with the remnant of Israel, who were the chosen ones of Israel (CD A I 7–8).[99] *The Similitudes of Enoch* implies that the righteous (or the Elect ones) would possess the Promised Land (cf. *1 En* 38:3–4; 39:4–5; 45:4–5). The righteous (or the Elect ones) in *the Similitudes*

---

interprets the meaning of the firstborn son in the NT in terms of the privileged status in his influential article, "He [Christ] is thus the πρωτότοκος, like them but above them in rank and dignity, since He remains their Lord … As there is no great emphasis on –tokos in the πρωτότοκος of R. 8:29, so it is also in Col. 1:18, where Christ is called πρωτότοκος ἐκ τῶν νεκρῶν." See Wilhelm Michaelis, "πρωτότοκος," in *TDNT*, *vol. 6* (ed. Gerhard Friedrich; Grand Rapids, Eerdmans, 1968), 877.

97 Jutta Leonhardt-Balzer, "Israel and the Community in Paul (Rom 9–11) and the Rule Texts from Qumran," in *The Dead Sea Scrolls and Pauline Literature* (ed. J-S. Rey; STDJ 102; Leiden: Brill, 2010), 277.

98 Leonhardt-Balzer, "Israel and the Community in Paul," 281–82.

99 Leonhardt-Balzer, "Israel and the Community in Paul," 283–84.

of Enoch are not all ethnic Israelites, but a chosen few amongst ethnic Israel.[100] Perhaps, "the Israel of God" in Gal 6:16 refers to the believers encompassing the Jews and the Gentiles.[101] Fourthly, in Philo, the concept of Israel extends to all seers of God including the Gentiles,[102] whilst certain conceptual links between Israel and ethnic Jews are also found.[103] Thus, the concept of Israel was complex in the Second Temple era. Accordingly, for our convenience, when the ethnic sense of Israel is highlighted, this work will use the term 'ethnic Israel.' Otherwise, if Israel means 'the people of God,' this study will use the term 'Israel.'

1.2.2 *Israel's Inheritance*

In ancient Israelite society, the concept of inheritance is closely related to the right to use the land. As Adrian Schenker observes, ברית (covenant) is translated διαθήκη in the LXX, and this connotes that the translators of the LXX understood ברית as the right to use the land in the Greco-Egyptian legal context.[104] In the OT and Jewish literature, inheritance language frequently expresses the expectation that Israel or the chosen few would possess and rule over the Promised Land (or the entire world). In the OT and Jewish literature, Israel, God and Davidic kings are nominated as divine heirs. In Ps 82:8, God (אלהים) inherits (תנחל) all the nations,[105] and the imperfect tense of תנחל indicates God's continuous possession of all the nations.[106] In Ps 94:5, 14 and

100 Martha Himmelfarb, *Ascend to Heaven in Jewish and Christian Apocalypses* (Oxford: Oxford University Press, 1993), 59. Collins notes that the righteous in *Similitudes* does not refer to general righteous people, but to a certain community. However, the specific identity of the community is unclear. See Collins, *The Apocalyptic Imagination*, 192–93.

101 Leonhardt-Balzer, "Israel and the Community in Paul," 278.

102 Ellen Birnbaum, *The Place of Judaism in Philo's Thought: Israel, Jews, and Proselytes* (BJS 90; SPhiloM 2; Atlanta: Scholars, 1996), 213.

103 Maren Niehoff, *Philo on Jewish Identity and Culture* (TSAJ 86; Tübingen: Mohr Siebeck, 2001), 95. Cf. *Q.G.* 2.65; *Virt* 212; *Praem* 84; *Abr* 56–57.

104 Adrian Schenker, "Le contrat successoral en droit gréco-égyptien et la διαθήκη dans la Septante," *ZAR* 6 (2000): 175–185. For the background of the ANE, see S.E. Loewenstamm, "The Divine Grants of Land to the Patriarchs," *JAOS* 94 (1971): 509–10; Moshe Weinfeld, "The Covenantal Aspect of the Promise of the Land to Israel," in *The Promise of the Land: The Inheritance of the Land of Canaan by the Israelites* (TLJS; Berkeley: University of California Press, 1993), 258–61.

105 Cf. Deut 32:8. If we consider Ps 82:1–17 as "a visionary prophetic revelation which looks into the depth of the heavenly world and proclaims to the worshiping community the juridical activity of Yahweh, Ps 82:8 should be understood as a spontaneous answer of the community." See Hans-Joachim Kraus, *Psalms 60–150* (trans. Hilton C. Oswald; Minneapolis: Fortress, 1989), 157.

106 Samuel L. Terrien, *The Psalms: Strophic Structure and Theological Commentary* (ECCSeries; Grand Rapids: Eerdmans, 2003), 590. Ps 82:8 may reflect the privilege of God pertaining to the Land in Lev 25:23: "כִּי־לִי הָאָרֶץ" (for the Land is mine).

4 Ezra 8:45, God's inheritance refers to the people of Israel, and in *Sir* 17:17b, Israel is God's portion (καὶ μερὶς κυρίου Ισραηλ ἐστίν). In Ps 2:8b, a Davidic king is given the nations as his inheritance (נחלה).[107] "Inheritance" is paralleled with "given the end of the earth as your possession (ואחזתך אפסי־ארץ)," and inheriting the nations reflects Jewish anticipation of the Davidic king's dominion over the nations.

When Israel is called an heir of God,[108] Israel's inheritance includes the Land, the entire world, wisdom (or truth), eternal life and glory. Israel inherits glory in Prov 3:35; *Sir* 4:13; *Sir* 37:26; 4Q525, and this implies the expectation that the Jews will be honoured at the eschaton. Some Jews expected to inherit Wisdom (*Sir* 4:16; 4Q416 4 3; 1QS 11 7),[109] and in *Sir* 24:24, the congregations of Jacob inherit the Torah. The ones chosen by God inherit (וינחי) Wisdom, knowledge and understanding as their everlasting possession (1QS 11 7).[110] Eternal life

---

107 Joachim Schaper argues that, in terms of textual similarities with *PsSol* 17–18, Ps 2 was understood in a messianic view by translators of the LXX. See Joachim Schaper, *Eschatology in the Greek Psalter* (WUNT II/76; Tübingen: Mohr Siebeck, 1995), 72–76. See also Schaper, *Eschatology in the Greek Psalter*, 126. Schaper does not discuss "inheritance" in LXX Ps 2:6, but focuses on LXX Ps 2:10–12. On the other hand, J.J. Collins states, "In all, then, we have very little evidence of messianism in Judaism in the period 500–200 BCE, but our evidence for Judaism in this period is scanty in any case." See J.J. Collins, *The Scepter and the Star: Messianism in Light of the Dead Sea Scrolls* (New York: Doubleday, 1995), 40. Fitzmyer and J. Lust also minimise the significance of messianism in the LXX. See Joseph A. Fitzmyer, *The One Who is to Come* (Grand Rapids: Eerdmans, 2007), 65–81; J. Lust, "And I Shall Hang Him on a Lofty Mountain: Ezek 17:22–23 and Messianism in the Septuagint," in *IX Congress of the International Organization for Septuagint and Cognate Studies: Cambridge 1995* (ed. B.A. Taylor; SBLSCS 45; Atlanta: Scholars, 1997), 231–50.

108 However, it does not mean that "all Israel has a share in the world to come" (e.g., m.Sanh 10.1). Rather, in the Second Temple period, some Jews believed that only the chosen few or the remnant of Israel (not the entire Jewish people) who are faithful to the Law would be saved at the eschaton. See Mark A. Elliott, *The Survivors of Israel: A Reconsideration of the Theology of Pre-Christian Judaism* (Grand Rapids: Eerdmans, 2000).

109 Cf. in *Sir* 24:6–7, wisdom obtains her inheritance in Israel.

110 We should note that in the Dead Sea Scrolls the meaning of inheritance is not monolithic. 4Q417 states that the Lord gives his spirit as inheritance to the weak of the people. The weak will realise the wonderful mysteries and know eternal glory. Every creature will receive understanding as their inheritance (lines 10, 19; cf. "inheritance of all living beings" in 4Q416 3 2). In this passage, inheritance is linked with renewed understanding. Cf. 4Q365 10 4; 4Q411 1 ii 9. In 1QS XI 4–8 and 1QS IV 22–2, inheritance for the chosen ones includes the transformation of the mind, i.e., the epistemological transformation (or the new creation). A motif of inheriting wisdom is also found in *Sir* 4:16 (in Greek and Syriac manuscripts): "If they remain faithful, they will inherit her (wisdom); their descendants will also obtain her." If so, 1QS re-interprets the precedent wisdom tradition pertaining to inheritance of wisdom as an eschatological event. In *Sir* 4:16, to inherit is nearly synonymous

was also considered an inheritance of Israel or the righteous (4Q418 69 ii 13–14; *Sib.Or.* 3:45; *1 En* 58:2).

If Israel's inheritance refers to a geographical entity, the inheritance spans from the Land of Palestine to the entire world (e.g., *1 En* 5:7; *Jub* 32:18–19; 1Q34+1Q34bis 3 ii 1–3; Josephus, *Ant* 1.282; 4.114–16). Sometimes, both the Land of Palestine and the entire world are mentioned together as Israel's inheritance (e.g., 4Q171). Moshe Weinfeld writes that the elected people had to merit the Land.[111] Simultaneously, inheriting the Land was a gift from God given to the people of God and the Land was a privilege of the Elect. Weinfeld observes that, in Second Temple literature, the concept of the Land is often spiritualised as the celestial Jerusalem. Yet, as Doron Mendels notes, Jewish political expectations to possess the physical land of Palestine are also evident in Hasmonean literature (i.e., *Sirach, Jubilees, 1 Maccabees, Eupolemus, the*

with to obtain in a parallel structure. So, to inherit in *Sir* 4:16 may be mentioned in a figurative sense. 4Q462 and 4Q475 are not well preserved, but we find some inheritance motifs. The period of darkness is over and the period of light has arrived (line 10). Light shone over Jacob and illuminated Zion (line 3). Inheritance is given to many, perhaps, the seeds of Jacob (line 7) and "his glory" (perhaps God's glory) will fill the waters and the earth. The fullness of the kingdom is with him (God) and the light is with them (the seeds of Jacob). This passage also reflects Jewish eschatological expectation pertaining to inheritance. The contents of inheritance for the Israelites is unclear, but may be related to glory and rulership implied in line 7. 4Q525 14 ii 13–14 says, "he will give you as inheritance; he will fill your days with goodness, [and] with abundant peace you will [...] you shall inherit glory; and when you are snatched away to eternal rest they will inhe[rit her ...] and in your teaching, all those who know you will walk together ..." In 4Q525 14 ii 14, you (the law observer) inherit glory (תנחל כבוד) with goodness and abundant peace. It is probable that glory refers to an attribute of God since inheritance (line 13) is juxtaposed with goodness and peace which is perhaps God's attribute in the context. If so, to inherit glory connotes participating in the glory of God, i.e., an attribute of God, as Kampen writes. See Kampen, *Wisdom Literature*, 110. In this sense, to inherit glory can symbolise the glorification of the law observers. However, it seems more probable that the expression, to inherit glory (תנחל כבוד) in line 14 originated in Prov 3:35a: "The wise will inherit glory (כבוד חכמים ינחלו)." Glory in Prov 3:35a is contrasted with disgrace in 3:35b, and so glory must refer to honour. *Sir* 37:26 also evokes Prov 3:35a: "One who is wise among his people will inherit honour (כבוד) ..." This honour cannot signify the divine glory. So, glory can be an abstract concept that was meant as honour or dignity (see also *Sir* 4:13: "whoever holds her [wisdom] fast inherits glory). Martínez and Tigchelaar translate כבוד in this verse as honour. See F.G. Martínez and E.J.C. Tigchelaar, *The Dead Sea Scrolls Study Edition* (Leiden: Brill, 1999), 1075. Cf. *1 Clement* 45:8 also refers to inheritance of glory.

111 Moshe Weinfeld, "The Inheritance of the Land: Privilege versus Obligation" in *The Promise of the Land: The Inheritance of the Land of Canaan by the Israelites* (TLJS; Berkeley: University of California Press, 1993), 220.

Testament of the Twelve, 1 En 85–90).[112] There are "many variants of the concept of 'greater' Eretz Israel, ranging from those adopting the borders achieved by David and Solomon, to the borders which were drawn by God in his division of the *oecumene* to its nations, including the Jews." However, as Mendels also states, "Perhaps the most frequent motif we have traced is the idea of the twelve tribes, which always implies the settlement of the entire land."[113] So, possession of the Promised Land is a common motif in Jewish literature, but the physical boundaries of the Promised Land which the Jews expected to take possession of were wide-ranging.

In Second Temple literature, Israel's exalted status and privileges are described in various manners, and the motif of inheritance was sometimes associated with the privilege of Israel distinct over the nations. That is, Israel was elected to inherit (i.e., to possess) the Promised Land or the entire world. Therefore, the motif of Israel's inheritance is pervasive in the OT and Jewish literature, and reflects that, in the Second Temple period, some Jews shared a common expectation to inherit (or possess) the Land of Israel or/and the entire world.[114]

1.3 Methodological Considerations

This work will adopt exegetical and tradition-historical methods, but the following linguistic considerations will also be borne in mind. This study does not presume that the meaning of a word is identical to the etymology or the history of the word (i.e, "illegitimate totality transfer"), as Barr notes.[115] So, "the speaker is aware only of the present state of language,"[116] and this study will investigate the meaning of the firstborn son in the synchronic context. However, as Silva

112 *The Animal Apocalypse* (*1 En* 85–90) is dated to the early Hasmonean period. See John J. Collins, *The Apocalyptic Imagination: An Introduction to Jewish Apocalyptic Literature* (Grand Rapids: Eerdmans, 1998), 67.

113 Doron Mendels, *The Land of Israel as a Political Concept in Hasmonean Literature* (TSAJ 15; Tübingen: Mohr Siebeck, 1987), 121. See also George W.E. Nickelsburg, *Ancient Judaism and Christian Origins* (Minneapolis: Fortress, 2003), 130–32.

114 E.g., 1QapGen ar IV 21; XVI 12; XXI 12; XXII 33; 4Q171 IV 12; 4Q179 1 i 12; 4Q269 2 14; 4Q285 1; 4Q365 23 5.

115 James Barr, *The Semantics of Biblical Language* (Oxford: Oxford University Press, 1961), 217–18. Barr notes, "The identity of the object to which different designations are given does not imply that these designations have the same semantic value. The mistake of supposing that it does we may for convenience call 'illegitimate identity transfer'."

116 Moisés Silva, *Biblical Words and their Meaning: An Introduction to Lexical Semantics* (Grand Rapids: Zondervan, 1983), 36.

agrees, diachronism and synchronism are not antithetical in linguistics.[117] In particular, 'context' functions to remove vagueness of the meaning of a word.[118] Vyvyan Evans, a cognitive linguist, states, "[W]ord meaning represents the activation of part of the encyclopaedic knowledge network activated by virtue of the specific context in which a word is embedded."[119] According to Evans, encyclopaedic knowledge contains background knowledge, common-sense knowledge and sociocultural knowledge. In human cognitive process, a lexical interpretation requires the encyclopaedic knowledge surrounding the context, and this knowledge is sometimes called "frame" or "semantic frame."[120] Thus, while this study will adopt tradition-historical methods, and observe how the traditions and the concept of the firstborn son are used and developed in each stage of the tradition history, we will also carefully explore literary and historical contexts where the concept of πρωτότοκος is referenced.

Therefore, in order to properly understand the concept of πρωτότοκος, we should first consider the sociocultural usage of πρωτότοκος (chapter 2), and secondly, we should carefully observe the context where the term "the firstborn son" is used in Jewish literature and the NT (chapters 3 and 4).

1.4 Overview of the Argument

This work offers a study of the meaning of πρωτότοκος in the NT paying specific attention to the term "the firstborn" in the OT and Jewish literature. A full account of the concept of the firstborn son in the NT requires a number of tasks including: 1) analysing the right of the firstborn son in Jewish society (chapter 2.2); 2) understanding the cultic offering of the firstborn (chapter 2.3); 3) tracing the concept of the firstborn son in the OT and Jewish literature (chapter 3); and 4) defining the meaning of the firstborn son in the NT (chapter 4). In particular, this work will first investigate the right of the firstborn son in inheritance in chapter 2, and then, will consider how the title of the firstborn son is used in the OT and Jewish literature in chapter 3. So, all the verses that employ the term "firstborn son" in the Pentateuch, Apocrypha, Pseudepigrapha, the Dead Sea Scrolls and Philo will be within the range of our study. In chapter 2, we will explore the concept of the firstborn son in inheritance and in the

117 Silva, *Biblical Words and their Meaning*, 38.

118 Silva, *Biblical Words and their Meaning*, 150.

119 Vyvyan Evans, "Word Meaning," in *The Cambridge Encyclopedia of the Language Sciences* (ed. Patrick C. Hogan; Cambridge: Cambridge University Press, 2010), 917–19.

120 Charles Fillmore, "Frames and the Semantics of Understanding," *Quaderni di Semantica* 6 (1985): 222–54.

cultic context in the Pentateuch and some relevant Jewish literature including Apocrypha, Pseudepigrapha, Philo and Talmudic literature. Josephus will not be specifically explored in this work, since he omits many references to the firstborn son in his *Judean Antiquities*, and he does not impose significant theological implications upon the term "the firstborn" (see section 2.3.2). In chapter 3, we will also consider all the verses which indicate the firstborn son of the patriarchs, or the firstborn son of God in the OT (Genesis, Exodus, Ps 89 and Jer 31), Apocrypha, Pseudepigrapha, Philo and the Dead Sea Scrolls. The scope of this study will be limited to the OT, Second Temple literature and the NT (and some post-canonical literature in chapter 4) but exceptionally, when we examine the institution of primogeniture in Jewish society (chapter 2.2), rabbinic literature will be included in the scope of our research due to lack of evidence in the Second Temple period.[121] So, we will analyse the context where the notion of the firstborn son lies, and will trace Jewish eschatological anticipations with regard to the concept of the firstborn son.

121 Nickelsburg warns two points about using rabbinic traditions for New Testament exegesis. Firstly, the rabbinic text should be read in their given contexts. Secondly, we should be careful to date rabbinic texts. Rabbinic texts consist of many layers. So "caution, honest scholarly tentativeness, and careful methodology" is needed for approaches to rabbinic datum. See George W.E. Nickelsburg, *Ancient Judaism and Christian Origins: Diversity, Continuity, and Transformation* (Minneapolis: Fortress, 2003), 25–26.

CHAPTER 2

The Firstborn Son in Jewish Society

2.1 Primogeniture in Greco-Roman Society

This chapter will explore the rights of the firstborn son in the Greco-Roman family. Primogeniture can be defined as an institution in which the firstborn male offspring possesses a special status with regard to inheritance rights.[1] In Rome, the oldest form of inheritance was intestate succession.[2] *Sui heredes* (automatic heirs under intestacy) automatically became heirs after *paterfamilias*'s death.[3] As Richard Saller states, the preferred inheritors are as following: (1) *sui heredes* (his own heirs); (2) *proximus agnatus* (close agnate); and (3) clansmen of the same *nomen*.[4] In actual practices, if the fathers' natural children were alive, they were preferred as inheritors.[5] As Lindsay observes, "The tie of blood is always seen as a very strong factor in assigning estates."[6] If there was no immediate heir on death and grandchildren were the only surviving heirs, the grandchildren of the head of the family could be legally designated as his heirs.[7]

Robert Jewett and Francis Lyall assume that the eldest brother in Greco-Roman society had priority in inheritance,[8] but I believe that they

1 Baruch Levine, "Firstborn," in *Encyclopaedia Judaica, vol. 7* (eds. Fred Skolnik and Michael Berenbaum; Detroit: Thomson, 2007), 45.

2 In Roman law, a son under *patria potestas* could not take possession of any property in his own right. The Roman father enjoyed usufruct to use his children's property acquired through his children's labours. See *Codex Iust* 6.61. On the other hand, children usually received inheritance from their father during his life time in Classical Greek society. In Athenian society, on their sixtieth birthday, fathers commonly transferred their property to their children. See Winfried Schmitz, *Haus und Familie im antiken Griechenland* (EGRA 1; München: Oldenbourg, 2007), 35–36; D.M. MacDowell, *The Law in Classical Athens* (AGRL; Ithaca: Cornell University Press, 1978), 132. Some elderly fathers in classical Athens hoped to postpone transferring their property to their children, because they wished to avoid maltreatment by their children after the transfer of the estate (e.g., Demosthenes, 47.34–35).

3 Hugh Lindsay, *Adoption in the Roman World* (Cambridge: Cambridge University Press, 2009), 100–101.

4 Richard P. Saller, *Patriarchy, Property and death in the Roman Family* (CSPESPT; Cambridge: Cambridge University Press, 1994), 163.

5 J.A. Crook, "Patria Potestas," *CQ* 17 (1967): 118.

6 Lindsay, *Adoption in the Roman World*, 121.

7 Justinian, *Inst.* 3.1.7.

8 Jewett, *Romans*, 502; Francis Lyall, "Legal Metaphors in the Epistles," *TynBul* 32 (1981): 94.

 | DOI:10.1163/9789004394940_003

misunderstood the variety and flexibility of inheritance practices in Greco-Roman society. In Greco-Roman society, one of the most significant aspects of inheritance was flexibility.[9] Inheritance was flexibly practised and all surviving sons usually had equal shares according to their lot (κλῆρος). Primogeniture was simply one of many options. For instance, in *Moralia* 483C–D (approximately, CE 100), Plutarch does not consider primogeniture as the norm for dividing inheritance, and he describes the fact that fluid inheritance practices led to conflicts between brothers. Perhaps, in the context which exhorts fraternal love, Plutarch conceived that primogeniture was not conducive in maintaining fraternal unity. In the Roman world, the younger son could be legally designated as his father's principal heir, and the father's decision to designate him could be legally justified. There were few legal rules which endorsed the rights of the firstborn son in respect of inheritance in Gaius' *Institutes* (the second century CE) and Justinian's *Digest* (e.g., *Digest* 35.1.12).[10] Rather, the will of the father determined how to apportion his property to his heirs.[11] Even though

9 Saller, *Patriarchy, Property and Death*, 180. See also eds., John Boardman, Jasper Griffin and Oswyn Murray, *The Oxford Illustrated History of Greece and the Hellenistic World*, 205. Cf. In inheritance custom of an ancient German tribe, the rights of inheritance fell to the most courageous son, not to the eldest son, in Tacitus, *Ger.* 32. Asian traditions also have different conventions regarding the portion for the eldest brother. For instance, Batu Khan of Kipchak Khante in thirteenth century Mongolia was the eldest brother and inherited the farthest land (Russian prairie) according to the Mongolian convention. In Korea, the firstborn son is addressed as jangnam (the eldest son) and is entitled to the privilege of receiving the largest portion of the inheritance and the responsibility to lead the whole (extended) family. Cf. Soo Ho Choi, "The Struggle for Family Succession and Inheritance in a Rural Korean Village," *JAR* 51 (1995): 329–46.

10 Saller, *Patriarchy, Property and Death in the Roman Family*, 161–62. Cf. Pindar (the fifth century BC) illustrates that three brothers inherited equal portions: "There grew from the waters of the sea, an island, which is held by the birthgiving father of piercing rays, the ruler of fire-breathing horses. And there he once lays with Rhodes, and begat seven sons who inherited from him the wisest minds in the time of earlier men; and of these one begat Cameirus, and Ialysus the eldest, and Lindus. Each had his own separate share of cities in their threefold division of their father's land, and their dwelling-places were named after them" (Pindar, *Olympian* 7. 69–75 [LCL translation]). Cf. in Aristophanes, *Birds* 1644–45, Poseidon says that Heracles, younger son of Zeus would be the heir of all the wealth of Zeus, if Zeus died. In Ancient Sparta, fathers designated a single heir among brothers, and brothers co-managed the family property as a joint-inheritance. See David Asheri, "Laws of Inheritance, Distribution of Land and Political Constitutions in Ancient Greece," *Historia* 12 (1963): 6. Cf. Cheryl Anne Cox, "Sibling Relationships in Classical Athens: Brother-Sister Ties," *JFH* 13 (1988): 391.

11 Saller, *Patriarchy, Property and Death in the Roman Family*, 161–62.

a father died intestate, the larger share of inheritance was not automatically conferred upon the eldest son (e.g., *Digest* 32.27.1; cf. *Digest* 38.16.5).

In Roman Egypt, primogeniture was similarly not exercised as the norm for inheritance. Some differences between Roman Egyptian and Greco-Roman customs of inheritance existed. Firstly, Roman Egyptians followed indigenous Egyptian practices in inheritance.[12] For instance, all children were legally independent from the father, whereas Roman children under their fathers' power could not hold their own property as long as their fathers were alive in Roman society.[13] Secondly, in contrast to Athenian inheritance customs, an heiress could receive the father's inheritance without marriage to her father's nearest male relative.[14] Thirdly, female heads occasionally governed the family if the husband had already died and their children were minors in Roman Egypt. On the basis of the Roman census returns, approximately 25 percent of household heads were female in Roman Egypt,[15] while female heads were relatively rare in Hellenistic Greek society (9.8 percent).[16] So, as Huebner observes, "Most of these women who acted as head of household in Roman Egypt were widows who had taken over the headship from their late husbands and were managing the estate, as long as their children were minors."[17] Fourthly, while the children usually inherited equal portions of the father's inheritance,[18] the eldest sons sometimes received an additional portion of property from the father.[19]

12 Sabine Huebner, *The Family in Roman Egypt: A Comparative Approach to Intergenerational Solidarity and Conflict* (Cambridge: Cambridge University Press, 2013), 51.

13 Huebner, *The Family in Roman Egypt*, 51.

14 Huebner, *The Family in Roman Egypt*, 130.

15 Huebner, *The Family in Roman Egypt*, 130. Cf. Peter Garnsey and Richard P. Saller, *The Roman Empire: Economy, Society, and Culture* (Berkeley: University of California Press, 1987), 130–36.

16 W. Clarysse and D. Thompson, *Counting the People in Hellenistic Egypt, Vol. 1: Population Registers* (CCS; Cambridge: Cambridge University Press, 2006), 301–2.

17 Huebner, *The Family in Roman Egypt*, 130.

18 One example of equality in inheritance was joint-inheritance (*consortium*) in Roman Egypt. In P.Mich. 3.186 (CE 72), Herakleides and Horos divide some property among houseyards and courtyards which they jointly-inherited from their father. The practices of joint-inheritance are often found in ancient Greek contract papyri (e.g., P.Mich.inv. 5579; P.Mich. 15.704; P.Tebt. 2.319; P.Mich. 18.785a). For more examples of Roman *consortium*, see Valerius Maximus 4.4.8; Pliny, *Ep.* 8.18.4; *Digest* 10.2.39.3; Gaius, *Inst.* 3. 154a–b; Livy, 41.27.2.

19 L.E. Tacoma, *Fragile Hierarchies: The Urban Elites of Third Century Roman Egypt* (MnemosyneSup 271; Leiden: Brill, 2006), 228.

However, as recent classicists observe, primogeniture was not dominant in Roman Egypt, and was never a norm of succession there.[20]

We should consider that an equal portion of inheritance was not defined as a mathematically equal amount. For example, in *Banquet* 4.34 (the fourth century BCE), Xenophon describes that he knows of brothers who received equal shares of an inheritance, but simultaneously reports that one of them took more than enough, and the other was in utter want and this implies that, indeed, two brothers received different amounts of inheritance despite these being designated as "equal shares." Equality in a Classical and Hellenistic Greek sense did not mean sameness or equal portion as in a modern sense. Concerning the Roman understanding of equality, as Bannon writes, "[A] father defined equality among his children based on their individual needs and capacities and in response to social or economic circumstances."[21] Equality was determined by a father's judgment and the brothers received differentiated portions by their needs, although these were designated as "equal shares." So, priority in inheritance was not automatically determined by birth rank.[22]

The hereditary succession of the father's life-time office was a complex matter in the Greco-Roman world.[23] In Aeschylus' family, family continuity was achieved through the children of Aeschylus' sister, Philopeithes.[24] In Ptolemaic Egypt, sons of soldiers were sometimes obliged to inherit and assume their fathers' military responsibilities. There was an expectation that a father should

20 E.g., Tacoma, *Fragile Hierarchies*, 208; Huebner, *The Family in Roman Egypt*, 50; Sarah B. Pomeroy, *Families in Classical and Hellenistic Greece: Representations and Realities* (Oxford: Clarendon, 1997), 206.

21 Bannon, *The Brothers of Romulus*, 32.

22 On the other hand, in Greco-Roman families, the older brothers were portrayed as holding primacy over their younger ones. For more detail on this aspect, see A.D. Clarke, "Equality or Mutuality: Paul' Use of 'Brother' Language," in *The New Testament in Its First Century Setting: Essays on Context and Background in Honour of B.W. Winter on His 65th Birthday* (eds. A.D. Clarke and P.J. Williams, et al.; Grand Rapids: Eerdmans, 2004), 159–63. See also J.M.G. Barclay, "There is Neither Old nor Young? Early Christianity and Ancient Ideologies of Age," *NTS* 53 (2007): 225–41.

23 De Coulanges notes that the family worship in the paternal religion was transmitted from male offspring to their male offspring. See Numa Denis Fustel de Coulanges, *The Ancient City: A Study on the Religion, Laws, and Institutions of Greece and Rome* (Kitchener: Batoche, 2001), 58. In Demosthenes, *Against Macartatus* 43.74 (the fourth century BCE), the eldest son was named after his grandfather because the name was fitting for the eldest son (ὥσπερ καὶ δίκαιόν ἐστιν), and it implies that the eldest son had some honoured status. However, it did not mean that the eldest son inherit the office of his father and grandfather.

24 Sarah B. Pomeroy, "Some Greek Families: Production and Reproduction," in *The Jewish Family in Antiquity* (ed. Shaye J.D. Cohen; BJS 289; Atlanta: Scholars, 1993), 160.

have coached and tutored his children in the duties and responsibilities of his professional role in Classical Athenian society (e.g., Xenophon, *Oeconomicus* 20.22). In the families of artists and the theatrical families, the special skills and techniques acquired by the father were generally handed down to his children.[25] Yet in this case, there was no unique status governing the role and responsibility of the eldest son.[26] The continuance of the knowledge and skills was not only achieved through their inheritance by the eldest son. The acquisition of the skills and knowledge was sometimes bequeathed to daughters' sons.

Nonetheless, there are at least two exceptions where the eldest sons inherited their fathers' office in ancient Greek society (particularly, in Classical Greece).[27] Primogeniture was exercised with regard to determining royal succession in the classical Greek world. In some cases, the younger brother ascended to the throne before the elder brother. In Diodorus Siculus, 11.38, king Gelon (the fifth century BCE), the younger brother, was enthroned, and before his death, handed over his kinship to Hieron, his eldest brother. However, in many other cases, the eldest brother had the priority for royal succession over his younger brothers. For instance, in *Descriptions of Greece* 1.5.4, Pausanias says "Aegeus, as the eldest son, became king of the Athenians." In *Alcibiades* 1.121c (the fourth century BCE), Plato writes, "When the eldest son, the heir to the throne, is born, first of all the king's subjects who are in his palace have a feast, and then forever after on that date the whole of Asia celebrates the king's birthday with sacrifice and feasting" [Loeb Translation] (cf. Plato, *Lysis* 209d). So, when the first son of the king was born, the son was expected to be the royal heir. Sophocles (the fifth century BCE) also states in *Oedious at Colonus*, 1284, "as eldest-born, I [Polyneices] thought it right to sit on your sovereign throne." Thus, the order of birth in the royal family was considered to be an important criterion to determine the royal line of succession in the classical Greek world.[28]

25 Pomeroy, "Some Greek Families," 159–60; Dana F. Sutton, "The Theatrical Families of Athens," *AJP* 108 (1987): 9–26.

26 Willy Clarysse, *The Petrie Papyri, vol. 1: The Wills* (CH; Brussels: Koninklijke Academie voor Wetenschappen, 1991), 37–39.

27 Artists' artistry was also inherited by descendants in the Ancient Greek society. See Pomeroy, *Families in Classical and Hellenistic Greece*, 155. See also Pliny the Elder, *Naturalis Historia*, 36.24.

28 In Livy 40.9, Perseus (the eldest son of the Macedonian king) spoke to his younger brother who was ambitious for the throne, "My brother, we have long lived with one another in no spirit of boon companions. You wish of course to be king. In the way of this ambition of yours stand my age, the rule of nations, the ancient custom of Macedonia, and indeed also the decision of our father [Loeb Translation]." This quotation implies the important principle of royal succession in Macedonia. Whereas the decision of the king was

By contrast, in the early Roman Empire, birth rank was not considered to be the norm in respect of royal succession. Royal successions in the early Roman Empire were often practised by means of imperial adoption, which was in conformity to the meritocracy pursed by Roman society.[29] For instance, in the early first century AD, Augustus adopted Tiberius and appointed him as successor of his imperial power (e.g., Tacitus, *Annales* 1.59). Nero was adopted by Claudius and enthroned instead of Britannicus (Claudius' natural son).[30] Thus, in the first-century Roman Empire, the imperial succession was usually determined by the successor's merit and quality instead of his birth rank.

The second exception is related to the succession of Classical Athenian priesthoods. Succession of an Athenian priestly family, such as the family of Eumopidai, has drawn scholarly attention as an example of primogeniture in relation to the father's office.[31] In the case of the Athenian priesthood, it seems that the deceased priest's priesthood was transmitted to the eldest son through inheritance.[32]

In brief, we do not find any evidence that primogeniture was not prevalent in Greco-Roman society. The prerogative of the eldest son in inheritance was not supported by Greco-Roman legal rules. Therefore, we conclude that primogeniture was uncommon in the Greco-Roman world. Exceptions are found in the Athenian priesthood and Greek Royal succession. As Sarah Pomeroy writes, "Primogeniture appears only in determining succession to the throne, where priority is given to the eldest son born after a king's accession" in Classical and Hellenistic Greek society.[33] In the next section, we will consider features of Jewish inheritance practices distinct from Greco-Roman customs (particularly, the institution of primogeniture).

---

significant with regard to the royal successor, the order of age was also a crucial principle, and the eldest son normally had priority as a royal heir over his younger brothers (royal primogeniture).

29 Michael Peppard, *The Son of God in the Roman World: Divine Sonship in Its Social and Political Context* (Oxford: Oxford University Press, 2011), 73.

30 Tacitus, *Annales*, 12.25; 12.68–69.

31 C. Hignett, *A History of the Athenian Constitution to the End of the Fifth Century BC* (Oxford: Oxford University Press, 1952), 64–65; J.K. Davies, *Athenian Propertied Families, 600–300 BC* (Oxford: Oxford University Press, 1971), 172–73; Kevin Clinton, "A Family of Eumolpidai and Kerykes Descended from Pericles," *Hesperia* 73 (2004): 39–57; William S. Bubelis, "Inheritance, Priesthoods and Succession in Classical Athens: The Hierophantai of the Eumolpidai," in *Families in the Greco-Roman World* (eds. Ray Laurence, *et.al.*; London: Bloomsbury, 2012), 95–105; Pomeroy, *Families in Classical and Hellenistic Greece*, 149–52.

32 Bubelis, "Inheritance, Priesthoods and Succession," 98.

33 Pomeroy, *Families in Classical and Hellenistic Greece*, 53.

2.2 Primogeniture in Jewish Inheritance Practices

This section will explore primogeniture (בכרה) in the Jewish family. It has been observed by scholars that the firstborn son was placed "second in rank to the *pater familias*" in terms of advantages and obligations.[34] It seems that the first-born son held preferential status in the Ancient Near East. Mendelsohn defines the position of the firstborn son in the Ancient Near Eastern family, as follows.

> We thus have evidence that the eldest brother was accorded a preferential status not only in Nuzi, Assyria, Syria, and Palestine, but also in Southern and Northern Babylonia in the period between the fall of Ur III and the rise of the Hammurabi empire. On the basis of the available data we may conclude that the preferential status of the first-born son had its origin and raison d'être in semi-nomadic and predominantly agricultural societies.[35]

In the Old Testament, בכר was meant as the firstborn son, and sometimes גדל (the eldest one) and ראש (head or the first) also refer to the firstborn.[36] The titles of גדל and ראש imply that the status of בכר is distinct and even higher than that of the younger brothers.

2.2.1 *Frederick E. Greenspahn and Primogeniture*

Did the first male offspring automatically become בכר (the firstborn son)? Otherwise, was the status of בכר assigned by one's father? This question is significant, since, if בכר is selected by his father, it means that בכר cannot be defined as the eldest son of the family, and that primogeniture did not exist in ancient Jewish society. It has been argued by scholars that primogeniture in the OT carries some prerogatives and duties with regard to the rights of inheritance.[37] In recent scholarship, however, an alternative view has been

34 E.g., I. Mendelsohn, "On the Preferential Status of the Eldest Son," *BASOR* 156 (1959): 39–40. 40; Roland de Vaux, *Ancient Israel: Its Life and Institutions* (London: Darton, Longman & Todd, 1961), 41.

35 Mendelsohn, "On the Preferential Status,"40. Cf. Baruch Levine, "Firstborn," 45.

36 For the uses of גדל in sense of the firstborn son, see Gen 27:1, 42; 44:12. For ראש, see 1 Chr 26:10–11. Von Rad also writes, "[T]he privilege of the first-born was absolutely uncontested in the ancient orient." See Gerhard von Rad, *Genesis: A Commentary* (trans. John H. Marks; OTL; Philadelphia: Westminster, 1973), 416.

37 Cf. Job 18:13; Zech 12:10. Tsevat mentions, "The size of the portion given to the firstborn (his normal inheritance plus a preferential portion) is not the same in the various cuneiform laws; but as far as we now know, usually the firstborn received twice as much as each succeeding son, but sometimes less," in M. Tsevat, "b^{e}khôr," in *TDOT, vol. 2* (eds. G. Johannes

emerging: i.e., the status of בכר was determined by the choice of the father, and primogeniture according to birth rank did not exist in Jewish inheritance practices.[38] Tikva Frymer-Kensky maintains:

> [In the ANE], the term, 'the first-born,' like the terms 'son,' 'father,' 'brother,' and 'sister,' is essentially a description of a particular juridical relationship which may be entered into by contract as well as by birth ... the designation of an individual as 'first-born' can also be a matter of choice [in the OT].[39]

Frymer-Kensky concludes that the firstborn son could be appointed by the father's choice, and that choosing the younger over the older is attested in many cases in the OT.

Frederick E. Greenspahn develops this perspective. He maintains that "the position of bekor was an assigned, not an automatic status, even if eldest sons were most likely to achieve its benefits."[40] In other words, בכר was not a status obtained through the first birth rank, but as a result of the father's decision. Greenspahn writes:

> The semantic ambiguity of the title bekor, which designates the beneficiary of whatever advantages that system had to offer, undercuts the utility of that term for demonstrating that the transmission of property and authority was based on automatic principles.[41]

Botterweck and Helmer Ringgren; Grand Rapids: Eerdmans, 1977), 124. Mendelsohn also states, "The reason for selecting a 'firstborn' was that the chosen son was by this act elevated to a privileged position in the family. The eldest son was entitled to a double share in the inheritance of the paternal estate in Assyria, Nuzi, Palestine," and, as it must now be assumed, also in Ugarit and Alalakh ... The contemporary texts from Larsa, although they do not employ the technical term SIB. TA, clearly indicate that the eldest son inherits a larger share (often amounting to a double portion) than do his younger brothers," in Mendelsohn, "On the Preferential Status," 39–40.

38 Frederick E. Greenspahn, *When Brothers Dwell Together: The Preeminence of Younger Siblings in the Hebrew Bible* (Oxford: Oxford University Press, 1994); Carol Bakhos, *Ishmael on the Border: Rabbinic Portrayals of the First Arab* (Albany: State University of New York Press, 2006), 22; Julie Faith Parker, *Valuable and Vulnerable: Children in the Hebrew Bible, Especially Elisha Cycle* (Providence: Brown University Press, 2013), 52.

39 Tikva Frymer-Kenksy, "Patriarchal Family Relationships and Near Eastern Law," *BA* 44 (1981): 214.

40 Greenspahn, *When Brothers Dwell Together*, 59. Cf. Knoppers, "The Preferential Status," 17.

41 Greenspahn, *When Brothers Dwell Together*, 69.

So, the status of בכר could be transferred, as in the case of Esau's having sold the right of the firstborn son to Jacob (Gen 25), and one did not become בכר by virtue of birth but by the appointment of one's father (or grandfather), as Isaac and Ephraim became בכר over Ishmael and Manasseh. Greenspahn also contends, "Esau was not disinherited, nor Jacob granted *patria potestas*. What was at stake was destiny, not property."[42] In the OT, the royal succession of Israel seems unrelated to birth rank.[43] David, Jehoram, Rehoboam, Hezekiah, Manasseh, Josiah and Jehoiakim were succeeded by younger sons. In 1 Chr 26:10–11, Hosah designates Shimri (his younger son) as ראש (chief) which may refer to the firstborn son. Greenspahn, therefore, concludes that Israel's system of succession and inheritance was not strictly bound to birth order and that the status of בכר is not automatic but could be earned or appointed.[44] Thus, the ambiguity of the concept of בכר justifies further investigation into the right of the firstborn son in inheritance.

2.2.2 *Primogeniture in Genesis and 1 Chronicles*

Some ambiguity is found when exploring the notion of the firstborn son in the OT and Jewish literature. Was the firstborn son "the first son" born to his father? The firstborn son can refer to "the firstborn male with the first issue of the womb, as such the aetiology of Levitical consecration in the Book of Numbers"[45] with particular reference to the sacrificial law. However, it should be noted that, in Deut 21:17, the firstborn son is defined not in terms of "the first issue of the womb," but in relation to the father (cf. Gen 49:3; Ps 78:51; 105:36).[46] Perhaps, as Levine observes, there were two distinct definitions of the firstborn in ancient Israelite society: a socio-legal one and a cultic one. The socio-legal definition is particularly concerned with legislation regarding inheritance. So, in this sense, the firstborn son is "a principal heir and successor of his father as head of the family."[47] The second definition of the firstborn son highlights the biological link of the firstborn son to the mother. Arguably, this definition originated in "the religious significance of the first products of the procreative

42 Greenspahn, *When Brothers Dwell Together*, 56.

43 Greenspahn, *When Brothers Dwell Together*, 80.

44 Greenspahn, *When Brothers Dwell Together*, 82.

45 Jon D. Levenson, *The Death and Resurrection of the Beloved Son: The Transformation of Child Sacrifice in Judaism and Christianity* (New Haven: Yale University Press, 1993), 56. Cf. Num 3:11–13; 8:13–18. Cf. "Consecrate to Me every first-born son; man and beast, the first issue of every womb among the Israelites is Mine," in Exod 13:2.

46 Tsevat, "b^ekhôr," 125; Levenson, *The Death and Resurrection of the Beloved Son*, 58.

47 Levine, "Firstborn," 45.

process in human and animal life."[48] In the Patriarchal narrative, the status of the firstborn son is defined in relation to the paternal line, with reference to the father's inheritance and the succession of his family as follows.

Some exegetes argue that the blessings to Jacob's sons in Gen 49 originated from the collections of tribal sayings, and that Gen 49:4 reflects a certain tribal offence of the Reubenites.[49] However, Reuben's sexual violation in Gen 35:22 and the curse given to him in Gen 49:3–4 are paralleled with the story of Ham's curse in Gen 9:20–27. As it is difficult to regard Ham's misdeed as a tribal offense, so there is no evidence to consider Reuben's sin as a tribal violation in the given text.[50] In Gen 49:3, Reuben is spoken of as the firstborn son of Jacob and the first fruits of Jacob's vigour: "the first fruit of my vigour, excelling in rank and excelling in power." This verse indicates that Reuben was biologically the eldest son of Jacob, and the firstborn son clearly held higher status than his younger brothers. However, Jacob's favour is taken away from Reuben (Gen 49:3–4). In Exod 6:14; Num 1:20, 26:5, Reuben is nominated as the firstborn son of Israel, and listed in the first place in all the tribes of Israel. However, the tribe of Reuben does not have leadership of Israel, and rulership is conferred upon the tribe of Judah: particularly, "your father's sons [Judah's brothers] shall bow down before you [Judah]," in Gen 49:8 and "a ruler came from him [Judah]," in 1 Chr 5:2. It is probable that supplanting Reuben's birthright in Genesis reflects the political decline of the tribe of Reuben.[51] Nonetheless, Reuben is still addressed as the firstborn son of Jacob (or Israel) in Gen 35:23; 36:15; 46:8; 49:3; Exod 6:14; Num 1:20; 26:5; 1 Chr 5:1. In 4Q252 IV (a commentary on Genesis 49:3–4), Reuben is also addressed as Jacob's firstborn son (בכר), the first fruit of Jacob's manhood, pre-eminent in stature and pre-eminent in strength. In *T.Jacob* 5:3, Reuben is also designated as the firstborn son. These verses denote that, in the biblical and extra-canonical literature, Reuben was called בכר even after Reuben was deprived of his birthright.

In Gen 48:22, Joseph was assigned a larger portion than his brothers, and so Joseph may have been bestowed a special privilege as the firstborn son by Jacob.[52] In Gen 49:26, Jacob blesses Joseph as follows: "The blessings of your father are stronger than the blessings of the eternal mountains, the boun-

48 Gershon Brin, *Studies in Biblical Law: From the Hebrew Bible to the Dead Sea Scrolls* (trans. Jonathan Chipman; JSOTSup 176; Sheffield: Sheffield Academic Press, 1994), 212–13.

49 E.g., John Skinner, *A Critical and Exegetical Commentary on Genesis* (ICC; New York: Charles Scribner's Sons, 1910), 515.

50 Victor P. Hamilton, *The Book of Genesis: Chapters 18–50* (NICOT; Grand Rapids: Eerdmans, 1995), 647–48.

51 F.M. Cross, "Reuben, Firstborn of Jacob," *ZAW* 100 (1988): 46–65.

52 So, Knoppers, "The Preferential Status," 119. Cf. 1 Chr 5:1.

ties of the everlasting hills; may they be on the head of Joseph, on the brow of him who was set apart from his brothers." In this blessing, the preferential portion is given to Joseph. Furthermore, Joseph's portion is increased by Jacob's blessing to Manasseh and Ephraim (Gen 48:6). In other words, through Jacob's blessings to Joseph's two sons (Manasseh and Ephraim), Joseph may be given the double portion that is the prerogative of the firstborn son.[53] Nonetheless, the title of the firstborn son is still retained by Reuben (49:3). So, in this story, the right of the firstborn son is transferred to Joseph, but the title of the firstborn son is determined by the order of age.

In Gen 41:51 and 48:14, 18, Manasseh is entitled בכר according to his birth rank. However, Jacob laid his right hand on Ephraim (Joseph's younger son), and Joseph intervenes in Jacob's blessing to Manasseh and Ephraim: "Not so. My father! Since this one [Manasseh] is the firstborn, put your right hand on his head" (Gen 48:18). This may show that it was a normal expectation that the eldest son became a successor of the family, and the same point also seems to be implied in Gen 49:3–9.[54]

In Gen 48:19, Jacob said that the younger (Ephraim) would be גדל (greater) than the elder brother, Manasseh. גדל (the greater) refers to the eldest brother in brotherly relationship. This suggests that the birthright was transferred to Ephraim. That is, it seems that Ephraim is designated as the eldest son through Jacob's blessing.[55] Brevard Childs insightfully states, "He [Joseph] does not form the part of the triad [Abraham, Isaac and Jacob] to whom the promise of the land and posterity is given, rather he becomes the first (Gen 50:24) to whom the promise to Abraham, Isaac and Jacob is reiterated."[56] So, Joseph is the bearer of the promise given to Abraham, Isaac and Jacob in Genesis. In Deut 33:13–15, Moses gives the blessing of material prosperity to Joseph and his land. In Deut 33:16b, Moses also says, "May these [blessings] come upon the head of Joseph, on the blow of the prince among his brothers." In Deut 33:17, Moses blesses the tribe of Joseph: "A Firstborn bull, majesty is his [Joseph]." The image of a firstborn bull is connected to militant images: "His horns are the horns of a wild ox; with them he gores the peoples, driving them to the

53 Sara Japhet, *I&II Chronicles: A Commentary* (OTL; Philadelphia: WJK, 1993), 133.

54 *Contra* Greenspahn, *When Brothers Dwell together*, 121.

55 In Jer 31:9, Ephraim is addressed as the firstborn son of God: "For I have become a father to Israel, and Ephraim is my firstborn." This story may also reflect that the tribe of Ephraim outranked the tribe of Manasseh in ancient Israel. Von Rad observes, "Obviously the more centrally located tribe of Ephraim had politically surpassed the fraternal tribe Manasseh. Our narrative will also make mysterious allusions to that fact." See von Rad, *Genesis*, 413.

56 Brevard Childs, *Introduction to the Old Testament as Scripture* (Minneapolis: Fortress, 1973), 156.

ends of the earth" (33:17ab). This blessing has some similarities with the blessing of Jacob in Gen 49:22–26. In the blessing, Jacob speaks of prosperity in Gen 49:22 and military blessings in 49:23. In Deut 33:13–17, Moses also blesses Joseph with the best ones that are highlighted by the six-fold "with the best of" in Deut 33:13–16. In Deut 33:16, Joseph is "upon the forehead of the foremost of his brothers." This privilege goes to both Ephraim and Manasseh, but Ephraim will have primacy over Manasseh (33:17b). Joseph is likened to "a firstborn bull," and the image of the firstborn is juxtaposed with the images of divine favour (33:16a), Joseph's primacy over other brothers (33:16b), and majesty (33:17). Furthermore, Joseph is not merely the firstborn son, but also a bull that gores the nations. This image of the firstborn evokes that the right of the firstborn son is transferred to Joseph (Gen 48:22; 49:26; 1 Chr 5:1).

In Gen 38:6–7 (cf. 1 Chr 2:3), Judah's eldest son, Er, is spoken of as בכר (the firstborn son), however, he is killed by YHWH because he was evil in the sight of YHWH (38:7). In 1 Chr 2:3, Judah's בכר is still Er in spite of his misdeeds, although the successor of Judah's family was Perez. This case also denotes that the title of the firstborn son (בכר) is determined by birth rank.

In 1 Chr 5:1–2,[57] Reuben is still addressed as the firstborn son of Israel, but also the right of the firstborn son was transferred to Joseph in 1 Chr 5:1–2, even though Judah had grown mighty among his brothers and had become a leader.[58] Two themes in 1 and 2 Chronicles are the kingship of the Davidic line and the Temple.[59] H.G.M. Williamson notes that Chronicles does not simply stress the legitimacy of the Southern monarchy, but includes both Southern and Northern kingdoms to the whole Israel.[60] Manfred Oeming develops this argument through his study on genealogy in 1 Chr 1–9. In Chronicles, the true Israel is defined as the nation who obeys the Law and participates in the Jerusalem cult. Jerusalem is the true centre of Israel, and the Northern tribes could belong to the true Israel (das wahre Israel) through participation in the Jerusalem cult.[61] Therefore, it is highly probable that the author of Chronicles

---

57 The composition and purpose of Chronicles have been highly disputed. E.g., Martin Noth, *Überlieferungsgeschichtliche Studien* (Darmstadt: Wissenschaftliche Buchgesellschaft, 1943); Frank M. Cross, "A Reconstruction of the Judean Restoration," *JBL* 94 (1975): 4–18; Sara Japhet, "The Supposed Common Authorship of Chronicles and Ezra-Nehemiah Investigated Anew," *VT* 19 (1968): 330–71.

58 *Contra* Greenspahn's observation in *When Brothers dwell together*, 58–59.

59 See David N. Freedman, "The Chronicler's Purpose," *CBQ* 23 (1961): 432–42.

60 H.G.M. Williamson, *Israel in the Books of Chronicles* (Cambridge: Cambridge University Press), 1977.

61 Manfred Oeming, *Das wahre Israel: die "genealogische Vorhalle" 1 Chronik 1–9* (BWANT 128; Stuttgart: Kohlhammer, 1990). See also J. Kegler, "Prophetengestalten im Deuteronomistischen Geschichtswerk und in den Chronikbüchern. Ein Beitrag zur Kompositions-und Redaktionsgeschichte der Chronikbücher," *ZAW* 105 (1993): 481–97.

did not intend to exclude the northern tribes from the whole of Israel in 1 and 2 Chronicles. In this context, Reuben is addressed as the firstborn son of Israel, even though the right of the firstborn son was transferred to Joseph. Particularly, Reuben's status as the firstborn son is stressed by the six-fold reiteration of בכר and its cognate words.[62] Accordingly, as Greenspahn concedes, Reuben is identified as בכר, "even after claiming that he had lost the bekora [the right of the firstborn son]."[63] On the other hand, Judah takes possession of the kingship of Israel in 1 Chr 5:1–2.[64] Thus, it seems that the author of Chronicles distinguishes the right of the firstborn son from the kingship of Israel in 1 Chr 5:1–2.

We can understand the next three points from this passage (1 Chr 5:1–2). Firstly, it seems that the title of בכר is assigned by birth rank. So, the title of the firstborn son is retained by Reuben in the OT and Jewish literature, even though it is simply nominal.[65] Secondly, the right of the firstborn son is transferred to Joseph and the kingship is given to Judah. Therefore, it seems that the title of בכר was determined by the order of age, but that the right of the firstborn son could be transferred to a younger brother (see also 4Q252 IV). However, the kingship of Israel is distinguished from the right of the firstborn son in 1 Chr 5:2 (cf. Gen 49:10: "The scepter shall not depart from Judah ... the obedience of the peoples is his"). Thirdly, the underlying political motivations in 1 Chr 5:1–2 are unclear, but it seems that the author of Chronicles follows the depictions of Jacob's blessing to Reuben, Judah and Joseph in Gen 48–49.

It is difficult to come to a conclusion regarding the concept of primogeniture through historically nuanced documents. However, it seems that the right of the firstborn son could be transferred to his brothers as a result of the father's decision.[66] Yet, the title of the firstborn son (בכר) was normally nominated according to chronological order.[67] Even after deprival of his birthright,

---

62 Japhet, *I&II Chronicles*, 132.

63 Greenspahn, *When Brothers dwell together*, 123. However, he also argues on the basis of the syntactical awkwardness in 1 Chr 5:1–3 that "the account of Reuben's losing the bekora has been inserted into a list of his descendants which identified him as Israel's bekor. Yet, it was no wonder to Jews that the title of the firstborn son was retained by the first male offspring, even after dispossessing bekora."

64 Cf. Josephus, *Ant* 7.14.8.

65 This is also confirmed in *Sifre to Deut.* 2.3.2.

66 This study will separately deal with the story of Jacob and Esau in detail in the next chapter.

67 Anderson and Knoppers espouse this view. See B.A. Anderson, "The Inversion of the Birth Order and the Title of the Firstborn Son," *VT* 60 (2010): 655–58; Gary N. Knoppers, "The Preferential Status of the Eldest Son Revoked?" in *Rethinking the Foundations: Historiography in the Ancient World and in the Bible, Essays in Honour of John Van Seters* (BZAW 294; ed. S.L. McKenzie, *et.al.*; Berlin: Walter de Gruyter, 2000), 115–26. Cf. Raymond

the eldest was still addressed as בכר in the OT. In addition, the right of the firstborn son in Jacob's family was not related to the rulership of Israel, because the right of the firstborn son in Jacob's family was transferred to Joseph and the rulership was conferred upon Judah in Gen 49:10 and 1 Chr 5:2. Conversely, Gen 43:33 explicitly connects the firstborn son (בכר) to the birthright (the firstborn son according to the birthright). So, in this verse, the eldest son (בכר) is the one who holds the birthright. Yet, one of the recurring features of OT narratives is that family relations were troubled. Consequently, it is not easy to conclude whether, in OT narratives, the situations where a younger brother is designated as a principal heir were conventional or anomalous. Before any definitive position can be arrived at, further analysis of the Deuteronomic legal rules on the right of the firstborn son and the later interpretations of the Law needs to be made.

2.2.3 *Primogeniture in Deuteronomic Family Law and Its Later Interpretations*

In ancient Israelite society, postmortem division of the father's property was procedural and practised according to the rules of Torah.[68] Three possibilities were proposed in Israelite inheritance practices.[69] Firstly, the brothers could split up the family, and divide up the father's property into portions. Secondly, some brothers could be excluded from the inheritance of the father's property. The third possibility is a minimal division. The brothers could reside in the father's estate instead of partitioning the property (e.g., Deut 25:5).[70] In this case, the eldest brother had leadership of the whole family. However, as Westbrook

Westbrook, *Property and the Family in Biblical Law* (JSOTSup 113; Sheffield: Sheffield Academic, 1991), 137. In 1 Chr 26:10, Hosah, a Korahite, designated his son Shimri as the chief although he was not the firstborn. In this verse, the head (the status of the firstborn) is designated by the father's decision, not biologically determined. However, we should point out that 1 Chr 26:10b states that Shimri was not בכר. In other words, the status as a successor of the family is designated by the father, but it would appear that the normal expectation was that the firstborn son is nominated to the principal heir and the leader of his brothers.

68 In Jewish inheritance practices, inheritance could not move from one tribe to another tribe. See Num 36:7; *B.Bathra* 112a. *Sir* 22:23 may denote that a non-family member could share in the inheritance of a neighbor: "Gain the trust of your neighbor in his poverty, so that you may rejoice with him in his prosperity. Stand by him in time of distress, so that you may share with him in inheritance." However, the priority in matters of inheritance is given to the family members. See de Vaux, *Ancient Israel*, 113–17.

69 S. Bendor, *The Social Structure of Ancient Israel: The Institution of the Family (Beit' ab) from the Settlement to the end of the Monarchy* (JBS 7; Jerusalem: Simor, 1996), 171.

70 Cf. David Daube, "Consortium in Roman and Hebrew Law," *The Juridical Review* 72 (1950): 71–91.

observes, undivided inheritance was adopted when the division of the inheritance was postponed due to financial or economic factors.[71] In Talmudic literature, there are some references to brothers who co-owned the father's estate, but this seemed to be temporary until the estate was partitioned.[72] Greenspahn writes that, in some cases, property was shared and co-owned by brothers,[73] but permanent co-ownership of property between brothers was not a Jewish convention. So, the existence of joint-inheritance in ancient Israel and the Talmudic period lacks evidence.

In the ANE, primogeniture was widespread in contrast to Greenspahn's arguments.[74] The family in the ANE was "patrilocal in residence" and "patripotestal in authority," and was a large extended family, which meant that "all the sons stay together in one household with the father, who remains the undisputed head of the family until his death."[75] When the father died, the firstborn son assumed the position of the head of the family.[76]

Like the ANE law, Deut 21:15–17 also protects the rights of the firstborn son in inheritance. In Deut 21:15–17, the Legal rule limits the authority of the male head of household with regard to the rights of dependent members in the family, and forbids arbitrary distribution of the eldest son's portion to the younger son, and seeks to safeguard the right of the eldest son and further, the rights of the hated wife.[77] בכר in Deut 21:15–17 is defined as the first issue of his procreative power (the firstborn male offspring of the father) and the right of the firstborn son is his (משפט בכורה; 21:17). Even though he is the son of the hated wife, the eldest son should receive a double share of all according to the right of the firstborn son. In this inheritance regulation, the position of the firstborn son is not designated by the father, but automatically nominated by birth rank. In this legal rule, the firstborn son is the special heir who could possess the

71 Westbrook, *Property and Family in Biblical Law*, 120. He also writes, "The co-heirship of brothers ended up with division of the inheritance. Ideally, this would take place by mutual consent, as in the case of Abraham and Lot," in Westbrook, *Property and Family in Biblical Law*, 140.

72 Heinrich W. Guggenheimer, *The Jerusalem Talmud Fourth Order: Neziqin Tractates Bava Qamma, Bava Mesia, and Bava Batra* (SJ 45; Berlin: Walter de Gruyter, 2008), 663–64.

73 Greenspahn, *When Brothers Dwell Together*, 81.

74 Cf. Frymer-Kenksy, "Patriarchal Family Relationships and Near Eastern Law," 209–14. Gershon Brin also notes that the double portion for the firstborn son was frequently found in the ANE (e.g., Larsa, Nuzi and Mari), in Brin, *Studies in Biblical Law*, 240–1. See also Jack R. Lundbom, *Deuteronomy: A Commentary* (Grand Rapids: Eerdmans, 2013), 603.

75 Frymer-Kenksy, "Patriarchal Family Relationships and Near Eastern Law," 210.

76 Frymer-Kensky, "Patriarchal Family Relationships and Near Eastern Law," 211.

77 Pressler, *The View of Women*, 15–6; Jack Lundbom, *Deuteronomy: A Commentary* (Grand Rapids: Eerdmans, 2003), 602.

double portion of the father's inheritance, and is defined according to birth order just like the firstlings in the cultic offering. The expression "in preference to (or in front of)" in Deut 21:16 also implies that the prerogative of the firstborn son is related to his primary position over his siblings in matters of inheritance. That is, the sons of the beloved wife could not have priority over the firstborn son in matters of inheritance. This regulation also underscores the significance of the firstborn status "by firmly tying this position to birthright."[78] Double portion is occasionally referenced in the OT (e.g., Elisha's portion from Elijah in 2 Kgs 2:9; and Joseph's portion in Gen 48:5, 22), and it is highly probable that the double portion in Gen 48 and 2 Kings 2:9 are linked with the portion for the firstborn son. Double portion (שנים), perhaps, refers to the two-third portion according to Zech 13:8.[79] However, some later interpretations read double portion (שנים) as two portions.[80] Perhaps, the double portion was not mathematically understood, and it is hard to determine the actual size of the portion on the basis of extant documents. Yet, the clear point in the given text is, as Levine observes, that a father should have acknowledged his firstborn son as his principal heir.[81]

The firstborn son is referenced in the context of Deut 25:6 with regard to the Levirate marriage. The brother of the deceased should be married to the widow of the deceased and take care of her (25:5).[82] If the brother was not married, the firstborn son should be both his son and the son of the deceased brother (cf. Ruth 4:21).[83] The eldest son of the widow and her deceased husband shall succeed (יקום) the deceased brother's name. Thus in this law, the firstborn son is the principal heir of the family of the deceased. As Jack Lundbom notes, "name" is associated with inheritance.[84] In this sense, the firstborn is the successor of the name of the deceased and a principal heir of the inheritance.[85] Wiping out a name (מחה) in Deut 25:6 may indicate a kind of curse in ancient

78 Knoppers, "The Preferential Status," 117.

79 Paul Watson, "A Note on the 'Double Portion' of Deuteronomy 21:17 and 2 Kings 2:9," *ResQ* 9 (1965): 70–75.

80 See *B.Bathra* 118b; Philo, *Spec Leg* 2.130; Josephus, *Ant* 4.249. Cf. *Sir* 12:4–5. See Brin, *Studies in Biblical Law*, 242–244.

81 Baruch Levine, "Firstborn," 45. See also Pressler, *The View of Women*, 16.

82 Cf. *B.Bathra* 108b, "Surely, levirate marriage only takes place where there is no son, but where there is a son there is no levirate marriage."

83 Lundbom, *Deuteronomy*, 708.

84 See *b.Yebam* 24a. Lundbom, 708. Cf. Josephus, *Ant* 4.254.

85 Peter C. Craigie, *The Book of Deuteronomy* (NICOT; Grand Rapids: Eerdmans, 1976), 314.

Jewish society (cf. Ps 9:5; 109:13; Judg 21:7).[86] Therefore, in Deuteronomic family law, בכר refers to the first male offspring and is determined by birth rank.

Nevertheless, Greenspahn claims, "Deuteronomy's treatment of inheritance is better understood as reflecting that book's general interest in protecting the weak and the vulnerable."[87] In this vein, he argues that Deut 21:15–17 does not represent actual Jewish inheritance practices:

> [T]his law protects an unloved mother by limiting her husband's power … favouritism had previously played a role in the bestowal of that status. At the same time, the regulation implicitly allows that practice to continue, but only within certain limits.[88]

So, we will examine whether Greenspahn's view is evidenced by Jewish authors in the Second Temple period and the Talmudic era. In *Spec Leg* 2.133–34, Philo explains primogeniture in Jewish inheritance practices as follows:

> The eldest son (πρεσβύτατος) does not share equally with his younger brothers, but is adjudged a double portion. The one reason for the prerogative of the eldest son is that his parents who before but man and wife, owe to the first-born the fact that they have later become father and mother. Another is their firstborn who began to use these names in addressing his parents. The third reason is the most important, that what was before their birth a house of barren stock has become fruitful for the preservation of the human race, a preservation which is sown in marriage and fructified in the birth of children, starting with the eldest.
>
> Loeb Translation

Philo does not understand Deut 21:15–17 as a legal rule to protect the weak. Rather, he considers Deut 21:15–17 as a universal regulation of the Jewish family and of inheritance. In *Spec Leg* 2.124–39, Philo elucidates Jewish inheritance

86 As Bendor observes, "It is well known that a name is not merely a means of identifying and remembering a person. A given name is charged with considerable emotional weight; it implies the circumstances of a person's birth, and may at times leave its imprint on his life. The name is also connected to the remembrance, the offspring, and the kinship group," in Bendor, *The Social Structure of Ancient Israel*, 124. Cf. Gen 48:16b: "and in them let my name be perpetuated and the name of my ancestors Abraham and Isaac."

87 Greenspahn, *When Brothers Dwell Together*, 57.

88 Greenspahn, *When Brothers Dwell Together*, 58.

practices,[89] and, in *Spec Leg* 2.133–34, he states that primogeniture was generally exercised in the Jewish family. In this verse, Philo describes how the biologically eldest son (πρεσβύτατος) should take possession of the double portion as a principal heir and the right of the eldest son is not determined by paternal decision, but is given according to birth rank. Thus, in Philo, the eldest son (πρεσβύτατος) has priority (πρεσβεία) in inheritance. The son of the discarded wife should also receive the privilege of the double portion (*Spec Leg* 2.139). Philo writes that the eldest son's privilege equalises the division between brothers, because the sons of the beloved wife already enjoyed the father's favour as their portions when the father was alive (*Spec Leg* 2.139). In this verse, it seems that Philo justifies the reason for unequal inheritance practices in Jewish families since Gentile readers were familiar with equal portions between brothers. Therefore, it seems that *Spec Leg* 2.133–34 reflects actual practices of primogeniture in Alexandrian Jewish society.

Philo sometimes allegorises the practices of primogeniture but it is certain that the allegories are based upon actual practices of primogeniture in Jewish families.[90] In *Sacr* 20, Philo states that the chief honour and rights belong to no one else but to the eldest son (πρωτότοκος) alone and that we love pleasure and hate virtue. That is, the hated wife symbolises virtue and the beloved wife signifies pleasure. Similarly, in *Sobr* 23, Philo writes that the beloved wife is a symbol of pleasure and the hated wife refers to prudence. The son of the hated wife is an emblem of the lover of pleasure and the son of the hated wife represents the lover of virtue (*Sobr* 24). However, there is little evidence in Philo's writings that Deut 21:15–17 is concerned with protecting the right of the weak and that the principal heir was determined by the father's will.

In *Ant* 4.249–50, Josephus also states that the right of the firstborn son should not be assigned to the younger son. Josephus does not understand Deut 21:15–17 as the law for the weak, and rather literally reads and applies the legal rule. The right of the firstborn son is a double share of the father's inheritance, and the firstborn son deserves to take possession of the double

89 Philo writes that sons have priority over daughters in inheritance since men take precedence over women in nature: "The heirs of parents are to be sons, and if no sons, then daughters (*Spec Leg* 2.124)." Yet, if virgins are left without a dower and not granted anything from their parents, they deserve to equally inherit their shares with the males (*Spec Leg* 2.125). If the deceased father did not leave children or brothers, the succession passed to the uncles on the father's side or to the aunts if there were no uncle, and then to the next nearest kinsfolk (*Spec Leg* 2.127).

90 Philo's allegories are based upon the literal meaning of the Bible. See Peder Borgen, "Philo," in *ABD* (New York: Doubleday, 1991), 338; Jutta Leonhardt-Balzer, "Jewish Worship and Universal Identity in Philo of Alexandria," in *Jewish Identity in the Greco-Roman World* (eds. Jörg Frey, Daniel Schwartz and S. Gripentrog; AGJU 71; Leiden: Brill, 2007), 43.

share. The right of the firstborn son is defined according to birth rank, and the firstborn son is treated as a principal heir in this verse.[91] Therefore, Philo and Josephus reveal that primogeniture was actually exercised in the Jewish family.

Several aspects of families and inheritance in the Second Temple period were changed in the Talmudic era. For example, matrilineal aspects of succession in the Second Temple period are minimised in contrast to the Talmudic era. In the rabbinic literature, the child of a Gentile mother and a Jewish father was a Gentile, and the child of a Jewish mother and a Gentile father was a Jew. However, the matrilineal principle of succession is not found in Second Temple literature.[92]

Yet, the Talmudic tradition does not give an account of significant changes in the status of the eldest son in family and inheritance practices. In the rabbinic tradition, while the rights and status of the firstborn son are specified, primogeniture continued to be protected by rabbinic interpretations. The concept of the firstborn son is strictly distinguished with regard to בכור לנחלה (the firstborn son with respect to inheritance) and בכור לכהן (the firstborn son with respect to redemption from a priest), in *Bekoroth* 46a: "There is one who is [counted as] a firstborn [with respect to] inheritance but not with respect to redemption by a priest; a firstborn with respect to redemption from a priest but not a firstborn [with respect] to inheritance." If one who did not have children before married a freed woman who had given birth to a son, the son was reckoned as the firstborn son with respect to inheritance, but not as the firstborn with respect to redemption by a priest (*Bekoroth* 47a). If the woman was a proselyte and gave birth to a son when she was a heathen, the son was not considered as the firstborn son (בכור) with respect to redemption by a priest, but with respect to inheritance (*Yev* 62a).[93] Yet, if she became a proselyte when pregnant, the son was the firstborn (בכור) with reference to redemption by a

91 In *Ant* 4.254–55, when Josephus explains the levirate marriage, the right of the firstborn son is not stressed. Josephus states, "Calling the child that is born by the name of the one who died, she should raise him as successor to the inheritance," and it seems that Josephus employs the reading of LXX Deut 25:16 or another tradition than MT Deut 25:16 in this verse. However, the reason for the omission of the right of the firstborn son is uncertain. Josephus specifically states the legal rules of the levirate marriage and the punishment for the brothers of the deceased brother, if the brothers eschewed marriage with the deceased brother's wife. Josephus writes that the levirate was coined to prevent the property of the deceased brothers from passing to another family. See Louis H. Feldman, trans., *Flavius Josephus: Judean Antiquities 1–4* (FJTC 3; Leiden: Brill, 2000), 428.

92 Shaye J.D. Cohen, *The Beginnings of Jewishness: Boundaries, Varieties, Uncertainties* (HCS 31; Berkeley: University of California Press, 1999), 273.

93 Levine, "Firstborn,"47.

priest (*Bekoroth* 47b).[94] In *Bekoroth* 47b, the firstborn in respect of inheritance is defined by the paternal line (the first fruits of his vigour). The firstborn as regards redemption by a priest is associated with the maternal line (opening the mother's womb). Therefore, בכור refers to the first male offspring, and was not designated by the father's will.

The complex and detailed legal expositions described in the rabbinic tradition[95] imply that the determination of the firstborn son in terms of inheritance and redemption was significant in Jewish life. Yet, despite the complexity of the determination of the firstborn son, one clear principle is found: the firstborn son is determined by the chronological order, and the right of the firstborn son is protected by the rabbinic tradition as shown below. In *B.Bathra* 123a, Reuben was the firstborn son of Israel, and his rights of the firstborn son were transferred to the sons of Joseph. However, Joseph was not reckoned in the genealogy of the firstborn son. In other words, the rights of the firstborn son could be removed from Reuben to Joseph, but rabbis interpreted that the title of the firstborn son in the genealogy was still Reuben's. This denotes that the birthright could be transferred by the father's decision, but that the title of the firstborn son in the genealogy was determined by chronological order. Yet, transferring the birthright to other sons by a paternal decision was rare in Jewish inheritance practices.[96]

In *B.Bathra* 130b, the father cannot make the son of the beloved the firstborn, and transferring the birthright is forbidden in this verse. *B.Bathra* 126b also writes, "One who says, 'my firstborn [בכור] X shall not take a double portion,' ... did not say anything since he stipulated against what is written in the Torah." This verse implies that "בכור" is not designated by a paternal decision but refers to the chronological order. This verse also denotes that a father's inheritance should be practised according to what is prescribed by the Torah. Furthermore, if the father partitions his property into equal portions for his sons, his testaments could be illegitimate. The firstborn son should possess double portions as principal heir and this rule was ordained according to Torah. Thus, the right of the firstborn son as a principal heir was supported by the rabbinic tradition. Therefore, the eldest son generally received the double portion of the father's inheritance as a principal heir according to birth rank.[97]

94 On the other hand, if one already had a son and married a proselyte woman who had never given birth, the son is the firstborn son to be redeemed by a priest, but not the firstborn son with reference to inheritance (*Bekoroth* 47a).

95 For another case of the determination of the firstborn son, see *Bekoroth* 48b–49b.

96 Guggenheimer, *The Jerusalem Talmud, Fourth Order*, 669.

97 Also see *B.Bathra* 133b.

Talmudic literature does not understand Deut 21:15–17 as a law to protect the right of the weak, but as an actual regulation in matters of inheritance.

Exceptionally, in *B.Bathra* 126a, Rabbi La declared that the right of the firstborn son is equal to that of the brothers. Rabbi La's opposing opinion may reflect some intra-disputes on primogeniture in Jewish society. However, Rabbi La's view seems to be a minority view in the context of *B.Bathra* 126a. Rather, a majority of rabbis in the Talmudic literature espouses primogeniture. Rabbi La's view is disputed by other Rabbis in the same paragraph of the halahka. For instance, Rabbi Haggai states that, if a father equally distributes his property to his sons, this declaration is an erroneous action. Rabbi Eliezer also argues that the action of the father cannot be permitted. So, we can infer that primogeniture was exercised in many cases despite intra-Jewish disputes. In other words, the eldest male offspring received a double portion in inheritance. If a father bequeathed to his firstborn son less than a double portion of his inheritance, the testament was regarded as illegitimate by a majority of rabbinic interpretations. Thus, the right of the firstborn son was protected by the rabbinic interpretations.

Yet, we find some exceptions. Firstly, the firstborn son did not take a double portion for expected future income, and the prospective income was equally distributed to sons and daughters (*B.Bathra* 125b; *Babli Bekoroth* 52b; *Sifre Deut.* 217). The double portion of the firstborn son was applied only to the existing property (the father's property at his death). Likewise, the firstborn son did not take a double portion in a loan (*B.Bathra* 124b). Secondly, the rabbinic tradition strictly divides inheritance with the father's gift (*B.Bathra* 156a).[98] The firstborn holds priority for the father's inheritance. However, if the father makes a will to equally distribute his property to his sons in the form of a testamentary gift, the father's testament is legitimate (*B.Bathra* 146b).[99] In other words, offering a gift to one's offspring could be a voluntary action, but inheritance should be exercised by the Torah.[100] Thirdly, the firstborn takes a double portion of the father's inheritance, but does not take a double portion of the mother's estate.[101] This shows that the right of the firstborn son in inheritance was conferred through the paternal line, not through the maternal line.

98 Deed of gift by a father is also found in P.Yadin 19.

99 Cf. Gen 25:5–6.

100 Guggenheimer, *The Jerusalem Talmud, Fourth Order*, 665. For reciprocal aspects of gift, see Seth Schwartz, *Were the Jews a Mediterranean Society?: Reciprocity and Solidarity in Ancient Judaism* (Princeton: Princeton University Press, 2010), 127–28.

101 *Bekoroth* 51b.

Therefore, in Deuteronomic family law and its later interpretations, the prerogatives and status of the firstborn son were fixed according to birth rank.[102] Greenspahn writes, "Where a single individual did receive more than others, it is not at all clear how that person was selected."[103] However, the interpretations of Deuteronomic family law by later Jewish authors enable us to conclude that primogeniture was actually exercised in ancient Jewish society, and that the principal heir was normally determined by birth rank. One of Greenspahn's problems is that he does not provide evidence to support his claim in Jewish biblical interpretations. Alternatively, it is evidenced that, at least in the Second Temple period and the Talmudic period, the prerogative of the firstborn son in matter of inheritance was protected according to Deuteronomic family law. Exceptionally, it was legitimate that the father could assign additional portions to his preferred children in the form of a testamentary gift in rabbinic interpretations. Thus, we conclude that primogeniture existed in the Second Temple period and the Talmudic era.

2.2.4 *Conclusion*

This section has attempted to specifically answer the question as to whether primogeniture existed in ancient Jewish society. A recurring motif of choosing the younger son over the older son in OT narratives does not demonstrate that primogeniture did not exist in ancient Israel. In OT narratives, the right of the firstborn son could be transferred to younger brothers, but the title of בכר was retained by the eldest son. However, OT narratives show that family relations were often in conflict, and this feature of OT narratives makes it problematic to come to a conclusion about the absence or existence of primogeniture in Israelite culture. Alternatively, Deuteronomic family law and its later interpretations provide clearer evidence as to whether primogeniture was practised in ancient Jewish society, at least in the Second Temple period and the Talmudic era. In several OT narratives, the right of the firstborn son was transferred from the firstborn male offspring to a younger child, but in Deuteronomic family law, the right of the biological firstborn son is protected. Philo and Josephus show that primogeniture was actually practised by Jewish families according to Deut 21:15–17. Rabbinic literature also offers detailed regulations to endorse the prerogative of the first male offspring. Therefore, we conclude that primogeniture existed in the Jewish family, at least in the Second Temple period and the Talmudic era. In these eras, the status and rights of the firstborn son

102 See also Dvora E. Weisberg, *Levirate Marriage and the Family in Ancient Judaism* (Waltham: Brandeis University Press, 2009), 109–11.

103 Greenspahn, *When Brothers Dwell Together*, 81.

generally were determined by birth rank, contrary to Frederick Greenspahn's view. The firstborn son was not socially determined but was customarily nominated by order of birth irrespective of his own merits or qualifications in the Second Temple period and the Talmudic era. In contrast to Greco-Roman families, the right of the firstborn son in matters of inheritance was protected by Deuteronomic legal rules. Thus, the biologically firstborn son in Jewish families was a principal heir and successor of the father's family who had a distinct status and privilege compared to his younger brothers. We should also bear in mind that the concept of the firstborn son was defined in respect of patrilineage insofar as it is related to inheritance. Therefore, in the Jewish family, בכר/πρωτότοκος was the eldest son of the father by birth order and the one who held privileges and special rights in inheritance.

2.3 The Firstborn in the Jewish Cultic Setting

In this section, we will investigate the notions of offering of the firstlings. Cultic uses of בכר (LXX: πρωτότοκος) denote that Israelites imposed a special religious significance upon their firstborn. Cultic offering of firstlings were not merely a Jewish custom, but we can trace the existence of similar sacrifices in various pagan settings. For instance, first fruits were offered to the gods in classical Athens (e.g., Xenophon, *Oeconomicus* 5.10).[104] Let us specifically consider the concept of offering firstlings in the OT and Jewish literature.

2.3.1 *The Firstborn in the Story of Cain and Abel (Gen 4:4)*

Some scholars understand the story of Cain and Abel as a conflict story between crop farmers (Cain) and shepherds (Abel), and claim that the story

104 See Greshon Brin, *Studies in Biblical Law: From the Hebrew Bible to the Dead Sea Scrolls* (trans. Jonathan Chipman; JSOTSup 176; Sheffield: Sheffield Academic Press, 1994), 181. Jon Levenson notes that burnt offering of the firstborn son was practised in ancient Canaanite customs. See Jon D. Levenson, *The Death and Resurrection of the Beloved Son: The Transformation of Child Sacrifice in Judaism and Christianity* (New Haven: Yale University Press, 1993), 18–24. He says, "[T]he distance between ancient Israel and its Canaanite cousins on this point [sacrifice of the firstborn son] was not so great as the heated prophetic critique suggests." Cf. Levenson, *The Death and Resurrection of the Beloved Son*, 36–7. However, it is unclear whether the ancient Canaanite customs were linked with the Jewish cultic offering of the firstborn. The offering of the firstborn son in the OT is not explicitly related to the sacrifice of the firstborn son. Reference to "תפדה" (redeem) in Exod 34:20 denotes that the firstborn of human son was exempted from the sacrifice. Cf. R.W.L. Moberly, *At the mountain of God: Story and Theology in Exodus 32–34* (JSOTSup 22; Sheffield: JSOT Press, 1983), 99.

reflects the nomadic origins of Israel.[105] However, evidence of the agrarian origins of Israel leads to the conclusion that this theory is no longer credible.[106] It seems that Abel's cult was accepted and Cain's offering was rejected because Abel's offering was firstlings and Cain's was "some product of the ground."[107] Some scholars argue that Cain's offering was rejected due to the quality of his offering.[108] They assert that Cain's offering was not the best quality of his grain ("some product of the ground"). Abel's offering (בכר) is contrasted with Cain's offering in the given text, however, Cain offered "מנחה" (an acceptable offering in the book of Leviticus; e.g., Lev 2:3–15; 5:13; 6:14–15) in Gen 4:3.[109] So, it is not clear that Cain did not offer the best.

Alternatively, acceptance of Abel's בכר stresses the significance and distinction of offering firstlings in contrast with other cultic offerings. As Claus Westermann highlights, some parallel structure is found between Gen 4:1–2 and 25:24–27 (the birth of Jacob and Esau):[110] 1) birth of two sons (4:1–2a; 25:24–26); 2) naming sons (4:1b; 25:25b, 26b); and 3) occupations of two sons (4:2b; 25:27). These two stories have a shared theme in that they are presented with a focus on the notion of the firstborn (בכר), while the firstborn in Gen 4 is an animal. בכר is a recurring motif in the Pentateuch, and the prior status and significance of the firstborn son are reflected within the Israelite cultic system. Thus, it seems that the story of Cain and Abel functions as a prologue of ordinances on the cultic offering of the firstborn in the Pentateuch.[111]

---

105 E.g., Sigmund Mowinckel, *The Two Sources of the Predeuteronomic Primeval History (JE) in Gen. 1–11* (Oslo: I Kommisjon Hos Jacob Dybwad, 1937), 27–28.

106 Norman K. Gottwald, *The Tribes of Yahweh: A Sociology of the Religion of Liberated Israel, 1250–1050 B.C.E.* (Maryknoll: Orbis, 1979), 448–59.

107 Greenspahn, *When Brothers dwell together*, 91.

108 E.g., Gordon J. Wenham, *Genesis 1–15* (WBC; Waco: Word, 1987), 104.

109 Umberto Cassuto maintains that Abel did his best to please God, whereas Cain only took his obligation, in Cassuto, *Commentary on Genesis, Part 1* (Jerusalem: Magnes, 1978), 205.

110 Claus Westermann, *Genesis: Kapitel 1–11* (BKAT I/1; Neukrichen-Vluyn: Neukirchener Verlag, 1974), 399.

111 Cf. "firstborn of Satan" in *Polycarp* 7:1. In his article, Dahl observes that the phrase "firstborn of Satan" is used in Christian documents and Talmudic anecdotes, and the usage is rooted in the Cain tradition which the devil is Cain's father. Polycarp uses this term to address those who do not confess that Jesus Christ came in the flesh. Dahl argues that "the firstborn of Satan" was a common label for heretics in the early church. See Nils Dahl, "Der Erstgeborene Satans und der Vater des Teufels (Polyk, 7,1 und Joh 8.44)," in *Apophoreta: Festschrift für Ernst Haenchen* (ed. Walter Eltester; BZNW 30; Berlin: Töpelmann, 1964), 70–84. See also Paul Hartog, *Polycarp and the New Testament* (WUNT II/134; Tübingen: Mohr Siebeck, 2002), 79.

2.3.2 *The Cultic Offering of the Firstborn*

As Saul Olyan observes, the rhetoric of hierarchy and holiness underlies the Israelite cult and this rhetoric is principally presented in the form of binary opposition between holy and common, and between clean and unclean.[112] The prescription of offering the firstborn is also posited within the hierarchical system in the Israelite cult. The Laws on the cultic offering of the firstborn can be divided into four themes: 1) the principle of consecration of the firstborn to God; 2) the principle relating to the firstborn of clean animals; 3) the principle relating to the firstborn of unclean animals; and 4) the principle relating to the firstborn of human beings.[113]

After the story of God's destruction of the Egyptians' firstborn sons and the Passover ordinance, the Lord prescribes cultic ordinances to Moses in Exod 13:1–16: 1) consecration of the firstborn (Exod 13:1–2); 2) unleavened bread (13:3–10); and 3) consecration of the firstborn (13:11–16).[114] The given context denotes that prescriptions relating to consecration of the firstborn have an association with the death of the Egyptian firstborn.

As Childs observes, Exod 13:1–2 functions as "a superscription for the subsequent teaching by Moses in 13:3–16."[115] Some interpreters separate Exod 13:1–2 from Exod 13:3–16, because numbers alter from the singular (Exod 13:1–2) to the plural (13:3–16), and iterations of sanctification language (the hiphil of קדש) in 13:1–2 resemble the P history (e.g., Num 3:3 and 8:17).[116] However, the hiphil of קדש is also employed in Deut 15:19, and as Noth states, it is unclear that Exod 13:1–2 was originally separated from Exod 13:3–16.[117] In Exod 13:14–16, the offering of the firstborn is enacted to commemorate the destruction of the firstborn Egyptians.[118] "Consecrate" (קדש) has various meanings, and can be interpreted as transferring "to the realm of the Temple and the *heqdesh*, that is, the making of a given object into holy property."[119] קדש (piel) conveys the sense of transferring the firstborn to the ownership of God (acquiring sanctity).

112 Saul M. Olyan, *Rites and Rank: Hierarchy in Biblical Representations of Cult* (Princeton: Princeton University Press, 2000), 15.

113 Brin, *Studies in Biblical Law*, 170.

114 Cf. Exod 11:5; 12:12, 29.

115 Brevard S. Childs, *The Book of Exodus: A Critical, Theological Commentary* (OTL; Louisville: WJK, 1974), 202–4.

116 Thomas B. Dozeman, *Exodus* (ECCSeries; Grand Rapids: Eerdmans, 2009), 287.

117 Martin Noth, *Exodus*, 101.

118 Concerning the reason for cultic offerings of the firstborn, Num 8:17 also says, "On the day that I struck down all the firstborn in the land of Egypt I consecrated them [the firstborn] for myself."

119 Brin, *Studies in Biblical Law*, 218. Cf. Exod 28:38; Lev 22:2; 27:14, 15, 16.

Exod 22:21–23:19 constitutes "the second section of the two main sections of legal materials," and can be divided into four sub-sections (22:12–17; 22:28–31; 23:1–9; and 23:10–19).[120] The second sub-unit in Exod 22:28–31 specifies responsibilities towards God and sacral actions and rites.[121] In Exod 22:29–30,[122] it is prescribed that the firstborn son of the Israelites should be given to God and firstlings of oxen and sheep should be given on the eighth day after their birth. This mandate is connected to God's promulgation ("You shall be people consecrated to me") in Exod 22:31. In the synchronic context of Exod 22:29–31, threefold uses of the expression "to me" highlight that it is God to whom they are offered and consecrated:[123] "the firstborn of your sons you shall give to me; on the eighth day you shall give it to me; you shall be people consecrated to God." "Given to God" does not necessarily imply divine service, rather it can be understood in terms of "an unqualified transferal to the divine realm."[124]

Exod 32–34 presents a renewal of the covenant, and forms a climax of the golden calf narrative which begins from Exod 32.[125] In Exod 34:10, the Lord declares the covenant with Israel ("I hereby make a covenant") and particularly says, "All that first opens the womb is mine, all your male livestock, the firstborn of cow and sheep. The firstborn of a donkey you shall redeem with a lamb, or if you will not redeem it shall break its neck. All the firstborn of your sons you shall redeem [NRSV]" (Exod 34:19–20).[126] As in Exod 13:1–16, the prescription relating to the firstborn is associated with the rules related to the festival of unleavened bread (Exod 34:18).

120 Carol Meyers, *Exodus* (Cambridge: Cambridge University Press, 2005), 199. This passage belongs to the book of covenant or the covenant code (cf. 24:7). For specific literary features of the covenant code, see Joe M. Sprinkle, *'The Book of Covenant': A Literary Approach* (JSOTSup 174; Sheffield: JSOT Press, 1994), 17–27. Sprinkle finds a chiastic structure in Exod 19:24; A (Exod 19)-B (Exod 20:1–17)-C (Exod 20:18–21)-B' (20:22–23:33)-A' (Exod 24). Alexander allows for the unity of Exod 20:22–24:11. See T. Desmond Alexander, "The Composition of the Sinai Narrative in Exodus xix 1–xxiv 11," *VT* 49 (1999): 20.

121 Meyers, *Exodus*, 200.

122 "You shall not delay to make offerings from the fullness of your harvest and from the outflow of your presses. The firstborn of your sons you shall give to me. You shall do the same with your oxen and with your sheep: for seven days it shall remain with its mother; on the eighth day you shall give it to me."

123 Cf. Sprinkle, *The Book of Covenant*, 173.

124 Brin, *Studies in Biblical Law*, 217.

125 Childs, *Exodus*, 610.

126 Blum regards Exod 34:11–27 as *Privilegrechts JHWHs*. He argues that Exod 34:11–27 was added in the final stage of the tradition history. See Erhard Blum, "Das Sog. 'Privilegrecht' in Exod 34,11–26: Ein Fixpunkt der Komposition des Exodusbuches?" in *Studies in the Book of Exodus* (BETL 126; ed. M. Vervenne; Leuven: Leuven University Press, 1996), 366.

Num 18:15 reads, "Everything that opens the womb of all flesh, whether man or beast, which they offer to the Lord, shall be yours [NRSV]."[127] Compared to Exod 13, 22 and 34, Num 18:15–16 provides more specific instructions with regard to the firstborn (cf. Lev 27:25). The firstborn of human beings and of unclean animals should be redeemed and that the redemption price is five shekels.[128]

> But the firstborn of a cow, or the firstborn of a sheep, or the firstborn of a goat, you shall not redeem; they are holy. You shall dash their blood on the altar, and shall turn their fat into smoke as an offering by fire for a pleasing odor to the Lord; but their flesh shall be yours.
>
> NRSV (Num 18:17–18a)

This principle relating to offering the firstborn is pertinent for the priests. Brin states, "... according to JE (i.e. Exod 13.12; 22 and 34) the firstlings were literally offered up as burnt-offerings. In the second stage (D), they were eaten by the owners, while in the third stage (P), they were given as gifts to the priests."[129] According to this theory, this text may originate in the priestly redaction (see Num 18:18). However, Deut 18:3 denotes that the shoulders, two cheeks and the stomach of the sacrifice belong to the priests. Accordingly, in Deuteronomy, it seems that the sacrifices of the firstlings were eaten by the owner, his household and the priest together. Furthermore, Exod 13, 22 and 34 do not describe specific regulations in practical terms with regard to offering the firstlings, so it is unclear that the regulations in Exod 13, 22 and 24 are in conflict with those in Num 18. זבח in Exod 13:15 does not necessarily indicate a burnt offering. Thus, it seems that the sacrifices of the firstlings were consumed by the owner and the priests together in the early stage. The thrust of this passage is that the firstborn is an offering distinguished from other offerings and that the meat

127 Cf. Num 10:36–37. Jacob Milgrom understands the structure of the Hexateuch in terms of the introverted structure centred on the promise and accomplishment. See Jacob Milgrom, *Numbers* (Philadelphia: Jewish Publication Society, 1990), 18. In this structure surrounding the promise and accomplishment, Lee finds the axis of Numbers in Num 13–14, which reports Israelites' exploration of the land of Canaan and their rebellion at Kadesh. See W. Lee, *Punishment and Forgiveness in Israel's Migratory Campaign* (Grand Rapids: Eerdmans, 2003), 290. After the event at Kadesh, a new generation is prepared to enter the land of Canaan (Num 15:1–36:13). Num 18:15–16 is located in this literary context.

128 The redemption price of the firstling of unclean animals was one and a half shekels in Josephus, *Ant* 4.70–71. Cf. Brin, *Studies in Biblical Law*, 205: "'Thou shalt redeem' implies with a thing of whatever value', or 'The Torah did not intend by the law of redemption with a lamb to make it difficult for one, but on the contrary, to make it easier for one'."

129 Brin, *Studies in Biblical Law*, 193.

could, therefore, be eaten by the priests (Num 18:18). Brin also acknowledges that the traditions relating to offering the firstborn in Num 18 are associated with the concept that the firstborn belongs to God.[130] As in Lev 27:26–27, the firstborn of human beings and unclean animals are redeemed in Num 18:15–16, and Num 18:16 provides specific regulations by which to redeem the firstborn of human beings (the redemption price was five shekels in silver).[131]

Deut 12:2–27 discusses the legitimate setting for cultic practices, i.e., the Temple.[132] Deut 12–26 reflects deuteronomic covenantal rules, and in particular, Deut 12:2–16:17 consists of *Privilegrecht Jahwes*, which prescribes the cultic laws and *Hoheitsrechte Jahwes*.[133] Deuteronomy was formed with a focus on two main rules: 1) serving only God; and 2) centralisation of the cultic location.[134] The instructions relating to the prescriptions for the firstlings in Deut 12:6, 17 are presented within the core of the text which also elucidates the requirements for a centralised location for cultic ritual (12:2–7, 13–14, 17–18, 26–27). Whilst Israelites could eat meat in their towns whenever they desired in Deut 12:21, the firstborn offering should be eaten at the place chosen by God, i.e., the Jerusalem Temple in Deut 12:6. Tithes should be offered to God, and the tithes are related to the most important agricultural products—crops, wine and oils (Deut 7:13; 11:14; 14:23; 18:4; 28:51).[135] In this context, the firstlings can be related to the first (ראשית) of all the fruits of the ground. The firstlings in Deut 12 are juxtaposed with images of the centralised temple, tithes and the first fruits.

Deut 14 describes deuteronomic regulations on tithes. Some scholars argue that "as well as the firstlings of your herd and flock" in Deut 14:23b is secondary and later added to the original text.[136] However, the composition of Deut 14 has

130 Brin, *Studies in Biblical Law*, 194–95.

131 This practice is spoken of as *Pidyon ha'ben* by the Jews. For specific information on *Pidyon ha'ben*, see Nissan Rubin, *Time and Life Cycle in Talmud and Midrash: Socio-Anthropological Perspectives* (Boston: Academic Studies Press, 2008), 65–89. Cf. Num 8:16–18; 33:4.

132 Timo Veijola, *Deuteronomium: Kapitel 1,1–16,17* (ATD 8,1; Göttingen: Vandenhoeck & Ruprecht, 2004), 264.

133 Friedrich Horst, "Das Privilegrecht Jahwes: Rechtsgeschichtliche Untersuchungen zum Deuteronium," in *Gottes Recht. Gesammelte Studien zum Recht im Alten Testament* (TB 12; München: Chr. Kaiser, 1961), 17–154.

134 Otto Kaiser, *Der Gott des Alten Testaments* (Theologie des AT 1: Grundlegung; Göttingen: Vandenhoeck & Ruprecht, 1993), 201. In Deut 12, the requirements relating to the cultic centralisation are reiterated four times, and this reiteration indicates the significance of the theme of the centralisation in Deut 12.

135 Veijola, *Deuteronomium*, 268.

136 Gottfried Seitz, *Redaktionsgeschichtliche Studien zum Deuteronomium* (BWANT 93; Stuttgart: Kohlhammer, 1971), 194; Horst, "Das Privilegrecht Jahwes," 76.

been greatly disputed. Irrespective of its composition history, the juxtaposition of the firstlings and tithes shows a close conceptual association between these two notions. We also find the juxtaposition of tithes and the offering of the firstlings in Lev 27:26–34 and Deut 12:17. The firstlings in Deut 14:21 are contrasted with abhorrent things and correspond with the image of tithes in the context in Deut 14:1–21. It seems that the offering of the firstlings is related to the election of Israel. In Deut 14:2, these regulations are also given to Israelites who are a holy people to the Lord and a chosen people and a treasured possession. The firstborn belongs to God (cf. Exod 13:2; Num 3:13; 8:17), as Israel belongs to God. In deuteronomic cultic laws, the firstborn is associated with the centralised images of the Temple. As Levenson observes in Deut 14:1–2:[137]

> Here filiation, consecration, and chosenness—three aspects of one reality—serve as the ground for laws (such as the dietary restrictions that follow) that differentiate Israel from those who are not God's sacred, chosen children. To call Israel's status as the son of God a figure of speech, without qualification, is to miss the thorough going *practical* difference that this status is intended to make in the lives of the chosen people.[138]

In this quotation, Levenson states that filiation, consecration and chosenness are three aspects of one reality. The image of the consecration of the firstborn son also conveys the same reality. In other words, the idea that Israel is the firstborn son of God (Exod 4:22) and that the firstborn belongs to the Lord (e.g., Exod 13:1–2, etc.) evokes the election of Israel.[139] Thus, the concept of the firstborn son in the Pentateuch is connected to Israel's self-perception as the firstborn son.

Deut 15:19–22a also reflects a deuteronomic theme associated with the centralisation of the Temple (par. 15:19–20). In Deut 15:21–22a, the blemished offering of the firstlings should not be sacrificed in the Temple, but they should be eaten in the owners' living area. As Veijola notes, "You and your household" in 15:20 refers to "you and your son and daughter, and your male and female servants, and the Levite who is within your gates" in 12:28. Ostensibly, in contrast to Num 18, Deut 15:19–20 prescribes that the firstlings should be eaten solely by the owner and his household. However, as seen above, the shoulder, the two

137 Deut 14:1–2: "You are children of the LORD your God. You must not lacerate yourselves or shave your forelocks for the dead. For you are a people holy to the LORD your God; it is you the LORD has chosen out of all the peoples on earth to be his people, his treasured possession."

138 Levenson, *The Death and Resurrection of the Beloved Son*, 42.

139 Levenson, *The Death and Resurrection of the Beloved Son*, 40.

cheeks and the stomach were consumed by the priest in Deut 18:3. Likewise, the firstlings were, perhaps, eaten by the owner, his family and the priests together in the Temple.[140]

Thus, the offering of the firstlings in the Pentateuch should be understood within the relevant contexts. In Exod 13, 34 and Num 18, the prescriptions relating to the firstborn are associated with the Passover and the unleavened bread. In Exod 22, Deut 12 and 14, the offering of the firstborn can be understood within the context of the harvest, tithes and the centralisation of the Temple. Yet, the cultic references to the firstborn in the Pentateuch are also related to the consecration of the firstborn (or the owner in Exod 22:30) and the significance of the firstborn.

We find discussions on the offering of the firstborn son in some Jewish literature. 1Q26 1+2; 4Q270 2; 4Q368 2; 11Q19 LX. In 4Q270 2 ii, offering of the firstborn is prescribed within the body of the cultic regulations with the warning against idolatry (frag. 2 col. I), the ordinance of tithes, and "the money of the assessments for the ransom of their souls" (frag. 2 col. II 7, 9). 4Q368 frag. 2 gives an exposition of Exod 34:11–24. After the warning against idolatry and the prescriptions of the festival of the unleavened bread, the text elucidates the reasons for the redemption of the firstborn, and states that every firstborn belongs to YHWH (v. 11). In 4Q423 3+4, the offering of the firstborn son is linked to divine sanctification. The text implies that some mysterious experience ("mystery of existence") is revealed through the cultic offering (vv. 2, 5). 11Q19 60 mentions בכר as the cultic offering. The offering of the firstborn is juxtaposed with all the wave-offering and all the holy offerings which are consecrated to God. These offerings with tithes are given to the levites. Thus, the offering of the firstborn son is occasionally mentioned in conjunction with tithes and this, perhaps, reflects the close association between the firstborn and tithes already established in the OT (Lev 27:26–32; Deut 12:17; Neh 10:37).

As for the offering of the firstborn, Philo writes that those which opened the mother's womb signify speech and reason in mankind in *Heres* 117–120. Reason enables human beings to comprehend things and speech to exercise the energy of the voice. Further, in *Heres* 120, those which opened the mother's womb represent the invisible and divine Word (Logos). In other words, the firstborn in *Heres* 117–20 symbolises the most significant part of the mind and the universe.

Josephus delineates the redemption of the firstborn in *Ant* 4.70–71, but he does not link the redemption and offering of the firstborn to the Passover and

140 So, Veijola, *Deuteronomium: Kapitel 1,1–16,17*, 305.

destruction of the firstborn Egyptians. The regulations relating to the firstborn son are simply referenced in the sense of temple offering (a regular payment to the temple) along with tithes and the corban. Five shekels for the firstborn Israelites and one and a half shekels for the firstborn animals should be paid to the priests. Whereas the Passover was regarded as the most significant Jewish festival in Josephus' writings, Josephus omits many details of the process of the cultic offering and the event of the destruction of the firstborn Egyptians (*Ant* 2.311–319).[141] Josephus does not mention a great cry of sorrow from the Egyptians over their firstborn sons in the whole land.[142] Philo's frequent references to the death of the Egyptian firstborn son are sharply contrasted with Josephus' silence on the same issue in his *Antiquitates Judaicae*. Perhaps, Josephus wanted to maintain a good relationship with the Egyptians, and it seems that his silence on this issue resulted from this reason.[143] Thus, Josephus does not ascribe any significant religious meaning to the notion of offering the firstborn son.

To sum up, in the Pentateuch, the firstborn should be consecrated to God, as Israel is distinct from the nations, and the cultic offering of the firstborn denotes the significance and centrality of the firstborn. Abel's בכר was accepted by God, but Cain's מנחה. God's acceptance of Abel's בכר implies the significance of offering the firstborn in the Israelite cultic system. Ordinance of the firstborn as the cultic offering is directly connected to the Lord's promulgation that every firstborn belongs to the Lord. The cultic ordinance pertaining to the offering of the firstborn in Exod 13 is linked with the designation of Israel as the firstborn son (Exod 4) and destruction of the Egyptian firstborn son (Exod 11–12). The firstborn is consecrated to the Lord, and offering of the firstborn commemorates the destruction of the Egyptian firstborn son and salvation of the Israelite firstborn. Philo maintains that offering of the firstborn

141 See Federico M. Colautti, *Passover in the Works of Josephus* (JSJSup 75; Leiden: Brill, 2002), 237.

142 The kindness of Egyptians that the MT and LXX do not tell is added in *Ant*. As Colautti observes, Josephus "does not mention either the prohibition against participation by the uncircumcised in the commemoration, or the law concerning the consecration of the firstborn." See Colautti, *Passover in the Works of Josephus*, 34.

143 For example, Feldman observes, "Whereas Exod 12:29–33 presents a detailed and vivid picture of the effect of the plague upon the firstborn of the Egyptians, Josephus is much briefer, presumably because he sought to emphasize the good neighbourly relations between the Egyptians and the Israelites. In particular, Josephus omits the statement (Exod 12:30) that there was not a house among the Egyptians where there was not someone dead," Louis Feldman, *Judean Antiquities 1–4: Translation and Commentary* (FJCT 3; Leiden: Brill, 1999), 250.

symbolically refers to the best and pre-eminent offering (*Congr* 98).[144] By contrast, in Josephus, offering of the firstborn is regarded as the temple payment and any wider significance in the cultural or historic context is not elucidated.

2.3.3 *The Levites as the Firstborn Son of Israel*

The priests in Israel were privileged to "wear holy garments, eat holy foods, and approach the deity" (cf. Num 16:9).[145] The priests were regarded as privileged in that they could approach close to God (cf. Exod 19:22).[146] Num 3:5–10[147] explains how the tribe of Levi was set before Aaron the priest to assist him. Num 3:11–13 reads that God accepted the Levites from among the Israelites as substitutes for all the firstborn in Israel. The next passage (Num 3:14–39) speaks of the lists and numbers of clans of the Levites and their specific functions. Num 3:40–51 returns to the issue of the firstborn son with respect to enrolment of the firstborn son and the role of the Levites as substitutes for the firstborn in Israel. Num 3:11–13 is directly linked with 3:40–51.[148] Num 3:40–51 provides the principles of the substitution and the practical details of Num 3:11–13. The calculations in Num 3:40–51 were made on the basis of the total number of the Levites in Num 3:14–39. The total number of the Levites was 22,000 and the number of firstborn males from one month and upwards in Israel was 22,273. Therefore, 273 firstborn males were redeemed for five shekels per child in Num 3:50.

As Brin notes, it seems that Num 3 is not considered to be a law, since the passage does not prescribe any instructions for future generations. Rather, Num 3 takes "the form of a story about the one-time act of exchange of the Levites for the firstborn during the generation of the desert."[149] Brin argues that this passage functions to show the relationship between the Levites and the firstborn, and answers the question as to why the redemption price

---

144 See also *T.Ong. Exod* 24:5.

145 Olyan, *Rites and Rank*, 28.

146 See Georg Steins, "Priesterherrschaft, Volk von Priestern oder was sonst? Zur Interpretation von Ex 19,6," *BZ* 49 (2001): 28–32. Cf. Olyan, *Rites and Rank*, 27.

147 The tradition of the Levites as the firstborn in Num 3 might be the post-exilic tradition. However, the composition of Num 3 is disputed. See Walter Zimmerli, "Erstgeborenene und Leviten: Ein Beitrag zur exilisch-nachexilischen Theologie," in *Near Eastern Studies in Honor of W.F. Albright* (ed. H. Goedicke; Baltimore: Johns Hopkins University Press, 1971), 459–69. In the literary structure, Num 3 belongs to the Sinai pericope (Exod 19:3–Num 10:10). See R.P. Knierim and G.W. Coats, *Numbers* (FOTL 4; Grand Rapids: Eerdmans, 2005), 9–17.

148 Brin, *Studies in Biblical Law*, 229.

149 Brin, *Studies in Biblical Law*, 233.

of the firstborn should be paid to the priests.[150] As Tsevat observes, "the law concerning the redemption of the firstborn of man is always connected with the appointment of the Levites" (e.g., Num 3:11–13, 40, 44; 8:16–18).[151] Perhaps, Num 3 implies the distinction of the Levites from the rest of the Jewish people. The link between the primacy of the Levites and the firstborn is reflected in Philo's writings. However, we should note that, in Numbers, the Levites are not identified with the firstborn.

In *Congr* 95–99, Philo maintains that the first fruits should be offered to God. He also writes that God sanctifies all the firstborn, and "took as their ransom the tenth, that is the tribe of Levi, that they should observe and maintain holiness, piety and the rites which are offered for the honour of God [Loeb translation]" (*Congr* 98). Philo states that the Levites represent Israel, and reason plays the same role in humankind as do the Levites in Israel.[152] The connection between the first fruits and the firstborn is linked to the Levites and to reasoning: "the first and best thing in us is the reason … We should offer the first fruits to God, who gave to it its fertility of thinking [Loeb translation]" (*Congr* 98). Therefore, the firstborn son and the first fruits symbolise the first and the best thing, and they are connected to reason and priesthood in Philo's writings.

In Philo's *Sacr* 118, ἀπαρχή refers to offering of the soul,[153] and the Levites are also designated as πρωτότοκος. In *Sacr* 119, the Levites symbolises Logos: "It is Reason, who has taken refuge with God and become his suppliant, who is here given the name of Levite [Loeb translation]." In other words, the Levites

150 Brin, *Studies in Biblical Law*, 234.

151 Tsevat, "b^{e}khôr," 126. De Vaux states, "Levites were consecrated to God as substitutes for the firstborn of the people (Num 3:12–13; 8:16–18)." See de Vaux, *Ancient Israel*, 42. Cf. Greenspahn, *When Brothers Dwell Together*, 21–22.

152 In Philo, *Spec Leg* 1.135–40, the first fruits and the firstborn males are given to the men consecrated to the priesthood, *i.e.*, the priests (1.136). Money can be given to the priests as a ransom for horses, asses, camels and similar animals. Children are inseparable from their parents in nature (1.137) and, in order that the parents may not be separated from their children, they equally value their firstborn male offspring (ἀπαρχή) at a fixed value regardless of the property of the parents or beauty of the children, since children are equally born to wealthy and poor parents (1.140). Philo associates the offering of the first fruits to the consecration of the firstborn son of the Israelites (1.137–38). That is, for Philo, the offering of the first fruits from agricultural products is analogous to the consecration of the firstborn son of human beings. Cf. the special status of Philo as the firstborn in *Spec Leg* 4.180.

153 *Sacr* 117. The offering the firstborn to God is "true to nature," because the firstborn is the one who opened his mother's womb (*Sacr* 102). Female offspring of the soul is vice and passion, and male offspring represents health of the soul and virtue. So the firstborn is the males, in *Sacr.* 102.

play the role among the Jews which is analogous to the reasoning part of the mind. The Levites are central among the Jews,[154] and Levi, who was perfectly virtuous among Jacob's sons, deserves the status of the firstborn son as Jacob was granted πρωτοτόκια: "Reuben the man of natural gifts must yield the rights of the elder to Levi, whose life is one of perfect virtue [Loeb translation]."[155] Reuben was the oldest in age, but the status of the firstborn, which Esau passed to Jacob, was given to Levi.[156] Thus, in Philo's writings, the Levites are the firstborn sons among the Jews, and the firstborn son refers to the same superior position as does reason in the mind. Yet, it should be noted that, while the Levites are associated with the status of the firstborn sons in Philonic literature, it does not convey that the firstborn son symbolises a priestly intermediary role.

Therefore, in the Pentateuch and some Jewish literature, the Levites are portrayed as privileged and as representatives of the whole of Israel. The notion of the Levites as cultic substitutes of the firstborn son also denotes the primary status of the Levites. In addition, the Levites as the firstborn sons in Philonic literature does not suggest that the concept of the firstborn son is linked with the intermediary notion.

2.3.4 *The First Fruits*[157]

As White notes, the offering the first fruits in the Pentateuch has a covenantal meaning.[158] In Lev 23:9–14,[159] the offering of the firstling sheaf is associated with the Festival of Weeks. The time of the presentation of the firstling sheaf coincides with the Festival of Unleavened Bread, so Lev 23:9–14 is probably related to a tradition of the Festival of Unleavened Bread.[160] In Num 18:12–13, the first fruits of all that are in the land of Israel should be offered to the Temple with all the best of the oil and all the best of the wine and of the grain. This denotes that the first fruits are conceptually related to the best products in Num 18:12–13. The first fruits refer to the head (ראש) of all fruits in Deut 26:2. The

154 *Sacr* 118.

155 *Sacr* 120.

156 As for the excellence of the Levites, see *Sacr* 127–133.

157 E.g., see Lev 23:9–14; Num 18:12; 2 Chr 31:5; Prov 3:9–10; Neh 10:35–37; Ezek 44:30; Mal 3:10. For the origin of the feast of the first fruits of wine in 11QT XIX 11–XXI 10, see John C. Reeves, "The feast of the First Fruits of Wine and the Ancient Canaanite Calendar," *VT* 42 (1992): 350–61.

158 See Joel White, *Die Erstlingsgabe im Neuen Testament* (TANZ 45; Tübingen: Francke, 2007), 43–64.

159 Traditionally, Lev 17–26 is viewed as the holiness code. See Jacob Milgrom, *Leviticus 1–16* (AB; New York: Doubleday, 1991), 61–63; N. Kiuchi, *Leviticus* (AOTC 3; Nottingham: Apollos, 2007), 16–18.

160 Erhard S. Gerstenberger, *Leviticus: A Commentary* (OTL; Louisville: WJK, 1996), 344.

first fruit does not belong to human beings but to God through sacral consecration. The first fruits were offered solely for the priests (Num 8:13; Deut 18:3–4; Neh 10:37; Ezek 44:30; cf. Exod 23:19; 34:26). The first fruits in Num 8:13 are juxtaposed with the most holy in Num 8:9 and the best in Num 8:12.

The notion of the first fruits is also related to that of the firstborn son. In Exod 34:26, the offering of the first fruits is referenced in the context of prescriptions related to the firstborn.[161] In Num 8:15, it is promulgated that offering of the firstborn (the first issue of the womb of all creatures, human and animal) should be given to the Levites and the firstborn of human beings should be redeemed. Arguably, the notion of the first fruits is connected to the holy, the best and the firstborn: particularly, "the best of the first fruits of your ground" in Exod 34:26 (cf. Prov 3:9).[162]

The first fruit in the OT is also mentioned in other figurative senses. Firstly, the first fruit symbolises the special status of the Jewish people. In Jer 2:3, Israel is addressed as the first fruit of God's harvest, which were sacred to God. This status of Israel as the first fruit is linked to Rom 11:16, James 1:18 and Rev 14:4 (cf. Hos 9:10). Secondly, the first fruit (ראשית) signifies 'the core' or 'the kernel' in Jer 49:35: "Thus says the LORD of hosts: I am going to break the bow of Elam, the first fruit of their might [NRSV]." Thirdly, the firstborn signifies temporal priority. In LXX Exod 22:29; LXX Num 8:16, 19; LXX Ps 77:51; 104:36; LXX Ezek 44:30, the sense of ἀπαρχή as temporal priority is stressed. The concept of ἀπαρχή in the sense of temporal priority is linked to Rom 8:23, 16:5 (1 Cor 16:15) and 1 Cor 15:20, 23 respectively concerning the Holy Spirit, the first convert and the resurrection.

In Philo's writings, the first fruit symbolises something beyond temple payment and temporal priority.[163] The firstborn son is frequently connected to the first fruit or the cultic offering, as discussed in the previous section.[164] In *Spec Leg* 2.162–175, Philo states that the Jewish people offer the first fruits as representatives of humankind, and the Jews serve as the priests for humankind.[165] The purpose of offering the first fruits is to worship the creator (*Decal* 160).

161 Cf. Exod 23:19: "The choice first fruits of your soil you shall bring to the house of the Lord your God." See also Lev 27:26; Exod 13:15; 34:26.

162 G. Delling, "ἀπαρχή," 483.

163 Specific discussions on Philo's theology and the first fruit in Philo will be offered in the following chapter.

164 E.g. *Congr* 7; *Conf* 124; *Spec Leg* 1.135, 138, 139, 248; *Virt* 95; *Abr* 196. Particularly, the first fruits are offerings for the priests in *Spec Leg* 2.222. Ἀπαρχή also means the best portion in *Post* 96. See Jutta Leonhardt, *Jewish Worship in Philo of Alexandria* (TSAJ 84; Tübinen: Mohr Siebeck, 2001), 198.

165 For specific information on the first fruits in Philo's writings, see Leonhardt, *Jewish Worship in Philo of Alexandria*, 190–98.

In this verse, the first fruit not only indicates temporal priority, but symbolises the best. In *Spec Leg* 2.136, the first fruit is also connected to πρωτότοκος as the status of Israel.

In *Jos* 194 and *Sacr* 107–9, the first fruits do not merely signify the first, but also the best offering. Ἀπαρχή is also linked to the inheritance of Israel.[166] The reason Israel inherited the Land is that the Jews should offer ἀπαρχή of the Land for God. In these verses, the Jews are the representative of all nations.[167] The first fruit is linked to the Jewish people in *Spec Leg* 4.180: "Nevertheless as Moses tells us the orphan-like desolate state of his people is always an object of pity and compassion to the Ruler of the Universe whose portion it is, because it has been set apart from the rest of the human race as a kind of the first fruits to the Maker and Father [Loeb translation]." That is, the Jewish people are consecrated as the first fruits among the whole human race, and this denotes that the Jews represent the whole of mankind and hold a primary status over the nations. In this verse, ἀπαρχή is associated with consecration of the Jews to God over the whole human race.

In 4Q423 2 1 and 4Q423 3+4 4, the ordinance of offering the first fruits should be observed, and these commands are connected to a mystic concept ("as he opened your ears through the mystery of existence" in line 5).[168] The text was not so well preserved, but might prescribe the strict observance of the decree on the offering of the first fruits, since the covenantal curse (perhaps for disobedience to the law of the Lord) is followed in line 6. The offering of the firstborn is juxtaposed with the first fruits in v. 4, which implies the conceptual link between the firstborn and the first fruit.

On the contrary, the offering of the first fruits in Josephus, *Ant* 3.251 is performed along with the sacrifice of the lamb and this corresponds to Lev 23:12. Yet, it seems that Josephus does not impose any special meaning on the offering of the first fruits in *Ant* 3.251. Josephus mentions the offering of the first fruits along with tithes in *Ant* 4.241. In the same vein as the redemption of the firstborn Israelites and animals, the offering of the first fruits is understood as a temple offering (a regular payment to the temple) or an offering for the Levites (or the priests). However, Josephus does not ascribe any other theological implications to the offering of the first fruits. In Josephus' writings, the first fruits does not symbolise the best offering.

166 *Spec Leg* 2.75–77.

167 *Spec Leg* 2.168.

168 Cf. 11QT 11 11; 11QT 18 14; 11Q19 19 2, 5, 12; 11Q19 21 16; 11Q19 37 10; 11Q20 3 23. Cf. *Aramaic Levi* v. 4: "everything desirable of the first fruits of the entire earth for food …"

In brief, πρωτότοκος is associated with the primacy within the hierarchy of the Jewish cultic system in Jewish literature. On the other hand, ἀπαρχή covers a broader semantic field: 1) the Temple payment; 2) the best offering; 3) the symbol of Israel's status; and 4) temporal priority.[169]

2.3.5 *Summary*

This section has explored the concept of offering the firstborn in the Jewish cultic setting. The firstborn in the cultic context is defined in terms of his maternal lineage, which differs from the definition of the firstborn son in inheritance in respect of the father. So, in the cultic sense, בכר/πρωτότοκος is the first male offspring of the mother. When בכר is mentioned in a cultic sense, it can be translated as the first offspring or the firstborn, since the term בכר does not necessarily refer to a human son in the cultic context. The offering of the firstborn in the Pentateuch and some Jewish literature is delineated in terms of hierarchy in the Jewish cultic system. In Exod 11–12, the offering of the firstborn is connected with the destruction of the firstborn Egyptians and recalls the distinct status and designation of Israel as the firstborn son. This notion of the firstborn and the first fruit reflects the theology of election in the Pentateuch and some Jewish literature. This cultic concept of the firstborn is inevitably linked with the self-perception of Israel as the firstborn son.

169 For ἀπαρχή in Philo, see 4.14.2. Cf. Leonhardt, *Jewish Worship*, 190–213.

CHAPTER 3

The Firstborn Son as Self-Perception of Israel

3.1 The Jacob Cycle (Genesis 25:19–35:22)

3.1.1 *The Text*[1]

In the previous chapter, we considered the concept of the firstborn son in the Jewish context. In the Jewish culture, the firstborn son was a principal heir of the father and a successor of the family. In this chapter, we will explore the meaning of the firstborn son, when it is used in relation to the self-perception of Israel in relation to her inheritance. Primary topics in the Jacob cycle can be captured within the following three motifs: birth, blessing, and land.[2] In the Jacob cycle, Gen 25:29–34 contains a paradigmatic function.[3] The principal issue of this unit in Gen 25:29–34 is the "transfer of the birthright."[4] We can

1 The composition and *Sitz im Leben* of this text have been widely disputed. Gunkel insists that the conflict between Esau and Jacob should be read in the national and historical perspective and that it implies the conflicts between herding and hunting peoples. See Herman Gunkel, *Genesis* (Macon: Mercer University Press, 1997), 316. However, his argument is overstated. Westermann notes that conflicts between the herdsmen and the hunters occur only in Gen 25, and that we should consider the conflict in Gen 27 as family stories (Familienerzählungen) which include one father, one mother and two sons. In addition, some scholars observe that the narratives in Gen 25:21–34 and Gen 27 are originally two separate stories which originate in different traditions. See Claus Westermann, *Die Verheißungen an die Vater: Studien zur Vatergeschichte* (FRLANT 116; Göttingen: Vandenhoeck & Ruprecht, 1976), 78–79; Greenspahn, *When Brothers Dwell Together*, 125. However, we should note that Gen 25:21–34 and Gen 27 can be understood in one large elaborated chiastic structure. See Michael Fishbane, "Genesis 25:19–35:22: The Jacob Cycle," in *Text and Texture: Close Readings of Selected Biblical Texts* (New York: Schocken, 1979), 40–62; J.P. Fokkelman, *Narrative Art in Genesis: Specimens of Stylistic and Structural Analysis* (BS 12; Assen: Van Gorcum, 1975), 86–122. Van Seters also finds the textual association between Gen 25:21–34 and Gen 27: "Genesis 27 is not an independent story unit because its very composition is based upon the earlier materials of 25:21–34." See John van Seters, *Prologue to History: The Yahwist as Historian in Genesis* (Louisville: WJK, 1992), 285. Cf. Erhard Blum, *Die Komposition der Vätergeschichte* (WMANT 57; Neukirchen-Vluyn: Neukirchener Verlag), 66–88.

2 Fishbane, "Genesis 25:19–35:22," 60.

3 Paul Vrolijk, *Jacob's Wealth: An Examination into the Nature and Role of Material Possession in the Jacob-Cycle* (VTSup 146; Leiden: Brill, 2011), 47.

4 Vrolijk, *Jacob's Wealth*, 47.

 DOI:10.1163/9789004394940_004

understand the relationship between the firstborn son (בכר) and the blessing (ברך) as the following symmetrical structure.[5]

A – oracle sought; Rebekah struggles in childbirth; בכרה: Gen 25:19–34[6]
B – interlude; strife; deception; ברך; and covenant with foreigner: Gen 26
C – deception; ברך; stolen; fear of Esau; flight from land: Gen 27:1–28:9
D – encounter with the divine at sacred site; and ברך: Gen 28:10–22
E – internal cycle opens; arrival; Laban at border; deception; and wage: Gen 29
F – Rachel fertile; Jacob increases the herds: Gen 30
E' – internal cycle closes; departure; Laban at border; deception; and wages: Gen 30
D' – encounter with divine beings at sacred sites; and ברך: Gen 32
C' – deception planned; fear of Esau; ברך; gift returned; and return to land: Gen 33
B' – interlude; strife; deception; and covenant with foreigner: Gen 34
A' – oracle fulfilled; Rachel struggles in childbirth; ברך; death; and resolution: Gen 35:1–22

We will analyse the specific meaning of the firstborn son (בכר) in the Jacob cycle in what follows.

3.1.2 *Analysis*

Von Rad argues that the meaning of the birthright is unclear and that, furthermore, "there is nothing in the oft-repeated promise to the patriarchs about each one binding himself always to the firstborn alone."[7] However, we obtain some clues on the meaning of the birthright from the text. First of all, what is the relationship between ברך (blessing) and בכרה (the right of the firstborn son) in the Jacob cycle?

Van Seters argues that ברך and בכרה do not have any relationship. Firstly, the legal claim concerning the inheritance or any other rights "over the preferential claim of the firstborn son" cannot be granted through blessing. Secondly,

5 Fishbane, "Genesis 25:19–35:22," 42. This structure is followed with some minor amendments by Rendsburg. See Rendsburg, *The Redaction of Genesis* (Winona Lake: Eisenbrauns, 1986), 53. Cotter and Fokkelman presents different internal structures, however, they concede the relationship between בכרה and ברך, in David Cotter, *Genesis* (CollBibCom; Collegeville: Liturgical, 2003), 181–197 and Fokkelman, *Narrative Art in Genesis*, 86–122.

6 As for the internal structure in 25:29–34, see Fokkelman, *Narrative Art in Genesis*, 95.

7 Gerhard von Rad, *Genesis: A Commentary* (trans. John H. Marks; OTL; London: SCM, 1961), 262. See also Vrolijk, *Jacob's Wealth*, 53.

Gen 27 indicates that Jacob was already given his share as the firstborn son, not through blessing, but by other means (25:29–34; 27:36).

We, however, find close associations between ברך and בכרה in the given text.[8] Firstly, we should note the interesting phonetic correspondence between ברך (blessing) and בכרה (the right of the firstborn son).[9] It seems that the phonetic correspondence is linked with the semantic association between ברך and בכרה in the given text. In particular, ברך and בכרה are closely associated in the parallel structure in Gen 27:36. Fokkelman finds the elaborated parallelism (AA'BB') in this verse as below.[10]

A Is he not rightly named *Ya'qob*?
A' For he has supplanted me these two times, *yaqebeni*:
B My birthright (*bekora*) he took away.
B' And behold, now he has taken away my blessing (*beraka*).

In this parallel structure, ברך and בכרה display a kind of alliteration.[11] In other words, this parallelism shows the close correspondence between the firstborn son and the blessing, even though they are not synonymous.[12] Secondly, the oracle in Gen 25:23 denotes the close association between ברך and בכרה. Isaac's blessing in Gen 27:29 that he will be lord over his brothers is closely associated with the oracle in Gen 25:23 that the older brother will serve the younger. The oracle in Gen 25:23 is implied in Esau's behaviour that sells his own right of the firstborn son, as Fokkelman states: "The importance of 'coming into the world first' and not after the other (25.25) is now expressed exactly by the word *bekora* …" In this context, we find the association between the right of the firstborn son and Isaac's blessing. Thirdly, the association between "he called his

8 Cotter, *Genesis*, 203; Wenham also states that this blessing in Gen 27 is the firstborn's blessing that Jacob is after. See Gordon Wenham, *Genesis* (WBC; Waco: Word, 1987), 209. Also see Levenson, *The Death and Resurrection of the Beloved Son*, 61.

9 Gordon Wenham notes, "It may also be significant that בכרה "rights of firstborn" is an anagram of ברך "blessing," the subject of chaps. 26–27 and a key theme in Genesis." See Wenham, *Genesis*, 178.

10 See Fokkelman, *Narrative Art in Genesis*, 99. Wenham also finds the same alliteration, in Wenham, *Genesis*, 211. Fishbane states, "The deception for the blessing-*berakhah* in chapter 27 is linked to and completes the first deception, for the birthright-*bekhorah*, in chapter 25." See Fishbane, "Genesis 25:19–35:22," 51.

11 Fokkelman, *Narrative Art in Genesis*, 99.

12 Walton states, "[T]he repeated use of the term by Jacob seems to indicate that the status of the firstborn is associated with the theme of the blessing." See Kevin Walton, *Thou Traveller Unknown: The Presence and Absence of God in the Jacob Narrative* (PBM; Carlisle: Paternoster, 2003), 22.

elder son Esau" in 27:1 and "so that I may bless you before I die" in 27:4 once again confirms the relationship between the firstborn and the blessing. In other words, the blessing should have been given to the firstborn son. Further, Fokkelman finds the close correspondence between the firstborn son and the blessing in the chiasm of 27:1–28:5.[13] This *inclusio* and Abrahamic blessing in 28:4 denote that the firstborn son in the Jacob cycle is related to the blessing, which is in the same line as the Abrahamic blessing.[14] Therefore, as Fishbane argues, the birth, the blessing, and the Land in Gen 28:4 are reiterations of the Abrahamic blessing in Gen 12:1–3.[15]

Fretheim argues that Isaac's blessing taken by Jacob is not related to the national blessing of Abraham, but it is only an individual blessing.[16] However, in several aspects, this interpretation warrants criticism. Firstly, it is evident that Gen 25:23–29 and 27:39 imply the national blessing. This oracle for superior status was not accomplished in Jacob's life-time, which means that this oracle is not an individual blessing to Jacob. Secondly, contrary to Fretheim's argument, any direct clue that Isaac wanted to make an individual blessing is not found in 27:4. Thirdly, Fishbane observes that the firstborn son/blessing narratives in the Jacob cycle have a thematic association with Abraham's covenant in Gen 12:1–3 in that the birth, the blessing, and the Land are primary factors

---

13 As seen above, Fishbane the relationship of ברך and בכרה (the blessing and the firstborn son) in the structure of the larger passage, that is, the *inclusio* between 25:19–34 and 35:1–22. See Fishbane, "Genesis 25:19–35:22," 42. As for Fokkelman's structure, see the following chiasm.

27:1–5	A. Isaac—son of the ברך and בכרה (the blessing and the firstborn son) (=Esau)
27:6–17	B Rebekah sends Jacob on the stage
27:18–29	C Jacob appears before Isaac, receives blessing
27:30–40	C' Esau appears before Isaac, receives anti-blessing
27:41–45	B' Rebekah sends Jacob from the stage
27:46–28:1–5	A' Isaac—son of the ברך and בכרה (the blessing and the firstborn son) (=Jacob)

Fokkelman, *Narrative Art in Genesis*, 98. However, many current scholars reject Fokkelman's view pertaining to Esau's anti-blessing in 27:30–40, and conceive that Esau was less-blessed than Jacob, but certainly blessed in some respects. See Bradford Anderson, "Election, Brotherhood and Inheritance: A Canonical Reading of the Esau and Edom Traditions," (PhD diss., Durham University, 2010), 67; 70–71; Levenson, *The Death and Resurrection of the Beloved Son*, 62.

14 Wenham states, "[F]undamental to the whole story is the conviction of the efficacy of the deathbed blessing." See Wenham, *Genesis*, 216.

15 Fishbane, "Genesis 25:19–35:22," 60.

16 T.E. Fretheim, "Which Blessing Does Isaac Give Jacob?" in *Jews, Christians and the Theology of the Hebrew Scripture* (eds. A. Ogden Bellis and J.S. Kaminsky; SBLSymS 8; Atlanta: SBL, 2000), 279–91. Cf. Anderson, "Election, Brotherhood and Inheritance," 88–89.

in both the Jacob cycle and Abraham's covenant.[17] Particularly, Isaac "blesses Jacob alone with mastery over his brothers and with the key Patriarchal provision, 'Cursed be they who curse you / Blessed be they who bless you' (Gen 27:29; cf. in Gen 12:3, to Abraham)."[18] Fourthly, Isaac's continuous blessing of Jacob in Gen 28:3–4 connotes a direct connection to Abraham's covenant.[19] In a similar vein, Anderson concludes, "While these blessings are obviously from Isaac to his sons, they also appear to establish the continued promised line of Abraham."[20]

After all, what does Esau sell Jacob? In order to answer this, we should compare what Jacob and Esau were ultimately given. We should note that both of the peoples (Israel and Edom) were strong and prosperous, and that Esau did not serve Jacob. Esau did not lose his positional priority as an older brother.[21] Both Esau and Jacob received their father's prosperity. Instead, the right of firstborn son/blessing for Jacob is related to the succession of the Abrahamic blessing as the Elect and the primacy of Jacob's descendants over other people.[22] We should note that the firstborn son in the Jacob cycle is closely connected to divine election.[23] Jacob is not biologically the firstborn son.[24] Yet it needs to be observed that Jacob was distinct on account of the elected position for his divinely ordained standing before his birth in the oracle of Gen 25:23. In other words, Jacob was not the firstborn son by nature, but he was elected as the firstborn son by God. This relation between the firstborn son and election is reiterated in Exodus. Therefore, as Anderson agrees, "Jacob not only has the

17 Fishbane, "Genesis 25:19–35:22," 60.

18 Levenson, *The Death and Resurrection of the Beloved Son*, 62.

19 "May God Almighty bless you and make you fruitful and numerous, that you may become a company of peoples. May he give to you the blessing of Abraham, to you and to your offspring with you, so that you may take possession of the land where you now live as an alien—land that God gave to Abraham," in Gen 28:3–4.

20 Anderson, "Election, Brotherhood and Inheritance," 89.

21 E.g., "He [Jacob] himself went on ahead of them, bowing himself to the ground seven times, until he came near his brother [Esau]," in Gen 33:3.

22 Cf. Levenson, *The Death and Resurrection of the Beloved Son*, 57.

23 Levenson maintains, "The special status of the firstborn son in the Hebrew Bible is inextricably associated with the theology of chosenness … The firstborn and the chosen are not, of course, synonymous, but their semantic fields overlap so extensively that an investigation of the one concept will inevitably illumine the other." See Levenson, *The Death and Resurrection of the Beloved Son*, 59–60.

24 On the other hand, Reuben is Jacob's biological firstborn son. He is acknowledged as the firstborn son in 49:3, but his status to receive the patriarchal blessing seems to be lost. It should be noted that Isaac is not Abraham's firstborn son, however, he is called the firstborn son in *Jub* 18:11, 15, which also denotes the close relationship between the nonbiological firstborn son and the election.

double share of the family inheritance and the honours of family succession, but he also has the blessing of his father, and appears to be the vessel to carry on the chosen line.[25]

In sum, the relationship between ברך and בכרה is still ambiguous and enigmatic, but we can draw a conclusion that the firstborn son in the Jacob cycle has a close association with the blessing,[26] and that the right of the firstborn son connotes the succession of Abraham's covenant and Jacob's primacy over Esau.[27] That is, the firstborn son refers to the "heir to the Abrahamic blessing,"[28] in the Jacob cycle.[29] In this vein, the firstborn son symbolises primacy over other peoples such as the Edomites.[30]

> It cannot be underscored enough that the man of whom this story is told is the eponymous ancestor of the nation, Jacob/Israel. At its deepest level the Jacob narrative is more than biography: it is the national history and speaks, therefore, of the self-conception of the people Israel and not merely of the pranks of the trickster from whom they are descended.[31]

This discussion of the firstborn son in the Jacob cycle is linked to the story of Exodus, and forms the background of the designation of Israel as the firstborn son in Exod 4:22 and the plague of the Egyptian firstborn sons in Exod 11–12.[32]

---

25 Anderson, "Election, Brotherhood and Inheritance," 96. Fishbane states, "The deception for the blessing-berakhah in chapter 27 is linked to and completes the first deception, for the birthright-bekhorah, in chapter 25." See Fishbane, "Genesis 25:19–35:22," 51.

26 Greenspahn states that Isaac's blessing to Jacob is related only to the numbers and strongness of Jacob's descendants. See Greenspahn, *When Brothers Dwell Together*, 56. However, as for the specific contents of Isaac's blessing, see van Seters, *Prologue to History*, 286; Fokkelman, *Narrative Art in Genesis*, 111.

27 Especially, see Gen 28:4.

28 Levenson, *The Death and Resurrection of the Beloved Son*, 65. Similarly. Syren states, "It seems also that the 'blessings' of the first-born sons are worked out in deliberate reference to the concept of God's election of Israel." See Roger Syrén, *The Forsaken First-Born: A Study of a Recurrent Motif in the Patriarchal Narrative* (JSOTSup 133; Sheffield: Sheffield Academic Press, 1993), 144.

29 Gunkel also argues, "[T]he blessing and the rights of the firstborn son is actually identical." See Gunkel, *Genesis*, 306.

30 E.g., "Be lord over your brothers," in Gen 27:29.

31 Levenson, *The Death and Resurrection of the Beloved Son*, 66.

32 We should note that another name of Jacob is Israel (cf. 35:10). See also Levenson, *The Death and Resurrection of the Beloved Son*, 36–42.

3.2 Exod 4:21–26

3.2.1 *The Text*

The text consists of the commission of Yahweh (4:21–23)[33] and the episode of Moses (4:24–26).[34] The speaker in 4:21–23 is Yahweh and the listener Moses. A new character in the Exodus cycle, Pharaoh, is introduced in 4:21 and the emphatic אני denotes the clear antithetical relationship between Yahweh and Pharaoh.[35] בכרי (my firstborn son) is paralleled with בני in 4:22, which is in apposition.[36] The apposition of בכרי was likely intended as "a kind of climax" in terms of the Hebrew word order.[37] There is also a parallel between my son, my firstborn son in 4:22 and your son, your firstborn son in 4:23. A new character, Zipporah, appears in 4:25. Wellhausen argues that 4:24–26 shows the origin of infant circumcision in Ancient Israel.[38] Since Wellhausen, many scholars have connected this text to the aetiology of Israel's circumcision ritual.[39] Some scholars take 4:25–26 as redundant, but "the repetition in vv. 25–26 may simply put an emphatic end to the narrative," as Propp notes.[40] In addition, מולת in 4:26 is a *hapax legomenon* in the OT, but it is likely "a derivative of מות"[41] and

33 There are debates on the composition and unity of 4:21–23 in the context, and also the similarity between 4:23 and 11:4 causes the redactional-critical discussions on this text. For example, Hyatt argues that fragments of 4:21–23 are misplaced in the current passage and it was originally located before 10:28 or 11:4. See J.P. Hyatt, *Exodus* (Grand Rapids: Eerdmans, 1971), 85. Some scholars argue that 4:21–23 is the passage. However, as Houtman notes, 4:21–23 fits the context: "That Moses (again; cf. 3:18ff) receives instructions and information as to how he is to speak and act before Pharaoh. Ahead of time he may know that it is going to be a difficult confrontation, topped off by a dramatic climax. From the perspective of the telling of the story, the gain of 4:21–23 is that already at this point the reader is given some information about what will happen." See Cornelis Houtman, *Exodus, vol. 1* (HCOT; Kampen: Kok, 1993), 432.

34 As for the textual variances of 4:24–26, See William Dumbrell, "Exodus 4:24–26: A Textual Re-Examination," *HTR* (1972): 285–290.

35 B.S. Childs, *The Book of Exodus: A Critical, Theological Commentary* (OTL; Philadelphia: Westminster, 1974), 102: "The conflict is over paternal power, and in the claim of the firstborn the God of Israel and the king of Egypt have clashed in a head-on encounter."

36 Houtman, *Exodus*, 430–31.

37 Houtman, *Exodus*, 431.

38 Julius Wellhausen, *Prolegomena to the History of Ancient Israel* (trans. J. Sutherland Black and Allan Enzies; Edinburgh: Adam and Charles Black, 1885), 340.

39 E.g., William Propp, *Exodus 1–18: A New Translation with Introduction and commentary* (AB; New York: Doubleday, 1999), 233–39.

40 Propp, *Exodus 1–18*, 220.

41 Houtman, *Exodus*, 438.

"another plural of abstraction: 'the act of circumcision'."[42] The preposition ל in 4:26 may mean "in reference to."[43]

3.2.2 *Analysis*

This section will focus on the meaning of the firstborn son and the contextual relations between 4:21–23 and 4:24–26. Exod 4:24–6 has caused "exegetes headaches."[44] The function of Exod 4:21–23 is more definite than Exod 4:24–26. Noth maintains that this passage implies the beginning of the tenth disaster (the death of the firstborn sons).[45] Propp also notes that Exod 4:21–23 foreshadows later incidents and the whole framework of the plagues: "4:22–23 is fulfilled in 11:4–8, 11:2–3 is fulfilled in 12:35–36. The separation of command and fulfilment both avoids monotony and creates coherence."[46] Particularly, Exod 4:22 is significant in the implication of the later plague of the first-born: "Yahweh kills the Egyptian firstborn but redeems his own firstborn, the entire nation of Israel."[47]

However, Exod 4:24–26 remains more problematic. The full discussion of the problems in 4:24–26 is beyond the scope of this study. Yet, this study will briefly organise current scholars' opinions. First of all, many scholars point out the paschal symbolism in 4:24–26.[48] For instance, we find the allusion or similar motifs in 4:24–26 with the Passover narrative.[49]

42 Propp, *Exodus 1–18*, 220.

43 Childs, *Exodus*, 100.

44 Houtman, *Exodus*, 432.

45 Noth states, "It already hints at the last of the plagues and with regard to this describes Israel as the 'firstborn son' of Yahweh, whose violation Yahweh will avenge on the 'firstborn son' of Pharaoh in accordance with the *ius talionis*," in Martin Noth, *Exodus: A Commentary* (trans. John Bowden; London: SCM, 1962), 47.

46 Propp, *Exodus 1–18*, 218.

47 Propp, *Exodus 1–18*, 217.

48 Fretheim, *Exodus* (IBC; Louisville: John Knox, 1991), 80; Bernard Robinson, "Zipporah to the Rescue: A Contextual Study of Exodus IV 24–26," *VT* 36 (1986) 452; Kosmala, "The Bloody Husband," *VT* 12 (1962): 23–24, Propp, "That Bloody Bridegroom (Exodus IV 24–26)," *VT* 43 (1993): 510. Robinson observes "the allusion to the Passover narrative" in Exod 4:24–26. See Robinson, "Zipporah," 452.

49 Cf. Propp, "That Bloody Bridegroom," 510; Kosmala, "The Bloody Husband," 23–24; Robinson, "Zipporah,"452–53. A similar pattern is found in the scene in front of Jordan at Gilgal in Jos 4:3, 8; 5:2–8.

Exod 4:21–26	The Passover narrative
Circumcision (4:25–26)	Circumcision (12:44, 48)
Blood (4:25)	Blood (12:22)
Night (4:24)[a]	Night (11:4;12:29–30)
The firstborn son (4:22–23)	The firstborn son (11:5; 12:29)

a Propp, *Exodus*, 218.

This clearly shows the close relationship between the meaning of 4:21–26 and of the Passover narrative.

Secondly, most scholars regard "Moses' feet" in 4:25b as a euphemism for Moses' genitals.[50] Accordingly, Zipporah's enigmatic action ([she] touched Moses' feet with [her son's foreskin]) in 4:25b can be interpreted as symbolic of the [re]circumcision of Moses.[51] Thirdly, many interpreters contend that the one who was attacked by Yahweh is Moses, not his son.[52] This third point leads us to the other difficult issue in Exod 4:24–26: why would God attack the man who was commissioned to set Israel free? Wellhausen[53] and Durham[54] argue that Moses' (not his son's) uncircumcision causes Yahweh's attack. According to their opinion, Moses' son was circumcised instead of Moses (i.e., vicarious circumcision). However, this concept of vicarious circumcision is not found in OT and ANE literature, and it is more probable that Moses was already circumcised.[55] On the other hand, Propp thinks that Yahweh attacked Moses owing to Moses' bloodguilt of murder in Egypt.[56] We cannot easily determine

50 E.g., Kosmala, "The Bloody Husband," 23.

51 Houtman, *Exodus*, 447; Propp, "That Bloody Bridegroom," 515; Kosmala, "The Bloody Husband," 16; Robinson, "Zipporah," 458.

52 Propp, *Exodus 1–18*, 238. Also see Houtman, *Exodus*, 447: "Consequently, to me it seems most likely that Moses is the implied object of 4:24."

53 Wellhausen, *Prolegomena*, 340.

54 John Durham, *Exodus* (WBC; Waco: Word, 1987), 58.

55 Robinson argues that it is unnatural that Moses was commissioned as a leader for Israel without the requirement for circumcision if Moses was not circumcised, and that it is highly probable that Moses was circumcised in eight days after his birth according to the tradition of Israel (Gen 17), because he was nurtured by Jewish parents for three months before he was cast into Niles, in Robinson, "Zipporah," 456–57. Geza Vermes collects the evidences in Early Jewish interpretations in Geza Vermes, "Baptism and Jewish Exegesis: New Light from Ancient Sources," *NTS* 4 (1957–8): 308–19. See also Houtman, *Exodus*, 447.

56 Propp, *Exodus*, 234–35. Robinson also contends that Moses needed atonement before he returned to Egypt, but he argues, "YHWH is angry with Moses for weakly trying to evade the duty of confronting the Pharaoh which has been placed on his shoulders, and

the meaning of God's attack towards Moses, but the clear point is, as Houtman observes, that "The context suggests that Moses' circumcision was in effect his consecration to this commission and the official beginning of the task."[57]

In addition, the meaning of "חתן דמים" in Exod 4:25 is still enigmatic.[58] No Akkadian lexical corresponding form with חתן is found.[59] Two possibilities concerning the lexical origin can be postulated on the basis of the Arabic *hatana*: 1) to cut or circumcise; and 2) family relations in relation to marriage such as the bridegroom,[60] son-in-law or father-in-law.[61] Whichever option we choose, scholars notice the close relation between circumcision and Israel's covenant in this phrase.

The meaning of Exod 4:24–26, therefore, still remains unclear. However, the clearest point in 4:24–26 is the significance of circumcision,[62] because this text denotes that Moses' life could be threatened due to omitting or conducting the circumcision improperly. Furthermore, Exod 4:21–26 shows the close association of the firstborn son, the circumcision and the covenantal people.[63] This point is strengthened by the relation between Exod 4:21–26 and the Passover narrative in Exodus. One of the important points in Exod 4:21–26 and the Passover narrative is that Israel is distinct from the nations. Yahweh says, "consecrate to me all the firstborn sons," in Exod 13:2, and he proclaims that "All Israel, man and woman, young and old, are Yahweh's collective firstborn son."[64] Furthermore, "any uncircumcised may not eat of [the Passover meal],"

although the men who meditated Moses' death are now dead, YHWH himself has begun to regret his choice of Moses." Thus, Robinson contends that 4:24–26 functions a kind of symbolic warning to Israelites who hesitate to leave Egypt. See Robinson, "Zipporah," 456.

57 Houtman, *Exodus*, 447–8.

58 For example, Propp translates this phrase into "bridegroom of bloodguilt" in relation to the blood of atonement, in Propp, *Exodus 1–18*, 239. Houtman understands this phrase as "one circumcised with blood," in Houtman 448. Interestingly, Robinson considers the meaning as "a son-in-law by virtue of the pouring out of blood" in terms of atoning blood in Propp's understanding. See Robinson, "Zipporah," 458. In addition, Robinson maintains that Moses' being rescued by his son's blood foreshadows the blood of the paschal lamb.

59 Dumbrell, "Exodus 4:24–26," 287.

60 Cf. Isa 62:5.

61 Cf. 2 King 8:27. See Dumbrell, "Exodus 4:24–26," 287. Also see Propp, "That Bloody Bridegroom," 496.

62 Child, *Exodus*, 104.

63 Nahum Sarna, *Exodus: The Traditional Hebrew Text with the New JPS Translation* (Philadelphia: JPS, 1991), 24–25. Also see F.C. Fensham, "Father and son as Terminology for Treaty and Covenant" in *Near Eastern Studies in Honor of William Foxwell Albright* (ed. H. Goedicke; Baltimore: Johns Hopkins University Press, 1971), 121–35.

64 Cf. Exod 4:22. See Propp, *Exodus 1–18*, 457.

in Exod 12:48. Thus, circumcision was the pivotal prerequisite to participate in the Passover celebration.

What does circumcision mean in Exodus? Propp observes, as we find in Gen 34:14–17 and Gen 17:10–14, "circumcision was a sign of Israelite identity. Not that the lack of a foreskin was uniquely Israelite—many neighbouring peoples were also circumcised. Rather, the operation acquired special significance as a rite of socio-religious initiation and a perpetual reminder of the covenant."[65]

In this context, Israel's position as the firstborn son of the Lord (Exod 4:22) is contrasted to the firstborn son of Pharaoh (Exod 4:23).[66] Egypt is a quintessential 'other' against Israel in Exodus, and Israel's identity is defined by contrast to the negative descriptions on Egypt.[67] In this context, designation of Israel as the firstborn son prefigures the Passover story surrounding the firstborn sons.

In sum, the firstborn son in Exodus 4:21–26 refers to the special and exclusive relation with his Father, Yahweh. The elected status of Israel as the firstborn son is contrasted with the destruction of the Egyptian firstborn son in Exod 11–12. Thus, Levenson states, "It is the special status of Israel, son of God, that explains why the Exodus is not a story of universal liberation at all but only of one nation's release, the release of the firstborn son to rejoin and serve his divine father."[68] Furthermore, the firstborn son in Exod 4:21–26 can be defined in relation to other peoples.[69] In other words, the firstborn son refers to the identity of Israel as the Elect and as a distinct people from Egypt and the nations (cf. Exod 19:6).[70] This point is confirmed in the story of the Passover, particularly, the story of circumcision and the tenth plague inflicted on the Egyptian firstborn sons, as noted above. The cultic notion of the offering the firstborn in the Pentateuch also highlights the distinct status of Israel as the firstborn son. In addition, the firstborn son of God is the circumcised people, and this point is emphasised in Exod 4:24–26 and the Passover narrative.[71]

65 Propp, "That Bloody Bridegroom," 513.

66 Greifenhagen, *Egypt on the Pentateuch's Ideological Map*, 77.

67 Greifenhagen, *Egypt on the Pentateuch's Ideological Map*, 156.

68 Levenson, *The Death and Resurrection of the Beloved Son*, 38.

69 It should be noted that the firstborn son in Exodus is implicitly the heir of Abrahamic blessing. As discussed above, Jacob is called the firstborn son and this firstborn son title is associated with the patriarchal blessing. Levenson notes the parallels between the Jacob cycle in Genesis and the Israel's story in Exodus. See Levenson, *The Death and Resurrection of the Beloved Son*, 67.

70 We also find the similar title connoting the primacy as Jewish ethnic identity in Exod 19:5–6: "my treasured possession out of all the peoples" and "the kingdom of priests and the holy nation."

71 The importance of circumcision with regard to the Canaan land is also found in Jos 5:2–8.

3.3 Psalm 89

3.3.1 *The Text*[72]

Psalm 89 is classified as a national lament (Volksklagelied),[73] or "communal lament over royal defeat."[74] Eaton and Johnson argue that Ps 89 reflects a ritual humiliation ceremony for the Israelite king, which is a similar rite for a Babylonian king in the Babylonian new year festival, depicting the king being attacked and saved by God and having power restored again.[75] This view is rejected by recent interpreters. For example, Ward observes: 1) Ps 89 does not describe anything about the ritual humiliation of a king; 2) Ps 89 does not depict any restoration after humiliation; 3) the exaltation of the king precedes the humiliation (the order of the humiliation is the opposite of the alleged humiliation ritual; and 4) no evidence of the existence of this humiliation ritual in Israel is found in the other psalms.[76] Therefore, the origin of Ps 89 in the context of a humiliation rite remains unconvincing.[77]

---

72 Some scholars maintain that Ps 89 is a composite and includes redactional additions, in terms of the modification of the contents, tones and metres, and in terms of the liturgical background. Particularly, Ps 89:39–52 is often regarded as a redactional addition due to its harsh tone. However, current scholars find the coherence and unity in Ps 89 according to the unifying motives and terms (25 key words reiterated). See James Ward, "The Literary Form and Liturgical Background of Psalm LXXXIX," *VT* 11 (1961): 323. Mitchell and Sarna also support the unity of the Psalm 89, in Sarna, "Psalm 89: A Study in Inner Biblical Exegesis," in *Studies in Biblical Interpretation* (New York: JPS, 2000), 378–80; Matthew Mitchell, "Genre Disputes and Communal Accusatory Laments: Reflections on the Genre of Psalm LXXXIX," *VT* 55 (2005): 515.

73 See Klaus Koch, "Königspsalmen und ihr ritueller Hintergrund; Erwägungen zu Ps 89,20–38 und Ps 20 und ihren Vorstufen," in *The Book of Psalms: Composition and Reception* (eds. Peter Flint and Patrick Miller; VTSup 99; Leiden: Brill, 2005), 19.

74 See Richard J. Clifford, "Psalm 89: A Lament over the Davidic Ruler's Continued Failure," *HTR* 73 (1980): 27. Clifford also considers this psalm as a lament for the Davidic ruler who is unsuccessful in battle or international politics, in Clifford, "Psalm 89," 47. For further discussion on the genre of Ps 89, see Floyd, "Psalm," 442–3.

75 See Aubrey Johnson, *Sacral Kingship in Ancient Israel* (Cardiff: University of Wales Press, 1967), 112: "as the celebration of Yahweh's universal Kingship is also the identical background to the present lament, it seems reasonable to infer that the defeat or humiliation of the Davidic king, which is indicated in these lines, is not any specific historical event, for indeed there is none that can be made to fit the scene, but is an important element in the ritual drama." This view is followed by John Eaton, *Kingship and the Psalms* (London: SCM, 1976), 109–11.

76 Ward, "Literary Form," 333–35.

77 As for the structure of Ps 89, this Psalm is traditionally divided into 89:1–19 (hymnic section), 89:20–38 (covenant oracle to David), and 89:39–52 (lament of the present situation), in Erhard Gerstenberger, *Psalms, Part 2 and Lamentations* (Grand Rapids: Eerdmans,

The historical background of Ps 89 has also been debated by exegetes. For instance, Clifford locates the background in Josiah's sudden death.[78] Anderson argues that Ps 89 was written after 520 BCE: "[A]gainst the background of the hope that the Davidic kingdom might soon be restored."[79] Ward maintains that the origin of the psalm lies in the "division of the Davidic-Solomonic kingdom, and the failure of Judah to realise its grandiose hope of universal dominion."[80]

Thus, the historical background of the psalm is controversial, yet it is highly likely that this psalm was written in the Exilic or post-Exilic period, as Tate notes.[81] Firstly, the temple motif is missing in this Psalm and this might indicate that, even after 515 BCE, Jerusalem was not yet rebuilt. Secondly, the lament in Ps 89:40–47 denotes the duration of the situation in suffering and destruction (particularly, the strong tone in Ps 89:45). These may depict the era when the Davidic dynasty was destroyed and the ancient covenantal hope and expectation were dimmed. Accordingly, it is highly probable that these laments denote desolation over the shattered Davidic dynasty and "the exilic hope for the restoration of the Davidic kingship and the nation."[82]

3.3.2 *Analysis*

Exegetes often interpret the firstborn son as meaning "an exalted status of privilege and power."[83] Yet, further issues need to be considered in order to elucidate the meaning of the firstborn son in Ps 89:27.

Firstly, the meaning of Ps 89:25 should be considered. Ostensibly, this verse may denote David's conquests against the personified and mythical enemies of YHWH.[84] However, the sea and the river is the common word pair which indicates the territory of David's kingdom (cf. Ps 72:8). Furthermore, Gerstenberger observes, "within Psalm 89 the attention is not on mythical battles and their festive enactments, but on Yahweh's great promises of the past

2001), 147; Michael Floyd, "Psalm LXXXIX: A Prophetic Complaint about the Fulfilment of an Oracle," *VT* 42 (1992): 447.

78 Clifford, "Psalm 89," 47.

79 A.A. Anderson, *The Book of Psalms: 73–150* (NCBC; Grand Rapids: Eerdmans, 1980), 631.

80 Ward, "Literary Form," 338.

81 Tate writes, "the psalm probably reflects different contexts and may have been used on various occasions … the arguments against the post-exilic period for the present psalm are weighty (e.g., silence about the destruction of Jerusalem and the temple and the deportation of large numbers of people)." See Tate, *Psalms 51–100* (WBC; Waco: Word, 1991), 416–17.

82 Gerald Wilson, "The Use of Royal Psalms at the 'Seams' of the Hebrew Psalter," *JSOT* 11 (1986): 91.

83 Tate, *Psalms*, 424; Anderson, *Psalms*, 642.

84 Johnson, *Sacral Kingship*, 24; Anderson, *Psalms*, 641.

and the sad state of his people in the present."[85] Even if we consider the expression of YHWH's cosmic expressions, there is no reason we should exclude the geographical meaning of this verse, because "the powers overcome by Yahweh (Ps 89:10–13) have their counterpart in the Davidic ruler's domination of an earthly kingdom (vv. 26)," as Tate writes.[86] Accordingly, we conclude that Ps 89:25 depicts the boundary of David's reign.

Secondly, we need to take into account the covenantal aspects in Ps 89:27. Many scholars admit that Ps 89 is covenantal "from first to last."[87] These covenantal features are fundamentally based on the Davidic covenant (e.g., 89:28–35), and the interpretation of Ps 89 should be taken into consideration in relation to 2 Sam 7, because motifs of 2 Sam 7 are reiterated in Ps 89 (e.g., 89:20, 26, 29).[88] Therefore, David is the covenantal leader of Israel.[89]

Timo Veijola argues that Ps 89 reflects the post-exilic era in which the Davidic covenant was applied to collective Israel. The identical phenomenon is found in Isa 55:3: "Incline your ear, and come to me; listen, so that you may live. I will make with you [Israel] an everlasting covenant, my steadfast, sure love for David." Ps 89 also uses certain concepts like בחיר ,בחור, and ברית, which are central in Isa 40–55, but not used in 2 Sam 7.[90]

Ps 89 extends Davidic covenant to collective Israel, and we find 'collective interpretations' of the figure of David in Ps 89, and Ps 89:40–45 clearly denotes this tendency:

> You have broken through all his walls; you have laid his strongholds in ruins. All who pass by plunder him; he has become the scorn of his neighbours. You have exalted the right hand of his foes; you have made all his enemies rejoice. Moreover, you have turned back the edge of his sword,

85 Gerstenberger, *Psalms*, 152. On the other hand, Tate merges two options: "a purely either/or choice between mythical and sociographic understandings of this language should be avoided." See Tate, *Psalms*, 423.

86 Tate, *Psalms*, 423.

87 Ward, "Literary Form," 331.

88 However, several strategic changes are found: 1) the Temple motif in 2 Sam 7:10–13 is missing; 2) the promise of respite from foreign enemies is limited to only David in Ps 89:23–24 and the threat to the Davidic royal line is stressed in Ps 89; 3) the father-son relationship between YHWH and the Davidic royal line is promised in 2 Sam 7:14 is applied to only David in Ps 89:27–8; and 4) Ps 89 reinterprets David as a dynastic symbol, while the threat of punishment for sin is "transferred from the son of David (as in 2 Sam 7:14) to the entire Davidic line." See Sarna, "Psalm 89," 383–85. Cf. Tate, *Psalms*, 417–18. Also see Timo Veijola, *Verheißung in der Krise: Studien zur Literatur und Theologie der Exilszeit anhand des 89. Psalms* (Helsinki: Suomalainen Tiedeakatemia, 1982), 48–59.

89 Ward, "Literary Form," 323; Clifford, "Psalm 89," 36.

90 Veijola, *Verheißung in der Krise*, 69.

> and you have not supported him in battle. You have removed the scepter from his hand, and hurled his throne to the ground. You have cut short the days of his youth; you have covered him with shame.
>
> SELAH [NRSV]

In this passage, the third person singular "He" refers to the figure of David, not Davidic kings. So, in Ps 89, David is identified with the nation of Israel, and the fall of the figure of David is a national fall of collective Israel. In other words, David is Israel herself in Ps 89. So, as Marttila, Pietsch and Veijola note, the psalmist ascribes Davidic covenant to the whole Israel in Ps 89.[91]

In the same context, the firstborn son (בכור) in Ps 89:27 should be understood as the title of Israel as in Exod 4:22. The firstborn son (בכור) in Ps 89:27 is not related to the divine origin or divine birth of a royal ruler in contrast to the son of God title in Ps 2:7b, which clearly indicates the divine origin of the Davidic king (cf. 2 Sam 7:14): "You are my Son. I have begotten (γεγέννηκα) you" (LXX Ps 2:7). It has been widely acknowledged that 'the son of God' title of the Davidic king in Ps 2:7 was derived from a royal protocol in the ANE. In ANE literature, evidence is broadly found that a royal ruler was called as the son of God. For example, in COS 1.36, King Sehetepibre is entitled as son of Re. In the ANE, divine origin and divine birth of a royal ruler are commonly associated with the immortality of kings and their divine power:

> COS 2.4C: "[King of Southern and Northern Egypt, M]en[mare, Son of Re, Sethos I Merenptah], given life. (c.i. [Vulture]). [Nekhbet …], may she endow him [with …], with life and dominion, [… like] Re every day."
>
> COS 2.4D: "King of Southern and Northern Egypt, Lord of Both Lands, Menmare Heir of Re, [Bodily Son of Re, his beloved], Lord of Crowns, [Sethos I Merenptah], beloved of Amun-Re, Lord of the Thrones of Both Lands, and given life like Re [forever]."
>
> COS 2.4E: "The Good god, strong in power, a hero valiant like Montu; Powerful one, powerful like him who begot him, illuminating Both Lands like Him of the Horizon. Mighty in strength like the Son of Nut, the strength of the Two Lords is in his actions."[92]

91 Veijola, *Verheißung in der Krise*, 141; Michael Pietsch, *'Dieser ist der Sproß Davids …': Studien zur Rezeptionsgeschichte der Nathanverheißung im alttestamentlichen, zwischentestamentlichen und neutestamentlichen Schrifttum* (WMANT 100; Neukirchen: Neukirchener Verlag, 2003), 115; Marko Marttila, *Collective Reinterpretation in the Psalms: A Study of the Redaction History of the Psalter* (FAT II/13; Tübingen: Mohr Siebeck, 2006), 144.

92 Translations taken from William W. Halo and K. Lawson, eds., *The Context of Scripture: Canonical Compositions, Monumental Inscriptions and Archival Documents from the Biblical World*, vols. 1–3 (Leiden: Brill, 2003). See also COS 2.4F; 2.5B; 2.14; KTU 1:16 i.14–15.

So, the son of God title in 2 Sam 7 and Ps 2 appears in the context of the divine birth of the royal ruler, and the divine origin of kings legitimised their rulership in the ANE.

However, it seems that the firstborn son in Ps 89:27 is not related to divine birth of a royal figure in the context. Divine birth of David is not presented in the context of Ps 89, but rather the firstborn son is referenced in the context of primacy and inheritance (e.g., Ps 89:25; cf. Gen 27:29). Furthermore, the firstborn son is not used as an honorary title of kings in extant ANE literature. We do not have any evidence that the term "the firstborn son" was used as a royal title in extant ANE literature. Thus, it is more reasonable to conclude that the firstborn son in Ps 89:27 originated in the title of Israel, and this reading fits well with the tendency of Ps 89 to link collective Israel to the figure of David. Accordingly, it is doubtful that the firstborn son in Ps 89:27 refers to the title of the Davidic king.

It should be noted that the firstborn son in Ps 89 exists within the pattern of the patriarchal blessings. In Ps 89, the firstborn son is clearly declared in the covenantal context, and we find the same patterns with the patriarchal blessing as in Gen 12:1–3 and 25:23; 27:27–29; 28:3–4: 1) the birth of the offspring in Ps 89:29, 36; 2) priority over the Gentiles in Ps 89:27; 3) election in Ps 89:19; 4) the Land in Ps 89:25; and 5) the exclusive relationship with God in Ps 89:26. Thus, in Ps 89, David is the heir of the patriarchal blessing for birth, the Land, election, superior status over the Gentiles, and an exclusive relationship with YHWH. The Yahweh community is also "the direct heir of promises given to the Davidic dynasty."[93]

Therefore, in Ps 89, the figure of David symbolises collective Israel. In this vein, we conclude that the title of the firstborn son in Ps 89:27 was derived from the title of collective Israel. So, the firstborn son in Ps 89:27 refers to the title of the chosen people possessing the supreme position and the divine inheritance. There is little evidence that the firstborn son was used as a royal title in ANE literature and the OT.

3.4 Jer 31:7–14

3.4.1 *The Text*

God's declaration of Ephraim as his firstborn son in Jer 31:9 is located in Jer 30–31, which is often called "the book of consolation." The first part (31:7) is

93 Gerstenberger, *Psalms*, 153. For further studies on the relationship between the Abrahamic and Davidic covenants, see Ronald Clements, *Abraham and David: Genesis XV and its Meaning for Israelite Tradition* (London, SCM 1967).

a petition for salvation, and the other parts (the second part: 31:8–9; the third: 31:10–11; and the fourth: 31:12–14) declare God's saving action.[94] The subject in the second (31:8–9) and fourth parts is "the Lord," (31:12–14) who promises salvation to Israel. The messenger formula in 31:7 opens this passage (31:7–14) with the conjunction כי, which does not occur in the other messenger formulae in 30:5, 18; 31:2, 15. This כי denotes the logical flow between the preceding unit (31:2–6) which depicts how Israel settles in the Land, and this unit (31:7–14) which portrays how they will arrive in the Land.[95]

3.4.2 *Analysis*

Before we define the firstborn son in Jer 31:9, we need to take the object of this oracle in Jer 7–14 into account. Who is Jacob or Israel in Jer 31:7, 9? Is he the northern kingdom or the future restored kingdom or "another name for the whole people of Israel"?

Some scholars argue that Jacob in 31:7, and Israel and Ephraim in 31:9 refer to the future restored kingdom.[96] We find that Judah and Israel are used in the same sense in Jer 2:3, 26, 31; 14:8; 16:14; 17:13; 18:6; 23: 3, 6, 7, etc. However, the expression of "the mountains of Samaria" in 31:5, and of the mountains of Ephraim in 31:6 should be considered as symbolic places of the northern kingdom.[97] Furthermore, there is no reason for Jeremiah to name the whole people of Israel as Ephraim, the prominent people of the northern kingdom.[98] Finally, we need to remember that Israel often refers only to the northern kingdom in Jeremiah.[99] In this vein, Lundbom maintains that Jacob and Ephraim (31:7, 9) indicate the northern kingdom, and that reference to the firstborn son in 31:9 points to the status of the northern kingdom as the firstborn son as in

94 G. Keown, P. Scalise, T. Smothers, *Jeremiah 26–52* (WBC; Waco: Word, 1995), 112.

95 Also see Georg Fischer, *Jeremia 26–52* (HThKAT; Freiburg: Herder, 2005), 149.

96 E.g. Parke-Taylor, *The Formation of the Book of Jeremiah: Doublets and Recurring Phrases* (SBLMS 51; Atlanta: SBL, 2000), 68.

97 Jack Lundbom, *Jeremiah: A New Translation with Introduction and Commentary, Vol. 2* (AB; New York: Doubleday, 2004), 357.

98 Nohfink argues that "Jacob" in 30:7, 18, "Israel" in 31:4, 21, "Ephraim" in 31:6, 9, 18, 20 and "Rachel" in 31:15 represent the northern kingdom, and that "their" in 30:21 means Josiah who extended the boundary of the southern kingdom to the north after the ruin of Assyria, and who wanted to rule over the northern area as he does the south. See N. Nohfink, "Der junge Jeremia als Propagandist and Poet. Zum Grundstock von Jer 30–31," in *Le Livre De Jérémie: Le Prophète et Son Milieu les Oracles et leur Transmission* (BETL 54; Leuven: Leuven University Press, 1981), 360.

99 E.g., Jer 3:6–18.

1 Chr 5:1–3.[100] Thus, we draw the conclusion that the poetic oracle in Jer 31:7–14 (and also 31:15–22) is especially given to the captives of the northern kingdom.[101]

What, then, does it mean that the northern kingdom is designated as the firstborn son in Jer 31:9? Holladay contends that this designation for the northern kingdom as the firstborn son is "over against Judah" as in 2 Sam 19:43.[102] However, the superiority of the northern kingdom over Judah is not found in the context of Jer 31. Rather, it is prophesied that Israel will return to Zion (the southern realm) and that they will worship YHWH there in 31:6. Therefore, it is not plausible that this designation of the northern kingdom as the firstborn son implies superior status over the southern kingdom.

Explicitly, Ephraim's designation as the firstborn son is related to the status of the beloved son as in 31:20. The father-son imagery is found elsewhere in Jeremiah (3:4, 19; 31:20). The father/son formula in Jer 31 may evoke 2 Sam 7:14a.[103] However, it is more probable that the designation of collective Israel as the firstborn son in Jer 31:9 is an allusion to Exod 4:22. God's paradigmatic declaration in Jer 31:1 alludes to God's promise in Exod 6:7 and 19:5–6: "At that time, says the LORD, I will be the God of all the families of Israel, and they shall be my people." This passage may demonstrate that the northern kingdom is still the chosen people after her destruction, and that the people of the northern kingdom still have a favoured position as the firstborn son with God, and a superior relationship to the other nations.[104] Jacob in Jer 31:7 and 11 implies that the title of the firstborn son in Jer 31:9 is related to the promise given to Jacob and his descendants. Ephraim is the chief of the nations (31:7) as Jacob was (Gen 27:29). Ephraim is elected from among the nations as Jacob was elected. The other nations cannot participate in the promise, but Ephraim does. Depictions of returning to the Promised Land in Jer 31:7–9 also implies that the concept of the firstborn son in Jer 31:9 is associated with the promise to possess the Promised Land. In conclusion, the restoration of Ephraim is the realisation of the divine promise (par. Jer 31:1), and Ephraim (the northern kingdom) is the recipient of the promise regarding this restoration.

Therefore, we can conclude that the designation as the firstborn son in Jer 31:9 denotes the title of Israel who possesses the elected status. In other words, this designation connotes that the northern kingdom still holds the

100 Lundbom, *Jeremiah*, 422, 425–26.

101 Cf. Jer 30:3; 31:27.

102 William Holladay, *Jeremiah 2: A Commentary on the Book of the Prophet Jeremiah Chapters 26–52* (Hermeneia; Philadelphia: Fortress, 1989), 185.

103 Georg Fischer, *Jeremia*, 152; Keown, et al., *Jeremiah*, 114.

104 See the unique expression of "the head of the nations" in Jer 31:7. Cf. Holladay, *Jeremiah* 2, 184.

divine promise and the privileged status amongst the nations in spite of their covenantal insincerity.

3.5 *Jubilees*

3.5.1 *The Text*[105]

The Book of Jubilees retells the biblical story of Genesis and the first half of Exodus.[106] The oldest Hebrew copy of *Jubilees* is 4Q216 which was copied possibly between 125 BCE and 100 BCE, and because some ancient Jewish literature (e.g., the Damascus Document XVI) quotes *Jubilees* as a work of authority, *Jubilees* must have been written earlier than this.[107] Great emphasis is placed on the covenant and the observance of the circumcision, the Sabbath, and the calendrical festivals in *Jubilees*. VanderKam situates the historical background of this book in the Maccabbean era and the preceding reign of Antiochus, who made attempts to remove the custom of circumcision and to abandon the covenant.[108] Echoes of Maccabean literature are also found in *Jubilees*.[109] Thus, *Jubilees* can be regarded as a result of resistance to assimilation in the era of Antiochus and later.

3.5.2 *Analysis*

3.5.2.1 *Jub* 2:13–33

Jubilees traces the unique and close relationship between God and Israel back to creation.[110] That is, Israel was elected and predestined as the special people of God in creation, and this point is stressed in *Jub* 1–2. However, why does *Jubilees* push back the election of Israel to the time of creation? It seems that

105 Most scholars consider *Jubilees* as the work of a single author. For arguments in favour of unity of *Jubilees*, See James C. VanderKam, "The Origins and Purposes of the Book of Jubilees," in *Studies in the Book of Jubilees* (ed. M. Albani, et al.; TSAJ 65; Tübingen: Mohr Siebeck, 1997), 3–24; VanderKam, *The Book of Jubilees* (GAP 9; Sheffield: Sheffield Academic Press, 2001), 17–18.

106 *Jubilees* is often categorised as an example of Rewritten Bible. See VanderKam, *The Book of Jubilees*, 93. The biblical text is perhaps not the Masoretic text of the Hebrew Bible, but rather the text closer to LXX or the Samaritan Pentateuch. See VanderKam, *The Book of Jubilees*, 94.

107 "And the exact interpretation of their ages about the blindness of Israel in all these matters, behold, it is defined in the book of 'the divisions of the periods according to their Jubilees and their weeks'," in CD XVI 2–4 [translated by F.G. Martínez].

108 VanderKam, *The Book of Jubilees*, 139–40.

109 VanderKam, *The Book of Jubilees*, 17–18.

110 VanderKam, *The Book of Jubilees*, 122.

Jubilees asserts that the Jewish religion is the true religion which has existed since the beginning against the background of the assimilation in the era of Antiochus.[111] We can encapsulate the notion of the covenant in *Jubilees* as follows:[112] 1) the covenant in *Jubilees* is one, and the contents of the covenant are always the same;[113] 2) the covenant in *Jubilees* does not denote universalistic aspects;[114] 3) the covenant in *Jubilees* is conditional in that it depends on the practice of Israel and individual members of the Jewish nation;[115] 4) the covenant is traced back to creation;[116] 5) the covenant highlights the importance of the Mosaic law;[117] 6) the covenant is depicted as a father-son relationship which cannot be broken in contrast to its conditional aspects;[118] and 7) circumcision in *Jubilees* is a mark of the Elect as distinct from the Gentiles, and it causes the ontological change of its bearers into heavenly beings.[119] Conversely, the uncircumcised belong to Belial, and they are under the anger of God.[120]

How, then, does *Jub* 2:13–33 rewrite the story of creation? *Jub* 2:15–33 basically reframes Gen 2:1–3, but the influence of Exod 31:12–17 is also found:[121]

111 VanderKam, *The Book of Jubilees*, 321.

112 Yet, we should also note, "Jubilees is not so much a covenantal book as an apocalyptic within a covenantal setting that inherently lends it authority." See James M. Scott, "Covenant," in *The Eerdmans Dictionary of Early Judaism* (eds. John J. Collins and Daniel C. Harlow; Grand Rapids: Eerdmans, 2010), 494.

113 VanderKam, *The Book of Jubilees*, 13; Huizenga, "The Battle for Isaac: Exploring the Composition and Function of the Aqedah in the Book of Jubilees," *JSP* 13 (2002): 47. Cf. *Jub* 19:27.

114 Huizenga, "The Battle for Isaac," 48: "Jubilees thus strongly emphasizes the need for Abraham to have an heir. The covenant is intended only for the physical line of Israel, and should that be lacking, the covenant cannot exist. There is no possibility of a 'spiritual' Israel."

115 Huizenga, "The Battle for Isaac," 50: "To keep covenant status means above all to practice circumcision and to marry only within Israel, as well as avoiding transgression in general." Also see William Gilders, "The Concept of Covenant in Jubilees," in *Enoch and the Mosaic Torah: The Evidence of Jubilees* (eds. Gabriele Boccaccini and Giovanni Ibba; Grand Rapids: Eerdmans, 2009), 180.

116 Gilders, "The Concept of Covenant," 181. Cf. *Jub* 1:5.

117 Gilders, "The Concept of Covenant," 181.

118 Gilders, "The Concept of Covenant," 181. Gilders writes, "*Jubilees* insists that the covenant does not create God's unique relationship with Israel. Rather, it enacts that relationship, which pre-exists the covenant," in Gilders, "The Concept of Covenant," 187.

119 Gilders, "The Concept of Covenant," 185. Cf. *Jub* 15:27.

120 "All the people of Belial will leave their sons uncircumcised just as they were born. Then there will be great anger from the Lord against the Israelites because they neglected his covenant, departed from his word, provoked, and blasphemed in that they did not perform the ordinance of this sign," in *Jub* 15:33c–34b.

121 J.T.A.G.M. Van Ruiten, *Primaeval History Interpreted: The Rewriting of Genesis 1–11 in the Book of Jubilees* (JSJSup 66; Leiden: Brill, 2000), 52–54.

1) observing the Sabbath in *Jub* 2:18–21, 26, 28, 29, 30, 31; Exod 31:13, 14, 16; 2) the Sabbath as the great sign in *Jub* 2:17, 21; Exod 31:13, 17; 3) the sanctification of Israel in *Jub* 2:19, 20, 21, 31; Exod 31:13; 4) the holiness of the Sabbath in *Jub* 2:23, 26, 27, 30; Exod 31:14, 15; 5) the phrases "six days shall work be done, and the seventh day the Sabbath" in *Jub* 2:17; Exod 31:51, 17; 6) capital punishment for the violation of the Sabbath in *Jub* 2:25, 27; Exod 31:14–15; 7) direction to Moses for teaching the law to the people of Israel in *Jub* 2:26, 29; Exod 31:13; and 8) the Sabbath should be observed by the whole offspring in *Jub* 2:24, 27, 33; Exod 31:16–17. Therefore, it can be concluded that *Jub* 2:13–33 rewrites the story of creation in Gen 2:1–3 according to the perspective of Exod 31:12–17.

Some differences between Gen 2:1–3 and Exod 31:12–17 is also detected in *Jub* 2:13–33. *Jub* 2:15–33 places an emphasis on Israel's separation from Gentiles. The Israelites are the chosen people in *Jub* 2:20. Israel is also elected as the firstborn son in *Jub* 2:20. Separation between light and darkness is mentioned in *Jub* 2:8–9, and this is linked to the separation of Israel and Gentiles: "I will now separate a people for myself from among my nations ... I have chosen the descendants of Jacob among all of those whom I have seen ... sanctified them for himself as a noteworthy people out of all the nations [*OTP* translation]" (*Jub* 2:19–21). The creation of the Sabbath is also addressed in terms of sanctification:[122] "I sanctified the Sabbath" (2:19). Israel is also said to be sanctified in 2:21. So, the sanctification of the Sabbath and the separation of Israel from the nations signal the privileged and central position of Israel amongst creation. Keeping the Sabbath also shows that Israel is a distinct people from the Gentiles, because the Sabbath is also sanctified from other days.[123] This privilege of Israel demonstrates the exclusive relationship with God and the pre-eminent status over the Gentiles.[124] Therefore, the story of creation in *Jub* 1–2 is used to reveal the primacy of Israel amongst creation and the separation of the Jews from the nations.

The firstborn son is located in the context of election: "I have chosen the descendants of Jacob among all of those whom I have seen" (*Jub* 2:20a). Jacob is addressed as the firstborn son in Gen 25–27 and *Jub* 19, and this denotes that the firstborn son refers to the title of the Elect. In *Jubilees*, Jacob is the centre of the covenant, and this point is confirmed in Abraham's blessings to Jacob[125]

122 Also see "the Lord God ... kept sabbath on the seventh day. He sanctified it for all ages and set it as a sign for all his works," in *Jub* 2:1.

123 Cf. "The creator of all blessed but did not sanctify any people(s) and nations to keep Sabbath on it except Israel alone," in *Jub* 2:31a.

124 Cf. S. Tzoref, "Covenantal Election in 4Q252 and Jubilees' Heavenly Tablets," *DSD* 18 (2011): 88–89.

125 See *Jub* 19:21–22.

which do not appear in Genesis. Thus, the offspring of Jacob are designated by God to hold the status of the firstborn son as the Elect who are pre-eminent over the Gentiles at the culmination of creation in *Jub* 2.[126]

3.5.2.2 *Jub* 18:9–16

Jub 18 retells the story of Akedah in Gen 22.[127] The first difference between *Jub* 18 and Gen 22 is that *Jub* 18 mentions that the life of Isaac, who is designated as the firstborn son in *Jub* 18:11, 15, was threatened by the prince Mastema, not by God. Mastema appears in *Jubilees* as a figure who threatens the covenant people with temptation or with actual attempts of destruction.[128] Mastema also makes an attempt to kill Israel's firstborn in *Jub* 49:2–4.[129] In contrast, all Gentiles are under the power of Mastema.[130] Four other motifs are added in *Jub* 18: 1) the Akedah is dated to the fourteenth of the first month; 2) Isaac is described as a firstborn son; 3) the slaughter of a sheep; and 4) the identification of the place of the Akedah with Mt. Zion.[131]

Isaac is not addressed as the firstborn son in Gen 22.[132] Yet in the Pentateuch, there are two distinct definitions of the firstborn son (בכר): 1) the firstborn son in respect of his father (e.g., Gen 49:3; Deut 21:17; Ps 78:51; 105:36); and 2) the firstborn son in respect of his mother (e.g, Exod 13:2, 12, 15; Num 3:11–13; 8:13–18). As concerns the first definition, the firstborn son is "a principal heir and successor of his father as head of the family."[133] In terms of inheritance, Isaac is not the firstborn son because Isaac is not the first offspring in Abraham's view. Instead, Ishmael is the biological firstborn son of Abraham.

The second definition is related to the cultic context. In the cultic sense, the firstborn is defined as the first male offspring from the mother's womb. Isaac

126 Gilders, "The Concept of Covenant," 187.

127 For further studies on Gen 22 and its interpretations in Jewish literature, See Davies and Chilton, The Aqedah: A Revised Tradition History, *CBQ* 40 (1978): 514; Geza Vermes, "Redemption and Genesis xxii," in *Scripture and Tradition in Judaism: Haggadic Studies* (StPB 4; Leiden: Brill, 1961), 193–227; Vermes, "New Light on the Sacrifice of Isaac from 4Q225," *JJS* 30 (1979): 140–46.

128 See Huizenga, *The New Isaac: Tradition and Intertextuality in the Gospel of Matthew* (NovTSup 131; Leiden: Brill, 2009), 86.

129 "[A]ll the powers of Mastema were sent to kill all of the firstborn …" in *Jub* 49:2. The firstborn son as the chosen line is the object of attack by Mastema. See Michael Segal, *The Book of Jubilees: Rewritten Bible, Redaction, Ideology and Theology* (JSJSup 117; Leiden: Brill, 2007), 197.

130 Cf. *Jub* 10:8.

131 Segal, *The Book of Jubilees*, 196.

132 Cf. Segal, *The Book of Jubilees*, 195.

133 Baruch Levine, "Firstborn," in *Encyclopaedia Judaica, vol. 7* (eds. Fred Skolnik and Michael Berenbaum; Detroit: Thomson, 2007), 45.

was the first male offspring in respect to Sarah and the promise of the seed of Abraham is also given to Sarah (Gen 17:15–16). Furthermore, God requires Abraham to offer Isaac as a cultic sacrifice and this means that the status of Isaac should be interpreted in the cultic context. We should also note that the genealogy in Gen 22:20–24 is matrilineal. So, Isaac is the firstborn son in relation to Sarah (his mother) in the given text, and this corresponds with the cultic definition of the firstborn son in the Pentateuch. In other words, Abraham was required to offer Isaac as the cultic offering of the firstborn. Accordingly, it is probable that the author of *Jubilees* perceived Isaac to be the firstborn son in respect of the mother in Gen 22.

Furthermore, we find some hints in the parallels between the Akedah and the story of Israel in the Exodus story:[134] 1) the firstborn son is the key to the events in both the Akedah and the Passover; 2) the Akedah on the mountain happens on the 14th day and Israel is rescued on the same day in *Jub* 49:1; 3) in *Jub* 18:17–19, the Akedah story is linked with the seven-day festival, and the only seven-day festival is the Passover festival (the Feast of Unleavened Bread);[135] 4) it is ordained in the heavenly tablets that the festival should be celebrated with "festal happiness" in *Jub* 18:18–19, and the night of the first Passover is "the beginning of joy" in *Jub* 49:2 and the Israelites "rejoice before the Lord" in *Jub* 49:22;[136] and 5) the Angel of the Presence who "stood" in *Jub* 18:9 and 48:13 rescues the firstborn son (Isaac and the firstborn sons of Israel) from Mastema.[137] Therefore, Huizenga argues, "These exact verbal links demonstrate that the author did more than simply construct the Akedah as a patriarchal aetiology of the Passover festival by means of timing and the ensuing feat."[138] So, the author of *Jubilees* links the title and destiny of Isaac to those of Israel. This is confirmed in *Jub* 16:18 when Isaac is given the title of Israel as in Exod 19:6; "he might become a kingdom of priests and a holy people."

134 Halpern-Amaru notes that the Akedah story in *Jubilees* and 4Q225 is combined with the Passover story. See B. Halpern-Amaru, "A Note on Isaac as First-born in 'Jubilees' and Only Son in 4Q225," *DSD* 13 (2006): 127–33. See also See also James C. VanderKam, "The Aqedah, Jubilees, and PseudoJubilees," in *The Quest for Context & Meaning: Studies in Biblical Intertextuality in Honor of James A. Sanders* (eds. Craig C. Evans and Shemaryahu Talmon; Leiden: Brill, 1997), 241–61; Cristina Grenholm, *The Old Testament, Christianity and Pluralism* (BGBE 33; Tübingen: Mohr Siebeck, 1996), 204–7. The expiatory aspects of the Aqedah tradition have been disputed. The connection between the Akedah and the Passover story is also found in 4Q225, *Exod. Rab.* 15:11, and *b. Ros. Has* 10b–11a.

135 Levenson, *The Death and Resurrection of the Beloved Son*, 177; Huizenga, "The Battle for Isaac," 42.

136 Huizenga, "The Battle for Isaac," 44–45.

137 Huizenga, "The Battle for Isaac," 45.

138 Huizenga, "The Battle for Isaac," 46.

If so, how does *Jubilees* describe Isaac's status which is distinct from that of Ishmael? Some positive descriptions seem to occur in *Jubilees*: 1) Abraham's blessing in *Jub* 20 goes to "all his children with their families and descendants";[139] 2) Ishmael came back to his father's house and enjoyed the Feast of Weeks with Abraham and Isaac in *Jub* 22:1–9; 3) Abraham prays for his sons (plural) to be "an elect people for you" and "inheritance" from the nations; and 4) in *Jub* 17:7, God or the messenger of God states that certain blessings go to Ishmael as in Gen 16:10–11 and 21:8.[140] In a similar vein, Mendels writes,

> *Jubilees*, which is full of aetiological stories referring to the events of the second century BC projects an extremely positive view of Ishmael, who was and remains a close relative of the Jews ... This contrasts sharply with the attitude to the 'Philistines' and Edomites, discussed above ... Ishmael is a sympathetic relative of the Jews, unlike Esau who is problematic.[141]

However, we should note that the positive descriptions of Ishmael do not go beyond the descriptions of Ishmael in the OT. In *Jub* 15:30–32, Ishmael is referenced and defined equally with Esau, and only Israel is stated to be sanctified and distinguished from all mankind:

> For the Lord did not draw near to himself either Ishmael, his sons, his brothers, or Esau. He did not choose them [simply] because they were among Abraham's children, for he knew them. But he chose Israel to be his people. He sanctified them and gathered [them] from all mankind.
> OTP translation, *Jub* 15:30–31a

In addition, *Jub* 16:17 denotes the separation of Ishmael and his descendants from Isaac and his descendants: "All the descendants of his [Abraham's] sons would become nations and be numbered with the nations. But one of Isaac's sons would become a holy progeny and would not be numbered among the nations [OTP translation]." Further, it is highly likely that the omission of Ishmael when Abraham is circumcised in *Jub* 15:24 was intentional: cf. "On that very

139 Roger Syren, "Ishmael and Esau in the Book of Jubilees and Targum Pseudo-Jonathan," in *The Aramaic Bible: Targums in their Historical Context* (eds. D.R.G. Beattie and M.J. McNamara; JSOTSup 166; Sheffield: Sheffield Academic Press, 1994), 311.

140 Syren, "Ishmael and Esau," 311. Also see Segal, *The Book of Jubilees*, 229–45; Tzoref, "A Note on Isaac," 82.

141 Doron Mendels, *The Land of Israel as a Political Concept in Hasmonean Literature: Recourse to History in 2. Century B.C. claims to the Holy Land* (TSAJ 15; Tübingen: Mohr Siebeck, 1987), 150.

day Abraham and his son Ishmael were circumcised" (Gen 17:26), and "On the same day Abraham was circumcised" (*Jub* 17:26). Thus, we conclude that Isaac and Israel have a distinct status from Ishmael and his descendants,[142] and that Isaac has primacy as the Elect over Ishmael in *Jubilees*.

Therefore, we should note that the firstborn son in *Jub* 18 demonstrates the sharp contrast of destinies between the chosen and the unchosen including Ishmael.[143] Isaac represents the circumcised and the chosen in the covenant line, and Ishmael signifies the uncircumcised and the unchosen.[144] So, Isaac's status is distinguished from that of Ishmael in *Jubilees*. The firstborn son in *Jub* 18:11, 15 is referenced in the context of the patriarchal blessing as follows: 1) the Land in *Jub* 18:15c; 2) the birth in *Jub* 18:15b; and 3) superior status over the Gentiles in *Jub* 18:15c. In this context, the firstborn son is associated with the line chosen by God.[145] Both Isaac and Israel procure the same blessings for the patriarchs,[146] and Isaac as the firstborn son is "a necessary and vital link between Abraham and Jacob."[147]

Furthermore, the title of the firstborn son in *Jub* 18:11, 15 is referenced in the context of the Akedah and the Passover story. In this vein, the title of the firstborn son can be related to the elected status of Israel in Exod 4:22 and Exod 12. This enables us to conclude that the firstborn son in *Jub* 18:11 and 15 refers to the title of Israel having the elected status in terms of primacy and inheritance.

3.5.2.3 *Jub* 19:26–29

Jacob's status in *Jubilees* is defined by comparison with Esau, as Isaac is defined in relation to Ishmael. Isaac warns Esau and Jacob to love each other in *Jub* 37. However, Esau's sons make a war against Jacob, which means violating Isaac's warning, and the consequence of the violations is "being uprooted" and the judgement: "you will complete a sin unto death, and your seed will be rooted out from under heaven" (*Jub* 26:34). The violation of Esau's sons justifies the eternal curse towards Esau's offspring in *Jub* 36:9–11.[148] Therefore, it is evident

142 Cf. *Jub* 17:4.

143 Segal notes, "The choice of Israel is meaningless without other nations, and therefore God chooses them from 'among my nations.' *Jub* 15:30–32 explicitly outlines the contrast between God's relationship with Israel and his connection to the other nations." See Segal, *The Book of Jubilees*, 179.

144 Huizenga, "The Battle for Isaac," 55.

145 Huizenga, "The Battle for Isaac," 49.

146 Cf. *Jub* 1:7; 14:7; 16:16; 18:15–16.

147 Huizenga, "The Battle for Isaac," 49.

148 Cf. Huizenga argues the doctrine of salvation according to works in *Jubilees*. See *Jub* 2:3, 23; 15:3. See also Huizenga, *New Isaac*, 88; Tzoref, "A Note on Isaac," 85. Tzoref writes, "The treatment of the non-Elect in Jubilees' Heavenly Tablets may reflect the exegetical

that Esau and his descendants are not chosen by God. In the same vein, Tzoref maintains,

> … both 4Q452 and the book of Jubilees exhibit discomfort with the fact that the book of Genesis records divine (or divinely sanctioned) blessings of the non-chosen sons of Elect individuals. Both texts highlight patriarchal blessings, especially those pertaining to offspring and the Land.[149]

Thus, Esau and his descendants represent the cursed under Mastema, and, by contrast, Jacob represents the heir of Abrahamic blessing and the superior and exclusive position over the nations.

Several differences between the blessing of Jacob in *Jub* 19 and Gen 27 can be found. Firstly, Abraham himself, not Isaac, prays for Jacob. This confirms that Jacob is the heir of the Abrahamic blessing more clearly than Gen 27, and *Jub* 19:17b and 27bc support this point.[150] Abraham directly names Jacob as his son in *Jub* 19:17, 29. This shows that the firstborn son title in *Jub* 19:29 implies the heir of the Abrahamic promise more directly than Genesis. Furthermore, Abraham in *Jubilees* asserts that the promise made to Jacob is the identical blessing given to Shem, Noah, Enoch, Malaleel, Enos, Seth, and Adam (e.g., *Jub* 19:24, 27). Secondly, *Jubilees* does not state that Jacob deceived Isaac in order to seize Esau's blessing, in contrast to Gen 27. Thirdly, Jacob in *Jubilees* is perfect and upright (cf. *Jub* 19:3), and this description of Jacob is not found in Genesis. Fourthly, in *Jub* 19, the Abrahamic promise is given to Jacob more explicitly than Gen 27:27–29. Fifthly, Mastema's threat appears in *Jub* 19:28 and this shows that Mastema is the one who is a threat to the covenantal line represented through Isaac, Jacob, and Israel. Sixthly, Jacob is the firstborn son as in Gen 25, 27, but is addressed as the firstborn son of God, not of Isaac, in *Jub* 19:29. So, the firstborn son in *Jub* 19:29 is not merely a human son, but the son of God like Israel in Exod 4:22.

On the other hand, the blessing of Jacob in *Jub* 19 is also related to the Abrahamic promise. In other words, the pattern of the Abrahamic promise for the birth, the Land, and the pre-eminent position is reiterated with the

---

development of Ps 69:27: 'May [my foe] be erased from the book of life, and not be inscribed with righteousness'." See Tzoref, "A Note on Isaac," 87.

149 Tzoref, "A Note on Isaac," 87.

150 "My daughter, take care of my son Jacob because he will occupy my place on the earth," in *Jub* 19:17b; "May he give you all the blessings with which he blessed Adam, Enoch, Noah, and Shem. Everything that he said to me and everything that he promised to give me may he attach to you and your descendants until eternity—like the days of heaven above the earth," in *Jub* 19:27bc.

designation of the firstborn son for Jacob in *Jub* 19:1) the birth (*Jub* 19:22); 2) the Land (*Jub* 19:17–18, 21); 3) primacy over Gentiles (*Jub* 19:17c–18); and 4) the exclusive relationship with God (*Jub* 19:18, 20).[151] We should also note that Jacob's inheritance is not only confined to the land of Canaan, but covers the entire earth.[152] In this sense, the title of the firstborn son in *Jubilees* connotes Jewish ethnic identity, and also symbolises the elected status of Israel possessing the primacy over Gentiles and the inheritance.

In conclusion, Jacob represents Abraham's true heir in *Jubilees*,[153] and Esau symbolises a contrasting figure to Jacob. Jacob is designated as the firstborn son who signals the elected position of Israel as Jewish ethnic identity and the true heir of the Abrahamic promise. Therefore, Israel, Jacob's descendants, is the elected people, and the status of the firstborn son is not extended to the Gentiles throughout the entirety of *Jubilees*.

3.6 4Q369

3.6.1 *The Text*

4Q369 was published in 1994, and it is called the "Prayer of Enosh" by Harold Attridge and John Strugnell,[154] although the second column of the fragments does not contain Enosh's prayer but that of a different person. The focus of the prayer is Israel and Jacob its founder.[155]

3.6.2 *Analysis*

4Q369 1 ii sheds light on the meaning of the firstborn son in ancient Jewish religion:

> And you made him a first-bo[rn] son to you [... like him for a prince and ruler in all your earthly land [... the] cr[own of the] heavens and the glory of the clouds [you] have set [on him ...] and the angel of your peace among his assembly. And h[e ... gave] him righteous statutes, as a father

151 See also *Jub* 22:30, 19:20, 21, 26.

152 "[H]is descendants will fill the entire earth," in *Jub* 19:21c.

153 VanderKam, *The Book of Jubilees*, 113.

154 H. Attridge and J. Strugnell, "The Prayer of Enosh," in *Qumran Cave 4. VIII: Para-biblical Texts: Part 1* (DJD 8; Oxford: Clarendon Press, 1994), 353–62.

155 James Kugel, "4Q369 'Prayer of Enosh' and Ancient Biblical Interpretation," *DSD* 5 (1998): 19.

> to [his] s[oul ...] his love your soul cleaves to for[ever] because by them [you established] your glory [...].[156]
>
> 4Q369 1 II 6–12

Who, then, is the firstborn son in 4Q369? Some scholars argue that it refers to an individual (Davidic) messianic figure. For instance, Xeravits argues for similarities between 4Q369 and Ps 89:[157] 1) in line 6, YHWH appoints his firstborn son; 2) in line 7, the author relates the political dominion to the status of the firstborn son; and 3) in line 10, YHWH appears as the father of the firstborn son.[158] Fletcher-Louis argues that the second half of 4Q369 has an individual focus (particularly, line 7) and he marshals the messianic reference to the firstborn son as in Ps 89:27.[159] However, Israel was also thought to have the status of a prince and ruler in Jewish literature. (e.g., Gen 27:28–29; *Sir* 33:21–23).

Other scholars note the collective meaning of the firstborn son (i.e., Israel). For example, Kugel observes: 1) 4Q369 1 ii 1 says, "You allotted his portion (נחלתו) to cause his Name to dwell there," and according to Deut 32:8–9, "his portion" (נחלתו) refers to Israel's homeland; 2) The rare word, splendour (צבי) of the earth in 4Q369 1 ii 2, refers to the home land of Israel in Ezek 20:6, 15; 3) in 4Q369 1 ii 5, "God's eye[s]" reminds us of the unique mention in Deut 11:2 and God's "glory is seen" recalls Isa 60:1–2, and both Deut 11:12 and Isa 60:1–2 refer to the home land of Israel; 4) In line 4, "to his seed for generations as an eternal possession" might be an allusion to "And I shall give this

156 The translation taken from Craig A. Evans, "A Note on the 'First-Born Son' of 4Q369," *DSD* 2 (1995): 193–95.

157 Geza Xeravits, *King, Priest, Prophet: Positive Eschatological Protagonists of the Qumran Library* (STDJ 47; Leiden: Brill, 2002), 89–94. Evans also argues that Ps 89 "offers three important parallels with 4Q369 1 ii 6–10": (1) David calls God his Father, which parallels 4Q369 1 ii 10; (2) Ps 89 says that God "will make him the firstborn," which parallels with 4Q369 1 ii 6; and (3) Ps 89 says that God's first-born will be "the highest of the kings of the earth," which partly parallels 4Q369 1 ii 7, in Evans, "A Note," 199.

158 So, Xeravits concludes, "It seems most probable that in 4Q369 1 ii the author consciously linked his work to the Davidic tradition already present in Psalm 89." See Xeravits, *King*, 94. Chester also writes, "This fragment is most naturally to be understood, then, as representing expectation of Davidic messiah who will be instrumental in bringing about the final kingdom of peace on earth." See Andrew Chester, *Messiah and Exaltation: Jewish Messianic and Visionary Traditions and New Testament Christology* (WUNT 207; Tübingen: Mohr Siebeck, 2007), 238. For similar interpretations, see John Collins, *The Scepter and the Star: the Messiahs of the Dead Sea Scrolls and other Ancient Literature* (New York: Doubleday, 1995), 165; J.D.G. Dunn, *Jesus Remembered* (Grand Rapids: Eerdmans, 2003), 709.

159 Crispin H.T. Fletcher-Louis, *All the Glory of Adam: Liturgical Anthropology in the Dead Sea Scrolls* (STDJ 42; Leiden: Brill, 2002), 197.

land to your seed after you as an eternal possession" (Gen 48:5); and 5) in line 2 ("you made him a first-bo[rn] son"), the verb, "made (שמתנו)" is the same verb used for designating Israel as the firstborn son in 4Q504.[160] Moreover, the verb, סמכת (setting on) in line 8 was used with reference to the blessing of Jacob in Gen 27:36–37: "'For he [Jacob] supplanted me [Esau] these two times. He took away my blessing.' Then he said, 'Have you not reserved a blessing for me?' Isaac answered Esau, 'I have already made him your lord, and I have given him all his brothers as servants, and with grain and wine I have sustained (סמכתיו) him ...'" In this vein, it is highly probable that line 8 evokes the idea that Jacob/Israel was given rulership over his brother/the nations.[161] Furthermore, in 4Q369 1 ii 1, "he may establish your name there [i.e. in his inheritance]" may imply that Israel (ישראל) has the name of God (אל), and that "he" refers to Israel. Hence, it is more probable that the firstborn son does not refer to a messianic figure, but recalls the designation of Jacob (or Israel) as the firstborn son.

While Kugel is correct to argue that the firstborn son in 4Q369 refers to a special relationship between God and Israel, he does not consider the concept of the firstborn son as a divine heir in the covenantal context. In 4Q369 ii 1–12, the firstborn son divides the portions of the Land (lines 1–2), and the name and the glory of God dwell in the Land (line 3). Line 4 implies that the Land was bestowed to the descendants as their eternal portion. The title of the firstborn son is referenced in the context of the distribution of the Promised Land. In this context, the firstborn son can be understood as the heir of the Promised Land (see "נחלתו" in 4Q369 1 ii 1). When a Davidic king is referred to as an heir, he inherits all nations in Ps 2:8 (MT and LXX). In extant Jewish literature, we do not find any verses where a messianic figure as the firstborn son participates in the partition of the Promised Land.

On the other hand, there are several pieces of evidence that Israel as the firstborn son is referenced in the context of inheritance or return to the Promised Land. For instance, in Jer 31:8–9, Israel (or Ephraim) is referred to as the firstborn son of God in the context of the return to their home land. In *Sir* 44:23 and *4 Ezra* 6:58–59, Israel is the firstborn son, which is the title of Israel as the heir of the Promised Land. Accordingly, it seems more reasonable to infer that the firstborn son in 4Q369 refers to the title of Israel, not a royal messiah.[162]

160 Kugel, "4Q369," 122–23, 137.

161 Kugel, "4Q369," 139–40. However, Kugel understands the status of Israel in terms of the Torah in Kugel, "4Q369," 145. We should note that the Torah does not explicitly occur in the context.

162 One may say that the firstborn son in 4Q369 1 ii 6 is described as singular, not as plural. However, Israel is mystified as a personal heavenly figure in ancient Jewish literature (e.g., *Conf* 146; *PrJos* A, 3).

We should also note that the eschatological inheritance pattern is embedded in 4Q369. Some Jewish literature reflects that the Jews (the chosen few or all of whole Israel) expected to receive their inheritance from God at the eschaton. Israel's Inheritance is a common motif in the OT and Jewish literature. In *1 En* 5:7 (*the Book of the Watchers*), the chosen inherit the entire world: "But to the Elect there shall be light, joy, and peace, and they shall inherit the earth." A motif of light, joy and peace is combined with the theme of the eschatological inheritance. The righteous in *2 Baruch*[163] includes the Law-observing proselytes and excludes apostate Jews.[164] In *2 Bar* 51:3, the righteous receive the undying world which is promised to them:

> As for the glory of those who proved to be righteous on account of my law, those who possessed intelligence in their life, and those who planted the root of Wisdom in their heart—their splendour will then be glorified by transformations and the shape of their face will be changed into the light of their beauty so that they may acquire and receive the undying world which is promised to them.
>
> OTP translation

In the end, the righteous are glorified by God, and this glorification encompasses the somatic transformation (see also *2 Bar* 51:11). The righteous dwell in the paradise surrounding the angels under the throne.

God distinguishes the Qumran members or collective Israel in order to make them holy among all the nations in 1Q34 3 ii 6 (cf. Exod 19:6).[165] In

163 The oldest extant text is Syriac manuscripts which were translated from Greek. *2 Baruch* is closely associated with *4 Ezra*. However, *2 Baruch* was more influenced by sapiential tradition than *4 Ezra* was. See Frederick J. Murphy, "Sapiential Elements in the Syriac Apocalypse of Baruch," *JQR* 76 (1986): 311–27. Most probably, *2 Baruch* was written between the two Jewish wars. See Collins, *The Apocalyptic Imagination*, 212–13. *2 Baruch* is usually divided into seven units (1:1–9:2; 10:1–12:5; 13:1–20:6; 21:1–34:1; 35:1–47:2; 48:1–77:26; 78:1). Frederick J. Murphy, *The Structure of Meaning of Second Baruch* (SBLDS 78; Atlanta: Scholars, 1985), 11–29. The unity of *2 Baruch* has been disputed. The core theme of *2 Baruch* is related to significance of observance of the Law.

164 Collins, *The Apocalyptic Imagination*, 221. This is contrasted with 4Q174 1 4 which describes that proselytes as well as Moabites, Ammonites and foreigners do not belong to the people of God. In 4Q174, proselytes can never enter the Temple. Restoration of the Promised Land is one of the core messages in *2 Baruch*. See Liv Ingeborg Lied, *The Other Lands of Israel: Imaginations of the Land in 2 Baruch* (JSJSup 129; Leiden: Brill, 2008), 288–89. In *2 Bar* 85:1–11, the author of *2 Baruch* articulates the hope that "we" would re-possess the Land which was lost: "we shall receive everything which we lost again by many times" (85:4b). Therefore, after the fall of Jerusalem, *2 Baruch* re-asserts the validity of the Covenant, and *2 Baruch* re-defines the heavenly area as the Promised Land.

165 Cf. Lev 20:26.

1Q34+1Q34bis,[166] the motif of inheritance is referenced in the context of the Exodus (or *Eisodus*). God also renewed the covenant for the Qumran members or collective Israel in the vision of glory.[167] The vision of glory (מראת כבוד) in line 6 alludes to "the appearance of the glory of the Lord (מראת כבוד יהוה)" in Exod 24:17. This indicates that glory in line 6 was denoted as divine glory and that, perhaps, "inheritance" in 1Q34+34bis is linked with the theme of the second Exodus. "The blessed" will rule over the entire world as their possession, because God has given the entire world to Israel as inheritance. So, dominion over the whole world is understood as an eschatological privilege given to a chosen people according to the covenant in 1Q34+1Q34bis: "and their dominion over the whole world. But the offspring of ma[n] has not understood all that you have given them as inheritance, and they do not know you" (1Q34+1Q34bis 3 ii 3). Thus, the chosen few (or collective Israel) were expected to inherit the whole world in light (line 1). Therefore, 1Q34+1Q34bis denotes the eschatological anticipation of the Qumran community relating to inheritance, and the image of inheritance is combined with motifs of glory and light.

The pesherist in 4Q171 3 ii 9–12 expounds the meaning of Ps 37:21–22.[168] In 4Q171 3 ii 10–12, the righteous does not refer to the whole people of Israel, but only the righteous among the whole people of Israel (i.e., the Qumran community) inherit the entire world and the high mountain of Israel. "Inheritance" in Ps 37:9 is re-interpreted in an eschatological sense in line 10. Inheritance for the righteous (i.e., the Qumran members) amongst the Israelites ranges

166 1Q34+1Q34bis is regarded as a festival prayer. The origin of 1Q34+1Q34bis has been disputed. Davila observes, "Overall it seems more likely than not that the Festival Prayers were composed outside the Qumran community and were adopted for use by its members." See James R. Davila, *Liturgical Works* (ECDSS; Grand Rapids: Eerdmans, 2001), 17. On the other hand, Charlesworth and Olson assume the origin of 1Q34+1Q34bis to be within the Qumran community. If 1Q34+1Q34bis was composed within the Qumran community, the earliest possible date would be around the middle of the 2nd century BCE. 1Q34+1Q34bis 3–5 ii is related to a festival that "mentions the giving of the covenant," and delineates the eschatological expectations through renewal of the covenant. Charlesworth and Olson presume that the festival is related to Pentecost. See James H. Charlesworth and Dennis T. Olson, "Prayers for Festivals," in *The Dead Sea Scrolls: Hebrew, Aramaic, and Greek Texts with English Translations: Pseudepigraphic and Non-Masoretic Psalms and Prayers, Vol. 4a* (eds. J.H. Charlesworth, et al.; Tübingen: Mohr Siebeck, 1994), 46–48.

167 Cf. Jer 31:31. See also CD VI 19.

168 4Q171 (4QpPsa (Psalms Pesher)) was perhaps written between AD 20 and 70 by the same scribe or school who produced 4Q161 and 4Q166. John Strugnell, "Notes en marge du volume V des Discoveries in the Judaean Desert of Jordan," *RevQ* (1969–71): 183. The pesherist of Psalm 37 makes a reference to an attempt of the Wicked Priest to kill the Teacher of Righteousness (4Q171 3 ii 8). Timothy H. Lim, *Pesharim* (CQS 3; Sheffield: Sheffield Academic Press, 2002), 38.

from Palestine to the entire world.[169] Thus, 4Q171 (4QpPsa) 3 ii 9–12 reflects the eschatological anticipation of the Qumran community in respect of inheriting the whole world and the Promised Land at the culmination of history.

Likewise, in 4Q369, Israel inherits the world and is designated as the firstborn son in the eternal light (line 6). Israel receives the heavenly status from God ("the crown of the heavens") in line 8. So, it seems that the firstborn son in 4Q369 is a boundary figure between heaven and earth (cf. *PrJos*; Philo, *Conf* 146–147).[170] Angelic powers (line 9) and rulership over the entire world (line 7) also highlight the heavenly status of Israel. Israel also appears as the heavenly assembly with the angel of peace (line 8). Therefore, 4Q369 reflects Jewish anticipation of inheritance which would be given to Israel (all of Israel or the Qumran members) at the culmination of history.

In short, we conclude that the firstborn son in 4Q369 refers to the status of Israel as a divine heir, and is the title ascribed to the Qumran community or Israel. Particularly, the title of the firstborn son in 4Q369 embodies the elected status of Israel possessing the Land and the entire world.

3.7 4Q504 (4QDibHam[a])

3.7.1 *The Text*

4Q504 belongs to Words of the Luminaries (4Q504, 4Q505 and 4Q506), which is regarded as a communal supplication which recalls the biblical history from Eden to Israel's disobedience and exile and which repeatedly invokes God to remember his mercy and wondrous works for Israel in the past on each day from Sunday to Saturday.[171] The prayers for the first six days are regarded as a similar genre with the communal lament of the Psalms.[172] 4Q504 1–2 iii expresses laments and supplications. 4Q504 perhaps dates from around 150 BCE, before the settlement of the Qumran community,[173] and the plural subject "we" implies that its *Sitz im Leben* is not a private situation, but a public setting.[174]

169 See also 4Q171 4 12; 4Q179 1 i 12; 4Q365 23 5; 11Q19 62 13; 11Q20 15 6–7.

170 Cf. C.T.R. Hayward, *Interpretations of the Name Israel in Ancient Judaism and some Early Christian Writings: From Victorious Athlete to Heavenly Champion* (Oxford: Oxford University Press, 2005), 193.

171 4Q504 8 *recto*; 4Q504 4 16; 4Q504 3 ii 4; 4Q504 1–2 ii 11.

172 James Davila, *Liturgical Works* (ECDSS; Grand Rapids: Eerdmans, 2000), 241.

173 Esther Chazon, "Words of the Luminaries," in *Encyclopedia of the Dead Sea Scrolls* (eds., Lawrence Schiffman and James VanderKam; Oxford: Oxford University Press, 2000), 989; Davila, *Liturgical Works*, 239.

174 Davila, *Liturgical Works*, 241.

3.7.2 *Analysis*

> 1 … […] 2 … […] reckoned […] Behold, 3 all the peoples are [like not] hing in front of you; [as] chaos and nothing/ [they] are reckoned in your presence. 4 We have [in]voked only your name; for your glory you have created us; 5 you have established us as your sons in the sight of all the peoples. For you called 6 [I]srael my son, my first-born and have corrected us as one corrects 7 his son. You have {created us} raised *Blank* us over the years of our generations 8 […] evil, illnesses, famine, thirst, plague, the sword 9 [… requi]tal of your covenant, for you chose us 10 [to be your people amongst all] the earth.[175]
>
> 4Q504 1–2 III 1–9A

4Q504 recalls the history from creation to the exile and contains many OT quotations and allusions.[176] In the context, this prayer calls on God to remember Israel's election and covenant, and can be associated with Ps 106, as James Davila observes. In line 6, Israel is called the firstborn son as in Exod 4:22 and this designation resembles *4 Ezra* 6:58 which calls Israel the firstborn son when supplicating God for Israel.[177] The quotation of Exod 4:22 in line 6 is connected to "and have corrected us as one corrects his son." This sentence reminds us, "God's discipline will be made for his firstborn son" in *PsSol* 13:9, and seems to reflect OT verses that God disciplines Israel as his son: "Know then in your heart that as a man disciplines his son so the Lord your God disciplines you," in Deut 8:5; "Hear, O my people, and I will admonish you; O Israel, if you would but listen to me," in Ps 81:8. 4Q504 6 15 also reads "as punishes [his sons …]." The firstborn son in *Sir* 17:18 is connected to discipline: "Whom, being his firstborn, he nourishes with discipline, and giving him the light of his love does not forsake him."[178] 4Q369 also relates the firstborn to the Torah.[179] This possibly implies the loving relationship between God and Israel as in 4Q504 1–2 iii,[180] and denotes that the firstborn son has a special status possessing the Torah, God's

175 The translations of the Qumran texts in this section taken from Florentino García Martínez and Eibert J.C. Tigchelaar, trans. *The Dead Sea Scrolls Study Edition* (Leiden: Brill, 1999), 1015.

176 E.g., Deut 4:29–30, 30:1–3 and Lev 26:40–45 in 4Q504 1–2 9–16; Lev 18:5 in 4Q504 6 17; and Exod 19:6 in 4Q504 4 10.

177 Davila. *Liturgical Works*, 249.

178 Cf. *LAB* 16:5.

179 See 4Q369 1 ii 5–6.

180 Particularly see, "all of us are your people … you are in our midst," in 4Q504 6 vi 10.

teaching and discipline.[181] We can observe the meaning and implications of the firstborn son as follows.

Firstly, the firstborn son in 4Q504 is to be understood as the distinct status apart from the Gentiles as in Exod 4:22. In line 3, the Gentiles (all the people) are like nothing and chaos before God. On the other hand, Israel was created for the glory of God, and God established them as his son in the presence of all nations in line 5.[182] In the context, the prayer recalls the designation of Israel as the firstborn son in line 6. Thus, the firstborn son in 4Q504 implies the distinct position of Israel separate from other peoples.

Secondly, the firstborn son in line 6 indicates the pre-eminence of Israel in that it illustrates the loving close relationship between God and Israel. God corrects Israel just like a son,[183] and God loves Israel more than all the peoples.[184] The discipline (or Torah) of Israel implies that God favours Israel over any other nations. Furthermore, only Israel is called God's son and firstborn son.

Thirdly, we should consider that election and covenant are premised throughout 4Q504. God especially chose Israel (e.g., 4Q504 1–2 iv 4; 4Q504 1–2 ii 15–16; 4Q504 1–2 iii 4–10), and this corresponds to the context of Exod 4:22 which designates Israel as the firstborn son in the context of election and covenant (Exod 19:4–6).[185] God's special election of Israel is stressed in 4Q504, and blessing (ברך) is bestowed solely on Israel.[186]

In addition, 1Q34+1Q34bis is formally similar with the Words of the Luminaries (4Q504, 4Q506).[187] In this vein, Charlesworth and Olson state that 1Q34+1Q34bis and 4Q504–506 probably "represent four copies of the same

181 It should be noted that possessing the Torah is sometimes regarded as evidence for the Jews' superiority to the nations in ancient Jewish literature. Torah and discipline are also connected to each other in Deut 8:1–6.

182 Also see, "you have favoured [us] with a h[oly] spirit," in 4Q504 4 5; "[a kingdom of] priest and a holy people [...] [... wh]ich you chose," in 4Q504 4 10–11; "You did favours to your people Israel among all [the] countries," in 4Q504 1–2 v 11; and "For you loved Israel more than all the peoples," in 4Q504 1–2 iv 4.

183 See 4Q504 1–2 iii 6.

184 See 4Q504 1–2 iv 5.

185 See "all of you are your people. You have lifted us wonderfully [upon the wings of] eagles and you have brought us to you" (4Q504 6 6–7); "You have seen what I did to the Egyptians, and how I bore you on eagles' wings and brought you to myself. Now therefore, if you obey my voice and keep my covenant, you shall be my treasured possession out of all the peoples. Indeed, the whole earth is mine, but you shall be for me a priestly kingdom and a holy nation. These are the words that you shall speak to the Israelites" (Exod 19:4–6). For the covenant, See 4Q504 1–2 iii 18; 4Q504 1–2 iv 6; 4Q504 1–2 v 8–9; and 4Q504 1–2 vi 8.

186 See 4Q504 1–2 iv 13; 4Q504 1–2 v 16.

187 Davila, *Liturgical Works*, 16.

document."[188] As seen in the preceding section, 1Q34+1Q34bis clearly shows the theme of the renewal of the covenant and the eschatological inheritance pattern. So, if 1Q34+1Q34bis and 4Q504–506 originally belong to the same document, "the firstborn son" in 4Q504 1–2 iii 6 can be another evidence that the firstborn son refers to the title of Israel as the heir of promise in the eschatological inheritance pattern.[189]

We, therefore, conclude that the firstborn son in 4Q504 refers to the distinct status of Israel as the Elect set apart from the Gentiles. It also indicates Israel's special relationship with God as in Exod 4:22. Thus, the firstborn son in 4Q504 means Israel's status as the Elect and as having pre-eminence over the nations.

3.8 *Sirach*

3.8.1 *The Text*

The author of *Sirach* is known as Jeshua ben Eleazar ben Sira,[190] and the date is traced back to the late second century BCE.[191] The text was originally written in Hebrew, and was translated into Greek by ben Sira's grandson in the era of King Euergetes around 132 BCE.[192] Most scholars maintain that *Sirach* was written before the reign of Antiochus IV (175–164 BCE), because the severe political and religious conflict in his era was not reflected in *Sirach*, and, furthermore, ben Sira praises Simeon the high priest who supported the Seleucid rulers in *Sir* 50:24.

In this vein, *Sir* 36 is often considered to be a later addition, perhaps, in the Maccabean era,[193] because of its harsh tone and urgent petition for the

188 James H. Charlesworth and Dennis T. Olson, "Prayers for Festivals," in *The Dead Sea Scrolls: Hebrew, Aramaic, and Greek Texts with English Translations: Pseudepigraphic and Non-Masoretic Psalms and Prayers* (eds. J.H. Charlesworth, et al.; Tübingen: Mohr Siebeck, 1994), 46.

189 For specific information, see the previous section (3.6) on 4Q369.

190 See *Sir* 51:30; 50:27.

191 John Collins, *Jewish Wisdom in the Hellenistic Age* (OTL; Edinburgh: T&T Clark, 1997), 23.

192 "I arrived in Egypt in the thirty-eighth year of the reign of King Euergetes, and during my stay I came across the reproduction of a good deal that is instructive. I therefore considered myself in duty bound to devote some diligence and industry to the translation of this book. Many sleepless hours of close application have I devoted in the interval to finishing the book for publication, for the benefit of those living abroad who wish to acquire wisdom and are disposed to live their lives according to the standards of the Law" (*Sir* Prologue, 8–10).

193 Collins, *Jewish Wisdom in the Hellenistic Age*, 23: "The book shows no awareness of the upheavals of the time of Antiochus IV Epiphanes (175–164). The only possible reflection of these events is found in the prayer in chapter 36, but this is so alien to the thought world

deliverance of Israel. However, as Skehan and Di Lella observe, the theme in *Sir* 35:22b–26 is linked to *Sir* 36:1–22. In *Sir* 35:14–22, the author is concerned with the poor and the oppressed, and he turns his focus from the individuals to Israel in *Sir* 35:22b–26, which, as Skehan and Di Lella argue, leads the prayer for the chosen people in *Sir* 36:1–22. Thus, the flow from *Sir* 35:22b–26 to 36:1–22 is natural.[194]

It is undeniable that *Sir* 36:1–22 has a clear covenantal aspect and implies a feeling of resistance against the reign of the Gentiles. The author of *Sirach* writes that true wisdom is not in Athens, but in Jerusalem, in *Sir* 24. He connects true wisdom to the Torah in *Sir* 1:26; 6:37; 10:19; 19:20 (cf. Ps 119:66), not to Hellenistic philosophy. These aspects may imply that the Jews were faced with assimilation by Hellenism in the second century BCE, and that the author had an interest in maintaining Jewish identity.[195]

This unit (36:1–22) can be divided into four sub-units.[196] The first (36:1–5) and the second units (36:6–12) contain the petition to humble and punish the Gentile enemies (presumably the Seleucid rulers) of Israel. The next unit (36:13–19) is the prayer for the restoration of Israel, especially for the restoration of the Land called Zion and Jerusalem, and the final unit (36:20–22) includes a plea for fulfilment of the prophecies for Israel and for hearing the prayer of God's servants. "God" in 36:1 and 22 forms an *inclusio*.

3.8.2 *Analysis*

3.8.2.1 *Sir* 36:1–22

The prayer in *Sir* 36:1–22 demonstrates that Israel is oppressed by the Gentiles, and petitions for the restoration of Israel (*Sir* 36:13–19), in particular, the return to the Promised Land (36:13) and the restoration of the nation of Israel (36:13–16).[197] The author describes Israel as the firstborn son (πρωτόγονος) in *Sir* 36:17. We find the title (the firstborn son) used in the covenantal context in *Sir* 36. The author is eager for the restoration of Israel's inheritance: "συνάγαγε πάσας φυλὰς Ιακωβ καὶ κατακληρονόμησον αὐτοὺς καθὼς ἀπ᾽ἀρχῆς" (36:10).

---

of Ben Sira that it must be regarded as a secondary addition, possibly from the Maccabean period."

194 P. Skehan and A. Di Lella, *The Wisdom of Ben Sira* (AB; New York: Doubleday, 1987), 420.

195 As for the relationship between *Sirach* and the Stoic philosophy, see Martin Hengel, *Judentum*, 288; S. L. Mattila, "Ben Sira and the Stoics: A Reexamination of the Evidence," *JBL* 119 (2000): 473–501.

196 Skehan and Di Lella, *The Wisdom of Ben Sira*, 420–423.

197 "Gather all the tribes of Jacob, and give them their inheritance, as at the beginning. Have mercy, O Lord, on the people called by your name, on Israel, whom you have named your firstborn. Have pity on the city of your sanctuary Jerusalem, the place of your dwelling. Fill Zion with your majesty, and your temple with your glory" (36:13–19).

Furthermore, Zion and Jerusalem are the earthly places where God will dwell (36:12–13). Israel's particularism is also shown in the given context. God will lift up his hand against the Gentiles (ἐπὶ ἔθνη) and let them see his might, and finally destroy and wipe them out.[198] By contrast, God will save the Israelites and they will inherit the Land.[199]

The title of the firstborn son in *Sir* 36:17 is linked to the inheritance of the Promised Land, and located in the context of particularism. Israel is the firstborn son, and the Gentiles cannot hold this status. Jacob is given inheritance (i.e., Palestine) and Israel is designated as the firstborn son. So, Israel as the firstborn son should be understood as the elected status of Israel in terms of inheritance. The notion of the firstborn son refers to the right to possess inheritance of Israel, i.e., the Promised Land, and it recalls the patriarchal blessing as in Gen 25–27 (cf. 28:4).

3.8.2.2 *Sir* 44:17–23

The tone of *Sir* 44:17–23 is not so particularistic as in 36:11–17, maybe since the given text is not linked to Israel's oppression by the Gentiles. Rather, in 44:21a, the author reminds his readers that the Abrahamic promise is essentially universalistic as in Gen 12:3: "Therefore the Lord assured him with an oath that the nations [ἔθνη] would be blessed through his seed." Further, this promise to Jacob is associated with the blessing of all people: "εὐλογίαν πάντων ἀνθρώπων" (44:22).

Sir 44:17–23 recollects Israel's ancestors including Noah, Abraham, Isaac and Jacob by name, after praising their virtues in 44:1–16. The context is clearly covenantal: "Everlasting covenants were made with him [a remnant]" (44:18). In particular, the author recalls the covenant made with the patriarchs: "Therefore, the Lord assured him [Abraham] with an oath that the nations would be blessed through his seed; that he would make him as numerous as the dust of the earth, and exalt his offspring like the stars, and give them inheritance from sea to sea and from the Euphrates to the ends of the earth" (44:21). Isaac is mentioned in respect of renewing the promise with God. As for Jacob, the author writes, in *Sir* 44:22–23:

198 *Sir* 36:2, 8. Cf. "Let survivors [of the Gentiles] be consumed in the fiery wrath, and may those who harm your people meet destruction. Crush the heads of hostile rulers who say, 'There is no one but ourselves'" (36:11–12).

199 As Goering notes, in the case of *Sirach*, "the land of Canaan is the subset of territory allotted to Israel, special wisdom is the subset of universal wisdom allotted to Israel. The ideas of portion and inheritance share in common with the concept of election the notion that a part has been separated from the whole." See Greg Schmidt Goering, *Wisdom's Root Revealed: Ben Sira and the Election of Israel* (SJSJ 139; Leiden: Brill, 2009), 101.

> The blessing of all people and the covenant he made to rest on the head of Jacob. He acknowledged him with his blessings, and gave him his inheritance; he divided his portions, and distributed them among twelve tribes. From his descendants the Lord brought forth a godly man, who found favour in the sight of all he made to rest on the head of Jacob; he acknowledged him as the firstborn son, and gave him his inheritance; he divided his portions, and distributed them among twelve tribes.
>
> *OTP* translation

We find reference to the firstborn son in 44:23, but there is a textual problem in this verse. LXX and NRSV read "ἐν εὐλογίαις αὐτοῦ" (in his blessings) in 44:23, however, according to MS B^{mg} and Syr, the phrase can be read as "as the first-born son (בבכר)." So the NASB also translates this "as the firstborn son," and Skehan and Di Lella support this reading.[200] On the other hand, MS B^{txt} and G read "with the right of the firstborn son (בבכרה)." Perhaps, the translator of the Greek *Sirach* understood "as the firstborn son" or "with the right of the firstborn son" in the sense of individual blessings or privileges, and accordingly, that he paraphrased it into "in his blessings." Furthermore, it seems that the reading of LXX unnecessarily reiterates the blessing of Jacob mentioned in the previous colon. Thus, "the theme of 'firstborn' is a major topic in the Jacob narratives, and it is only understandable that Ben Sira pays his attention to this motif in his portrayal of the patriarch Jacob."[201] Therefore, it is highly probable that the original phrase contains "the firstborn son" or "the right of the firstborn son."

We should note that the firstborn son (or the right of the firstborn son) is juxtaposed with inheritance in 44:23: "he [the Lord] acknowledged him [Jacob] as the firstborn son, and gave him his inheritance." This parallelism shows that the concept of the firstborn son (or the right of the firstborn son) is closely

200 Skehan and Di Lella, *The Wisdom of Ben Sira*, 504. Most interpreters follow this reading. E.g., G.H. Box and W.O.E. Oesterley, "Sirach," in *The Apocrypha and Pseudepigrapha of the Old Testament in English with Introductions and Critical and Explanatory Notes to the Several Books, vol. 1* (ed. R.E. Charles; Oxford: Clarendon, 1913), 484; James K. Aitken, The Semantics of 'Glory' in Ben Sira: Traces of a Development in Post-Biblical Hebrews?" in *Sirach, Scrolls and Sages: Proceedings of a Second International Symposium on the Hebrews of the Dead Sea Scrolls, Ben Sira and the Mishnah, Held at Leiden University, 15–17 December 1997* (eds. T. Muraoka and J.F. Elwolde; STDJ 33; Leiden: Brill, 1999), 12; Marko Marttila, *Foreign Nations in the Wisdom of Ben Sira: A Jewish Sage Between Opposition and Assimilation* (DCLS 13; Berlin: Walter de Gruyter, 2012), 167; Pancratius C. Beentjes, "Ben Sira 44:19–23—the Patriarchs: Text, Tradition, Theology," in *Studies in the Book of Ben Sira* (eds. G. Xeravits and J. Zsengeller; JSJSup 127; Leiden: Brill, 2008), 224–25.

201 Marko Marttila, *Foreign Nations in the Wisdom of Ben Sira*, 167.

associated with the notion of inheritance in 44:23. Furthermore, inheritance in 44:23 is paralleled with inheritance given to the seeds of Abraham in 44:21: "give them an inheritance from sea to sea and from the Euphrates to the ends of the earth." The context in this passage is also associated with the Promised Land as in 36:11–17. The author recollects the patriarchal blessing in 44:21–23, and this blessing is related to the inheritance, namely, the Promised Land. Furthermore, the blessing of Jacob (44:22) includes the blessing for the nations (ἔθνη) just like the blessing of Abraham in 44:21. So, the blessing of Jacob (44:22–23) is the reiteration of the Abrahamic promise. So, in this context, the firstborn son refers to the heir of inheritance (44:23) (i.e., the Abrahamic promise). Thus, the firstborn son in 44:23 is an allusion to Jacob's elected status, and simultaneously to the right to inherit the Promised Land (and also the entire world (44:21)).

Can the status of Israel as the firstborn son in *Sir* 44:21–22 include the priestly role of Israel in the context of *Sir* 44:19–22, because the firstborn son is referenced in the context of the blessing of Abraham? It is not deniable that *Sir* 44:17–12 shows some universalistic features. In *Sir* 44:19–21, the blessing for Abraham implies the priestly role of Israel (44:21a), but also contains the blessing for Israel (44:21b–22): The descendants of Abraham would be multiplied and would be honoured by other peoples, and would occupy the whole earth. While Isaac and Jacob would be blessing to the Gentiles (*Sir* 44:22), the title of the firstborn son is bestowed upon Jacob in 44:22 and it is mentioned in the context of blessings that Jacob received. The title of the firstborn son is juxtaposed with the promise of the Land within the same sentence. The firstborn son was a principal heir of the father's property, so it seems that the term "the firstborn son" is paralleled with the inheritance of the Land. Thus, it is unclear what relationship the title of the firstborn son has with the priestly role of Israel.

In summary, the firstborn son title in *Sir* 44:23 is also the status of the chosen people, and is related to the right to inherit the Promised Land (44:23) and also the entire world (44:21). The given text signals the universalistic aspects, but the blessing and the elected status are fundamentally associated only with Jacob and the Israelites, and are believed to be fulfilled in and through them.

3.9 *Prayer of Joseph*

3.9.1 *The Text*

The fragment A in *Prayer of Joseph* (*PrJos*) is preserved in Origen's commentary on the Gospel of John 2:31 in the shape of a partial quotation of its Greek translation. The original language of this prayer is presumed to be Aramaic, however, the original text is not extant. Origen writes that this prayer is "an apocryphon presently in use among the Hebrews." The date is inferred to be first or second century CE and in particular, Smith maintains that "the various parallels to both Hellenistic and Aramaic materials would suggest a first-century date."[202] It seems that *PrJos* was developed from the tradition of Jacob's blessing to Joseph's sons in Gen 48, and the main story deals with the conflict between Israel and Uriel over the issue of heavenly rank.[203]

3.9.2 *Analysis*

In *PrJos*, Israel is not a people, but a heavenly or pre-existent being as the firstborn son (A, 3), an angel of God (A, 1), a ruling spirit (A, 1) a man seeing God (A, 2), the first minister before the face of God (A, 8), and a chief captain of the power of the Lord (*PrJos* C). As Smith notes, "it is striking that many of Jacob-Israel's titles are applied by Philo to the Logos, by rabbinic literature to Michael, by Jewish mystical literature to Metatron and by Jewish Christianity to Jesus."[204] The patriarchs are claimed to have existed since creation (A, 1). Jacob-Israel is an angelic being, and is mentioned to have tabernacled in heaven and earth (A, 4).

What, then, is the meaning of the firstborn son in *PrJos*? M.R. James writes that, in *The Shepherd of Hermas* 58:3, the seven holy angels were denominated as created first, and in Clement of Alexandria, *Str.* 6.143, seven is "the first begotten rulers of the angels."[205] The seven [angels] in *Her.* and *Str.* may have originated either in Jewish (e.g., *Pirke R.Eliezer*, 4) or in Christian tradition (e.g., Rev 1:4; 3:1; 4:5; 5:6; 8:2) which also reflects angelological speculations in ancient Judaism. In this context, James states, "If Jacob is the first begotten of every living thing, is he the senior to Abraham and Isaac? ... it is even possible that the words of Christ in John viii. 58, 'Before Abraham was, I am,' are to be regarded as showing a consciousness, and containing a contradiction, of

202 J.Z. Smith, "Prayer of Joseph," in OTP, *vol.* 2 (New York: Doubleday, 1985), 700.

203 M.R. James writes that *PrJos* contains "a dying speech of Jacob" which evokes Gen 49, and some prayers uttered by Joseph may also have been contained in the lost parts of *PrJos*. See Montague Rhodes James, *The Lost Apocrypha of the Old Testament: Their Titles and Fragments* (London: SPCK, 1920), 26.

204 J.Z. Smith, "The Prayer of Joseph," in *Religions in Antiquity: Essays in Memory of Erwin Ramsdell Goodenough* (ed. Jacob Neusner; Leiden: Brill, 1970), 259. The close connection between *PrJos* and *Conf* 146 will be discussed in 3.14.4. Smith also notes that *PrJos* is a precious source that enables us to understand the later development of Metatron and Merakavah traditions. See Smith, "The Prayer of Joseph," 260.

205 James, *The Lost Apocrypha of the Old Testament*, 27–28.

such beliefs."[206] In this view, πρωτόγονος παντὸς ζῴου may be read as formed before creation.

Yet, it seems clear that the competition between Israel and the angel originated in the story of Jacob's wrestling with an angelic figure in Gen 32 (particularly see A, 5: "wrestled with me ...").[207] In this vein, it is highly probable that the firstborn son in *PrJos* is an allusion to Jacob's status as the firstborn son in Gen 25:27. Furthermore, the firstborn son in *PrJos* is connected to Jacob (A, 1). Therefore, the firstborn son evokes the status as the chosen one originally given to Jacob in Gen 25–27 (A, 2–3).

We should also note that the firstborn son is "the firstborn of every living thing to whom God gives life" (πρωτόγονος παντὸς ζῴου in *PrJos* A, 3). Thus, the idea of the firstborn son is connected to creation, particularly, the superiority over every creature including angels. We find that the theme of election is related to the idea of creation in the book of Isaiah and Jewish literature in various ways.[208] That is, creation is for Israel, and the centre of creation is Israel as in *4 Ezra* 6:58 and *Jub* 1–2. In *Spec Leg* 2.164–166, Philo also describes the ascent of the Jewish nation over all created beings, and depicts that the Jewish nation was chosen for the service of the Uncreated and Eternal. It seems that "the firstborn son of over living being" in *PrJos* A, 3 can be understood in the similar context with *Spec Leg* 2.164–166 which delineate the centrality of the Jewish nation over all creation. Therefore, "the firstborn son of every living thing to whom God gives life" in *PrJos* reflects the election theology of Israel which is related to creation. In other words, Israel as the firstborn son is the special one who has a pre-eminent status amongst creation (cf. *Jub* 2:20). Jacob (A, 1) represents collective Israel and the angelic Israel symbolises the heavenly status of Israel who has sovereignty over all things (cf. Frag. C). While the firstborn son is not referenced in the context of inheritance, the story of *PrJos* reframes

206 James, *The Lost Apocrypha of the Old Testament*, 26–27.

207 C.T.R. Hayward, *Interpretations of the Name Israel in Ancient Judaism and Some Early Christian Writings: From Victorious Athlete to Heavenly Champion* (Oxford: Oxford University, 2005), 218. Cf. J.Z. Smith finds the origin of the firstborn son in *PrJos* A, 3 in Exod 4:22. See Smith, "The Prayer of Joseph," 268. The conflict between Jacob/Israel and Uriel elicited a multiplication of interpretations. Some scholars argue that Uriel should be identified with Christ and so, *PrJos* originated in an anti-Christian polemic. See J.T. Marschall, "Prayer of Joseph," in *Dictionary of the Bible*, vol. 2 (ed. J.R. Hastings; New York: Scribner, 1888), 362; R.H. Charles, *The Ascension of Isaiah* (London: Black, 1900), 39. Yet, this interpretation lacks evidence.

208 For example, *Jub* 1–2; *4 Ezra* 6:59; *PsSol* 18:10–12. Cf. Isa 40:26; 48:12–13; 51:16. See also J.D.G. Dunn, *Christology in the Making: An Inquiry into the Origins of the Doctrine of the Incarnation* (London: SCM, 1980), 73.

the status of Israel as an angelomorphic heavenly figure (or a boundary figure between heaven and earth).[209]

In conclusion, the title of the firstborn son in *PrJos* is related to Jacob and Israel.[210] So, the firstborn son in *PrJos* is the title given to Jacob and Israel, and symbolises the heavenly status of Israel. The firstborn son in *PrJos* is "the firstborn son of every living thing to whom God gives life," and this notion reflects Israel's election theology that signals the centrality of Israel in every branch of creation including the angels like Uriel. So, the firstborn son in *PrJos* should be understood as the elected and privileged status of Israel.[211]

3.10 *Liber Antiquitatum Biblicarum*

3.10.1 *The Text*

Biblical Antiquities or *Liber Antiquitatum Biblicarum* (LAB) was presumably written in Palestine before the Jewish war against the Roman Empire in CE 66.[212] It is highly probable that the original text of the *Biblical Antiquities* was written in Hebrew.[213] *Biblical Antiquities* can be categorised as midrash or as a rewritten Bible,[214] like Josephus's *Jewish Antiquities* and *the Book of Jubilees*. *Biblical*

209 Hayward, *Interpretations of the Name Israel*, 204. Contra Jarl E. Fossum, *The Name of God and the Angel of the Lord: Samaritan and Jewish Concepts of Intermediation and the Origin of Gnosticism* (WUNT 36; Tübingen: Mohr Siebeck, 1985), 318. He connects the concept of the firstborn son in *PrJos* to the demiurgic activity.

210 Morray-Jones writes, "Jacob's victory over the angel is similarly associated with performance of the celestial liturgy in rabbinic midrashim, which explain that the angel begged Jacob to release him so that he could return to heaven in time to lead the morning worship." He refers to *Gen.R* 78,1–2; *bHul* 91b; and *CantR* 3,6. See Christopher R.A. Morray-Jones, "The Body of the Glory: Approaching the New Testament from the Perspective Of Shiur Koma Traditions," in *The Mystery of God: Early Jewish Mysticism and the New Testament* (eds. C. Rowland and C.R.A. Morray-Jones; CRINT 12; Leiden: Brill, 2009), 562. See also Smith, "The Prayer of Joseph," 280.

211 The concept of the firstborn son in *3 En* 44:10 can be understood in a similar context.

212 Frederick Murphy, *Pseudo-Philo: Rewriting the Bible* (Oxford: Oxford University Press, 1993), 3, 6–7.

213 Daniel Harrington, "Pseudo-Philo," in *OTP, vol. 2* (ed., James Charlesworth; New York: Doubleday, 1985), 298–99.

214 Murphy, *Pseudo-Philo*, 4–5. Cf. Harrington writes, "The expression 'rewritten Bible' is used simply to refer to those products of Palestinian Judaism at the turn of the era that take as their literary framework the flow of the biblical text itself and apparently have as their major purpose the clarification and actualization of the biblical story," in Daniel Harrington, "Palestinian Adaptations of Biblical Narratives and Prophecies," in *Early Judaism and its Modern interpreters* (SBLBMI 2; eds. R. Kraft and G.W. Nickelsburg; Atlanta: Scholars, 1986), 239. Also see Bruce Fisk, *Do You Not Remember: Scripture,*

Antiquities is thought to reflect "the mainstream scribal Judaism,"[215] or "the milieu of the Palestinian synagogues at the turn of the common era."[216] *LAB* shows an ambiguous attitude to Gentiles. In *LAB* 11:3, Israel alone receives the Law and the Israelites are honoured over the nations.[217] In this vein, Israel is an elected and distinct nation from the nations in *LAB*. However, in *LAB*, the Gentiles could also learn and observe the Law (11:1–2). Pseudo-Philo also highlights the existence of the righteous in the midst of the corrupt generations (e.g., 1:16; 4:11, 16; 6:3; 16:4–5).[218]

3.10.2 *Analysis*

As Bruce Fisk notes, *LAB* 18 does not simply retell Num 22–24, but also evokes the Akedah story in Gen 22. Fisk points out the original elaborate parallels between Num 22:19, 21, 22bc, 32; 23:1–2a, 2b, 3, 6, 7–12, 14b, 15, 17, 18–26, 29–30a, 30b; 24:1–9 and Gen 22:1, 3, 5, 6b, 9, 10, 11–12, 13b, 16–18, 19.[219] That is, the Balaam cycle in Num 22–24 has a relationship to the Akedah story in Gen 22, and *LAB* is also aware of the tradition that the Balaam cycle is linked to the Akedah story.[220]

For example, *LAB* 18:7b says, "Behold I know that when you offer [*offeras*] burnt offerings [*holocaustomata*] to God, God will be reconciled with men. Now seek again from your Lord and beg with as many burnt offerings [*holocaustis*] as he wishes. But if he should forgive my wrongdoings, you will have your reward and God will receive [*accipiet*] his offerings [*oblationes*],"[221] and this verse is paralleled with *LAB* 18:5b:

> 'Your [Abraham] seed will be like the stars of the heaven,' when I lifted him above the firmament and showed him the arrangements of all the

---

Story and Exegesis in the Rewritten Bible of Pseudo-Philo (JSPSup 37; Sheffield: Sheffield Academic Press, 2001), 25–27.

215 Murphy, *Pseudo-Philo*, 7.

216 Harrington, "Pseudo-Philo," 300.

217 Nickelsburg, *Jewish Literature Between the Bible and the Mishnah*, 267.

218 Stephen Westerholm, "Paul's Anthropological 'Pessimism' in Its Jewish Context," in *Divine and Human Agency in Paul and His Cultural Environment* (LNTS 335; eds. John M.G. Barclay and Simon Gathercole; London: T&T Clark, 2006), 93.

219 Fisk, *Do You Not Remember*, 244–46.

220 Fisk, *Do You Not Remember*, 247–49.

221 The original text and the translation taken from Howard Jacobson, *A Commentary on Pseudo-Philo's Liber Antiquitatum Biblicarum: With Latin Text and English Translation, Vol. I* (AGJU 31; Leiden: Brill, 1996), 118–19.

> stars? I demanded his son as a burnt offering [*holocaustomata*] and he brought him to be placed on the altar. But I gave him back to his father and, because he did not object, his offering [*oblatio*] was acceptable [*acceptabilis*] before me, and in return for his blood I chose them ...
>
> OTP translation

In this vein, as Fisk notes, in LAB 18, Balaam can be regarded as "a quasi-Abraham figure."[222]

Thus, LAB combines the Balaam cycle in Num 22–24 and the Akedah story in Gen 22. In particular, this is related to the meaning of the firstborn son in LAB 18:6. God states that he spoke to Abraham in a vision, and promised his seeds like the stars of the heaven (18:5). God also chose Jacob and blessed him (18:6). Significantly, Jacob is designated as Abraham's son (18:6) and also God called [*vocavit*] Jacob as the firstborn son (*primogenitum*).

The notion of the firstborn son is reinterpreted within the tradition of the Akedah and the Balaam cycle. The focus of God's promise in LAB 18 is placed on the Land in 18:1, the seed in 18:5a (cf. Gen 22:17), the blessing of intimacy in 18:5c (cf. Gen 18:17; I [God] will reveal everything I am doing to Abraham), and "the blessing of the divine presence," in LAB 18:6 (cf. Gen 32:9–12, 24–27).[223] The firstborn son in LAB 18:6 is located in the context which retells the biblical story of Balaam's encounter with Balak in Num 22–24, and in the wider context, LAB 15–18 defends "God's covenantal loyalty."[224] In LAB 18:4–6, God recalls "God's special relationship with Israel"[225] to Balaam in his dream, and God reminds Balaam of God's promise to Abraham in LAB 18:5–6.

The title of the firstborn son given to Jacob in LAB 18:6 reflects the story of the firstborn son in Gen 25–27. We should note that Jacob is not merely called the son of Abraham, but also the firstborn son of God in 18:5–6. Arguably, the firstborn son in 18:6 represents the elected and distinct status as the heir of the Abrahamic promise (18:5). Accordingly, whilst LAB shows some universalistic attitudes towards the Gentiles, the title of the firstborn son still symbolises the elected status and primacy of Israel.

222 Fisk, *Do You Not Remember*, 247.

223 Fisk, *Do You Not Remember*, 238–40.

224 Fisk, *Do You Not Remember*, 193.

225 Murphy, *Pseudo-Philo*, 85.

3.11 *4 Ezra*

3.11.1 *The Text*

4 Ezra is believed to be originally written in Hebrew,[226] but is transmitted only in Latin and several ancient languages such as Armenian, Syrian, Coptic, Georgian and Ethiopic.[227] Generally, scholars think that *4 Ezra* was written after the destruction of Jerusalem in CE 70, and understand the three heads in *4 Ezra* 11 and 12 to symbolise Vespasian, Titus and Domitian the emperors, and the twelve-winged eagle in the same chapters to refer to the twelve emperors from Caesar to Domitian.[228] Accordingly, *4 Ezra* is assumed to have been written in the late first century in the era of Domitian (CE 81–96).[229] Generally, *4 Ezra* is divided into seven sections: 1) 3:1–5:19; 2) 5:20–6:34; 3) 6:35–9:25; 4) 9:26–10:59; 5) 10:60–12:51; 6) 13:1–58; and 7) 14:1–48. *4 Ezra* describes the vision in the mediation of the angels, but the first three paragraphs are not visionary and consist of the conversation between Ezra and the angels.[230] Generally, the unity of *4 Ezra* is undisputed by most scholars.[231]

3.11.2 *Analysis*

4 Ezra begins with the question concerning the destruction of Jerusalem:

> In the thirtieth year after the destruction of our city, I, Salathiel, who am also called Ezra, was in Babylon. I was troubled as I lay on my bed, and my thoughts welled up in my heart, because I saw the desolation of Zion and the wealth of those who lived in Babylon. My spirit was greatly agitated, and I began to speak anxious words to the Most High.
>
> *4 EZRA* 1:1–3

Ezra, then, develops the questions from his anxiety about the destruction to theodicy or the problem of justice.[232] The privileged status of Israel is also specifically stated according to the patriarchal promise in *4 Ezra* 3:13–16:

> [W]hen they were committing iniquity before you, you chose for yourself one of them, whose name was Abraham; and you loved him and to him

226 Michael Stone, *Fourth Ezra: A Commentary on the Book of Fourth Ezra* (Hermeneia; Minneapolis: Fortress, 1990), 10–11.

227 Collins, *The Apocalyptic Imagination*, 156; Stone, *Fourth Ezra*, 3–8.

228 Stone, *Fourth Ezra*, 10.

229 Collins, *The Apocalyptic Imagination*, 156.

230 Collins, *The Apocalyptic Imagination*, 158.

231 Bruce W. Longenecker, 2 *Esdras* (GAP 1; Sheffield: Sheffield Academic Press, 1995), 24.

232 Collins, *The Apocalyptic Imagination*, 159.

> only you revealed the end of the times, secretly by night. You made with him an everlasting covenant, and promised him that you would never forsake his descendants; and you gave to him Isaac, and to Isaac you gave Jacob and Esau. And you set apart Jacob for yourself, but Esau you rejected; and Jacob became a great multitude.
>
> OTP translation

However, *4 Ezra* relates the failure of Israel to the "universal human situation."[233] Adam often appears as a sinner in *4 Ezra*.[234] Further, the evil human inclination has been associated with Israel and the problem of justice. Membership of the covenantal people is meaningless for their individual salvation, because the exceptional individuals can be saved by observing the commandments.[235] Therefore, Collins rightly observes, "The basis of salvation is individual merit, not membership of a covenant people."[236] The whole of ethnic Israel will not be saved in the end. Rather, those who are to be saved are the small number who remain after divine judgment: "Many have been created, but few will be saved" (8:3).[237]

The author of *4 Ezra* describes Israel's hopeless situation in terms of Israel's disobedience to the Law, and the author urges Israel to obtain divine mercy through observing the Law.[238] The Mosaic Law is still glorious, and the chosen ones should obey this: "the Law, however, does not perish but remains in its glory" (9:37). Israel is comforted in 12:46–51:

> Take courage, O Israel; and do not be sorrowful, O house of Jacob; for the Most High has you in remembrance, and the Mighty One has not forgotten you in your struggle. As for me, I have neither forsaken you nor withdrawn from you; but I have come to this place to pray on account of the desolation of Zion and to seek mercy on account of the humiliation of our sanctuary. Now go, every one of you to his house, and after these days I will come to you. So the people went into the city, as I told them to do. But I sat in the field seven days, as the angel had commanded me;

233 Collins, *The Apocalyptic Imagination*, 160.

234 Cf. *4 Ezra* 3:4–11, 21–26; 7:116–26; *2 Bar* 4:3; 17:3; 18:1–2; 23:4–5; 48; 46; 54:15, 17–19; 56:6.

235 *4 Ezra* 3:35–36.

236 Collins, *The Apocalyptic Imagination*, 162. In similar token, Bruce Longenecker writes, "To claim, then, the author is assured of 'God's enduring purpose of covenantal election and his attendant mercy' upon ethnic Israel is to miss the whole purpose of 4 Ezra," in Longenecker, *Eschatology and the Covenant: A Comparison of 4 Ezra and Romans 1–11* (JSNTSup 57; Sheffield: Sheffield Academic Press, 1991), 151. Also see *4 Ezra* 14:27–36.

237 See also *4 Ezra* 5:41; 6:25; 7:27; 9:7–8; 12:34; 13:16, 19. The last generation motif also occurs in *PsSol* 18:5–6. See Stone, *Fourth Ezra*, 148.

238 Longenecker, *Eschatology and the Covenant*, 155.

> and I ate only of the flowers of the field, and my food was of plants during those days.
>
> OTP translation

Thus, Israel is encouraged to obey the Law to achieve her ultimate survival. We may conclude, therefore, that the relationship between Jewish particularism and individual legalism is ambiguous in *4 Ezra*, that the notion of Israel is redefined in terms of individual obedience, and that the true Israelites amongst Israel are those who obey the Mosaic Law in *4 Ezra*.

In *4 Ezra* 7:90, the observers of the Law shall see God's glory with great joy. The observers of the law will receive rest and immortality and shall inherit what is to come. They will also receive their reward when glorified (7:98). Their face will shine like the sun (7:97), and this implies the somatic transformation of those who observe the Law. In this passage, those observing the Law will be distinguished from sinners in the final judgment and will be protected in rest by angels. Finally, they will receive the inheritance and reward in glory. It should be noted that inheritance is referenced in respect to the eschatological glory.

In this context, Israel is addressed as the firstborn son (6:58), and Ezra states Israel's right to take possession of the entire world in *4 Ezra* 6:58–59. *4 Ezra* 6:58 is located within the unit of *4 Ezra* 6:38–50, which begins the third vision in *4 Ezra*.[239] This unit is divided into two sub-units of 6:38–54 and 6:55–59. The first sub-unit describes creation in the beginning over six days (the *Hexaemeron*). In the second sub-unit (6:55–59), Ezra asks why Israel is ruled by other nations, if creation is for Israel: "All this I have spoken before thee, O Lord, because you have said that it was for us that you created this world ... If the world has indeed been created for us, why do we not possess our world as an inheritance? How long will this be so?" (6:55, 59). We should bear in mind the contrast between the other nations in 6:56 and Israel (we thy people) in 6:58. The emphatic "we" in "we thy people" in 6:58 functions as the contrastive. So, the author of *4 Ezra* implies in 6:58 that Israel ("we thy people") is distinct from the nations. In 6:58, Israel is addressed with several titles: 1) the firstborn son (*primogenitum*); 2) only begotten;[240] 3) kin;[241] and 4) dear

239 Stone, *Fourth Ezra*, 179. Cf. the first vision in 3:4–36 and the second vision in 5:23–30.

240 A juxtaposition of "only begotten (*unigenitum*)" with "firstborn son (*primogenitum*)" (6:58) is also found in *PsSol* 18:2, where two titles (only begotten and firstborn son) also refer to Israel.

241 The meaning of "kin" (*aemulatorem*) is unclear. See Karina Martin Hogan, *Theologies in Conflict in 4 Ezra: Wisdom Debate and Apocalyptic Solution* (JSJSup 130; Leiden: Brill, 2008), 129.

one.[242] All these titles can be understood to signify the chosenness of Israel in terms of the close and loving relationship between Israel and God. Furthermore, Israel is clearly distinguished from other nations in the given text:

> As for the other nations which have descended from Adam, you have said that they are nothing, and that they are like spittle, and you have compared their abundance to a drop from a bucket. And now, O Lord, behold, these nations, which are reputed as nothing, domineer over us and devour us.
>
> *OTP* translation (6:56–57)

Accordingly, Israel still holds the centred and elected position among the nations in *4 Ezra* 6.

The firstborn son in 6:58 is related to inheritance (cf. 6:59: "possess our world as an inheritance"). The world was created as Adam centred, (6:54) and Adam can be viewed as the first Israelite (6:45–59). Israel is the centre of the world, and is elected by God in order to inherit the world (6:59).[243] The highlight of Israel's covenantal membership in *4 Ezra* is weaker than in other Jewish literature, however, the title of the firstborn son is still used in the sense of the elected status with regard to the Land, election and creation.[244]

We conclude, therefore, that the firstborn son in *4 Ezra* 6:58 denotes Israel's status distinct from the Gentiles.[245] The firstborn son in *4 Ezra* appears in the context of creation, Israel's election, glory and the inheritance of the world (*saeculum*). Accordingly, the concept of the firstborn son in *4 Ezra* is associated with an eschatological heir of the inheritance concerning the entire world

242 "Dear one" in *4 Ezra* 6:58 may evoke Hos 11:1–4 and the Song of Songs 1:9, 15; 2:1,13; 4:1, 7. See Hogan, *Theologies in Conflict in 4 Ezra*, 129.

243 *Saeculum* (original ארץ) in *4 Ezra* 6:59 can be translated into 'the world' or 'the Land.' Elliott prefers the latter option (the Land). See Mark A. Elliott, *The Survivors of Israel: A Reconsideration of the Theology of Pre-Christian Judaism* (Grand Rapids: Eerdmans, 2000), 101. However, the context of creation (*Propter nos creatum est saeculum* (6:59)) fits better with the former option (i.e., the world). Most scholars accept this reading. E.g., Michael Stone and Matthias Henze, *4 Ezra and 2 Baruch: Translations, Introductions, and Notes* (Minneapolis: Fortress, 2013), 39; Masanobu Endo, *Creation and Christology: A Study on the Johannine Prologue in the Light of Early Jewish Creation Accounts* (WUNT II/149; Tübingen: Mohr Siebeck, 2002), 26; Johannes Tromp, *The Assumption of Moses: A Critical Edition with Commentary* (Leiden: Brill, 1993), 141; Jonathan A. Moo, *Creation, Nature and Hope in 4 Ezra* (FRLANT 237; Göttingen: Vandenhoeck & Ruprecht, 2011), 152.

244 For the Esau-Jacob passage in *4 Ezra* 6:7–10, see Stone, *Fourth Ezra*, 181.

245 In particular, see distinctions of the destinies between Jacob and Esau in *4 Ezra* 3:16. Cf. Hogan, *Theologies in Conflict in 4 Ezra*, 137.

(6:59). The inheritance should be given to Israel (or the Law observers) with immortality, glorification and the somatic transformation (7:96–98). Therefore, the title of the firstborn son in *4 Ezra* 6:58 is the title of Israel denoting her elected status by God which is associated with primacy and inheritance.

3.12 *The Psalms of Solomon*

3.12.1 *The Text*

It seems that *The Psalms of Solomon* [*PssSol*] was written by a pious Jew in or around Jerusalem who observed the Mosaic Law (3:7, 8; 4:8; 9:6; 13:7; 14:1–3). *PssSol* is believed to have been originally written in Hebrew, but only its Greek and Syriac translations are extant.[246] Scholars trace the date of the *PssSol* through the identification of allusions to Jewish historic events,[247] and view *PssSol* in relation to the historical period of Pompey. Perhaps, *PssSol* reflects the historic events that a certain opponent is welcomed to Jerusalem by the officers in 8:16–18, and he (Pompey) desecrates the Temple in 2:2, and he leaves from Jerusalem to go to Egypt and is assassinated in Egypt in 2:26.[248] This chronology closely matches Pompey's timeline, and accordingly, scholars postulate that *PssSol* was written around 48–40 BCE after Pompey's death.[249]

PssSol is well known for its expectation of the Messiah and the kingship of God (cf. *PsSol* 5:18–19; 17:3–4, 21, 32). The Gentiles are portrayed in the *PssSol* as those who are rejected by God due to their lawlessness (2:2, 19–25; 7:1–3; 8:23; 17:13–15). On the other hand, the psalmist is deeply concerned with the oppression of Israel, and is eager for the royal reign of God and the Messiah. The psalmist anticipates that Gentiles will be expelled by the Messiah (chapter 17), and Israel will be ruled by him (18:7–8). God-designated Israel will be placed above all the nations forever (9:8–11). And the nations will glorify God and come to see the glory of God from the end of the world: "bringing as gifts her sons who had fainted, and to see the glory of the Lord with which God glorified her" (*PsSol* 17:31).

---

246 Kenneth Atkinson, *An Intertextual Study of The Psalms of Solomon: Pseudepigrapha* (Lewiston: Edwin Mellen, 2001), 398.

247 Wright, "Psalms of Solomon," in *OTP, vol.* 2 (New York: Doubleday, 1985), 641.

248 "And I did not wait long until God showed me his insolence pierced on the mountains of Egypt, more despised than the smallest thing on earth and sea," in 2:26. The Greek text is from Atkinson, *The Psalms of Solomon.*

249 Wright, "Psalms of Solomon," 641; Marinus de Jonge, *God's Final Envoy: Early Christology and Jesus' Own View of His Mission* (Grand Rapids: Eerdmans, 1998), 45; Atkinson, *The Psalms of Solomon*, 419.

3.12.2 *Analysis*

3.12.2.1 *PsSol* 13:9

In *PsSol* 13, the psalmist remarks that his community was saved from crisis, namely the sword, famine and pestilence of the sinners (13:1–2). God will save the righteous in 13:7, and "the sinner may not rejoice over the righteous," in 13:8. God will admonish (νουθετήσει) the righteous as a beloved son (υἱὸν ἀγαπήσεως), and God's discipline (παιδεία) will be made for his firstborn son in 13:9.[250] *PsSol* 13 demonstrates that the sinners (the Gentiles) will be judged and punished. The righteous, however, will be admonished and treated as the firstborn son.[251] The firstborn son is paralleled with υἱὸν ἀγαπήσεως in 13:9, and this denotes that the firstborn son is the special one beloved by God. We should also note that the one who is admonished by God is Israel in Deut 8:5 and Ps 81:8: "Know then in your heart that as a man disciplines his son so the Lord your God disciplines you" (Deut 8:5); "Hear, O my people, and I will admonish you; O Israel, if you would but listen to me" (Ps 81:8). In *Sir* 17:17–18, God also disciplines the firstborn son, i.e., Israel. *PsSol* 13:9 also reflects this tradition. The Gentiles will be judged, but the righteous will be treated as the firstborn son in *PsSol* 13. Eventually, the firstborn son is the title of Israel who is admonished by God and who is distinct from the sinners (i.e., Gentiles).

3.12.2.2 *PsSol* 18:4

PsSol 18 functions as the summary and the conclusion of the whole *PssSol*.[252] *PsSol* 18 can be divided into two sections: 1) the divine rule through the Messiah in 18:1–9; and 2) the divine rule of the cosmos in 18:10–12.[253] The nations will be judged in 18:3a, but God's love will be given to the seed of Abraham in 18:3b. *PsSol* 18 reiterates the motif of παιδεία for the firstborn son as in *PsSol* 13:9 (Cf. *Sir* 18:13; 4Q504 1–2 iii 5–6 ("For you called Israel my son, my first-born and have corrected us as one corrects")).[254] Παιδεία will recover the soul from ignorance (ἀπὸ ἀμαθίας) to the obedience.[255] "The seed of Abraham" is juxta-

250 A similar image about God's discipline towards his firstborn son is also found in *Sir* 18:13 and 4Q504 1–2 iii 5–6. Cf. Bussino Severino, *The Greek Additions in the Book of Ben Sira* (trans. Michael Tait; AnBib 203; Rome: Gregorian & Biblical, 2013), 228.

251 Atkinson, *The Psalms of Solomon*, 263.

252 Atkinson, *The Psalms of Solomon*, 383.

253 Atkinson, *The Psalms of Solomon*, 382.

254 While ἐν ἀγνοίᾳ evokes *PsSol* 13:7, υἱὸν πρωτότοκον μονογενῆ recalls *PsSol* 13:9. See Patrick Pouchelle, "Prayers for Being Disciplined: Notes on ΠΑΙΔΕΥΩ and ΠΑΙΔΕΙΑ in the Psalms of Solomon," in *The Psalms of Solomon: Language, History, Theology* (eds. Eberhard Bons and Patrick Pouchelle; EJL 40; Atlanta: SBL press, 2015), 129.

255 For specific information of the motif of discipline in *PssSol*, see Pouchelle, "Prayers for Being Disciplined," 115–132. Schaper notes that the discipline (or the instruction) would

posed with "the firstborn son" in a synonymous parallelism in *PsSol* 18:3b–4a: "Your love is for the seed of Abraham, an Israelite, and your discipline is for the firstborn son, an only child (μονογενής)." In *PsSol* 9:9, the psalmist writes, "You [God] chose the seed of Abraham above all the nations, and you placed your name upon us," and he petitions the restoration of the inheritance according to the Abrahamic covenant (9:1, 9, 10). Israel is designated as the firstborn son and μονογενής in 18:4. Μονογενής evokes Isaac's title in LXX Gen 22:12, and the seed of Abraham (18:3b) is connected to the title of firstborn son (18:4). In *Jub* 18:15, Isaac is addressed as the firstborn son. So, in the context, the title of the firstborn son in 18:4 is related to the Abrahamic promise. Israel is the descendants of Abraham (18:3) and the firstborn son (18:4). Israel has a distinct destiny from the Gentiles (18:4–5), and fits the meaning of the firstborn son (18:4–5). Therefore, the title of the firstborn son refers to the title of Israel which represents the elected status of Israel as the descendant of Abraham.

3.13 *Joseph and Aseneth*

3.13.1 *The Text*

The story of Joseph's marriage to Asenath in Gen 41:45[256] is retold and expanded in an ancient Jewish novel, *Joseph and Aseneth* (*JosAs*). *JosAs* can be placed "within the broad category of a Greco-Roman romance or novel"[257] or can be categorised as "the rewritten Bible."[258] Its original language is highly likely Greek because it is certain that the original text of *JosAs* was influenced by the Septuagint.[259] The extant texts have been handed down mainly in Syriac, Armenian, Latin and Middle English.[260] It is difficult to date *JosAs*, but most scholars agree that *JosAs* was composed between the second century BCE and

be given through the rule of a messianic figure in *PsSol* 18:4. See Joachim Schaper, *Eschatology in the Greek Psalter* (WUNT II/76: Tübingen: Mohr Siebeck, 1995), 75.

256 Gen 41:45: "Pharaoh gave Joseph the name Zaphenath-paneah; and he gave him Asenath daughter of Potiphera, priest of On, as his wife. Thus Joseph gained authority over the land of Egypt [NRSV]."

257 Ross Kraemer, *When Aseneth Met Joseph: A Late Antique Tale of the Biblical Patriarch and His Egyptian Wife, Reconsidered* (New York: Oxford University Press, 1998), 10.

258 Susan Docherty, "Joseph and Aseneth Rewritten Bible or Narrative Expansion," *JSJ* 35 (2004): 45–46.

259 Gideon Bohak, *Joseph and Aseneth and the Jewish Temple in Heliopolis* (Atlanta: Scholars, 1996), xii.

260 Kraemer, *When Aseneth Met Joseph*, 8.

the second century CE.[261] It is improbable that *JosAs* is a Christian literature because we do not find any Christian aspects or any indication of its author's familiarity with the Christian theological concepts of the NT.[262]

There are some debates on the textual problems of *JosAs*. Scholars categorise the extant texts of *JosAs* into the four discrete families, labelled as family A, B, C and D. Yet, it is most probable that the short text (D) is an abbreviated version of the long text (B). So, Burchard explains the priority of the long text (B), and argues that some expressions in family D seems redundant as recensional expansions.[263] This view is supported by the majority of scholars.[264] So, this study will assume that the longer text is closer to the original text.[265]

The provenance of *JosAs* is uncertain, but it is highly probable that it was written in a Diaspora Jewish setting.[266] John J. Collins argues, "While the religion of *Joseph and Aseneth* preserves sharp boundaries over against polytheism, these boundaries are not identical with the boundaries of ethnic descent."[267] He also notes, "Jacob's significance is not his ethnic origin."[268] Yet, Aseneth continues to recall that Joseph is the son of Jacob (i.e., "the shepherd") who came from the land of Canaan (e.g., 4:13; 6:5; 13:10)," and these expressions may stress Joseph's ethnic origin as an Israelite. While the Jews in *JosAs* do not boast of their supremacy over the nations, we should note that the author of *JosAs* accentuates the sharp distinction of the Jewish people from the Egyptians. Monotheism is a major factor that distinguishes the Jews from the

261 For the current scholarly consensus, see Bohak, *Joseph and Aseneth and the Jewish Temple in Heliopolis*, xiii. Humphrey argues that *JosAs* was "written in Greek between 100 BCE and the early second century CE." See Edith Humphrey, *The Ladies and the Cities: Transformation and Apocalyptic Identity in Joseph and Aseneth, 4 Ezra, the Apocalypse and the Shepherd of Hermas* (Sheffield: Sheffield Academic Press, 1995), 30.

262 John J. Collins, "Joseph and Aseneth: Jewish or Christian?" *JSP* 14 (2005): 97–112; Randall Chestnutt, *From Death to Life: Conversion in Joseph and Aseneth* (Sheffield: Sheffield Academic Press, 1995), 75.

263 Indeed, Burchard does not view B as a family, but "as a group of witnesses which have much in common to distinguish them from A, C, and D." Christoph Burchard, "The text of *Joseph and Aseneth* reconsidered," *JSP* 14 (2005): 83–94.

264 E.g., Nickelsburg, *Jewish Literature*, 271; Randall Chestnutt, *From Death to Life: Conversion in Joseph and Aseneth* (JSPSup 16; Sheffield: Sheffield Academic Press, 1995), 64; Uta Barbara Fink, "Textkritische Situation," in *Joseph und Aseneth* (ed. Eckart Reinmuth; SAPERE 15; Tübingen: Mohr Siebeck, 2009), 33–44.

265 This study will use the Greek text of *JosAs* (the long text) edited by Uta Fink. See Fink, "Text, Übersetzung and Anmerkungen," in *Joseph und Aseneth*, 56–129.

266 J.M.G. Barclay, *Jews in the Mediterranean Diaspora: From Alexander to Trajan (323 BCE–117 CE)* (Berkeley: University of California Press, 1996), 204.

267 John J. Collins, *Between Athens and Jerusalem: Jewish Identity in the Hellenistic Diaspora* (Grand Rapids, Eerdmans, 2000), 234.

268 Collins, *Between Athens and Jerusalem*, 234.

Gentiles in *JosAs*.[269] Aseneth goes through painful processes (chs. 10–13) to be accepted by the Jewish community in *JosAs*, and this indicates that the process of the conversion could be not so easy for proselytes. While some Jews such as Gad and Dan is described more negatively than Pharaoh, this may signal that there were some actual social discords or internal disputes among the Diaspora Jews.[270] So, the negative descriptions of Gad and Dan do not imply that the author of *JosAs* forsakes the distinction of the Jews from the Gentiles. Thus, the author of *JosAs* does not negotiate the demarcation between the Jews and Gentiles, but rather implies some cultural antagonism towards the pagan culture, and explains how Joseph preserves his Jewish identity, even though he himself is married to a Gentile woman (cf. Gen 41:45).

3.13.2 *Analysis*

The meaning of the firstborn son (πρωτότοκος) in *JosAs* is a neglected theme in current scholarship. The title of firstborn son is ascribed to Joseph (as the firstborn son of God) and also to Pharaoh's son (as the firstborn son of Pharaoh). We have to consider the following six points. Firstly, Joseph functions as an idealised role model for the ancient Jews. In *Jubilees* 39:5, Joseph is handsome as in *JosAs*, and wise enough to interpret Pharaoh's dreams as in Genesis. In *LAB* 8:10, Joseph does not attempt any vengeance against his brothers, when they arrived in Egypt. In Josephus, *Ant* 2.198, Joseph is wondrous in virtue (θαυμάσιος τὴν ἀρετὴν γενόμενος) and in good command of everything (πάντα διοικῶν) through his reason (λογισμῷ). As Gruen mentions, Joseph is an ideal statesman in Philo's *De Josepho*.[271] Joseph is innocent in nature (*Jos* 5), fearless, wise and abstinent (*Jos* 107). In Philo, *Somn* 1.78, Joseph is described as the priest and minister of the mind (θεραπευτής τοῦ νοῦ). As Gruen notes, "Hellenistic Jews writing in Greek, mostly in the Diaspora, developed the image of Joseph beyond the one-dimensional ideal of virtuous self-control."[272] Similarly, Joseph in *JosAs* serves as the role of an ideal Israelite and also as a representative of Israel.

Secondly, Joseph is addressed as the son of God in *JosAs*. For example, Aseneth describes that Joseph is "your" [God's] son (ὅτι υἱὸς σοῦ ἐστι) in 13:10. In this case, it seems that the title 'son' does not originate in the messianic title 'son of God,' but it can be viewed as the title of Israel as used in LXX Exod 4:22.

---

269 Barclay, *Jews in the Mediterranean Diaspora*, 205.

270 Chestnutt, *From Death to Life*, 107–8.

271 Erich Gruen, *Heritage and Hellenism: The Reinvention of Jewish Tradition* (Berkeley: University of California Press, 1998), 81.

272 Gruen, *Heritage and Hellenism*, 79.

In the same verse (13:10), Joseph is the son of God because (διότι) he is the shepherd's [i.e., Jacob's] son from the land of Canaan (υἱὸς σοῦ ἐστι, κύριε, διότι εἶπόν μοι οἱ ἄνθρωποι ὅτι Ἰωσὴφ τοῦ ποιμένος ὁ υἱός ἐστι ἐκ γῆς Χαναάν). That is, Joseph is the son of God (υἱὸς σοῦ ἐστι) because he is the son of Jacob. The connection between "the shepherd's son from the land of Canaan" (ὁ υἱὸς τοῦ ποιμένος ἐκ γῆς Χαναάν) and "the son of God" (Ἰωσὴφ ὁ υἱὸς τοῦ θεοῦ) is also found in 6:2, 5, and 6. Thus, we may conclude that "your son" in 13:10 refers to the title of Israel (descendants of Jacob).

Thirdly, the title 'firstborn son' (πρωτότοκος) is one of the titles ascribed to Joseph (4:11; 18:11; 21:4; 21:20 and 23:10). In *JosAs* 21:20, Joseph is designated as the firstborn son (πρωτότοκος) of the great king (i.e., God). We find the clue to the meaning of πρωτότοκος in 21:4 and 23:10. Joseph is addressed as the son of God and the firstborn son (ὁ υἱὸς τοῦ θεοῦ ὁ πρωτότοκος) in 21:4 and 23:10. This expression is evocative of the phrase υἱὸς πρωτότοκός μου Ισραηλ in LXX Exod 4:22 (in particular, the juxtaposition of υἱός and πρωτότοκος). Thus, it seems that the title 'firstborn son' reflects the title of Israel in LXX Exod 4:22.

Fourthly, Pharaoh's firstborn son is addressed as 'Pharaoh's son' (23:2, 7, 10, 17; 24:5, 7, 12, 14, 19); 25:1–2; 26:7; 27:2–7) and also 'the firstborn son' (1:7; 23:1–2; 25:4; and 29:8). Pharaoh's 'firstborn son' (πρωτότοκος) does not simply refer to the eldest son. If the author envisaged the sense of the eldest son, the term πρεσβύτατος may be more fitting for this sense. Instead, the death of Pharaoh's firstborn son (πρωτότοκος) in *JosAs* 29 reminds the readers of the event of the destruction of the Egyptian firstborn sons in LXX Exod 11–12. Furthermore, the conflicts between Joseph (the firstborn son of God) and Pharaoh's firstborn son in *JosAs* may creatively reshape and retell the conflict between Israel (the firstborn son of God) and Egypt in LXX Exod.

Fifthly, the title 'firstborn son' is also used in the marriage story of Joseph and Aseneth. For example, in 4:11, Joseph is addressed as the 'son' and 'firstborn son' of the king [i.e., God] during the conversation about Aseneth's marriage: "οὐχί, ἀλλὰ γαμήσομαι τῷ υἱῷ τοῦ βασιλέως τῷ πρωτοτόκῳ" (No, but I will be married to the firstborn son of the king). Joseph is also designated as the 'firstborn son' of God in 18:11 and 23:11, which is also located in the context of Aseneth's marriage story. We should note that there is a love triangle in *JosAs* (Joseph–Aseneth–Pharaoh's firstborn son). Pharaoh's firstborn son also seeks to be married to Aseneth, but the final victor for the marriage turns out to be Joseph. It seems that the designation of Joseph as the 'firstborn son' functions to stress the rivalry between Joseph and Pharaoh's firstborn son in this context. As mentioned above, the conflict between Joseph (the firstborn son of God) and Pharaoh's firstborn son is evocative of the conflict between Israel and Egypt in the Exodus story. Moreover, the supremacy of Joseph as the firstborn son over Pharaoh's firstborn son is proved through the death of Pharaoh's firstborn son (29:7). In particular, the lamentation of Pharaoh over his firstborn son's death in *JosAs* 29:9 recalls the sorrow of Pharaoh and Egyptians over their firstborn sons in LXX Exod 12:30. This leads us to conclude that the title 'firstborn son' ascribed to Joseph is associated with the title of Israel as the firstborn son of God in Exod 4:22.[273]

Finally, we should consider whether the title 'firstborn son' in *JosAs* can be understood as a Davidic messianic title. We should note that the role of Joseph in *JosAs* is passive overall, whereas his beauty and excellence are stressed throughout *JosAs*.[274] While Joseph in *JosAs* plays a role as a representative of Israel, he is not illustrated as a military leader of his tribes. So, it is reasonable to conclude that Joseph does not function as a Davidic messianic figure in *JosAs*.

Summing up, the title 'firstborn son' in *JosAs* is used in the context of rivalry between Joseph and Pharaoh's firstborn son, and this shows that the motif of the firstborn son is evocative of the conflicts between Israel and Egypt in Exodus, and also of the destruction of the Egyptian firstborn sons in LXX Exod 11–12. On this basis, it can be concluded that the title 'firstborn son' ascribed to Joseph has its origin in the title of Israel (LXX Exod 4:22).[275] Arguably, the Diaspora Jews could find an ideal role model from Joseph in *JosAs*, and Joseph's title 'firstborn son' and his victory over Pharaoh's firstborn son function to encourage them to remember and solidify their Jewish identity, which is superior to the pagan or Gentile identity. Thus, the concept of the firstborn son in *JosAs* refers to the title of Israel and is associated with the self-perception of the Jews.

3.14 Philo

3.14.1 *Introduction*

3.14.1.1 Life

Philo was a first-century diaspora, Alexandrian Jew who was the inheritor of Jewish intellectual and religious tradition, and who was also politically active.

273 For other Exodus motifs in *JosAs*, see Erich Sänger, "Berkehrung und Exodus," *JSJ* 10 (1979): 22–27.

274 Christoph Burchard, *Untersuchungen zu "Joseph und Aseneth," Überlieferung-Ortsbestimmung* (Tübingen: Mohr Siebeck, 1965), 182.

275 For more specific discussions on the title of the firstborn son in *JosAs*, see Kyu Seop Kim, "The Meaning of the Firstborn Son in Joseph and Aseneth," *JSJ* 49 (2018): 404–416.

He recounted the oral tradition which was handed down by the "elders of the nations."[276]

First-century Jews, who believed that the Jewish people would achieve global supremacy, generally held two different perspectives about how this vision would be fulfilled. On the one hand, some Jews thought that this should be accomplished by violent means, evidenced by the armed revolt which was raised in CE 41 by Alexandrian Jews. Alternatively, others attempted to consolidate their position and status through peaceful means, using the inspiration of their religion which they asserted was granted the Law by God. Philo adhered to the latter perspective.[277]

3.14.1.2 Philosophy and Allegorical Interpretations of the Bible

Philo's writings are well-known for his adaptation of Platonism, particularly "contemporary Alexandrian Platonism" which was influenced by Stoicism and Pythagoreanism.[278] However, we should also note that he was a Jew, faithful to the Mosaic Law, and that many elements of his thought were deeply rooted in Jewish tradition.[279] Philo firmly believed that the scripture and the Mosaic Law were of universal and eternal significance.[280]

---

276 J.M.G. Barclay, *Jews in the Mediterranean Diaspora: From Alexander to Trajan (323 BCE–117 CE)* (HCS 33; Berkeley: University of California Press, 1996), 161. See also *Mos* 1.4.

277 Peder Borgen, "Philo," in *ABD, vol. 5* (New York: Doubleday, 1991), 336; Berndt Schaller, "Philon von Alexandreia und das 'Heilige Land'," in *Das Land Israel in biblischer Zeit: Jerusalem-Symposium 1981 der Hebräischen Universität und der Georg-August-Universität* (ed. Georg Strecker; GTA 25; Göttingen: Vandenhoeck & Ruprecht, 1983), 176.

278 John Dillon, *The Middle Platonists: 80 B.C. to A.D. 220* (Ithaca: Cornell University Press, 1996), 182; Barclay, *Jews in the Mediterranean Diaspora*, 164. As for the Stoic influence, "No Platonist at Philo's time could escape the influence of Stoicism both in terminology and doctrine.... Was Philo more deeply shaped by Stoicism? I think he probably was, but in ways that were largely episodic and unsystematic," in A.A. Long, "Philo on Stoic Physics," in *Studies in Philo of Alexandria: Philo of Alexandria and Post-Aristotelian Philosophy* (SPA 5; Leiden: Brill, 2008), 139–40. As for the difference between Stoicism and Philo, Mattila notes: 1) "Philo's Nature is not fully immanent like Stoic Nature, for she [Nature] is in contact with the transcendent Logos and the world of forms, and the paradigms from which she shapes the corporeal objects lie beyond the material realm"; 2) Philo denies material *pneuma* pervading all things; and 3) Philo remains God's transcendence in contrast of Stoic Pantheism. See Sharon Lea Mattila, "Wisdom, Sense Perception, Nature, and Philo's Gender Gradient," *HTR* 89 (1996): 120, 123–24.

279 Barclay writes, "[T]he whole gamut of Hellenistic culture is subordinated to Moses, pressed into service to endorse *his* original achievement." [Italics author's] in Barclay, *Jews in the Mediterranean Diaspora*, 173.

280 Barclay, *Jews in the Mediterranean Diaspora*, 172. See also Maren Niehoff, *Philo on Jewish Identity and Culture* (TSAJ 86; Tübingen: Mohr Siebeck, 2001), 247.

Philo uses both allegorical and literal interpretations in his exegesis of the scripture. Philo's allegorical interpretations of scripture are based on Platonic dualism. According to *Abr* 147, the obvious meaning of the text is accessible to all, but only a few can perceive the hidden meaning.[281] Philo applies his allegorical interpretations to the status of the Jewish and pagan peoples. He relates the concept of Platonic dualism demarcating heaven and earth (soul and body) to the distinction between Israel and the other nations.[282]

However, Philo does not neglect the literal meaning of the text, and rather, as Borgen writes, for Philo, "the allegorical interpretation never invalidates the literal,"[283] and "the literal meaning always comes first and the allegory is based on it."[284] Philo combines this allegorical and literal approach in his exegesis of the scripture, and he highlights the allegorical interpretation over the literal meaning, however, he also stresses the literal meaning as a counter to "over-spiritualisation."[285] In this vein, Borgen notes that Philo's allegorical interpretations have "affinities with the hermeneutical concept of prophecy and fulfilment."[286]

3.14.1.3 Covenant

Attempts to allegorically interpret the covenant are made in Philo's writings. For instance, Philo addresses the covenant as Logos.[287] Philo also writes, "The covenant of God is an allegory of his gifts of grace, and it may not be that any of his gifts should be imperfect."[288] Abraham is an example of excellent reason and speech, and the blessing of Abraham is associated with logos-excellence or good reasoning/speech.[289] Abraham is also portrayed as the mediator between

281 Barclay, *Jews in the Mediterranean Diaspora*, 166. See also *Vit Cont* 78.

282 Borgen, "Philo," 339.

283 Borgen, "Philo," 338. Especially see *Mig* 89–93.

284 Jutta Leonhardt-Balzer, "Jewish Worship and Universal Identity in Philo of Alexandria," in *Jewish Identity in the Greco-Roman World* (eds. Jörg Frey, Daniel Schwartz and S. Gripentrog; AGJU 71; Leiden: Brill, 2007), 43.

285 Borgen, "Philo," 338.

286 Borgen also notes, "Philo also adapts allegorical interpretation to the Jewish notion of election, which he uses to claim for the Jews and their sacred writings elements from Greek philosophy, education, ethics, and religion. Conversely, to Philo, allegorical interpretation is a way in which the wisdom of the laws of Moses and Jewish religious institutions can be disclosed to the world." See Borgen, "Philo," 338.

287 *Somn* 2.237.

288 *Sacr* 57. See also *Mut* 52.

289 See Phoebe Makiello, "Abraham and The Nations in the Works of Philo of Alexandria" in *Abraham, the nations, and the Hagarites: Jewish, Christian, and Islamic Perspectives on Kinship with Abraham* (eds. M. Goodman, G. van Kooten and J. van Ruiten; TBN 13; Leiden: Brill, 2010), 141, 143.

God and the rest of humankind in *Migr* 126; *Gig* 64, and as Minister of God.[290] Isaac is an heir of Wisdom and virtue given by nature.[291] On the other hand, Ishmael is depicted as a sophist. Jacob is a practiser of reason and speech.[292] Inheritance is also allegorically interpreted (e.g., *Sacr* 4), and Reason is connected to the land of the Canaanites (e.g., *Sacr* 90).[293] The Promised Land "from the river of Egypt to the great river Euphrates" symbolises moral progress from mortal bodily passion to the imperishable (*Heres* 315–16; *Q.G.* 4.182–83; *Heres* 314; *Somn* 2.255; *Sacr* 57).

However, Philo does not only understand the covenant from an allegorical and abstract perspective. We need to bear in mind that Abraham also appears as the founder of the Jewish people (twelve tribes) in *Abr* 77. The land of Palestine is depicted as the inheritance of the patriarchs and their offspring in Philo's writing (*Somn* 1.175; *Spec Leg* 2.168). Sandmel argues that Philo has no interest in the actual land of Palestine.[294] However, the actual land of Palestine is regarded as significant in *Spec Leg* 2.162–75. After the defence against the charge of Jewish misanthropy, Philo establishes that the Jews would occupy the land of Palestine which at that time belonged to others. Philo contended that the Jews would possess the Land and the cities [of Palestine] as their inheritance, and they would offer the first fruits as a sacred duty.[295] That is, the Jews were granted the Land in order to offer the first fruits of the Land as representatives of the whole human race.

Philo's designation of Jerusalem as "mother city" in *Flacc* 46 also uncovers Philo's understanding about Jewish expectations of a return to the homeland.[296] Some references to Jerusalem, which was called "mother city," are found in

290 Cf. Logos as the minister of God in *Migr* 175; *Heres* 234.

291 *Sobr* 8–9.

292 For Philo's interpretation of the patriarchs, see *Somn* 1.168; *Conf* 79–81. For Jacob, see *Congr* 129; *Agr* 51.

293 E.g. *Heres* 69: "Therefore, my soul. If you feel any yearning to inherit the good things of God, leave not only thy land, that is the body, thy kinsfolk, that is the senses, thy father's house, that is speech, but be a fugitive from yourself also and issue forth from yourself."

294 Samuel Sandmel, *Philo's Place in Judaism: A Study of Conception of Abraham in Jewish Literature* (New York: KTAV, 1971), 102.

295 "First, because they do not continue forever wandering broadcast over islands and continents and occupying the homelands of others as strangers and vagrants, open to the reproach of waiting to seize the goods of others. Nor have they just borrowed a section of this great country for lack of mans to purchase, but have acquired the Land and cities for their own property, a heritage in which they live as long established citizens and therefore offer first-fruits from it as a sacred duty," in *Spec Leg* 2.168.

296 *Spec Leg* 1.67–70. Cf. Sarah Pearce, "Jerusalem as 'Mother City' in the Writings of Philo of Alexandria," in *Negotiating Diaspora: Jewish Strategies in the Roman Empire* (ed. John Barclay; JSPSup 45; London: T&T Clark, 2004), 20.

Jewish literature such as LXX Isa 1:26 and Josephus, *Ant* 3.245, and the mother land was understood as the homeland. In *Somn* 1.181, Philo explicates Jacob's return from Laban's house as "return from imprisonment of the body" and as the return to the Land according to the promise, and Philo calls the Land the mother city. In other words, the mother land can be viewed in the context of return to the Promised Land. Jerusalem as "mother land" in *Flacc* 46 can also be considered in the same way. That is, Philo regards Jerusalem as the homeland. Niehoff argues that Philo's usage of Jerusalem as mother city aims to encourage Jews to think of Jerusalem as their homeland.[297] This usage can be understood as a device to maintain a distinct Jewish identity in the multi-ethnic setting of first-century Egypt. As Niehoff writes, "While Judea was thus not the physical homeland of most Jews, Philo made its capital the symbolic centre of Jewish ethnicity."[298]

3.14.1.4 Israel

Philo's concept of Israel is complex and is beyond the scope of this study. Therefore, in this section, we will briefly discuss the relationship between Israel and the Jews in Philo's writings. Philo interprets Israel as seers of God.[299] Birnbaum argues that Israel in Philo contains a more comprehensive meaning which is open to non-Jews. That is, Israel encompasses not only the Jews, but all seers of God including the Gentiles.[300] Birnbaum observes that Israel is not addressed as ἔθνος, πολιτεία or λαός, but γένος.[301] Israel refers to seers of God, and yet, "Philo does not speak about the Jews as being able to see God, an ability he associates predominantly with Israel."[302] Additionally, she does not make a connection between worshipping God and seeing God.[303] Rather,

---

297 For the similar point, see Schaller, "Philon von Alexandreia und das 'Heilige Land'," 182.

298 Niehoff, *Philo on Jewish Identity and Culture*, 33–4: "… Jerusalem possessed the central sanctuary to which all Jews should be looking," in Niehoff, *Philo on Jewish Identity and Culture*, 33–35. Niehoff's opinion on mothercity is endorsed by Pieter W. van der Horst, *Philo's Flaccus: The First Pogrom* (PACS 2; Leiden: Brill, 2003), 42. Cf. Leonhardt-Balzer, "Universal Identity," 41.

299 E.g., *Heres* 78; *Somn* 1.171; *Spec Leg* 3.38; *Mut* 81; *Migr* 125; *Conf* 56.

300 Ellen Birnbaum, *The Place of Judaism in Philo's Thought: Israel, Jews, and Proselytes* (BJS 90; SPhiloM 2; Atlanta: Scholars, 1996), 213.

301 See Birnbaum, *The Place of Judaism*, 163, 189. As for the notion of γένος, see Birnbaum, *The Place of Judaism*, 56: "he [Philo] may understand this γένος as a class of people that can see in addition to or instead of as a race united by birth that inherits this ability." Also see *Congr* 20, 42.

302 Birnbaum, *The Place of Judaism*, 163.

303 Birnbaum, *The Place of Judaism*, 211.

seeing God is only "intellectual activity."[304] According to Birnbaum, individuals can see God through their noetic or spiritual eyes,[305] and seeing God is "the highest philosophical goal."[306] Birnbaum's thesis helps us to perceive Philo's universalistic view of Israel.

However, we also detect some conceptual links between Israel and the Jews in Philo. Firstly, Philo's references to Abraham imply a close relationship between Israel and the Jews, because Abraham is the founder of the Jewish nation (ἀρχηγέτος τοῦ ἔθνους) and the paradigmatic visionary of God.[307] Abraham was also the most ancient member of the Jewish nation (τοῦ τῶν Ἰουδαίων ἔθνους ὁ πρεσβύτατος γένος) in *Virt* 212. Secondly, γένος can be understood with reference to ἔθνος in *Praem* 84: τοῦτο τὸ γένος οὐ μακρὰν ἀπῴκισται θεοῦ ... ὡς, κἂν εἰ πύθοιτό τις, ποῖον ἔθνος μέγα, προσφυῶς ἄν τινας ἀποκρίνασθαι (This people [γένος] does not live far from God ... if someone asks which makes the nation [ἔθνος] great, one can properly answer). In other words, γένος and ἔθνος can be understood as related concepts in *Praem* 84. Thirdly, Philo writes that only Jews worship God, even though he acknowledges that some Greeks and barbarians do also recognise the supreme God in *Spec Leg* 2.165–66: "In this sense, the Jews are the one truly worshipful community in the world; they are the nation with the clearest vision of God, the people thus naturally most God-beloved."[308] Jewish ritual in Philo's writings is related to seeing God.[309] We should note that Jewish worship in Philo is not merely symbolic and allegorical, but also that actual and literal observance of worship according to the teaching of the Torah is significant in Philo's writings. "Holy nation" (ἔθνος ἅγιον) (cf. Exod 19:6) is also linked with "he who sees God" in *Abr* 56–57. Fourthly, in *Q. G.* 2.65, Israel is also designated as "the beloved and elected people by God." This denotes that the concept of Israel contains an ethnic notion (cf. *Q. G.* 2.75). We conclude, therefore, that the concept of Israel is still related to the Jewish people, even though the notion of Israel in Philo is open to all seers of God including the Gentiles in some respects.

The privilege of the Jews among the nations is a significant theme in Philo. Firstly, Philo writes that the Jews are a priestly people among all other peoples: "The Jewish people is to the whole world what the priest is to the state. For the

304 Birnbaum, *The Place of Judaism*, 212.

305 Birnbaum, *The Place of Judaism*, 212. Cf. Makiello, "Abraham and The Nations in the Works of Philo of Alexandria," 160–61.

306 Birnbaum, *The Place of Judaism*, 191.

307 *Abr* 276; *Heres* 279. See also Niehoff, *Philo on Jewish Identity and Culture*, 95.

308 See also Barclay, *Jews in the Mediterranean Diaspora*, 174.

309 Jutta Leonhardt, *Jewish Worship in Philo of Alexandria* (TSAJ 84; Tübingen: Mohr Siebeck, 2001), 277.

holy office in very truth belongs to the nation because it carries out all the rites of purification and both in body and soul obeys the injunctions of the divine laws …" (*Spec Leg* 2.163). Thus, Philo proposes Israel's special position among the nations in that the Jewish nation acts as a priestly people for humankind.[310] Secondly, the Jews are the most beloved nation by God in *Abr* 98.[311] Thirdly, Philo states in *Spec Leg* 4.180–81 that the Jewish people is consecrated as distinct from the whole human race, because the founders of the race (ἔθνος) are righteous and virtuous. In *Mos* 1.149, Philo also states that the Jews are distinct from all other nations of the human race.[312]

Leonhardt-Balzer identifies particularistic and universalistic aspects of Jewish rites in Philo. She argues that Philo does not define Jewish identity by negation, but stresses that the Jews surpass other nations in a positive way. Leonhardt-Balzer finds evidence in Philo's depictions of the Jewish rites. It is evident that Philo holds "a clear concept of ethnicity" which distinguishes the Jews from the other nations.[313] Philo endeavours to integrate various intellectual traditions into the Jewish tradition, but Philo accords primacy to Jewish heritage.[314] Philo adheres to literal observation of the Jewish rites according to the Torah.[315] He perceives the significance of the Temple in Jerusalem and does not imply that local synagogues and the Temple were in conflict. Both the local synagogues and the Temple function to form a Jewish particularistic identity. Philo also views the Jewish rites as superior to any pagan rites.[316] On the other hand, Leonhardt-Balzer notes that the Jewish rites in Philo contain universalistic aspects. For example, the Jewish rites were inspired by Moses through the divine Logos, and this inspiration makes the Jewish cults relevant in the context of the universal order of the cosmos, and renders them superior

310 *Spec Leg* 2.163–64; *Mos* 1.149. In Philo's writings, the priests are considered to be consecrated apart from other people in a special level of holiness (*Spec Leg* 1.102), and to deserve their exalted status, in Martha Himmelfarb, *A Kingdom of Priests: Ancestry and Merit in Ancient Judaism* (JCC; Philadelphia: University of Pennsylvania Press, 2006), 151. Himmelfarb also observes, "Thus Philo claims here that the priesthood of all Israel is not only chronologically prior to the selection of a distinct group of priests but also ontologically prior: the nation is the archetype of the priesthood, even of the high priesthood." See Himmelfarb, *A Kingdom of Priests*, 159.

311 Cf. *Abr* 89–98.

312 See Leonhardt-Balzer, "Universal Identity," 52.

313 Leonhardt-Balzer, "Universal Identity," 34.

314 Leonhardt-Balzer, "Universal Identity," 35, 53.

315 Leonhardt-Balzer, "Universal Identity," 52.

316 Leonhardt-Balzer, "Universal Identity," 53.

to any Greco-Roman cults.[317] Thus, we conclude that Jewish ritual in Philo simultaneously has particularistic and universalistic aspects.[318]

In addition, Philo proposes that Jewish theology is the best philosophy, and identifies the Jews as well-educated and philosophical people.[319] Philo distinguished the Jews from the Egyptians and revealed the Jewish people as "the elite of world civilization."[320] The Jews are "quitting the objects of sense-perception and going after those of the mind," namely "transcendence of worldly matter."[321] They are identified as those who have "passed over all created objects" (*Spec Leg* 2.166).[322]

3.14.2 *The First Fruit (ἀπαρχή) in Philo*

In Philo's writings, the firstborn son is often linked with the first fruits or the cultic offering.[323] The first fruit in Philo has broad usage, as Leonhardt-Balzer categorises:[324] 1) The first fruit which is related to the Jewish harvest festival in *Spec Leg* 2.41 and to thanksgiving in *Sacr* 74; 2) the first fruit which alludes to the privileged position of Israel in *Spec Leg* 4.180–81; 3) the first fruit which refers to the income for the priests in *Spec Leg* 4.98; 4) expression of piety in *Mos* 1.318; *Spec Leg* 1.131; 5) virtuous actions and lives in *Somn* 2.172; *Prov* 15; *Spec Leg* 4.97–99; and 6) offering of the soul in *Spec Leg* 1.76–78; *Sacr* 117–19; and 7) symbol of the best part in *Heres* 113–19. Ἀπαρχή is also linked to the

317 Leonhardt-Balzer, "Universal Identity," 39.

318 Thus, Leonhardt-Balzer writes that the Jews are privileged as the nation of priests and philosophers, and "In this privilege lies the key to their unique identity which is defined by absolute universalism based on utmost particularism," in Leonhardt-Balzer, "Universal Identity," 53.

319 See Barclay, *Jews in the Mediterranean Diaspora*, 176. He points out *Decal* 96–101; *Mos* 2.209–16; *Spec Leg* 2.61–63.

320 Niehoff, *Philo on Jewish Identity and Culture*, 75. She also notes, "The cases of Gaius, Flaccus and others had in his view clearly shown that the Jews enjoyed God's special beneficence and protection," in Niehoff, *Philo on Jewish Identity and Culture*, 76.

321 Niehoff, *Philo on Jewish Identity and Culture*, 84. See also *Migr* 20.

322 Niehoff, *Philo on Jewish Identity and Culture*, 95. See also Barclay, *Jews in the Mediterranean Diaspora*, 173: "Although Philo refers often enough to the Jewish people as a 'nation' (ἔθνος), their ethnicity is defined less in genealogical terms than by reference to their common 'constitution', the holy πολιτεία of Moses. Such an emphasis enables Philo to portray the superiority of Jews in cultural rather than racial terms." However, Barclay also admits, "Nevertheless, the Jewish tradition is still 'ancestral', and Jews continue to be blessed by the merits of the fathers," in Barclay, *Jews in the Mediterranean Diaspora*, 173.

323 E.g. *Congr* 7; *Conf* 124; *Spec Leg* 1.135, 138, 139, 248; *Virt* 95; *Abr* 196. Particularly, the first fruit is an offering for priests in *Spec Leg* 2.222, ἀπαρχή also means the best portion in *Post* 96. See Leonhardt, *Jewish Worship*, 198.

324 See Leonhardt, *Jewish Worship*, 190–213. As for the material meaning of ἀπαρχή, see Leonhardt, *Jewish Worship*, 213.

inheritance of Israel.[325] The reason Israel inherited the Land is to offer the ἀπαρχή of the land to God, and the Jews are the representative of all nations like ἀπαρχή.[326] The first fruit is linked to the Jewish people in *Spec Leg* 4.180:

> Nevertheless as Moses tells us the orphan-like desolate state of his people is always an object of pity and compassion to the Ruler of the Universe whose portion it is, because it has been set apart out of the whole human race as a kind of first fruits to the Maker and Father.
>
> Loeb translation

That is, the Jews are consecrated as the first fruit among the whole human race, and this denotes that the Jews represent the whole of humankind and have primacy over the nations. The usage of ἀπαρχή is complex in Philo, but its link to the firstborn son in the context of election is apparent as will be demonstrated in the next section.

3.14.3 *The Firstborn Son in the Stories of Blessing and Curse*

In Philo's allegorical treatises,[327] the term "the firstborn son" is frequently referenced in the stories of election and curse. In *Legum Allegoriae* 3.87, Philo highlights that it was promised to Isaac that he would receive the blessing, before he was born. This same notion is found in the case of Jacob and Esau

325 *Spec Leg* 2.75–77.

326 *Spec Leg* 2.168.

327 Philo's works can be divided into three categories: 1) biblical commentaries; 2) apologetic or historical treatises and 3) philosophical treatises. Philo's three great commentary series consists of Questions and Answers on Genesis and Exodus, allegorical commentaries and expositions of the Law. Kenneth Schenck, *A Brief Guide to Philo* (Louisville: WJK, 2005), 14. Philo's allegorical commentaries include: *Legum Allegoriae* 1–3 (Gen 2–3); *De Cherubim* (Gen 3:24–4:1); *De Sacrificiis Abelis et Caini* (Gen 4:2–4); *Quod Deterius Potiori Insidiari Soleat* (Gen 4:8–15); *De Posteritate Caini* (Gen 4:16–25); *De Gigantibus* (Gen 6:1–4a); *Quod Deus Sit Immutabilis* (Gen 6:4b–12); *De Agricultura* (Gen 9:20–21); *De Plantatione* (Gen 9:20–21); *De Ebrietate* (Gen 9:20–21); *De Confusione Linguarum* (Gen 11:1–9); *De Migratione Abrahami* (Gen 12:1–6); *Quis Rerum Divinarum Heres Sit* (Gen 15:2–18); *De Congressu Quaerendae Eruditionis Gratia* (Gen 16:1–5); *De Fuga et Inventione* (Gen 16:6b–14); *De Mutatione Nominum* (Gen 17:1–5, 16–22); *De Somniis* 1 (Gen 28:10–22; 31:10–13); and *De Somniis* 2 (Gen 37:8–11; 40:9–11, 16–17; 41:17–24). Cf. Schenck, *A Brief Guide to Philo*, 16–17. The basic order of Philo's allegorical treatises is a sort of progression from chapter to chapter. See David Runia, "The Structure of Philo's Allegorical Treatises: A Review of Two Recent Studies and Some Additional Comments," *Vigiliae Christianae* 38 (1984): 213. Cf. John Dillon, "The Formal Structure of Philo's Allegorical Exegesis," in *Two Treatises of Philo of Alexandria: A Commentary on De gigantibus and Quod Deus sit immutabilis* (eds. J. Dillon and D. Winston; BJS 25; Chico: Scholars, 1983), 77–87.

(*Leg Alleg* 3.88). When they are in the womb, God declares that Jacob is "a ruler, leader and master," and that Esau is "a subject and a slave":

> For God the maker of living beings knows well the different pieces of his own handiwork, even before He has thoroughly chiselled and consummated them, and the faculties which they are to display at a later time, in a word their deeds and experiences.
>
> Loeb translation (*Leg Alleg* 3.88)

In this vein, Jacob is the one endowed with reason. On the other hand, Esau is innately irrational and a slave by nature, "of servile ethos underserved to a free man."[328] Jacob is frequently described as practiser in many parts of Philo's writings, but this does not imply that one can attain perfection only through adhering to certain practices. Jacob was bestowed with certain qualities and he practised and developed his mind and virtue by utilising and developing these qualities (or natural excellence in *Leg Alleg* 3.196). Philo implies that Jacob was elected to be rational before he was born and that he achieved perfection by drawing on his innate qualities. As Barclay observes, "Indeed, at many points Philo specifically denies that human virtue is what merits divine grace, or is itself in anyway self-generated."[329] On the other hand, it cannot be expected that Esau becomes a practiser like Jacob, since he is innately irrational, namely without quality.[330]

In *Leg Alleg* 3.188–94, Jacob who took over Esau's birthright is the one "[who is] first in virtue has received the things that are first, which indeed were his portion; for he has received the blessing also accompanied by perfect

328 *Leg Alleg* 3.195. Cf. Peder Borgen, *Philo of Alexandria: An Exegete for His Time* (NovTSup 86; Leiden: Brill, 1997), 52.

329 J.M.G. Barclay, "'By the Grace of God I Am What I Am': Grace and Agency in Philo and Paul," in *Divine and Human Agency in Paul and His Cultural Environment* (eds. J.M.G. Barclay and S.J. Gathercole; LNTS 335; London: T&T Clark, 2008), 144. Similarly, Makiello notes, "[Philo] intimates the importance of blessing, understood as excellent reason and speech, whilst emphasising its divine provenance: a good mind is gift from God to those souls which are worthy, that is, those that entertain thoughts of God," in Makiello, "Abraham and The Nations," 143.

330 It seems that the election of Abel, the patriarchs and Israel fits with the Aristotelian idea that grace is given to the deserved. However, as Barclay notes, "'worthy' [ἄξιος] in Philo means 'capable,' not 'deserving,' and Philo's concern is lest God's gifts be arbitrary or wasted ... Philo stresses the causative dynamics of grace to the extent that, in deepest reality, or at least at its ultimate stages of ascent, the soul is represented as inactive or passive, to avoid any implication of synergism." See Barclay, "By the Grace of God I Am What I Am," 157.

prayers."[331] In this context, Esau who relinquishes his birthright, but who nevertheless regards the blessing as his own,[332] symbolises bodily passion, and Jacob who seized Esau's heels is the one who "shall not let go the heel of his adversary, passion."[333]

In *De Sobrietate*, with special reference to Noah's prayer for blessing and curse, Philo explains that an older person is superior to a younger one, that an older brother is more blessed than a younger brother, and that the differentiation is rooted in virtue and mind, not with regard to literal ages. In other words, 'being younger' means "lack of a reasonable understanding."[334] In this way, Philo justifies the curse and the blessing in Noah's prayer. A younger son means rebelliousness and defiance (*Sobr* 6), and Isaac can be older than Ishmael and an heir of Abrahamic promise according to the faculty of soul. The son of the wife who is hated can be the firstborn son (πρωτότοκος), because the wife who is loved means "pleasure" and the wife who is hated is a figure of prudence.[335] For this reason, the son of the wife who is hated is "first in rank and precedence- and again, 'to him belong the rights of the firstborn,' by the law of nature, not by the no-law which prevails among men."[336] Jacob was younger in years, but older in worth and value. Therefore, "Esau is forced to surrender the inheritance of the firstborn to the rightful claims of Jacob."[337] This point is also applied to Joseph's sons (*Sobr* 27), the curse to Ham (*Sobr* 31), Noah's prayer for Shem (*Sobr* 59) and Isaac's seed (*Sobr* 65). That is, "Jacob trained in the wrestling-bout with the passions with the angels of reason to prepare him for the conflict." We should note that election and blessing for Jacob is connected to the excellence of the Jews: "Once more Jacob is the source of the twelve tribes, of whom the oracles say that they are 'the palace and priesthood of God,' thus following in due sequence the thought originated in Shem, in whose houses it was prayed that God might dwell."[338] Thus, in *De Sobrietate*, Philo maintains that the reversal of the status of the firstborn son depends on one's moral and intellectual quality.

331 *Leg Alleg* 3.192.
332 *Leg Alleg* 3.195–96.
333 *Leg Alleg* 3.190.
334 *Sobr* 11.
335 *Sobr* 23. Cf. Makiello observes, "In Migr 71 and Mut 128, Philo brings *eulogia* (blessing) in close connection with *eulogystia* (which normally denotes circumspection or prudence) … It is clear that Philo is playing upon the different meaning of *eulogistia* which can denote 'blessing' …" in Makiello, "Abraham and The Nations," 141.
336 *Sobr* 25.
337 *Sobr* 26.
338 *Sobr* 65.

This point is also confirmed in *De Sacrificiis Abelis et Caini*, which explains the reason why Abel's offering was accepted and why Cain's was not (cf. Gen 4:2–4). That is, God's acceptance was due because Abel's offering was ἀπαρχή or πρωτότοκος.[339] First of all, *Sacr* also associates the aspects of the mind and of virtue to the status of the older brother and the heir. Philo writes, "good and evil will be separated and set apart from each other and no longer have the same habitation,"[340] when Philo states, "two nations are in thy womb ... two peoples shall be separated from thy womb" in Gen 25. Accordingly, Cain is older in years, but Abel is more virtuous, and so "Abel should take the lead" for this reason.[341] This point is also applied to Esau and Jacob: "For he shows us Esau, who is named after his folly, as elder in point of age, but it is to the younger brother named from his discipline and practice of things excellent, even Jacob, that he awards the prize of precedence (πρεσβεία)."[342] Therefore, the birthright (πρωτοτόκια or πρεσβεία) belongs to Jacob, and "all that is supreme in value, and all to which virtue gives its place of honour, belong not to any of the wicked, but to the lover of wisdom only," namely Jacob.[343] In the story of Esau and Jacob, "Jacob, who overthrew the seat and foundation of passion," deserves the birthright (πρεσβεία), although Jacob is younger in years. Therefore, in this context, it is justified that Jacob was granted the birthright.[344] In addition, Jacob's exchanging the birthright with Esau means passing Esau's inheritance to Jacob.[345]

In *Sacr* 77, Philo explains the meaning of being older: "By 'elder' is meant he that is worthy of honour and privilege and elevated status, and to approve such was the task entrusted to Moses, the friend of God." As for the meaning of the first, Philo writes:

> The first in order are those in which we became at once participators, when we came into existence, taking nourishment, growth, sight, hearing, taste, smell, touch, reason, mind, the parts of the soul, the parts of the body, their activities, in general their natural movements and states.

---

339 *Sacr* 88.

340 *Sacr* 4.

341 *Sacr* 14.

342 *Sacr* 17.

343 *Sacr* 18. See also *Virt* 207. As Wilson writes, "Jacob's acquisition of his brother's birthright (πρωτοτόκια) is likened to the victory of the sage over passion ..." See Walter T. Wilson, *On Virtues: Introduction, Translation and Commentary* (Philo of Alexandria Commentary Series; Leiden: Brill, 2011), 402.

344 *Sacr* 42.

345 *Sacr* 135.

> The first in worth and value are righteous conduct, virtues, and virtuous actions.[346]
>
> Loeb translation

The first fruit (ἀπαρχή) occasionally refers to an offering of the soul,[347] and the Levites are also called πρωτότοκος in *Sacr* 118. Philo's designation of the Levites as πρωτότοκος evokes LXX Num 3:12: "I hereby accept the Levites from among the sons of Israel as substitutes for all the firstborn (ἀντὶ παντὸς πρωτοτόκου) that open the womb among the Israelites. The Levites shall be mine." In *Sacr* 119, the Levites symbolise Logos: "It is Reason, who has taken refuge with God and become His suppliant that is here given the name of Levite." In other words, the Levites play the analogous role among the Jews as reason plays in the mind. The Levites hold a pivotal role within the Jewish community,[348] and Levi, who was perfectly virtuous among Jacob's sons, deserves the status of the firstborn son as Jacob was granted πρωτοτόκια: "Reuben the man of natural gifts must yield the rights of the elder to Levi, whose life is one of perfect virtue."[349] In other words, Reuben was the oldest in age, but the status of the firstborn, which Esau passed to Jacob, was given to Levi.[350]

Philo also argues that the death of the Egyptian firstborn sons symbolises the most dominant aspect of blind passion in *Sacr* 134. After the destruction of the Egyptian firstborn sons, "the sanctification of the elder and precious offspring of Israel who has clear vision of God" is achieved. Thus, Philo develops the link between the first fruit (or cultic offering) and the firstborn, and also elaborates the cause of election and curse in the Pentateuch. Accordingly, we conclude that Philo claims the status of Israel "by negation" to some degree, because Philo accepts the strategy of the Pentateuch to distinguish Israel' status from that of Egypt and stresses Israel's superiority over Egypt through the destruction of the Egyptian firstborn sons and through the sanctification of the Israelite firstborn sons. Philo's frequent references to the death of the Egyptian firstborn son are contrasted with Josephus' silence on the same issue in his *Antiquitates Judaicae*. Feldman argues that Josephus wanted to improve relations between the Israelites and the Egyptians, and that his silence on

346 *Sacr* 73. Also see *Sacr* 52.

347 *Sacr* 117. The offering the firstborn to God is "true to nature," because the firstborn is the one who opened his mother's womb (*Sacr* 102). Female offspring of the soul is vice as passion, and male offspring is health of soul as virtue. So the firstborn is the males (*Sacr* 102).

348 *Sacr* 118.

349 *Sacr* 120.

350 As for the excellence of Levites, see *Sacr* 127–33.

this issue is intended to advance this objective.[351] We should note that, in the writings of Philo, the title of the firstborn son is not ascribed to the Gentiles. The title is used only for the Elect, the Israelites, and the Levites, if the title of the firstborn son is attributed to a specific person or people. Philo also employs the title of the firstborn son in relation to the privilege of election. Therefore, the firstborn title is not used for the non-Elect, and functions to distinguish the Elect from the non-Elect. In Philo, the firstborn son refers to the privileged status of the Elect, Israel, and the Levites, and this notion is depicted in the context of the annihilation of the Egyptian firstborn son.[352]

Quis Rerum Divinarum Heres Sit opens by the question; who can be Abraham's heir? Abraham says that he has no seed and his heir is Damascus Eliezer, the son of Masek: "'Master, what will you give me? I go hence childless. The son of Masek, he who was born in my house, is this Damascus Eliezer.' And again he says 'Since you have given me no seed, he that was born in my house shall be my heir.'" Philo allegorically interprets the story of Abraham, and highlights Abraham's boldness of speech: "But the man of worth has such courage of speech, that he is bold not only to speak and cry aloud, but actually to make an outcry of reproach, wrung from him by real conviction, and expressing true emotion."[353] This discourse on boldness of speech is linked to Moses. Moses' speeches in Exod 5:22, 23; 32:32; Num 11:12, 13, 22 are considered in terms of frankness of speech and of friendship. In *Heres* 63, Abraham's heir inherited a divine and incorporeal thing. In *Heres* 101, Philo argues that the heir is the inheritor of Wisdom. Philo also writes that the firstborn son is the one who opens the mother's womb, and an heir in *Heres* 49, when Philo describes the firstborn son of the wife who is hated. Additionally, The Levites also hold the status of the firstborn son who opens the mother's womb in *Heres* 124. In *Heres* 251–56, Jacob is the heir of Wisdom, but Esau is not, because "[Jacob's] mind within the body still lives to virtue and rules that body instead of being ruled by it," in *Heres* 256. In *Heres*, the firstborn son is referenced to explain Abraham's heirship. The firstborn son in *Heres* is linked to Abraham's heir, who

351 For example, Feldman observes, "Whereas Exod. 12:29–33 presents a detailed and vivid picture of the effect of the plague upon the first-born of the Egyptians Josephus is much briefer, presumably because he sought to emphasise the good neighbourly relations of the Egyptians and the Israelites. In particular, Josephus omits the statement (Exod 12:30) that there was not a house among the Egyptians where there was not someone dead." See Louis H. Feldman, *Judean Antiquities 1–4: Translation and Commentary* (FJTC 3; Leiden: Brill, 1999), 250. Josephus also remarks nothing about Esau's despising his birthright (cf. Gen 25:34). See Louis H. Feldman, *Josephus's Interpretation of the Bible* (Berkeley: University of California Press, 1998), 318.

352 See Borgen, "Philo," 339.

353 *Heres* 19.

inherits the Land (*Heres* 313–14). The Land is again linked to divine wisdom in *Heres* 314: "The land whose fruit is the sure and steadfast apprehension of the wisdom of God …"

In *Post* 62, Abraham/Sarah, Isaac/Rebecca and Jacob/Leah are delineated as the possessors of virtues. Soul is also older than body (or Egypt), and virtue is older than vice (or Zoan). Nature determines who the firstborn son (πρεσβύτατος) is, not by length of time, but by worth. In this sense, Israel is the firstborn son in *Post* 63:

> He [Israel] who sees God, the original Cause of being, is the recipient of honour, as earliest offspring of the Uncreated One, conceived by virtue the object of the hatred of mortals, and as he to whom there is a law that a double portion, the right of the firstborn, should be given as being the eldest.
>
> Loeb translation

In this quotation, Philo interprets the status of the firstborn son (cf. Exod 4:22) in terms of Deuteronomic inheritance law (i.e., primogeniture). This denotes that Philo understood the firstborn son as the title of Israel in terms of inheritance (i.e., primogeniture). So, Israel as the firstborn son takes possession of a double portion amongst the nations and this further symbolises primacy over Israel's neighbours, i.e., Egypt and Zoan.[354]

In *Congr* 95–99, Philo maintains that "we" should offer "our first fruits" to God. He also writes that God sanctifies all the firstborn, and "took as their ransom the tenth, that is the tribe of Levi, that they should observe and maintain holiness and piety and the rites which are offered for the honour of God," in *Congr* 98. The connection between the first fruit and the firstborn is applied to the Levites and to reasoning: "the first and best thing in us is the reason … We should offer first-fruits to God, who gave to it its fertility of thinking," in *Congr* 98. Therefore, the Levites represent Israel, and reason in humankind is a parallel or equivalent concept.

In summary, the first fruit (a cultic offering) and the firstborn son are often associated with each other. Ἀπαρχή symbolises offering to God or living up to the best thing in the mind and virtue, and it is justified in this context that God accepted only Abel's offering. In Philo, the one who has the right of the firstborn refers to the one who holds this distinct rational quality. By this token, Israel as the firstborn son is γένος who has this distinct rational quality. In other words, the Elect (e.g., Jacob, Israel and Levites) are those who have

354 Particularly, see "accordingly" in *Post* 63.

already innately (or by birth) achieved or demonstrated their distinct quality, which makes them worthy (ἄξιος) as the firstborn.[355] Nonetheless, as in *Leg Alleg* 3.196, the quality of the firstborn son is bestowed through divine agency, not by human quality. As Logos is the firstborn son, so Jacob, Israel and the Levites are the firstborn son. Also, as Logos is superior to other parts of the body and mind or of the universe, so Jacob, Israel and the Levites are superior to other beings or γένος. Therefore, in Philo, the concept of the firstborn is associated with the superiority of the Elect and the heirship of the Abrahamic promise. The heir inherits the Land, which is allegorically connected to noetic, virtuous or divine qualities, particularly divine Wisdom. We will explore the divine Logos as the firstborn son in the next section.

3.14.4 *Logos as the Firstborn Son*

Philo in his writings calls Logos the other God,[356] and indicates that Logos functions as a mediator between God and creature[357] and is located at the centre of the cosmos.[358] In Philo's writings, Logos is the intermediate reality between God and the cosmos, and can be identified with the pattern of the intermediary figure in middle-Platonism as well as with the Stoic principle of 'rationality' which pervades the cosmos.[359]

Tobin explores three functions of Logos in Philo:[360] 1) Logos has a cosmological function and is the highest among all beings which can be intellectually perceived; 2) Logos is also anthropological and the paradigm after which Human being are created, but it is not human; and 3) Logos is analogical and

355 However, we should note that as Barclay observes, "worthy" in Philo's writings means "capable," not "deserving." See Barclay, "By the Grace of God I Am What I Am," 157.

356 *Somn* 1.65.

357 Leonhardt-Balzer, "Der Logos und die Schöpfung: Streiflichter bei Philo (Op 20–25) und im Johannesprolog (Joh 1,1–18)" in *Kontexte des Johannesevangeliums: Das vierte Evangelium in religions- und traditionsgeschichtlicher Perspektive* (WUNT 175; eds. Jörg Frey and Udo Schnelle; Tübingen: Mohr Siebeck, 2004), 298.

358 E.g., *Heres* 223.

359 David Runia, *Philo of Alexandria and the Timaeus of Plato* (PA 44; Leiden: Brill, 1986), 450. Cf. Peter Schäfer, *The Origins of Jewish Mysticism* (Tübingen: Mohr Siebeck, 2009), 159: "Philosophically, Philo adopts the Stoic concept of Logos as the chief power immanent in the world." As for the Stoic influence in Philo's doctrine on Logos, Dillon writes, "Through the influence of the Logos, the Ideas become seminal reason-principles, a concept borrowed from the Stoics." See Dillon, *The Middle Platonists*, 159. Dillon also observes Platonic aspects of Philo's Logos. See Dillon, *The Middle Platonists*, 161. See also Francesca Calabi, *God's Acting, Man's Acting: Tradition and Philosophy in Philo of Alexandria* (SPA 4; Leiden: Brill, 2007), 85. Leonhardt-Balzer points out that Philo's Logos contains both transcendent and immanent aspects. See Leonhardt-Balzer, "Der Logos," 300.

360 Thomas Tobin, "Logos," in *ABD*, *vol. 4* (New York: Doubleday, 1991), 350–51.

"the Logos was meant to guide the human soul to the realm of the divine." As Tobin notes, Logos is not simply a metaphor or "a straightforward description of a being other than God." Rather, "It was a real aspect of the divine reality through which God was related, although indirectly, to the universe." Thus, Logos exists beyond the personal or impersonal categories, and it is "the source of the intelligibility of the universe."[361]

Logos and Wisdom are virtually identical in Philonic literature.[362] Philo identifies Logos with Wisdom (*Leg All* 1.65; *Heres* 191; *Somn* 2.242–45; *Opif* 100), and ascribes the same attributes to both of them.[363] LXX Ps 118 translates דברך into "your Logos" (λόγος σου; e.g., LXX Ps 118:9, 16, 17, 25, 28). Schäfer argues that, when considering these links between Logos and Wisdom, Philo may have been influenced by postbiblical Wisdom theology.[364] We conclude, therefore, that Philo's doctrine of Logos is a combination of Hellenistic philosophy and Biblical interpretation.[365]

Scholars are in agreement that the firstborn son (πρεσβύτατος, πρωτόγονος and πρωτόγονος) is used as the title of Logos in Philo,[366] but we are not aware of anyone who has traced and categorised the meanings of the firstborn son

361 Tobin, "Logos," 351. Runia also contends as follows: 1) "The Logos as place of the noetic cosmos. The κόσμος νοητός as plan or model for the visible cosmos is to be located nowhere else but in the divine Logos, or can even be said to coincide with the Logos of God as he is actually engaged in the act of creation"; 2) "Logos as instrument of creation"; 3) "The Logos as replacement for the cosmic soul"; and 4) The Logos and the microcosm, in Runia, *Philo of Alexandria*, 447–49. See also Leonhardt-Balzer, "Creation, the Logos and the Foundation of a City: A Few Comments on *Opif* 15–25," in *Philo und das Neue Testament: Wechselseitige Wahrnehmungen* (eds. Roland Deines and Karl-Wilhelm Niebuhr; WUNT 172; Tübingen: Mohr Siebeck, 2004), 332; Leonhardt-Balzer, "Der Logos," 300. The notion of Philo's Logos should also be considered in terms of Hellenistic-Jewish Wisdom speculation. See Tobin, "Logos," 350; Francesca Calabi, *God's Acting, Man's Acting: Tradition and Philosophy in Philo of Alexandria* (Leiden: Brill, 2007), 85.

362 However, we should also note that, in *Fug* 109, Logos is called the son of God and Sophia. Sophia is also addressed as the mother of all things and Logos in *Det* 115–16.

363 See Tobin, "Logos," 350.

364 Schäfer, *The Origins of Jewish Mysticism*, 159.

365 See Leonhardt-Balzer, "Creation," 344. Williamson compares Logos with exalted personal intermediary figures such as Moses. See Ronald Williamson, *Jews in the Hellenistic World: Philo* (Cambridge: Cambridge University Press, 1989), 115–16. However, Hurtado denies that Moses is a semi-divine figure in Philo: "Williamson mistakenly takes *Somn* 1.164–65 as a 'prayer addressed to Moses' (when in fact it is purely a literary device), and he fails to take account of the considerable difference represented by the devotional practice of early Christians." See Larry W. Hurtado, "Does Philo Help Explain Christianity?" in *Philo und das Neue Testament: Wechselseitige Wahrnehmungen* (eds. Roland Deines and Karl-Wilhelm Niebuhr; WUNT 172; Tübingen: Mohr Siebeck, 2004), 81, 90.

366 Cf. Wisdom is addressed as *primogenitum ante omnem creaturam* in Latin *Sir* 24:3.

as the title of Logos in Philo.[367] Montefiore states, “The Logos, since it stands for the intelligible universe, is the firstborn Son,”[368] and offers his evidence in Philo, *Deus* 31, where the intelligible world is addressed as the elder son.

Yet, this view is not compelling. In *Deus* 31–32, Philo uses a kinship metaphor in order to explain the relationship between the perceptible universe and the intelligible universe: i.e., the present (αἰσθητός) universe is God’s younger son (νεώτερος υἱός θεοῦ), and the intelligible (νοητός) is the elder son (πρεσβύτερος). That is, Philo discusses his Platonic cosmology concerning the physical world and the ideal world, explaining that the intelligible universe is superior to the perceptible universe. In this metaphor, God the creator is spoken of as the father of the perceptible and the intelligible world, and the two worlds are two sons, i.e., God’s creatures. In these verses, the notion of Logos is not explicitly used to symbolise the intelligible universe in the context. So, contrary to Montefiore’ view, the term ‘the firstborn son’ (πρωτότοκος, πρεσβύτατος or πρωτόγονος) is not used for this concept of Logos, and Philo does not use ‘the elder son’ (πρεσβύτερος) as titular in *Deus* 31–32. We will consider the concept of Logos as the firstborn as follows.

3.14.4.1 *Heres* 119

Philo uses the kinship metaphors relating to the eldest son in order to express certain attributes of Logos. In *Heres* 119, Philo also likens Logos to the firstborn son:

> That is true too of one who opens the womb of all from man that is reason and speech, to beast, that is sense and body. For he that opens the womb of each of these, of mind, to mental apprehensions, of speech, to the activities of the voice, of the senses, to receive the pictures presented to it by objects, of the body, to the movements and postures proper to it, is the invisible, seminal artificer, the divine Word, which will be fitly dedicated to its Father.
>
> Loeb translation (*Heres* 119)

In this verse, Philo explains the meaning of ἀρχή and an attribute of Logos through a cultic metaphor. As a cultic sense, the firstborn (πρωτότοκος) is the

367 Cf. Matthew Vellanickal asserts that, in Philo, Logos’ quality of being the firstborn son refers to the mediatorship of men to become sons of God, in Matthew Vellanickal, *The Divine Sonship of Christians in the Johannine Writings* (AnBib; Rome: Pontifical Biblical Institute, 1977), 361. However, it is doubtful that Philo’s concept of the firstborn son conveys the notion of the mediatorship as shown below.

368 Montefiore, *Hebrews*, 36. Ronald Williamson follows this view without any critiques. See Ronald Williamson, *Philo and the Epistle to the Hebrews* (ALGHJ 4; Leiden: Brill, 1970), 417.

one which opened the womb of all these things, and "πρωτογενή" (the first in generation) evokes the cultic ordinance of the firstlings in LXX Exod 13:2 (ἁγίασόν μοι πᾶν πρωτότοκον πρωτογενὲς διανοῖγον πᾶσαν μήτραν). In *Heres* 118, the first in time, value and generation are God's possessions, and they are reason and speech (ὁ λογισμός καὶ λόγος). Thus, in *Heres* 119, πρωτότοκος stresses the attribute of Logos as the first and supreme one with regard to the cultic offering of the firstborn.

3.14.4.2 *Conf* 60

In *Conf* 60, Philo writes that there are two kinds of "rising" (Ἀνατολή) in the soul: the better and the worse: "The better is when the beam of the virtues rises like the rays of the sun; the worse when virtues pass into the shadow and vices rise above the horizon." In *Conf* 63, Philo explains the meaning of Zech 6:12: "Behold, a man whose name is the rising (Ἀνατολή)." "Rising" in *Conf* 63 is arguably related to a messianic figure (particularly see *Conf* 64–65).[369] Philo writes that this man is composed of soul and body (σώματος καὶ ψυχής), and that he is not incorporeal. The name of "rising" (Ἀνατολή) means the eldest son (πρεσβύτατος υἱός and πρωτόγονος), whom the father of all raised up (ἀνέτειλε). In *Conf* 63, Philo utilises πρεσβύτατος υἱός and πρωτόγονος as a kinship metaphor in order to explain the meaning of "rising" as an archetypal pattern which is an attribute of Logos.[370] So, the firstborn son in *Conf* 63 is a kind of kinship metaphor which connotes the role of the eldest son as an archetype.

3.14.4.3 *Somn* 1.215

In *Somn* 1.215, Philo compares the role and status of the divine Logos with those of the High Priest, and understands the Jewish cult allegorically. The term 'the firstborn son' (πρωτόγονος) in *Somn* 1.215 is juxtaposed with the concept of "High Priest," and perhaps, symbolises the supreme status of the divine Logos. However, it also seems that the concept of the firstborn son is also linked with μίμημα αἰσθητόν (perceptible copy). Therefore, the origin of the firstborn son is unclear in this verse.

369 Horbury argues that "rising" in *Conf* 63 refers to a messianic figure. See William Horbury, *Jewish Messianism and the Cult of Christ* (London: SCM, 1998), 94. See also Charlene McAfee Moss, *The Zechariah Tradition and the Gospel of Matthew* (BZNW 156; Berlin: Walter de Gruyter, 2008), 34–35. Hecht argues that a messianic term ("rising") is utilised symbolically to represent Logos in *Conf* 63. See Richard D. Hecht, "Philo and Messiah," in *Judaisms and their Messiahs at the turn of the Christian Era* (eds. Jacob Neusner, et al.; Cambridge: Cambridge University Press, 1987), 148.

370 Moss writes that the firstborn son in *Conf* 63 evokes Zech 12:10 ("They will weep and mourn over him as over their firstborn son"). See Moss, *The Zechariah Tradition*, 33.

3.14.4.4 *Agr* 51

In *Agr* 51, Logos is nominated as πρωτόγονος υἱός. God governs everything including the earth, the water, the air, the fire and living creatures. Logos as the firstborn son received the role for the holy care of "this herd" (ἡ ἐπιμέλεια τῆς ἱερᾶς ταύτης ἀγέλης), and the role is likened to viceroyship of the great king (μεγάλου βασιλέως ὕπαρχος). Πρωτόγονον υἱόν is an example of Philo's kinship metaphors, used in order to explain the role and the supreme status of Logos over all creatures.

In *Leg All* 3.175; *Det* 118; *Mig* 6; *Heres* 205; *Somn* 1.230, Philo addresses Logos as the eldest of all created things: e.g., "Manna is the divine Logos, the eldest (πρεσβύτατον) of all beings" (*Det* 118).[371] It is common in ancient literature that a divine being was called the eldest. Sophocles also addresses earth as the eldest of gods, and he states that earth is the immortal and the unwearied in *Antigone*, 332. In *Timaeus* 40c, Plato writes, "She [earth]… is creator of night and day, and is the first and eldest (πρώτη καὶ πρεσβυτάτη) of all the gods which have come into existence in heaven [my translation]." In this verse, earth was admired most of all because earth is the eldest among all the gods. The designation of Earth as the eldest can be literally understood since Earth is the primordial and oldest goddess in Greek myth.[372] On the other hand, Heracles, Dionysus (or Osiris) and Pan were regarded as the youngest gods in Greek myth by the ancient Greeks: "Among the Greeks, Heracles, Dionysus, and Pan are held to be the youngest of the gods [Loeb translation]" (Herodotus, 2.145.1).

Yet, the title of the eldest is also ascribed to the god who is not literally the oldest. For instance, in Plato, *Symposium* 178B, Eros is the first among all the gods (πρώτιστον μὲν ἔρωτα θεῶν μητίσατο πάντων; cf. Parmenides, *fr.* 132). In Diogenes Laertius, 4.5.26, Eros also refers to "the first of the immortal gods, the eldest of all the children whom old Erebus and queenly Night brought to birth in the depths beneath the wide Ocean." In the second century CE, Oppian also states that Eros is the oldest (παλαίτατος) among the blessed gods.[373] A similar concept is found in the 4th century Greek papyrus written (Anonymous, *Moral Maxims* in *Selected Papyri* 3, no. 116 [Loeb]): "Eros is the oldest (παλαίτατος) among all the gods." Eros is the son of Aphrodite and Ares, and he is not literally the oldest of the gods. Thus, the designation of Eros as the eldest (or the oldest) may denote that being the oldest is associated with certain positive attributes.

---

371 In *Ebr* 30 and *Fug* 109, God is the father of Logos. In *Fug* 109, Wisdom is the mother of Logos.

372 Hesiod, *Theogony*, 116–18.

373 Oppian, *Halieutica*, 4.23.

Thus, Logos as "the eldest" in *Agr* 51 does not simply denote the age of the Logos, but also indicates that Logos holds a higher rank than other creatures. In Greco-Roman society, the eldest had a higher status than his younger brothers. In *Moralia* 486F–487A, Plutarch exhorts that the eldest brother should take primacy in every matter over his other brothers. In Demosthenes, *Against Macartatus* 43.74, the eldest son was named after his grandfather because the name was fitting for the eldest son (ὥσπερ καὶ δίκαιόν ἐστιν), and it implies that the eldest son had some distinct status. The order of age contained a crucial cultural value in Greco-Roman society. Seniority was often associated with some higher status within human relationships.[374] In *Sacr* 77, Philo states, "By 'elder' is meant he that is worthy of honour and privilege and high place." Thus, the order of age was significant in the Greco-Roman world and related to singular qualities. The older brother had a higher rank amongst his brothers, and the seniority of the older brother was respected by his younger siblings.[375] Therefore, Logos as the eldest son in *Agr* 51 (perhaps, also in *Somn* 1.215) is associated with the seniority and the supreme status of Logos, and designating Logos as the firstborn son cannot be considered as a unique feature of Hellenistic Jewish speculation about Logos (or Wisdom). It was common that a divine figure was designated as the eldest in ancient literature.

3.14.4.5 *Conf* 124

On the other hand, the status of Logos in Philo's Hellenistic Jewish speculation is associated with the status given to Israel. In *Conf* 124, Philo states that Cain did not offer his first fruits, but Abel brought the eldest (πρεσβύτατον) of the flock to the altar. In this verse, Abel's offering of the eldest symbolises "confessing that even the causes which come higher in the chain of causation owe their existence to the Cause which is highest and first of all," and Philo adds, "The impious man thinks the opposite …"

3.14.4.6 *Conf* 145–46

In *Conf* 145–46, Philo considers the concept of sonship and the status of the firstborn son (πρωτόγονος):

374 For instance, *On the Embassy* 2.22, Aeschines writes "… as soon as we were come to Macedonia, we arranged among ourselves that at our audience with Philip the eldest should speak first, and the rest in the order of age [Loeb Translation]." This verse shows that the order of speech was arranged according to order of age, and it implies that the oldest person was respected and would have the right to speak first. In *Politics* 1.1252b, Aristotle says, "every household is under the royal rule of its eldest member [Loeb Translation]," and this verse connects seniority to authority.

375 Cf. Cicero, *Cato Maior de Senectute*, 38.

> But they who live in the knowledge of the One are rightly called "Sons of God," as Moses also acknowledges when he says, "Ye are sons of the Lord God" and "God who begat thee", and is not He himself thy father?" Indeed with those whose soul is thus disposed it follows that they hold moral beauty to be the only good, and this serves as a counterwork engineered by veteran warriors to fight the cause which makes Pleasure the end and to subvert and overthrow it. But if there be any as yet unfit to be called a Son of God, let him press to take his place under God's Firstborn (πρωτόγονος), the Word, who holds the status of the eldest (πρεσβύτατος) among the angels, their ruler as it were. And many names are his, for he is called, "the Beginning," and the Name of God, and His Word, and the Man after His image, and "the seer," that is Israel.
>
> Loeb translation

In this citation, Logos is called πρωτόγονος who holds the status of the eldest (πρεσβύτατος) among the angels.[376] Accordingly, it is likely that the status of the firstborn is related to the supremacy over the other angels. Furthermore, we find the identification of Logos with Israel in this context. Israel is the name of Logos in the last line. Birnbaum argues that the concept of Israel becomes abstract in this verse. We also find similar abstraction in *Somn* 1.175, where Philo addresses Jacob as Wisdom. Both Israel and Jacob are designated as Logos and Wisdom, and also the firstborn son.[377] We should note that various parallels between *The Prayer of Joseph* and *Conf* 146 are found, and these parallels can give us a clue on the meaning of the firstborn son in *Conf* 146:[378] 1) "angel of God" in *PrJos* and "the firstborn of angels" in *Conf* 146; 2) "ruling spirit" in *PrJos* and "archangel" in *Conf* 146; 3) "Israel" in *PrJos* and *Conf* 146; 4) "a man who sees God" in *PrJos* and "the seer" in *Conf* 146; 5) "firstborn of every living thing to whom God gives life" in *PrJos* and "His firstborn" in *Conf* 146; 6) "archangel of the power of the Lord" in *PrJos* and "archangel" in *Conf* 146; and

376 Cf. Jean Daniélou, *Philo of Alexandria* (trans. J.G. Colbert; James Clarke & Co, 2014), 121.

377 Philo illustrates Jacob as the heir of Abrahamic promise and inheritor of the four quarters of the world, in *Somn* 1.173–76, and describes Jacob as Wisdom in *Somn* 1.175. Philo also writes that every nation will be blessed through Jacob in *Somn* 1.177. Philo also platonically interprets the promise of return to the Land, and presents the foreign land outside the land of Palestine as "body" in *Somn* 1.181. After these interpretations, Logos is designated as High Priest in *Somn* 1.214, and as the firstborn son in *Somn* 1.230.

378 Birnbaum, *The Place of Judaism*, 75. It is Edmund Stein who first observed these similarities between *Conf* 146 and *PrJos*. See Edmund Stein, "Zur apokryphen Schrift 'Gebet Josephs,'" *Monatsschrift für Geschichte und Wissenschaft des Judentums* 81 (1937): 282–83. Similarly, Darrell D. Hannah, *Michale and Christ: Michael Traditions and Angel Christology in Early Christianity* (WUNT II/109; Tübingen: Mohr Siebeck, 1999), 89–90.

7) "chief captain among the sons of god" in *PrJos* and "archangel" in *Conf* 146. As for these similarities, Stein writes, "eine zufällige Übereinstimmung ist hier kaum denkbar." Yet, Stein assumes the priority of *Conf* 146,[379] but as Birnbaum notes, the date of *PrJos* is not clear, so it is unclear which one depends on whom.[380] Philo's designation of Logos as the firstborn son in *Conf* 145–46 could be rooted in a similar tradition about the angelomorphic Israel with *PrJos*, but some differences exist between *Conf* 146 and *PrJos*. Firstly, in *PrJos*, Israel is not designated as Logos, contrary to *Conf* 146. Secondly, in the extant portions of the *Prayer of Joseph*, Jacob and Israel are not described as the image of God.[381] As Robert Hayward notes, "Israel's equation with an angel is made indirectly via this Logos, who is the most senior of those beings and image of God." These differences lead us to infer that *PrJos* and *Conf* 146 did not directly rely on each other, but they merely share a similar tradition about heavenly Israel, and each author utilised the tradition according to their purposes and contexts.

Thus, on the basis of these parallels, it can be inferred that *Conf* 146 and *PrJos* share a similar tradition on heavenly Israel. Several scholars also observe that the title of the firstborn son in *PrJos* originated in Exod 4:22 (see section 3.9.2).[382] In *Conf* 146, Philo connects the names of the Logos to the title of Israel: "And many names are his, for he is called, 'the Beginning,' and the Name of God, and His Word, and the Man after His image, and 'the seer,' that is Israel." In *Conf* 146, Philo also mentions the title of Israel (i.e., the son of God) in *Conf* 146 (cf. Exod 4:22; Jer 31:9, 20; Hos 11:1; cf. Exod 6:6–8; Isa 63:16): "... they who live in the knowledge of the One are rightly called 'Sons of God,' as Moses also acknowledges." Furthermore, in *PrJos*, the title of the firstborn son is used as the title of heavenly Israel. So, in terms of the shared tradition about heavenly Israel as discussed above, it is probable that the title of the firstborn son in *Conf* 146 also originated in the title of Israel. Accordingly, it is a natural inference that the title of the firstborn son in *Conf* 146 is related to the title of Israel (i.e., the firstborn son of God (e.g., Exod 4:22; Jer 31:9)).[383]

Riemer Roukema maintains that, in Philo's writings, the designation of Logos as the firstborn son is not derived from LXX Exod 4:22, because Philo

379 Stein, "Gebet Josephs," 283.

380 Birnbaum, *The Place of Judaism*, 75.

381 C.T.R. Hayward, *Interpretations of the Name Israel in Ancient Judaism & some Early Christian Writings: From Victorious Athlete to Heavenly Champion* (Oxford: Oxford University Press, 2005), 198.

382 E.g., Smith, "The Prayer of Joseph," 268; Morray-Jones, "Shiur Koma Traditions," 561. See also section 3.9.2.

383 For the concept of Israel in Philo, see section 3.14.1.4.

uses πρωτότοκος nowhere in his writings "as a designation of the Logos."[384] Robert Hayward asserts that πρωτόγονος refers to a supernatural reality and is a different concept from πρωτότοκος in Philo's writings.[385] Fee and McDonough also argue that Philo's πρωτόγονος is not related to πρωτότοκος.[386] However, as discussed above, it seems that the title of πρωτόγονος in *Conf* 146 originated in the title of Israel (e.g., Exod 4:22; Jer 31:9), and shares a similar tradition with *PrJos*. In this vein, the term πρωτόγονος in *Conf* 146 can be related to πρωτότοκος which is the title of Israel in LXX Exod 4:22.

We must also bear in mind that Philo addressed Jacob and Israel as Wisdom and Logos, and that Israel is the seer of God endowed with Logos, and that this notion distinguishes Israel from other γένη like Egypt and Syria. Therefore, we conclude that Philo's designation of Logos as the firstborn son is associated with the status of Israel. This point is also confirmed in the analogous relationship between the patriarchs/Israel/the Levites and Logos which shares the same metaphors as follows:

The patriarchs/Israel/the Levites	**Logos**
Firstborn Son	Firstborn Son
Mediator (Abraham; *Migr* 120)	Mediator
Minister of God (Abraham; *Migr* 126; *Gig* 64)	Minister of God (*Migr* 175; *Heres* 234)
Wisdom (Jacob; *Somn* 1.175)	Wisdom
High Priest (*Spec Leg* 2.163–64)	High Priest (*Somn* 1.215)[a]
The seer of God (e.g., *Abr* 56–57)	The seer of God (*Conf* 146)

a The designation of Israel and Logos as the high priest may imply that Israel and Logos has a priestly role distinct from all others.

Thus, in Philo's writings, the patriarchs, Israel and the Levites form analogous relationships with Logos.[387] The function of the patriarchs, Israel and the Levites are contiguous with that of Logos. In this context, Philo's Hellenistic

384 Roukema, *Jesus, Gnosis and Dogma*, 152.

385 Hayward, *Interpretations of the Name Israel*, 200.

386 Fee, *Pauline Christology*, 297; Sean M. McDonough, *Christ as Creator: Origins of a New Testament Doctrine* (Oxford: Oxford University Press, 2009), 177.

387 Hayward notes that, in Philo's *Mut*, "Jacob–Israel appears as a 'boundary' figure, 'on the cusp,' as it were, of earth and heaven." See Hayward, *Interpretations of the Name Israel*, 167. Hays also writes that Logos is also a supernatural reality as a boundary figure between heaven and earth. See Hayward, *Interpretations of the Name Israel*, 161–64.

Jewish speculation about Logos is linked with the status and title given to Israel in *Conf* 146 (cf. *PrJos*).

Israel as the firstborn son is distinct from other γένη. Logos is also distinct from other creatures in the universe, and from bodily or irrational part in human beings. Thus, the status of Logos as the firstborn in *Conf* 146 is associated with Israel's superiority and privilege. The excellence of Logos is stressed in Philo's writings, but a similar excellence is also ascribed to Israel.[388] So, it seems that the designation of Logos as the firstborn son in *Conf* 146 is related to the status of Israel.[389]

To summarise, the meaning and the origin of Logos as the firstborn son is not monolithic, and can be categorised as follows. Firstly, in Hellenistic literature, a divine (or quasi-divine figure) was commonly designated as the eldest (πρεσβύτατος) which signifies the supreme status. In this vein, the firstborn son in Philo is used as a metaphor which stresses the pre-eminent status of Logos (cf. *Leg All* 3.175; *Det* 118; *Mig* 6; *Heres* 205; *Somn* 1.230). In *Agr* 51, πρεσβύτατος υἱός is employed as a kinship metaphor expressing the primacy of Logos. Secondly, in *Conf* 63, πρεσβύτατος υἱός, πρωτόγονος is related to the concept of archetype. Thirdly, in *Heres* 119, Logos' concept as the firstborn son originated in the Jewish cultic concept of the firstborn (πρωτότοκος) which refers to the first and supreme one. Fourthly, in *Conf* 146, the status of Logos as the firstborn son is associated with that of Israel. It seems that *Conf* 146 shares a similar tradition with *PrJos*. In addition, πρωτότοκος, πρεσβύτατος and πρωτόγονος are interchangeably used in Philo's literature in several cases. For instance, in *Sobr* 22, the firstborn (πρωτότοκος) is used together with the eldest (πρεσβύτατος) without distinction. In *Conf* 124, Abel's offering of the firstling is called πρεσβύτατος. In *Conf* 145–46, πρεσβύτατος and πρωτόγονος are employed together in the identical senses. Israel is addressed as πρωτόγονος (*Post* 63; *Fug* 208). Yet, it should be borne in mind that πρωτόγονος is rarely used when Philo uses the concept of the firstborn in a cultic sense. Πρωτότοκος is not used in the sense of archetype in Philo's writings. When the firstborn son means archetype, πρωτόγονος is used (*Conf* 63; cf. *Somn* 1.215).

388 See *Ebr* 36–7. Cf. Borgen, "Philo," 339.

389 Logos in Philo is pre-existent, and the designation of Logos as the firstborn in *Conf* 146 may also imply that Logos was born before all creation. So, perhaps, the title of the firstborn son in *Conf* 146 has a double force in the sense of the pre-existence and the status of Israel.

3.14.5 *Conclusion*

In this section, we have explored the concept of the firstborn son in Philo. In Philonic literature, the title of the firstborn son refers to the superiority of the Elect and the heirship of the Abrahamic promise, and is not ascribed to the Gentiles or the non-Elect. The title is used solely for the Elect, the Israelites, and the Levites, when the title is attributed to a specific person or people. In *Post* 62, the firstborn son as the title of Israel is understood in terms of inheritance (i.e., double portion), and this implies that Israel is the one who holds primogeniture amongst the nations. Philo philosophically and allegorically interprets the stories of blessing and curse, and these interpretations are concerned with Philo's elaborations about whom the firstborn sons are, and what 'being older' means. In Philo, the firstborn son refers to the status of the Elect. Philo adopted a universalistic interpretation on the meaning and the range of Israel in certain respects, but we should note that the notion of the firstborn son contains particularistic implications, because the status of the firstborn son is linked with that of the Elect (particularly, the patriarchs, Israel, and the Levites), and because the non-Elect such as Cain, Ham, Esau, and the Egyptians are described as innately inferior to the firstborn sons; as Abel, Shem, Jacob, the Israelites, and the Levites. Furthermore, the status of the firstborn is reinforced by the negative description of the non-Elect (i.e., by their being forsaken).

Philo employs the concept of the firstborn son to elaborate his election theology. The title of the firstborn son is sometimes associated with Israel's election and the primacy of the Elect, the Israelites, or the Levites over the non-Elect (par. *Post* 63). The prerogative of Israel in Philo's writing is linked to the Jews. We should also note that the status of the firstborn son is related to the innate rational quality of the ones who are designated as the firstborn son. The non-firstborn sons imply that they are innately undeserving as the firstborn son, or the Elect. That is, they are irrational, innately disqualified, intellectually inferior, and slaves. Israel and the Jews are elected by God as pre-eminent over the nations. Thus, the firstborn son is related to the elected status of Israel, and Israel is the Elect and special γένος in Philo's writings. In addition, when the firstborn son refers to Logos, the sources are various. Yet, in *Conf* 145–46, Philo's designation of Logos as the firstborn son is related to Israel's status as the firstborn son.

CHAPTER 4

Πρωτότοκος in the New Testament

4.1 Romans

In this chapter, we will explore the meaning of πρωτότοκος in Rom 8:29. For this purpose, we will first investigate the background of Romans (section 4.1.1) and the pre-Pauline tradition in Rom 8:29–30 (section 4.1.2), and then consider the concept of inheritance in Romans (section 4.1.3.1) and the meaning of 'the son' in Rom 8:3 and 32 (section 4.1.3.2).

4.1.1 *The Background*

Romans was written to the Jewish and Gentile congregations in Rome.[1] "Now I am speaking to you Gentiles" in Rom 11:13a signals that Gentile believers were among the letter-recipients. Yet, the Gospel which Paul wished to preach to "you who are in Rome" is both for the Jew and for the Greek in Rom 1:15–16,[2] and this implies that Paul includes the Jewish believers as his letter-recipients. Juxtapositions of Jewish and Roman names in Rom 16 also suggest that Romans was not written solely for the Gentile believers.[3]

Wolfgang Wiefel explains the background of Romans in terms of the Claudian expulsion of Jews from the city of Rome in CE 49.[4] Claudius expelled

---

1 Halvor Moxnes observes that the Roman churches consisted of Jews and Non-Jews. See Halvor Moxnes, *Theology in Conflict: Studies in Paul's Understanding of God in Romans* (Leiden: Brill, 1980), 97. It is difficult to infer the proportion of the Jewish and the Gentile believers at the churches in Rome. However, it is apparent that the Roman churches were not a single congregation unlike the Corinthian church. See Andrew D. Clarke, "Jew and Greek, Slave and Free, Male and Female: Paul's Theology of Ethnic, Social and Gender Inclusiveness in Romans 16," in *Rome in the Bible and the Early Church* (ed., Peter Oakes; Carlisle: Paternoster, 2002), 109. Also see Peter Lampe, *Christians at Rome in the First Two Centuries: From Paul to Valentinus* (London: T&T Clark, 2003), 74; Philip Esler, *Conflict and Identity in Romans: The Social Setting of Paul's Letters* (Minneapolis: Fortress, 2003), 111, 114–15; Klaus Haacker, *The Theology of Paul's Letter to the Romans* (Cambridge: CUP, 2003), 12.

2 Grieb notes that the complex arguments of Romans are based on the story of God's action in Christ, and that the sub-narratives of this story can be construed as the defence of God's righteousness (or his covenantal faithfulness). See A. Katherine Grieb, *The Story of Romans: A Narrative Defense of God's Righteousness* (Louisville: WJK, 2002), 24–25.

3 However, the primary recipients of Romans must be Gentile Christians. See Peter Oakes, *Reading Romans in Pompeii: Paul's Letter at Ground Level* (SPCK: London, 2009), 150.

4 Wolfgang Wiefel, "The Jewish Community in Ancient Rome and the Origins of Roman Christianity," in *The Romans Debate* (ed., K.P. Donfried; Peabody: Hendrickson, 1991), 85–101.

 | DOI:10.1163/9789004394940_005

Jews from Rome in response to disturbances which arose from a person called *Chrestus*.[5] If *Chrestus* refers to Christ (indeed, it is highly probable), it is plausible that the disturbances were triggered by the conflicts between the Jews and the Jewish Christians.[6] After the death of Claudius in CE 54, Jews were allowed to return to Rome. Consequently, it is probable that core members of the Christian communities in Rome would be replaced with the Gentile believers after the expulsion of the Jews in CE 49. However, the scope of the Claudian expulsion may be small, and we do not specifically know how the expulsion impacted on the Christian communities in Rome.[7] Accordingly, Wiefel's theory cannot be evidenced, even though his theory has some attractive implications.[8]

Yet, we can infer that Romans reflects some ethnic tensions inside the Roman churches.[9] In Rom 16:3–5, it is arguable that Priscilla and Aquila were not incorporated into the Gentile house church, and that there was a church that met in their house (κατ᾽οἶκον αὐτῶν ἐκκλησίαν).[10] It is highly probable that Rom 9–11 and Rom 14–15 reflect intra-tensions between Jewish and Gentile Christians in Rome.[11] A theme of reconciliation between Jewish and Gentile Christians underlies Rom 14:1–15:13,[12] particularly in the verses below.

> Accept one another, therefore, just as Christ has accepted you, for the glory of God. For I tell you that Christ has become a servant of the circumcised on behalf of the truth of God in order that he might confirm the promises given to the patriarchs, and in order that the Gentiles might

5 Suetonius, *Claudius*, 25.4: "The Jews, who by the instigation of one *Chrestus* were evermore tumultuous, he banished Rome." This happened in CE 41 or 49. The expulsion of the Jews were exercised twice in CE 41 and 49, and some scholars consider that the first banishment was a limited and short-term measure (perhaps, the ban of the right of gathering), and that the second is a broader and more thorough measure, namely, expulsion. See Dunn, *Romans 1–8*, xlv–liv. Cf. Acts 18:2.

6 Dunn, *Romans 1–8*, 60.

7 D.H. Slingerland, *Claudian Policymaking and the Early Imperial Representation of Judaism at Rome* (Atlanta: Scholars, 1997); Oakes, *Reading Romans*, 74.

8 However, through two expulsions of Jews in Rome (CE 19 and 49), it is probable that Jewish communities in Rome was turbulent even in Paul's era. See William S. Campbell, *Paul and the Creation of Christian Identity* (London: T&T Clark, 2008), 77. He writes, "[Paul] would still have been aware that at the centre of Roman administration and the visual embodiment of the imperial ideology any group, especially a Jewish one, which appeared to challenge Roman cultural and political domination would be in great danger."

9 Moxnes, *Theology in Conflict*, 78.

10 See Lampe, *Christians at Rome*, 74–75.

11 See Grieb, *The Story of Romans*, 7; Campbell, *Paul and the Creation of Christian Identity*, 76.

12 Cf. Rom 1:16; 2:10–11.

> glorify God for his mercy. As it is written, 'Therefore I will confess you among the Gentiles, and sing praises to your name'.
>
> ROM 15:7–9

Rom 15:7–13 is the conclusion to the body of the letter (1:16–15:13).[13] As we see above, in Rom 15:7, Paul reiterates the exhortation of Rom 14:1 in generic form, and tells the letter-recipients to accept one another in unity and harmony.[14] Thus, it is highly plausible that Romans reflect some intra-conflicts between Jewish and Gentile believers at Rome.

What does Paul say about the proper relationship between Jewish and Gentile believers in Romans? Did Paul write Romans in order to warn against the Gentile believers' sense of superiority to the Jewish believers? Does Paul advocate primacy of the Jewish believers in Romans? Although some scholars argue in favour of the primacy of Jews in Romans,[15] equality between Jews and Gentiles, and not the continuing primacy of Jews, is more clearly one of the key motifs of Romans. In Romans, Jews and Gentiles are equal in respect to sinfulness (1:18–3:20), justification (3:21–4:25), the new status in Christ (5:1–8:39), and the divine plan (9:1–11:36).[16] Paul gives this as the reason for his "eagerness to proclaim the gospel to you also who are in Rome" (1:15), and applies the need of the gospel to Jews and Gentiles alike: "For I am not ashamed of the gospel; it is the power of God for salvation to everyone who has faith, to the Jew first and also to the Greek" (1:16). Furthermore, Paul states that God shows no partiality in judgement and reward (2:11). Thus, Jews and Gentiles are equal in that both of them need the gospel and divine salvation.[17]

---

13 Joseph Fitzmyer, *Romans: A New Translation with Introduction and Commentary* (New York: Doubleday, 1993), 705–6. N.T. Wright also observes that Rom 15:7–13 is the climax of the entire letter, in N.T. Wright, *Climax of the Covenant*, (Minneapolis: Fortress, 1991), 235. Also see Robert Jewett, *Romans: A Commentary* (Minneapolis: Fortress, 2007), 501.

14 Oakes writes that, in Rom 15:7, Paul "asks his hearers to 'welcome one another,' writing in a context where he backs this up with points relating to Jews and Gentiles" (i.e., Rom 15:8–12). See Oakes, *Reading Romans*, 76. Indeed, the conflict between the Jews and the Gentiles results from their long-running enmities.

15 E.g., Markus Barth argues that Paul's view on Israel changed from negative to positive perspective. See Barth, *The People of God* (Sheffield: JSOT Press, 1983), 45; J. Christiaan Beker, *Paul the Apostle: The Triumph of God in Life and Thought* (Minneapolis: Fortress, 1980), 69–74; Richard H. Bell, *The Irrevocable Call of God: An Inquiry into Paul's Theology of Israel* (Tübingen: Mohr Siebeck, 2005), 421; Caroline J. Hodge, *If Sons, Then Heirs: A Study of Kinship and Ethnicity in the Letters of Paul* (Oxford: Oxford University Press), 66.

16 Daniel Jong-Sang Chae, *Paul as Apostle to the Gentiles: His Apostolic Self-Awareness and its Influence on the Soteriological Argument in Romans* (Carlisle: Paternoster, 1997).

17 Jouette Bassler also examines the notion of divine impartiality in the OT and the Jewish literature and argues that this concept provides the theological axiom in Romans and

Yet one may maintain that God's impartiality does not mean the equality of Jews and Gentiles, and that "first to the Jews and then to the Greeks" (Rom 1:16; 2:9–10; 3:1–4; cf. 11:18, 28–29) implies the Jews' higher rank over the Greeks.[18] Yet, this expression too can be interpreted in terms of the equality of Jews and Gentiles. Firstly, τέ implies the equality of Jews and Gentiles, because it neutralises πρῶτον.[19] Secondly, when Paul mentions "the Jews first" in 1:16 and 2:9–10, the context does not indicate that Jews are in primacy over the Gentiles. Instead, it may refer to temporal priority. In 2:9, divine judgment is given first in time to Jews, which cannot imply the primacy of Jews.[20] Moreover, παντί in Rom 1:16 demonstrates that the only condition for salvation is faith, and that this condition encompasses both Jews and Gentiles. Thus, the faith as the condition for salvation implies equality between Jews and Gentiles,[21] since salvation is based on faith in Christ, not on merit or ethnicity.

Alternatively, the idea of "the Jews first" may refer to the uniqueness[22] of Jews, not the primacy of Jews. Jews are unique in salvation history through election and the divine promise, which will finally accomplished (cf. Rom 11:1; 15:8). Their uniqueness does not necessarily signify their primacy. In Christ, Jews and Gentiles now share the privileges which were promised in the OT, and election in Romans does not provide a basis on which the Elect can boast of their primacy over the non-elect. Conversely, for Paul, the chosen are those who do not deserve to be elected (Rom 9–11), and the election removes the human boast.[23]

However, God's equitability to Jews and Gentiles does not mean that Jews and Gentiles were incorporated into 'a third race.' The Jewish identity is still valid in Christ, and the Jews are still a unique people. Yet, simultaneously, Jews

---

other Paul's letters. She mentions, "God accepts both Jew and Gentile without distinction on the common basis of faith." Bassler, *Divine Impartiality: Paul and a Theological Axiom* (Chico: Scholars, 1982), 187–88.

18 So, Dunn, *Romans 1–8*, 37. Cranfield also maintains that the paradox is the essence of Romans in that Romans asserts the gospel without distinction, but with primacy of the Jews. See C.E.B. Cranfield, *The Epistle to the Romans*, vol. 1 (Edinburgh: T&T Clark, 1975), 91. Cf. Cranfield, *The Epistle to the Romans*, 87.

19 So, Cranfield, *The Epistle to the Romans*, 91.

20 "Here will be anguish and distress for everyone who does evil, the Jew first and also the Greek, but glory and honor and peace for everyone who does good, the Jew first and also the Greek" in Rom 2:9–10.

21 Chae, *Paul as Apostle to the Gentiles*, 84. See also Grieb, *The Story of Romans*, 41–42; Nils A. Dahl, *Studies in Paul: Theology for the Early Christian Mission* (Minneapolis: Fortress, 1977), 79.

22 E.g., Rom 9:4–5; 11:1–2; 11:28–29.

23 See Sigurd Grundheim, *The Crux of Election: Paul's Critique of the Jewish Confidence in the Election of Israel* (Tübingen: Mohr Siebeck, 2005), 194, 197.

and Gentiles are equal in status. It seems that Paul did not intend to extinguish Jews' and Gentiles' ethnic identities and reconstruct a new ethnic identity into "a third race." For example, Paul states, in 1 Cor 7:18, "Was anyone at the time of his call already circumcised? Let him not seek to remove the marks of circumcision. Was anyone at the time of his call uncircumcised? Let him not seek circumcision." This verse implies that the original ethnic identities of the believers can co-exist with the new identity acquired after their conversions.[24]

In Romans, Paul does not entitle the church or the Gentile believers as Israelites. Jews are still addressed as Ἰσραηλῖται (Rom 9:4) and Paul exhorts them to accept the weak (most probably, Jewish Christians), and to respect their way of life (Rom 14:22–15:3). When, in Rom 14, Paul exhorts the believers in the Roman churches, Paul addresses them as "*your*" brothers, and the genitive "your" stresses and evokes the emotional attachment to the believers and the co-responsibility between brothers in Rome. In Rom 14, when Paul says not to judge the weak but to tolerate them, Paul asks in 14:10, "Why do you pass judgment on your brother? Or you, why do you despise *your* brother? For we will all stand before the judgment seat of God," and, in 14:15, "If *your* brother is being injured by what you eat, you are no longer walking in love. Do not let what you eat cause the ruin of one for whom Christ died." In these exhortations, Paul explains the relationship between believers as a kind of sibling relationship, which is evocative of the emotional attachment to and the co-responsibility with other siblings in the ancient family system.[25] The obligations of brothers include the mutual care and sharing of resources within the kinship group. Thus, Paul's sibling language in Rom 14 highlights his exhortations to the Gentiles to accept and tolerate the Jewish believers and, furthermore, recalls Paul's discussions on the family of Abraham in Rom 4.[26] In other words, the Gentile believers were expected to treat the Jewish believers as brothers in the family of Abraham, to offer mutual care to them and respect to their way of life.[27]

---

24 See also Esler, *Conflict and Identity in Romans*, 140.

25 David G. Horrell, "From ἀδελφοί to οἶκος θεοῦ: Social Transformation in Pauline Christianity," *JBL* 120 (2001): 309; Aasgaard, *My Beloved Brothers and Sisters: Christian Siblingship in Paul* (London: T&T Clark, 2004), 21; Klaus Schäfer, *Gemeinde als 'Bruderschaft': Ein Beitrag zum Kirchenverständnis des Paulus* (Frankfurt: Peter Lang, 1989), 319–21.

26 Cf. Robert Jewett, "The Law of the Co-Existence of Jews and Gentiles in Romans," *Int* 39 (1985): 341–56. In Amos 5:25, Amos states that Israel is a family (בַּיִת; οἶκος). See also Jacob Neusner, *Judaism and its Social Metaphors: Israel in the History of Jewish Thought* (Cambridge: Cambridge University Press, 1989), 112–44.

27 In addition, the imperial background of Romans should also be considered. Paul's political attitudes towards the Roman Empire has been disputed among scholars. Some scholars argue, on the basis of Rom 13:1–7, that Paul was in favour of or did not have

In summary, it is evident that one of Paul's primary purposes in Romans was to solve the internal discord between the Jewish and Gentile believers in Rome. It seems clear that the equality between the Jewish and the Gentile believers underlies one of the key messages in Romans. However, the original ethnic identities of the believers could co-exist with the new identity obtained after their conversions.

4.1.2 *Non-Pauline Tradition in Rom 8:29–30?*

For several reasons, some exegetes identify non-Pauline or pre-Pauline tradition in Rom 8:29–30.[28] Firstly, Otto Michel takes account of non-eschatological features in Rom 8:28–30 contrasting to typical eschatological accounts in Rom 8:19–27.[29] Michel writes that Rom 8:28–30 shows a certain independence in that Paul emphasises the action of God in Rom 8:28–30, which is contrasted with the previous eschatological images in 8:18–27. Particularly, according to Michel, Rom 8:28 seems like a precedent tradition which originated in ancient Judaism, and it also seems that 8:29–30 is the continuation (Fortführung) and

a specific interest in the Roman Empire. Yet, we can infer that Paul had some political interest in the Roman Empire. Firstly, Rome was a capital city of the Roman Empire and was regarded as a political central place in the Mediterranean world. If so, it is meaningful for Paul to send his letter to the believers who lived in Rome, and to discuss an issue on the ethnic equality and the status of Jews against this background. Secondly, some terms which was significant for the Roman imperial ideology are used in Romans: εὐαγγέλιον, πίστις, δικαιοσύνη, εἰρήνη and σωτήρ. In particular, εὐαγγέλιον is not used except for 2 Sam 4:10 in the LXX, and recalls the Roman εὐαγγέλιον which allegedly brought peace to the world. See Dieter Georgi. Moreover, in 1 Thess 5:3, Paul cites a Roman propaganda, peace and security (εἰρήνη καὶ ἀσφάλεια), and this indicates that he was not completely disinterested in the ideology of *Pax Romana*. See J.A.D. Weima, "'Peace and Security' (1 Thess 5.3): Prophetic Warning or Political Propaganda," *NTS* 58 (2012): 331–359. Thus, we cannot rule out the possibility that, in Romans, Paul was conscious of the Roman imperial ideology.

28 So, Ernst Käsemann, *An die Römer* (HNT 8a; Tübingen: Mohr Siebeck, 1973), 233; Jacob Jervell, *Imago Dei: Gen. 1.26f im Spätjudentum, in der Gnosis und in den paulinischen Briefen* (FRLANT 58; Göttingen: Vandenhoeck & Ruprecht, 1960), 272; Ulrich Luz, *Das Geschichtsverständnis des Paulus* (BEvT 49; München: Kaiser, 1968), 250–51; Wilckens, *Der Brief an die Römer (Röm 6–11)*, 151; Henning Paulsen, *Überlieferung und Auslegung in Römer 8* (WMANT 43; Neukirchen-Vluyn: Neukirchener Verlag, 1974), 156–61. Among Anglophon scholarship, see Thomas Tobin, *Paul's Rhetoric in the Contexts: The Argument of Romans* (Grand Rapids: Baker, 2005), 294–95. On the other hand, Osten-Sacken argues that 8:18–30 is the precedent tradition which originated in the Hellenistic Christianity. See P. von der Osten-Sacken, *Römer 8 als Beispiel paulinischer Soteriologie* (FRLANT 112; Göttingen: Vandenhoeck & Ruprecht, 1975), 78–104.

29 Otto Michel, *Der Brief an die Römer* (KEK 4; Göttingen: Vandenhoeck & Ruprecht, 1957), 274.

justification (Begründung) of Rom 8:28. Secondly, Ulrich Luz claims that Paul demonstrates glorification (freedom of the glory of the children of God) in 8:21 as a future eschatological event, but that glorification in 8:30 is articulated in the aorist tense (ἐδόξασεν).[30] Thirdly, the objects in 8:29–30 are the third person plural (those who …), but in the adjacent context, the objects are the first person plural "us." Fourthly, words rarely used in the undisputed Pauline letters are employed intensively in this passage: e.g., πρωτότοκος, προγινώσκω, προορίζω and σύμμορφος.

However, Rom 8:29–30 is not diverted from the thematic threads of Rom 8 and Paul's own theology.[31] Glorification (ἐδόξασεν) in Rom 8:30 fits with the discussions concerning glory in Rom 8:18, 21, and also corresponds with συνδοξασθῶμεν in Rom 8:17.[32] Paul understands transformation (μεταμορφούμεθα) and glorification in the present tense in 2 Cor 3:18,[33] and Paul also states, "So if anyone is in Christ, there is a new creation (2 Cor 5:17a)," in the present sense. Accordingly, Paul does not envisage that transformation and glorification are entirely future eschatological events. Εἰκών in Rom 8:29 appears in the undisputed Pauline letters (Rom 8:29; 1 Cor 15:49; 2 Cor 3:18; 4:4; cf. Col 1:15; Phil 2:6). The notion of conformity to Christ is also employed by Paul in the undisputed Pauline letters (1 Cor 15:49; Gal 4:19; Phil 3:10). Προγινώσκω and προορίζω are used in Rom 11:2 and 1 Cor 2:7 (cf. Eph 1:5, 11). Therefore, there is no reason to conclude that Rom 8:29–30 is a non-Pauline tradition or interpolation, and it is also plausible that Rom 8:29–30 reflects Paul's own theology, while it is probable that Paul could have utilised the theological concepts of the preceding traditions.[34]

In addition, Luz, Osten-Sacken and Wilckens contend that Rom 8:29b (εἰς τὸ εἶναι …) breaks up the sequence of five aorist verbs between Rom 8:29a and 8:30.[35] However, this break does not demonstrate that Paul cites a non-Pauline tradition in Rom 8:29b. Perhaps, 8:29b (εἰς τὸ εἶναι …) is Paul's parenthesis,[36] and was written in order to elucidate the ultimate goal of conformity to the

---

30 Luz, *Geschichtsverständnis*, 250–51.

31 Cf. Andrzej Gieniusz, *Romans 8:18–30: Suffering Does Not Thwart the Future Glory* (USFISFCJ 9; Atlanta: Scholars, 1999), 80.

32 J. Kürzinger, "σύμμορφος τῆς εἰκόνος τοῦ υἱοῦ αὐτοῦ (Rom 8,29)," *BZ* 2 (1958): 296.

33 Seyoon Kim, *The Origin of Paul's Gospel* (WUNT II/4; Tübingen: Mohr Siebeck, 1981), 254. Cf. 2 Cor 3:18.

34 If Paul utilised a preceding tradition in Rom 8:29, the tradition may be linked with an early Christian baptismal tradition. See Käsemann, *An die Römer*, 233; Luz, *Das Geschichtsverständnis des Paulus*, 251; Jervell, *Imago Dei*, 275.

35 Luz, *Geschichtsverständnis*, 251; Osten-Sacken, *Römer 8*, 69; Wilckens, *Der Brief an die Römer (Röm 6–11)*, 165.

36 For an example of Paul's parenthesis, see Rom 9:5b.

image of the son of God in 8:29a.[37] Again, even though it is possible that Rom 8:29b originated in a pre-Pauline tradition, Paul could also have utilised the preceding tradition for his own purpose.

4.1.3 *The Meaning of the Firstborn Son in Rom 8:29b*

4.1.3.1 Inheritance in Rom 4 and 8

In order to understand the meaning of the firstborn son in Rom 8:29, we should also consider the inheritance motif in Romans. The story of Israel is one of the significant sub-narratives in Romans.[38] God elected Israel (Rom 9:4–5), and Israel was captivated by the universal power of sin (Rom 3:9). The eschatological saving action of God is performed for Israel (Rom 15:8–9), and God remains sincere to his people. The Gentiles who believe in the "servant to the circumcised" (i.e., Christ) take part in the story of Israel (e.g., 11:17–24; 15:8–10, 27).[39] The story of Israel in Romans is also closely associated with a question: "Who are the true descendants of Abraham?" As Morna D. Hooker notes, "The belief that gentiles have been incorporated into the people of God is an essential part of Paul's 'story' of how God's purpose for the world is being accomplished."[40] The promise of inheritance originally granted to Israel was fulfilled in Christ, and the Gentile believers as well as the Jewish believers can be the true descendants of Abraham (Rom 4) according to the Spirit[41] and grace.[42] Paul elucidates who the true seed of Abraham is in Rom 4 and 9:6–7. The true seed of Abraham will inherit the promise given to Abraham as an heir of the entire world (Rom 4:13–14). Paul also states that all of the physical children of Abraham are not regarded as his true seed (Rom 9:6–7). The Jews and the Gentiles all are under accusation and sin, and they are justified by faith, not by works of law

37 As Mayordomo observes, Paul's writing style differs from modern logical styles. See Moises Mayordomo, *Argumentiert Paulus logisch?: Eine Analyse vor dem Hintergrund antiker Logik* (WUNT 1/188; Tübingen: Mohr Siebeck, 2005), 241.

38 Bruce W. Longenecker, "Sharing in Their Spiritual Blessings?: The Stories of Israel in Galatians and Romans," in *Narrative Dynamics in Paul: A Critical Assessment* (ed. B.W. Longenecker; Louisville: WJK, 2002), 58–64. Bruce Longenecker notes two kinds of linearity in Romans. Firstly, ethnic Israel has a special relationship with God in covenantal linearity (9:4–6, 11:28 (cf. 3:1–2)). Secondly, Gentile Christians participate in elective grace given to ethnic Israel in organic linearity (11:17–24).

39 Longenecker, "Sharing in Their Spiritual Blessings?" 73–74.

40 Morna D. Hooker, "'Heirs of Abraham': The Gentiles' Role in Israel's Story: A Response to Bruce W. Longenecker," in *Narrative Dynamics in Paul*, 96. See also Grieb, *The Story of Romans*, 50–51. However, Grieb does not observe the significance of the motif of inheritance.

41 Grieb, *The Story of Romans*, 50.

42 N.T. Wright, "Romans and the Theology of Paul," in *Pauline Theology, vol. 3* (eds. D.M. Hay and E.E. Johnson; Minneapolis: Fortress, 1995), 40.

(3:21–28). In Rom 4, Abraham is first and foremost revealed as the model justified by faith, not by works of law. Gentile Christians are also justified by faith, and they can claim that Abraham is their ancestor, because Abraham was justified by faith while uncircumcised. In this vein, Paul considers that Abraham's offspring extends to the uncircumcised (Gentile Christians).[43] Jewish and Gentile Christians alike are addressed as children of God and heirs in Rom 8:17, and were incorporated into the family of God as adoptive sons (8:15, 23; 9:4). The eschatological blessings (8:17, 28–30) are also given to Gentile Christians without discrimination. Therefore, "Who are the true heirs of divine promise (or the true seed of Abraham)?" was one of Paul's key questions in Romans.[44]

In Rom 4:1, Paul addresses Abraham as "our ancestor according to the flesh," but also presents Abraham as the prototype of Jewish and Gentile Christians alike. It is difficult to infer the proportion of the Jewish and the Gentile believers at the churches in Rome, but it must have been important to embrace cultural diversity when different races met each other at the Roman churches.[45] In Rom 4, Paul re-categorises Jewish and Gentile groups in conflict into a common in-group identity through designating Abraham as the common ancestor of Jewish and Gentile Christians. So, "he [Paul] presents Abraham not as a figure who gathers in non-Judeans and excludes Judeans, but as one who incorporates both social categories."[46] In this context, Abraham's blessings are given to Jewish and Gentile Christians alike in Rom 4.[47]

Romans 4 illustrates the family of Abraham.[48] Paul introduces Abraham as our father as described in Josephus, *Ant* 1. 158; *Odes* 9:55, 73; *4 Macc* 16:20; 17:6; *GkApEzra* 2:6; 3:10, which is modified by "according to the flesh" in Rom 4:1, and it allows us to conclude that Paul envisages Abraham as the father of the Jews.

43 Andrew T. Lincoln, "The Stories of Predecessors and Inheritors in Galatians and Romans," in *Narrative Dynamics in Paul* (ed. B.W. Longenecker; Louisville: WJK, 2002), 184–89.

44 This work does not deny that Romans deals with the universal human dilemma. In Romans, Paul answers the following questions: "How, in the face of coming judgment, can anyone (Jew and Gentile) find 'salvation'? How (in other words) can sinners find a gracious God?" Westerholm writes that, in Romans, Paul answers, "God shows himself gracious by providing, in Christ, justification for all (Jew and Gentile alike) who believe." See Stephen Westerholm, *Justification Reconsidered: Rethinking a Pauline Theme* (Grand Rapids: Eerdmans, 2013), 21. In Romans, a Gentile problem is intertwined with the problem of essential sinfulness of humankind, and making too sharp antithesis between these two problems can be a false dichotomy.

45 Possibly, the Roman churches consisted of the Jews and the non-Jews. See section 4.1.1.

46 Esler, *Conflict and Identity in Romans*, 189.

47 Dahl, *Studies in Paul*, 129.

48 Orrey McFarland, "Whose Abraham, Which Promise? Genesis 15.6 in Philo's *De Virtutibus* and Romans 4," *JSNT* 35 (2012): 108; Michael Cranford, "Abraham in Romans 4: The Father of All Who Believe," *NTS* 41 (1995): 88.

Paul also states that Abraham is the father of the circumcised and the uncircumcised in Rom 4:11–12. This leads us to a conclusion that Abraham's being πατὴρ πάντων ἡμῶν in Rom 4:16 means that he is the father of the circumcised and the uncircumcised alike and that the Gentile believers belong to the family of Abraham.[49]

Rom 4 is linked with Rom 8 in some respects. The same kinship language is used in Rom 4 and 8: father (Abraham as father in 4:1, 11, 12, 18; God as father in 8:15); and heir in 4:13, 14; 8:17 (cf. seed in 4:13, 18). "Εἰς τὸ εἶναι αὐτὸν πρωτότοκον" in Rom 8:29 evokes "τὸ κληρονόμον αὐτὸν εἶναι κόσμου" in 4:13. The two chapters (Rom 4 and 8) contain discussions concerning inheritance. In Rom 4:13, the descendant of Abraham inherits the world (τὸ κληρονόμον αὐτὸν εἶναι κόσμου, ἀλλὰ διὰ δικαιοσύνης πίστεως), and Christ is designated as the firstborn son in Rom 8:29. Gentile Christians do not have to become Jews in order to be heirs of the promise. Rather, they receive inheritance in union with Christ as joint-heirs of Christ (8:17) according to the Spirit. The Jewish and Gentile believers alike are given "τὰ πάντα" by God in Rom 8:32. It is highly likely that "τὰ πάντα" in Rom 8:32 reflects "κόσμος" in 4:13.[50] Inheriting the world in *1 En* 5:7; *4 Ezra* 6:59; *Sir* 44:21; *Jub* 22:14; 32:19; 1Q34+1Q34bis 3 ii 3 is associated with universal sovereignty. The promise that Israel would rule over the whole world is also found in *Jub* 22:11–12 and 32:18–19. Thus, in Romans, Gentile Christians take part in the promise previously given exclusively to the Jews.

The heir (singular) of the Abrahamic promise in Rom 4:13 is Christ. Jesus is a Jew, the representative of Israel and the heir of the promise. The Gentile believers share in the inheritance given to the Jews as the joint-heirs of Christ though union with Christ in Rom 8:17. Thus, Rom 4 discusses the children of Abraham, and in Rom 8, the children of God is delineated, and Paul returns to the discussion about the true descendants of Abraham in Rom 9:7. In this context, it seems that the family of Abraham in Rom 4 refers to the same entity with the family of God in Romans 8. So, Rom 4 and Rom 8 contain analogous discussions concerning who the true heirs are, and should be read in terms of sub-narratives relating to Israel's inheritance.

In addition, we should also observe that Rom 8:28–30 is linked with Rom 8:17. Shared elements between Rom 8:17 and Rom 8:28–30 can be demonstrated as below:

---

49 Nils Dahl, *Studies in Paul: Theology for the Early Christian Mission* (Minneapolis: Fortress, 1977), 129.

50 So, Wilckens, *Röm 6–11*, 172; Otto Michel, *An die Römer*, 280; James M. Scott, *Adoption as Sons of God: An Exegetical Investigation into the Background of ΥΙΟΘΕΣΙΑ in the Pauline Corpus* (WUNT II/48; Tübingen: Mohr Siebeck, 1992), 249; Mark Forman, *The Politics of Inheritance in Romans* (SNTSMS 148; Cambridge: Cambridge University Press, 2011), 106–7.

Shared elements	Rom 8:17	Rom 8:28–30
Family terms	τέκνα κληρονόμοι συγκληρονόμοι	υἱοῦ αὐτοῦ (8:29) πρωτότοκον (8:29) ἀδελφοῖς (8:29)
Prefix "συν-" words	συγκληρονόμοι συμπάσχομεν συνδοξασθῶμεν	συνεργεῖ (8:28) συμμόρφους (8:29)
Glorification and cognate words	συνδοξασθῶμεν	ἐδόξασεν (8:30)

As shown above, we find some shared elements in Rom 8:17 and 8:28–30. Firstly, whilst words with the συν-prefix do not occur in 8:18–25 except for 8:22, συνεργεῖ and συμμόρφους appear in 8:28–29. Secondly, family language is found in Rom 8:17 and 8:29. Moreover, αὐτόν in Rom 8:29 refers back to Christ in Rom 8:17. We should note that there is no explicit mention of Christ and no Christological discussion in Rom 8:18–27. Αὐτόν in Rom 8:29 is the first reference to Christ since the mention of συγκληρονόμοι δὲ Χριστοῦ in Rom 8:17, so αὐτόν in Rom 8:29 points back to Christ in Rom 8:17. In other words, Christ as "the firstborn son among many brothers" in Rom 8:29 corresponds to the joint-heir in Rom 8:17. This point enables us to read Rom 8:29 in reference to the motif of inheritance in Rom 8:17. Before specifically considering the meaning of the firstborn son in Rom 8:29, we will briefly explore the meaning of "his own son" in Rom 8:32.

4.1.3.2 His Own Son in Rom 8:32

The origin of Paul's Son Christology is a notoriously difficult issue. So, the comprehensive research of the origin of 'the son' title is beyond the scope of this work. The origin of the son of God in the NT can be associated with Jesus' self-consciousness, Wisdom, Israel or messianic sonship, and some contemporary scholars focus on royal messianic rhetoric, particularly after publications of the Dead Sea Scrolls.[51] For instance, Ulrich Müller argues that the title of the

51 Cf. John 1:49. Particularly see 4Q246. See John J. Collins, *The Scepter and The Star: The Messiahs of the Dead Sea Scrolls and Other Ancient Literature* (Grand Rapids: Eerdmans, 2010). As with this usage in Jewish literature outside DSS, see *4 Ezra* 7:28; 13:32, 37, 52; 14:9.

son of God originated in a messianic title,[52] and that the title of the son of God in Rom 1:3 signals that early Christians understood that crucified Christ was raised by God and that Christ was the Davidic son of God on the basis of 2 Sam 7:14 and Ps 2:7.[53] C.F.D. Moule also writes that the son of God in Paul's letters is rooted in the concept of the messianic son of God. Moule states that the son of God in the era of Jesus was an "actual synonym for the Messiah,"[54] and that another tradition relating to the angelic son of God was later merged with this original meaning.[55] Thus, some recent scholars tend to find the origin of the son of God Christology in Jewish messianic tradition.

Yet, there are some aspects in the son of God Christology in Rom 8:32 which cannot be fully explained by the messianic definition. The son in Rom 8:32 should be considered in the context of 'surrender (or giving up) formula:' the reason for the surrender (God's love) + the verb of the surrender (παραδίδωμι or δίδωμι) + the object of the surrender (the son); (e.g., John 3:16, Rom 8:32, Gal 2:20, Rom 5:10, 1 John 4:10).[56] In this vein, the similarity of the pattern in John 3:16 and Rom 8:32 is conspicuous:

> οὕτως γὰρ ἠγάπησεν ὁ θεὸς τὸν κόσμον, ὥστε τὸν υἱὸν τὸν μονογενῆ ἔδωκεν, ἵνα πᾶς ὁ πιστεύων εἰς αὐτὸν μὴ ἀπόληται ἀλλ᾽ ἔχῃ ζωὴν αἰώνιον.
>
> JOHN 3:16

> ὅς γε τοῦ ἰδίου υἱοῦ οὐκ ἐφείσατο ἀλλ᾽ ὑπὲρ ἡμῶν πάντων παρέδωκεν αὐτόν, πῶς οὐχὶ καὶ σὺν αὐτῷ τὰ πάντα ἡμῖν χαρίσεται.
>
> ROM 8:32

Similar patterns are found in both verses: the verbs of giving up (παραδίδωμι and δίδωμι) are used and the object of the surrender is the son (τὸν υἱὸν). These similar patterns may indicate that the formula with regard to the

52 Ulich B. Müller, "'Sohn Gottes'—ein messianischer Hoheitstitel Jesu," *ZNW* 87 (1996): 1–32. See also H.-W. Kuhn, "Rom 1,3f und der davidische Messias als Gottessohn in den Qumrantexten," in *Lese-Zeichen für Annelies Findeiss zum 65. Geburstags am 15. März 1984* (eds. C. Burchard and G. Theissen; Heidelberg: Wissenschaftlih-theologisches Seminar, 1984), 103–13. Likewise, A. Yarbro Collins and J.J. Collins also states, "… [Paul's] portrayal of Jesus as the son of God is closely related to his status as messiah," in Collins and Collins, *King and Messiah as Son of God: Divine, Human, and Angelic Messianic Figures in Biblical and Related Literature* (Grand Rapids: Eerdmans, 2008), 122.

53 Müller, "Sohn Gottes," 7. See also Georg Strecker, *Theology of the New Testament* (ed. Friedrich W. Horn; trans. M. Eugene Boring; Louisville: WJK, 2000), 81–82.

54 Moule, *The Origin of Christology*, 28.

55 Moule, *The Origin of Christology*, 30–31.

56 Werner R. Kramer, *Christ, Lord, Son of God* (trans. Brian Hardy; London: SCM, 1966), 114.

Rom 8:32	LXX Gen 22
οὐκ ἐφείσατο	οὐκ ἐφείσω (vv. 12, 16)
τοῦ ἰδίου υἱοῦ	τοῦ υἱοῦ σου τοῦ ἀγαπητοῦ (vv. 12, 16)

surrender of the son of God was broadly confessed in early Christianity. What, then, is the origin of this confession? It is widely argued that, when the verb παραδίδωμι refers to the suffering and the crucifixion of Christ, it originates in LXX Isa 53:6, 12.[57] Yet, the one who was surrendered in LXX Isa 53:6, 12 is the servant of the Lord, not the son of God.

So, we should consider where the son of God in the surrender formula originate, because the title of the son is consistently used with the verb of giving up in the surrender formula (e.g., John 3:16; Rom 8:32). For this purpose, we need to examine an intriguing allusion to the Akedah story in Rom 8:32.[58]

Romans 8:32 and LXX Gen 22:12, 16 share the same verb (φείδομαι) and indicate "not sparing the son" in common. Daniel Schwartz claims that Rom 8:32 alludes to the vengeance story of Gibeonites in 2 Sam 21:1–9.[59] However, it is unreasonable to assume that Paul envisions the story of Gibeonites in

57 Cilliers Breytenbach, "The Septuagint Version of Isaiah 53 and the Early Christian Formula 'He Was Delivered for Our Trespasses'," in *Grace, Reconciliation, Concord: The Death of Christ in Graeco-Roman Metaphors* (NovTSup 135; Leiden: Brill, 2010), 84; Martin Karrer, *Jesus Christus im Neuen Testament* (Grundrisse zum Neuen Testament; Göttingen: Vandenhoeck & Ruprecht, 1998), 82–83.

58 This allusion has been observed by many scholars. For example, Thomas Söding, "Sühne durch Stellvertretung: Zur zentralen Deutung des Todes Jesu in Römerbrief," in *Deutungen des Todes Jesu in Neuen Testament* (WUNT I/181; eds. Jörg Frey and Jens Schröter; Tübingen: Mohr Siebeck, 2005), 394; Helmut Merklein, *Studien zu Jesus und Paulus II* (Tübingen: Mohr Siebeck, 1998), 32; Oscar Cullmann, *The Christology of the New Testament* (London: SCM, 1959), 292–93; W. Sanday and A.C. Headlam, *The Epistle to the Romans* (Edinburgh: T&T Clark, 1902), 219; Alan Segal, "'He who did not spare his son': Jesus, Paul and the Aqedah," in *From Jesus to Paul: Studies in Honour of Francis Wright Beare* (eds. P. Richardson and J.C. Hurd; Waterloo: Wilfrid Laurier University, 1984), 169–84; N.A. Dahl, "The Atonement-An Adequate Reward for the Akedah? (Ro 8:32)," in *Neotestamentica et Semitica: Studies in Honour of Matthew Black* (ed., E.E. Ellis and Max E. Wilcox; Edinburgh: T&T Clark, 1969), 15–16; Peter V.D. Osten-Sacken, *Römer 8 als Beispiel paulinischer Soteriologie* (FRLANT 112; Göttingen: Vandenhoeck & Ruprecht, 1975), 310; Otto Michel, *Die Brief an die Römer* (KEK; Göttingen: Vandenhoeck & Ruprecht, 1955), 214; Hans-Joachim Schoeps, *Paul: the Theology of the Apostle in the Light of Jewish Religious History* (London: Lutterworth, 1961), 148.

59 D.R. Schwartz, "Two Pauline Allusions to the Redemptive Mechanism of the Crucifixion," *JBL* 102 (1983): 263–66.

Rom 8:32, which is unfitting to the flow of Romans 8. Furthermore, David *spared* Mephibosheth (2 Sam 21:7), whereas Abraham and God did *not spare* Isaac and Jesus. Also, Mephibosheth was not in the filial relationship to David, whereas Isaac and Jesus are addressed respectively as Abraham' son and God's son. Therefore, Schwartz's claim remains unconvincing. Instead, most scholars note an allusion of the Aqedah tradition in Rom 8:32.[60] Thus, it seems clear that Paul envisages the Aqedah tradition in Rom 8:32.

Nils Dahl argues that the ancient Aqedah story contains the implication of the atonement, and that the Aqedah allusion in Rom 8:32 can be related to the Aqedah tradition in terms of Jesus' atoning death.[61] Yet, it is not clear that the Aqedah tradition in the NT and the second temple literature was interpreted in the context of the atonement. So, Dahl's interpretation was not broadly accepted by scholars.[62]

Rather, 'his own son' in Rom 8:32 is not merely connected to Isaac, but also to a representative of Israel and an heir of promise in Jewish literature. Firstly, some ancient Jews understood the Aqedah story as a *Vorlage* that the Israelite firstborn sons were saved, and linked it with the Passover story. For instance, the author of *Jubilees* considers Isaac as the firstborn son in the Aqedah story (*Jub* 18:11). In *Jub* 18:11, Isaac is explicitly addressed as the firstborn son, and in *Jub* 18:17–19, the Aqedah story is connected to the seven-day festival, and the only seven-day festival is the Passover festival.[63] So, the author of *Jubilees* interprets the Aqedah story in light of the Passover story (more specifically, see section on *Jub* 18:9–16 in this work). The link between the Aqedah and the Passover story is also found in 4Q225, *Exod. Rab.* 15:11, and *b. Ros. Has* 10b–11a. Thus, the tradition which links the Passover story with the Aqedah narrative existed in Second Temple Judaism.[64] In this tradition, the Aqedah story functions to prefigure the Passover story and to foreshadow that God would protect the Israelite firstborn sons under divine favour in Exodus, as God protected Isaac. Isaac in this tradition is not simply the son of Abraham, but also the representative of Israel. That is, the Aqedah narrative is also the story of the threat

60 E.g., Sanday and Headlam, *Romans*, 219; Larry W. Hurtado, *Lord Jesus Christ: Devotion to Jesus in Earliest Christianity* (Grand Rapids: Eerdmans, 2005), 105; Wilckens, *Röm 6–11*, 172; Mark Forman, *The Politics of Inheritance in Romans* (Cambridge: CUP, 2011), 106–7.

61 Dahl, "Atonement," 15–29. Cf. J. Swetnam, *Jesus and Isaac: A Study of the Epistle to the Hebrews in the Light of the Aqedah* (AnBib 94; Rome: Biblical Institute, 1981), 10.

62 E.g., Robert J. Daly, "The Soteriological Significance of the Sacrifice of Isaac," *CBQ* 39 (1977): 74. The following study argues that the Aqedah tradition in the second temple period does not contain the atoning implication. P.R. Davies and B.D. Chilton, "The Aqedah: A Revised Tradition History," *CBQ* 40 (1978): 514–36.

63 Levenson, *The Death and Resurrection of the Beloved Son*, 177.

64 Cf. Halpern-Amaru, "A Note on Isaac," 129.

given to the heir of the promise. So, Isaac is a representative of Israel and an heir of promise in this context. Understood along these lines, it can be said that 'his own son' in Rom 8:32 evokes Israel.

Secondly, the Aqedah allusion in Rom 8:32a is used together with the expression πῶς οὐχὶ καὶ σὺν αὐτῷ τὰ πάντα ἡμῖν χαρίσεται (8:32b). Giving everything in Rom 8:32b recalls Paul's mention of inheriting the world in Rom 4:13.[65] Isaac is the representative of Israel in *LAB* 18:5, and the Aqedah story is closely linked with the heirship of Israel in *LAB* 18 (see section 3.10.2). In 4Q475 line 7, we find the mention that God will let the beloved son inherit all: "[...] beloved son and he will let him inherit it all (בן אהוב והורישו את כולה)." In this verse, the beloved son is evocative of Isaac in the Aqedah story (LXX Gen 22:12, 16: τοῦ υἱοῦ σου τοῦ ἀγαπητοῦ), and perhaps refers to Israel, and is directly connected to the motif of inheriting all.[66] Thus, some ancient Aqedah narratives are overlapped with the story of Exodus, and Isaac or the beloved son refers to the heir of promise. It is notable that the motif of inheritance is referenced in the context of the Aqedah allusion in Rom 8:32. In this vein, the son in Rom 8:32 can refer to the heir of promise.

Thirdly, whereas Rom 8:32 is the Aqedah allusion, Rom 8:32 can also be related to Rom 11:21 in a lexical perspective: εἰ γὰρ ὁ θεὸς τῶν κατὰ φύσιν κλάδων οὐκ ἐφείσατο, μή πως οὐδὲ σοῦ φείσεται (Rom 11:21).[67] We detect a certain pattern between 8:32 and 11:21: God did not spare his son (8:32) and also the natural branches (i.e., Israel in 11:21). If we admit the lexical connection between two verses, the Aqedah allusion in Rom 8:32 can be inevitably linked with the notion of Israel. Therefore, the son in Rom 8:32 is connected to the sonship of Isaac in the Aqedah story, and also to the sonship of Israel. So, "his own son" in Rom 8:32 corresponds to the descendant of Abraham who inherits the world in 4:13, in that both are linked with Isaac.

To summarise, the son of God in Rom 8:32 can be interpreted in the story of Israel and her inheritance (Rom 8:14, 15, 29, 32; cf. Rom 4:13). Specifically, "his own son" in 8:32 is linked with the Aqedah story, and refers to Jesus Christ as the heir of promise.

---

65 E.g., Wilckens, *Röm 6–11*, 172; Otto Michel, *An die Römer*, 280; Käsemann, *An die Römer*, 230. Paul may focus on all things necessary for believers' glorious future in Rom 8:32, so it is certain that the motif of dominion is included in "τὰ πάντα" in Rom 8:32.

66 Likewise, in LXX Jer 38:20, Israel is designated as υἱὸς ἀγαπητὸς, and this title is linked with the title of πρωτότοκός as the title of Israel (LXX Jer 38:9) and the motif of returning to the Promised Land (LXX Jer 38:16).

67 Richard B. Hays, *Echoes of Scripture in the Letters of Paul* (New Haven: Yale University Press, 1989), 61–62.

4.1.3.3 The Firstborn Son in Rom 8:29

Let us consider the immediate context of Rom 8:29. Rom 8:18–30 is usually viewed as a climax of Rom 6–8 and further, a climax of Rom 1:18–8:30.[68] Rom 8:18–30 foreshadows Paul's discussion in Rom 9–11: Christians and Jews are described in the same terms (brothers (8:29 and 9:3), adoption (8:15, 23 and 9:4), children of God (8:16–17 and 9:8), the glory (8:18 and 9:4), calling (8:28 and 9:7, 24), election (8:28, 33 and 9:11)).[69] Rom 8:28c states "τοῖς κατὰ πρόθεσιν κλητοῖς οὖσιν" (those who love God are called according to his purpose), and the calling in Rom 8:28c is elucidated in Rom 8:30: "οὓς δὲ προώρισεν, τούτους καὶ ἐκάλεσεν· καὶ οὓς ἐκάλεσεν, τούτους καὶ ἐδικαίωσεν ..." Rom 8:29–30 following ὅτι in Rom 8:29 forms a conclusion in terms of certainty of the future glory delineated in Rom 8:18–30, and 8:29 also elaborates that the purpose (πρόθεσις) in Rom 8:28 is Christ-centered.[70]

Πρωτότοκος in Rom 8:29 is referenced in the context of election (κλητοῖς in Rom 8:28; ὅτι οὓς προέγνω, καὶ προώρισεν in Rom 8:29; ἐκάλεσεν in Rom 8:30; and κατὰ ἐκλεκτῶν θεοῦ in Rom 8:33) and inheritance (κληρονόμοι, συγκληρονόμοι in Rom 8:17). In this context, we should consider that the notion of the firstborn son in Rom 8:29 is overlapped with the concept of inheritance. In Jewish literature, Israel as the firstborn son is God's legitimate heir in respect of possession of Palestine or the entire world (see chapter 3). Israel's title as the firstborn son offers a reason as to why the Israelites are entitled to possess Palestine or the entire world. The usage of the firstborn son as the heir of divine promise fits well with the context of Rom 8 surrounding inheritance, and the firstborn son as the divine heir in Rom 8:29 recalls the notion of the seed (σπέρμα; singular) of the promise in Rom 4:13. In addition, these motifs match well with the concept of sonship and inheritance in Rom 8:32 discussed in the previous section.

Furthermore, the allusions to Exodus (or the second Exodus) in Rom 8 advocate our interpretation. The motif of enslavement (δουλείας) in Rom 8:15 is reminiscent of the Exodus motif (e.g., δουλείας in LXX Exod 20:1).[71] The groaning of Israel (cf. Rom 8:22) is also a central motif in the Exodus account (Exod 2:23, 24),[72] and the groaning of the Spirit in Rom 8:26 may be an echo of

---

68 E.g., Andrzej Gieniusz, *Romans 8:18–30: "Suffering Does not Thwart the Future Glory"* (USFISFCJ; Atlanta: Scholars, 1999), 51–52; Dunn, *Romans 1–8*, 467.

69 Cf. Nanos, *The Mystery of Romans*, 112.

70 Wilhelm Thüsing, *Per Christum in Deum: Studien zum Verhältnis von Christozentrik und Theozentrik in den paulinischen Hauptbriefen* (NTAbh 1; Münster: Aschendorff, 1965), 124. See also Dunn, *Romans 1–8*, 466–67; Gieniusz, *Romans 8:18–30*, 268.

71 Sylvia C. Keesmaat, *Paul and His Story: (Re)Interpreting the Exodus Tradition* (JSNTSup 181; Sheffield: Sheffield Academic Press, 1999), 104. See also Keesmaat, *Paul and His Story*, 111.

72 Keesmaat, *Paul and His Story*, 107.

God's anxiety for his beloved son, Israel (Jer 31:10). The son of God is led by the Spirit of God in Rom 8:14, and this is also evocative of God's leading of Israel in the wilderness.[73] The motif of glory is widely used in the context of the second Exodus (e.g., Isa 40:5; 43:7). The motif of inheritance can be also understood as an Exodus motif (e.g., Jos 15:1; 18:5–7; Ezek 45:8). The term 'firstborn son' is used in this context, and our reading of the firstborn son in Rom 8:29 as the title of Israel (Exod 4:22) accords well with this context.

The story of Israel in Rom 8 is also associated with the concept of the image in Rom 8:29a. The concept of εἰκών in Rom 8:29 recalls that a human being was created according to the image of God (e.g., Gen 1:26; *Sir* 17:3; *Wis* 2:23). Yet, in this case, εἰκών is not modified by God, but by the son of God (τῆς εἰκόνος τοῦ υἱοῦ αὐτου). Perhaps, the concept of the son of God may be related to the notion of the exalted or heavenly son of God in the Jewish background. Dunn observes that the concept of εἰκών in Rom 8:29 is linked with the story of creation of mankind in Genesis, and that εἰκών refers to the exalted Christ to whom the believers should be conformed (Rom 8:29; 2 Cor 3:18; 4:4; cf. 1 Cor 15:21).[74] Seyoon Kim finds the origin of the concept of εἰκών in the Merkabah tradition such as Ezek 1–2. Particularly, Kim argues that the concept of εἰκών originated in the Christ epiphany on the way to Damascus, that Paul interpreted his experience through the Merkabah tradition, and that he understood Christ as εἰκών.[75] Kim observes the theophanic throne visions in Ezek 1 and Jewish literature and considers their relationship with the son of God in 4Q246 and 4QFlor I 10–14 and with the son of man in Dan 7. In addition, Kim argues that Paul could regard the presence of εἰκών as the appearance of Wisdom of God, and then understood Christ as the son of God on the basis of the Jewish tradition which identifies Wisdom with the son of God.[76]

Yet, most scholars overlook the fact that the concept of εἰκών is connected to Jacob and Israel in early Jewish interpretations of the OT (e.g., *b. Hul.* 91b). In this context, εἰκών refers to the *Urbild* of Israel, not simply the prototype of humankind. Several ancient Jewish authors state that the image (צלם) of Jacob was engraved on the glorious throne in the heaven. This tradition is related to the story of Jacob's dream in Gen 28:12: "And he dreamed that there was a ladder set up on the earth, the top of it reaching to heaven; and the angels of God were ascending and descending on it [NRSV]." *Tg. Ps.-J. Gen* 28:12 reads "… and on that day they (i.e., angels) ascended to the heavens on high, and

73 Keesmaat, *Paul and His Story*, 133.
74 Dunn, *Christology in the Making*, 106–7.
75 Kim, *The Origin of Paul's Gospel*, 334–82.
76 Kim, *The Origin of Paul's Gospel*, 364.

said, 'Come and see Jacob the pious, whose image is fixed on the Throne of Glory'."[77] We also detect similar mentions in *Tg. Neof. Gen* 28:12, *Gen. Rab.* 82:2, *Lam. Rab.* 2:2 and *Num. Rab.* 4:1, etc.: e.g., "Would you annoy me thus were it not for the image of Jacob which is engraved on my throne (*Lam. Rab.* 2:2)"; "The Holy One, blessed be He, said to Jacob: You are exceedingly precious in my sight, for I, as it were, set your image on my throne, and by your name the angels praise me and say: Blessed be the Lord, God of Israel (*Num. Rab.* 4:1)."[78] Thus, the image of Jacob was engraved on the glorious throne in this tradition, and the concept of glory may be related to the divine glory in the Merkabah tradition as in Ezek 1:26–28.[79] Arguably, the Merkabah motif was merged into the Adam tradition in this case. Adam was linked with the concept of glory in the second temple period.[80] In this vein, if Jacob is juxtaposed with the concept of the image, the notion of Adam is implied in the motif of the image of Jacob.[81] Thus, as Bunta observes, "Jacob's image is defined in terms used in Second Temple literature and early rabbinic literature in regard to Adam's special status as the image of God."[82]

We also have to consider that the concept of the heavenly Adam is linked with Israel in the Dead Sea Scrolls. "The chosen ones" in 1QS do not refer to whole Israel, but to the community members of Qumran.[83] In this document, the members of the Qumran community define themselves as the true Israel or the righteous remnant. In 1QS IV 22–24, the ones chosen for the covenant shall belong to the glory of Adam (lines 22–23). The community rule also implies that the restoration of Israel is the restitution to the original and glorious state of Adam ("the glory of Adam"). Thus, the notion of Adam is linked with the restoration of the people of God as the new Israel in 1QS.[84]

77 M. Maher, trans, *Targum Pseudo-Jonathan: Genesis* (ArBib 1b; Collegeville: Liturgical Press, 1992), 99–100.

78 Adapted from H. Freedman and N. Simon, eds., *Midrash Rabbah: Numbers* (London: Soncino Press, 1961), 94.

79 Jarl Fossum, *The Image of the Invisible God* (NTOA 30; Göttingen: Vandenhoeck & Ruprecht, 1995), 140; Christopher Rowland, "John 1.51, Jewish Apocalyptic and Targumic Tradition," *NTS* 30 (1984): 504; David Halperin, *The Faces of the Chariot* (Tübingen: Mohr Siebeck, 1980, 121.

80 Crispin H. T. Fletcher-Louis, *All the Glory of Adam: Liturgical Anthropology in the Dead Sea Scrolls* (STDJ 42; Leiden: Brill, 2002), 101–2.

81 Silviu Bunta, "The Likeness of the Image: Adamic Motifs and צלם Anthropology in Rabbinic Traditions about Jacob's Image Enthroned in Heaven," *JSJ* 37 (2006): 73.

82 Bunta, "The Likeness of the Image," 83.

83 Crispin H.T. Fletcher-Louis, *All the Glory of Adam: Liturgical Anthropology in the Dead Sea Scrolls* (Leiden: Brill, 2001), 96.

84 Cf. Israel inherited the cosmic rulership over the world promised to Adam in *4 Ezra* 6:45–59.

In addition, it was not an unfamiliar notion in Jewish literature that the heavenly counterpart of Jacob–Israel resides in the heaven in a glorious state (e.g., *PrJos* A and Philo, *Conf* 145–146). *The Similitudes of Enoch* also offers a similar example about the heavenly Israel. *The Similitudes of Enoch* consists of the three parables (*1 En* 38–44; 45–57; 58–69) and two epilogues (*1 En* 70–71), and re-assures "the righteous" that their destiny is secure in the hands of "that Son of Man."[85] The first chapters of the three parables introduce the theme of each parable. In *1 En* 38, the evil and the powerful kings are destroyed, and the secret of the righteous is related to their final destiny.[86] Whereas eschatology in *the Similitudes of Enoch* is dualistic, *the Similitudes of Enoch* implies that the righteous (or the Elect ones) would possess the Promised Land (e.g., *1 En* 38:3–4; 39:4–5; 45:4–5). In *1 En* 39 (*the Similitudes of Enoch*), the righteous (or the elect ones) are not all Israelites, but the chosen few.[87] The Elect ones dwell in heaven as the heavenly assembly with the Elect one (39:6). In *1 En* 45:3 (the second parable), the Elect one sits on the seat of glory:[88] "my Elect one shall sit on the seat of glory and make a selection of their deeds, and their resting places will be without number, their souls shall be firm within them when they see my Elect one, those who have appealed to my glorious name."[89] In *the Similitudes of Enoch*, the Elect one on the heavenly throne is a heavenly representative (or *doppelgänger*) of the righteous.[90] We have already considered in the previous chapter that the image and the firstborn son in Philo's works are linked with the concept of the heavenly Israel (see section 3.14.4). So, the notion that the image of Jacob exists in the heaven can be related to the heavenly Israel tradition is already found in the second temple literature.

By the same token, the conformity to the image in Rom 8:29a can be related to the theme of the restoration of the people of God as the sons of God, not simply the transformation of universal humanity (cf. 1QS IV 22–23). As discussed above, the early rabbinic tradition on the image of Jacob originates

85 Collins, *The Apocalyptic Imagination*, 191.

86 Cf. Christopher Rowland, *The Open Heaven: A Study of Apocalyptic in Judaism and Early Christianity* (Eugene: Wipf and Stock, 2002), 161.

87 Martha Himmelfarb, *Ascend to Heaven in Jewish and Christian Apocalypses* (Oxford: Oxford University Press, 1993), 59. Collins notes that the righteous in *Similitudes* does not refer to general righteous people, but to a certain community. However, the specific identity of the community is unclear. See Collins, *The Apocalyptic Imagination*, 192–93.

88 Rowland and Morray-Jones, *The Mystery of God*, 558–63. Jarl Fossum observes that Jacob was enthroned on the heavenly throne. Jarl Fossum, *The Image of the Invisible God*, 140–41.

89 For the heavenly throne, see also *1 En* 47:3; 62:2–3; 63:2.

90 John J. Collins, "The Heavenly Representative: The 'Son of Man' in the Similitudes of Enoch," in *Ideal Figures in Ancient Judaism: Profiles and Paradigms* (eds., G.W.E. Nickelsburg and J.J. Collins; Missoula: Scholars, 1980), 111–33.

in the combination of Adam–heavenly Israel–Merkabah traditions. Through understanding this Jewish tradition, it can be concluded that Jacob–Israel was connected to the concept of the image, and the concept of the image in Rom 8:29a does not merely originate in the Wisdom tradition, but can be related to the heavenly Jacob–Israel tradition. If so, it is not inconceivable that the image in Rom 8:29a refers to the image of the true people of God (i.e., εἰκών τοῦ υἱοῦ αὐτου). Accordingly, both the image and the firstborn son can be related to the notion of Jacob and Israel. This suggests that Paul understood Christ in terms of heavenly Israel and the true member of God's people. Thus, we can construe Rom 8:29 in terms of the restoration of the family of God. The image can be the *Urbild* of the true representative of Israel, and the conformity to the image means the transformation into a true member of the family of God.[91]

The brothers in Rom 8:32 can be also defined as the members of the family of God, and not merely related to universal mankind. Sibling language was used as the ethnic insider-designation within Jewish groups.[92] The Jews addressed one another as brothers in the sense of shared ethnicity.[93] The kinship metaphors in Jewish literature are structuralised on the basis of one central metaphor: "God and Israel are a family," and commonly varied in the following expressions: "Israel is the son of God" (Exod 4:22; Jer 31:9, 20; Hos 11:1; cf. Exod 6:6–8); "Israel is the heir of God" (see 1.2.2); "Israelites are brothers to one another"; "Israel is the house of God" (*T.Mos.* 3:7 and *PsSol* 9:11); "God is the father of Israel" (Deut 32:6; Ps 89:26; 103:13; Isa 63:16; 64:8). The notion of a brother often refers to the concept of a blood relative or a family member in ancient Israel, and Israel's brotherhood in the family of God implies the notion which distinguishes themselves from others such as the Gentiles and foreigners, and

91 Examples of family metaphors in Rom 8: 1) siblings in 8:12, 29; 2) the relationship of the father of the son (or adoption) in 8:14, 15, 16–17; 3) inheritance in 8:17; 4) ἀββά (Aramaic term addressed to God as Father) in 8:15; and 5) the firstborn son in 8:29.

92 For ethnic dimensions of Paul's sibling language, see Kyu Seop Kim, "Reframing Paul's Sibling Language in Light of Jewish Epistolary Forms of Address," *HTS Teologiese Studies/Theological Studies* 71 (2015): 1–8.

93 For the usage of sibling language for ethnic insider designation, see Lev 19:17; 25:25, 35, 39; 25:46 (see the expression, "your brother, the sons of Israel); Num 16:10; 18:2; 18:6; 20:3; 25:6; Deut 1:16, 28; 3:18, 20; 15:8–12; 17:20; 18:15, 18; 19:18–19; 20:8; 22:1–4; 24:7; Neh 5:1; 8:10; Est 10:3; Ps 22:23; 133:1; Isa 66:20; Jer 7:15; 29:16; 31:34; 34:9, 14, 17; Ezek 33:30; 47:14; Mic 5:2; 7:2; Zech 7:9; *2 Bar* 77:1–3; *T.Isaac* 7:10; *T.Mos* 3:7; 11Q5 Col. XIX, 17; CD-A Col. VI 18–Col. VII 4; 11Q19 Col. LVI, 12–15; 1QS 4, 8–10; *4 Ezra* 12:12; *2 Bar* 33:2; 77:5, 12, 17; 78:2, 3, 5; 80:4; 82:2; 84:8; 85:7; *LAB* 22:6; 27:12, 14; 46:1, 2; 56:1; *Judith* 8:14; 8:22; *Tob* 1:3, 10, 16; 2:2; 4:12–13; 5:6; 5:13–14; 6:7, 11, 14, 16; 7:3–4, 9; 7:11; 9:2; 10:13; 11:8; 14:4; 14:7; *1 Macc* 2:40–41; 2:65; 5:13; 5:16; 5:25; 6:22; *2 Macc* 1:1; 12:6; *3 Macc* 4:12; *Sir* 40:24; Philo *Virt* 82; P.Yadin 49; TAD A3.6. Cowley 40; P.Princet. 73; *CIJ*. ii no. 1489 and etc.

which assigns solidarity as members of the same family sharing in a common blood relationship and ancestry. Sibling titles do not refer to a regional, but to an ethnic concept (e.g., *2 Macc* 1:1) and sibling titles should be understood in terms of "family of Abraham" which was accepted by the Jews. So, sibling language in Jewish literature was employed for ethnical and religious insider-designation as a member of the family of Abraham.

Thus, Paul designated the Jewish and Gentile believers as brothers, and this signals that the membership of *familia Dei* was extended to the Gentile believers.[94] Ancient Jewish letter writers rarely addressed their Gentile recipients as brother(s), and it seems that the Jews avoided calling their Gentile recipients in sibling language. However, Paul does not hesitate to designate his Gentile recipients as brothers in his letters. In Rom 8:29, the Gentile believers as well as the Jewish believers are expressed as "many brothers," and it is probable that this expression signals the fulfilment of God's promise to Abraham concerning many descendants (cf. Abraham as the "father of many nations" (Rom 4:17–18); "I will make your offspring as numerous as the stars of heaven, and will give to your descendants all these lands" (Gen 26:4). "Among many brothers" in Rom 8:29b evokes the divine promise given to Abraham that God would multiply Abraham's seeds (Gen 15:5; 22:17; 26:4). Israel as the firstborn son was a distinct heir of divine inheritance and a pre-eminent people over the nations. However, in Rom 8:29, Christ is designated as the firstborn son and shares in his inheritance with Gentile believers (8:17), and "brothers" (i.e., the believers) can partake in the promise and inheritance originally given to the Jews. The eschatological blessings (calling, adoption, inheritance and glory) enjoyed by the Gentile believers in Rom 8:18–30 originally pertain to ethnic Israel (Rom 9:4).[95] Abraham is the common ancestor of Jewish and Gentile Christians (4:11–12; 9:5). Therefore, it is evident in Romans that the Gentile believers are a part of the people of God, and shared in the symbolic universe of ethnic Israel.[96]

In this context, Paul writes that Christ is the firstborn son among many brothers in 8:29.[97] In some Jewish literature, the privilege as the firstborn son and the divine favour are granted solely to Israel (chapter 3). The firstborn son in the OT and Jewish literature refers to *sui heredis* and the favoured one

94 See Esler, *Conflict and Identity in Romans*, 248–49.

95 Cf. *Digest* 1.7.35: "A person's rank is not lowered by adoption, but it is raised." Adoption in Roman society implies upward mobility of class in many cases. So, in this context, it is also understandable that Paul mentions adoption in the list of privileges of the Jews in Rom 9:4.

96 Campbell, *Paul and the Creation of Christian Identity*, 59.

97 Cf. Osten-Sacken connects Rom 8:29b to Rom 4:25. See Osten-Sacken, *Römer 8 als Beispiel paulinischer Soteriologie*, 281.

distinct from the Gentiles. However, the Gentile believers as well as the Jewish believers take part in the inheritance of the firstborn son as the joint-heir of Christ the firstborn son in Rom 8:17. The Gentile believers are not the firstborn son of God in *familia Dei*, but they legitimately share in the inheritance and the promise given to the firstborn son (i.e., Christ).

In section 2.2 and 2.3, we concluded that πρωτότοκος refers to the eldest son and the principal heir in the Jewish family, when it is mentioned in respect of his paternal lineage. The term πρωτότοκος is juxtaposed with "the son of God" in Rom 8:29a and "many brothers" in Rom 8:29b. So, it seems that the kinship concept of πρωτότοκος does not disappear in Rom 8:29, and that πρωτότοκος in Rom 8:29 refers to the eldest son, whereas it is simultaneously the title of Israel. This usage corresponds with Heb 2:10 (cf. Heb 2:11, 16) which indicates that God brings many children to glory.[98] The firstborn son in Rom 8:29 can be the eldest brother to his many brothers (i.e., believers) in the terms of temporal priority,[99] and Rom 8:29 implies the believers' glorification through resurrection.[100] So, Christ is the eldest brother of his fellow heirs (cf. Rom 8:17), the forerunner of the glory, and the heir of God's promise in the context of Israel's inheritance. In Jewish culture, the eldest son enjoyed the privilege as the father's principal heir (section 2.2), and it seems that the title of πρωτότοκος as the privilege of Israel does not exclude the temporal sense of πρωτότοκος. Thus, the term πρωτότοκος has a double force in the sense of the eldest brother of the believers (i.e., many brothers) and the title of Israel as the heir of the promise.

We should also note that the firstborn son in Rom 8:29 is a kind of bridging concept between Rom 8 and 9. In Rom 9–11, Paul discusses how God's election of Israel can be understood as a merciful and impartial action to the Jews and the Gentiles.[101] In Rom 9, Paul demonstrates that God who was merciful to Jacob is also merciful to the Gentiles. We should note that the key word in the Jacob cycle (Gen 25–27) is the firstborn son (בכר). In Gen 25–27, the right of the firstborn son is transferred to Jacob from Esau, and God chose Jacob over Esau and the seeds of Jacob over the descendants of Esau (section 3.1). The story of Moses and the Pharaoh (Rom 9:14–18) also recalls Israel's story surrounding the

98 Martin Karrer, *Jesus Christus im Neuen Testament* (NTD 11; Göttingen: Vandenhoeck & Ruprecht, 1998), 201. Cf. Wilckens, *Der Brief an die Römer (Röm 6–11)*, 164.

99 E.g., Arland J. Hultgren, *Paul's Letter to the Romans: A Commentary* (Grand Rapids: Eerdmans, 2011), 329; Wilckens, *Röm 6–11*,164; Colin G. Cruse, *Paul's Letter to the Romans* (PNTC; Grand Rapids: Eerdmans, 2012), 357.

100 Rudolf Pesch, *Römerbrief* (Die Neue Echter Bibel; Stuttgart: Echter, 1985), 73.

101 David R. Wallace, *Election of the Lesser Son: Paul's Lament-Midrash in Romans 9–11* (Minneapolis: Fortress, 2014), 237.

firstborn son and the election in Exod 4 and 12 (section 3.2).[102] Accordingly, it is apparent that the motif of the firstborn son in Rom 8:29 prefigures the discussions which follow concerning the election of the Jews and Gentiles in Rom 9.[103]

Thus, this reading of the firstborn son in Rom 8:29 fits well with Paul's Gentile inclusion strategy. The firstborn son in Jewish literature symbolises the primacy of Israel and her heirship in relation to the divine promise. The Jews perceived themselves as the firstborn son of God. In Rom 8:29, Paul demonstrates that Christ is the firstborn son. Accordingly, the Gentile believers also participate in the inheritance given to the firstborn son as joint-heirs. In Romans, Paul overturns the original image of the firstborn son pertaining to the primacy and the chosenness of ethnic Israel, and designating Christ as the firstborn son implies that, as joint-heirs of Christ, the believers (both Jewish and Gentile) can equally take part in the promise and the inheritance of the firstborn son (Cf. Rom 8:17).

One could ask whether πρωτότοκος in the NT should be translated as 'the firstborn' or 'the firstborn son,' since πρωτότοκος literally means 'the first begotten.' In general, πρεσβύτατος or πρεσβύτατος υἱός is broadly used in the sense of the eldest son in ancient Greek literature.[104] However, the NT authors do not utilise πρεσβύτατος, or πρωτόγονος (which is at times used in Philonic literature), but consistently use πρωτότοκος in Rom 8:29, Col 1:15, 18, Heb 1:6 and Rev 1:5.[105]

102 See Exod 4:22; 12:1–51.

103 As discussed above, Rom 8:18–30 foretells the motifs in Rom 9–11: Christians and Jews are described in the same terms (brothers (8:29 and 9:3), adoption (8:15, 23 and 9:4), children of God (8:16–17 and 9:8), the glory (8:18 and 9:4, 23), calling (8:28 and 9:7, 11, 24), election (8:28, 33 and 9:11) and πρόθεσις (Rom 8:28 and 9:11). Accordingly, Rom 8:18–30 functions to provide a link between Rom 1–8 and Rom 9–11. This implies that the theme in Rom 8:18–30 is connected to the theme concerning Israel and God's purpose in Rom 9–11.

104 E.g., Philo, *Det.* 118; *Conf.* 147; Plutarch, *Nicias* 15; Hesiod, *Theogony* 234; Aristotle, *Politics* 5. 1305b; Plato, *Hipparchus* 228b; Plato, *Alchibiades* 1.121c; Plato, *Lysis* 204e; *Phaedrus* 259; Pindar, *Olympian* 7.69–75; Plutarch, *Moralia* 489E; Plutarch, *Artaxerxes* 1; Aeschines, *On the Embassy* 149; Josephus, *Ant* 7.163; Josephus, *War* 2.4.3; Apollonius, *Argonautica* 1.157; Thucydides, 1.20.1; Strabo, 12.3.29; Homer, *Iliad* 6.23; Aeschines, 2.147. Cf. Philo refers to Abraham as πρεσβύτατος of the Jewish nation in Philo, *Virt.* 212.

105 In the Classical era, πρωτότοκος seems to have been originally articulated as paroxytone: i.e., "πρωτοτόκος." E.g., Aristotle, *Historia Animalium* 546a12; 564a30; Plato, *Theaetetus* 151c; 161a. However, in the Hellenistic period, it was proparoxytone: i.e., "πρωτότοκος" (e.g., P.Lips. 28.15 (the fourth century CE); P.Lond. 1.312 (the first century CE); Nicander of Colophon, *Anthologia Palatina*, 9.213 (the second century BCE)). In the LXX, πρωτοτόκος is consistently proparoxytone. The examples above are taken from H.G. Liddell and R. Scott, *A Greek-English Lexicon* (Oxford: Clarendon, 1996), 1545.

In the Hebrew Bible (both the MT and the LXX), there are two distinct definitions of the firstborn:[106] 1) the firstborn in terms of paternal lineage (e.g., Gen 49:3; Deut 21:17; Ps 78:51; Ps 105:36); and 2) the firstborn in terms of maternal lineage (e.g, Exod 13:2, 12, 15; Num 3:11–13; 8:13–18). With regard to the first definition, בכר/πρωτότοκος is the eldest 'son' who is 'a principal heir and successor of his father as head of the family.' For instance, in 1 Chr 5:1 (the MT and the LXX), Reuben is addressed as the firstborn son (בכר/πρωτότοκος) of Israel. In Gen 48:18 (the MT and the LXX), Manasseh is the firstborn son (בכר/πρωτότοκος) of Joseph. The firstborn son (בכר/πρωτότοκος) takes possession of primogeniture in Deut 21:15–17 (the MT and the LXX). On the other hand, the second definition is related to a cultic offering which includes human sons and the offspring of animals. בכר/πρωτότοκος in MT and LXX texts is often concerned with consecration to God as a cultic offering (Exod 13:2, 12; 22:29b; Num 3:13, 8:17; Deut 15:19) and belonging to God (Exod 13:2; Lev 27:26; Num 3:13, 8:17). Accordingly, in a Jewish context, when בכר/πρωτότοκος is used in respect of the father, it can be translated as "the firstborn son," since a daughter is not designated as בכר/πρωτότοκος in the OT (the MT and the LXX). On the other hand, when בכר/πρωτότοκος is employed in a cultic sense, it can be translated as "the firstborn" which can refer to both human sons and the offspring of animals.

The Septuagint offers some examples as to how πρωτότοκος was used as kinship language. LXX translates בכר by other nouns than πρωτότοκος in several cases. For instance, LXX Deut 25:6 translates בכר as παιδίον. In LXX Job 18:13, the original "the firstborn son of death" is translated into "death (θάνατος)." In LXX Exod 13:12, the firstborn son is translated as "everything opening the womb (πᾶν διανοῖγον μήτραν)," and it might be because the translators wanted to avoid unnecessary reiterations of the same words.

However, in most cases, πρωτότοκος is the Greek equivalent of בכר in LXX texts, and πρωτότοκος in LXX texts refers to the first male offspring in a cultic sense and to the eldest son as a kinship concept. The translators of the LXX uses the phrase υἱὸς πρωτότοκος in the sense of the firstborn son in LXX Deut 21:15, but, in most cases, πρωτότοκος was employed as the Greek translation of בכר (e.g., LXX Gen 27:19; LXX Gen 48:18; LXX Exod 4:22; LXX Deut 21:16–17; in LXX Gen 49:3, "Ρουβην, πρωτότοκός μου σύ"). So, in some cases of the LXX, πρωτότοκος without υἱός can refer to "the firstborn son," when it is used in respect of the father.

106 See chapter 2 (particularly, sections 2.2.4 and 2.3.5). See also Baruch Levine, "Firstborn," in *Encyclopaedia Judaica, vol. 7* (eds. Fred Skolnik and Michael Berenbaum; Detroit: Thomson, 2007), 45.

Thus, when the term πρωτότοκος in the LXX is used as a cultic offering, it can be translated by "the first male offspring" or "the firstborn" in English. On the other hand, the term πρωτότοκος is employed as a kinship concept, it can be translated as "the firstborn son (of the father)."

While it is unclear that the term πρωτότοκος in Rom 8:29 reflects the usage in LXX texts, a proper translation of πρωτότοκος in Rom 8:29 can be "the firstborn son." Firstly, πρωτότοκος is mentioned in relation to "the father" and "inheritance" (8:15), "many brothers" and "the son of God" (8:29). We do not find the cases that בכר/πρωτότοκος refers to the eldest daughter in the OT (the MT and the LXX) and extant Jewish literature. This may imply that, when πρωτότοκος is used in relation to the father, πρωτότοκος without υἱός refers to the eldest 'son' in the Jewish usage. Secondly, when the term πρωτότοκος reflects the concept of the cultic offering, it can refer to "the firstborn" or "the first offspring" of the mother. Yet, the term πρωτότοκος in Rom 8:29 is used in respect of the father and inheritance (Rom 8:3, 15, 17, 32). Accordingly, a proper translation of πρωτότοκος can be "the firstborn son."

Finally, we should consider the messianic sense of πρωτότοκος in Rom 8:29. Whilst we did not find messianic usage of the firstborn son in chapter 3, it is probable that early Christians re-interpreted the title of the firstborn son in Ps 89:27 in a messianic sense. We should note that the title of the firstborn son is ascribed to Jesus Christ, the Messiah.[107] Further, the messianic sense of πρωτότοκος is compatible with its sense as the title of Israel, as the title of 'son of God' can also be understood in terms of the title of Israel as well as a messianic title.[108] In the same vein, it is probable that the firstborn son refers to the title of Israel as well as a messianic title (or a representative of Israel).

---

107 Matthew Novenson analyses early Jewish messianic language, and considers Paul's Christ language in a messianic sense. See Matthew V. Novenson, *Christ among the Messiahs: Christ Language in Paul and Messiah Language in Ancient Judaism* (Oxford: Oxford University Press, 2012). Novenson also argues that it is highly probable that Christ is not a proper name, but a Greek honorific (κύριος (title)—Jesus (name)—Χριστός (cognomen)) such as Imperator (title)—Caesar (name)—Augustus (cognomen). See Matthew Novenson, *Christ among the Messiahs*, 87–97. For the messianic sense of Christ, see also Martin Hengel, "'Christos' in Paul," in *Between Jesus and Paul: Studies in the Earliest History of Christianity* (Philadelphia: Fortress, 1983), 68. Cf. Horbury writes, "The principal New Testament titles of Christ, therefore, themselves suggest that messianism was an important factor in the rise of the cult of Christ," in Horbury, *Jewish Messianism and the Cult of Christ*, 150.

108 Wanamaker considers the title of 'sons of God' in terms of Israel's title. See Charles A. Wanamaker, "The Son and the Sons of God: A Study in Elements of Paul's Christological and Soteriological Thought," (Ph.D. diss., University of Durham, 1980), 409. Josef Blank notes that Paul's son-of-God Christology is based upon Jesus' self-consciousness as the

Yet, some scholars press further on the messianic concept of πρωτότοκος in Rom 8:29. James M. Scott maintains that πρωτότοκος in Rom 8:29 should be read in terms of "the same adoption of the Son according to the Davidic promise" as described in Rom 1:4.[109] Scott links υἱοθεσία in Rom 8:15, 23 to divine adoption particularly in 2 Sam 7:14 and Rom 1:3–4 in terms of messianic rulership.[110] However, I have two critiques that I will address. Firstly, it is doubtful that 2 Sam 7:14 and Ps 2:7 should be interpreted in terms of adoption.[111] The sonship of the Davidic king is not expressed in terms of the legal institution of adoption, but articulated in birth language. As discussed in section 3.3.2, the Ancient Near Eastern concept of 'the son of God' in relation to the kinship is expressed in birth language, and this birth language stresses the divine origin of the kingship and the everlasting regime of the king. The sonship of the Davidic king in 2 Sam 7:14 and Ps 2:7 falls on this category, and it is unclear that birth language in 2 Sam 7:14 and Ps 2:7 matches with the ancient concept of adoption. Secondly, although Scott attempts to find his evidences for messianic adoption in *Jub* 1:24 and *TJud* 24:3, it is doubtful that *Jub* 1:24 and *TJud* 24:3 indicates the notion of messianic adoption and rulership:

> … And I shall be a father to them, and they will be sons to me. And they will all be called sons of the living God….
>
> *JUB* 1:24b–25a; OTP translation

> And the heavens will be opened upon him to pour out the spirit as a blessing of the Holy father … And you shall be sons in truth, and you will walk in his first and final decrees.
>
> *TJUD* 24:3–4; OTP translation

The authors of *Jub* and *TJud* mention the plural "sons," not "the son," and we do not trace any concept of messianic adoption and rulership in these verses. Instead, it is more reasonable for sonship in *Jub* 1:24 and *TJud* 24:3 to be read

son of God (Sohnesbewusstsein). See Josef Blank, *Paulus und Jesus: Eine theologische Grundlegung* (SANT 18; München: Kösel, 1968), 301–2.

109 James M. Scott, *Adoption as Sons of God: An Exegetical Investigation into the Background of YIOTHESIA in the Pauline Corpus* (WUNT II/48; Tübingen: Mohr Siebeck, 1992), 255.

110 Scott, *Adoption as Sons of God*, 266. The similar interpretation is found in Georg Strecker, *Theology of the New Testament* (ed. Friedrich W. Horn; trans. M. Eugene Boring; Louisville: WJK, 2000), 82; Mark Forman, *The Politics of Inheritance in Romans* (SNTSMS 148; Cambridge: Cambridge University Press, 2011), 119.

111 A. Yarbro Collins and J.J. Collins, *King and Messiah as Son of God: Divine, Human, and Angelic Messianic Figures in Biblical and Related Literature* (Grand Rapids: Eerdmans, 2008), 20. *Contra* Mowinckel, *He That Cometh*, 78.

in the light of Israel's collective sonship as conveyed in Exod 4:22, not as the sonship of David in 2 Sam 7:14, contrary to Scott's view. Therefore, it is not compelling that the firstborn son in Rom 8:29 should be read in terms of Rom 1:4, and it is also unclear that the concept of adoption (υἱοθεσία) of the believers in Rom 8:15 should be understood in terms of messianic rulership and adoption.

Following Scott, Michael Peppard maintains that πρωτότοκος in Rom 8:29 indicates that Christ is an adopted son of God,[112] and proposes P.Lips. 28 as the evidence that an adoptee was addressed as πρωτότοκος: "The contract stipulates that the adopted son will 'be you legitimate and firstborn son [πρωτότοκος], as if begotten to you from your own blood.'"[113] Peppard also maintains that "the 'firstborn' in Greek often connotes 'privilege more than primogeniture'." However, his view also warrants criticism. Firstly, Peppard does not consider the Jewish concept of πρωτότοκος. In the Jewish context, when it is used in respect of the father, πρωτότοκος is linked with primogeniture as well as privilege (chapter 2). The firstborn son is referenced in the context of inheritance as discussed in this section, and should be interpreted as the heir of the father. Secondly, the term πρωτότοκος in P.Lips. 28 may be associated with the status of an adoptee, and ostensibly it may conveys an implication that an adoptee is regarded as a legitimate son.[114] However, P.Lips. 28 does not suggest that the term πρωτότοκος means adopted son. Because, while the term πρωτότοκος was associated with the status of an adoptee in P.Lips. 28, it does not imply that the term πρωτότοκος was generally identified with an adopted son. Furthermore, it is doubtful that, in the Greco-Roman context, an adopted son was usually called πρωτότοκος, since the status of an adoptive son was lower than a biological son.[115] According to Roman law, the right of adopted sons were weaker than the right of natural sons.[116] In *Digest*, 1.7.23, adoptees cannot be legally sons of the adopter's wife. In *Inst.* 1.25, adoptees were excluded from some social duties such as guardianship. In *Digest*, 37.4.8.11, it is stated that "they [adoptees] are *not entirely* strangers (*nec enim in totum extranei sunt*) to the family," and

112 Michael Peppard, *The Son of God in the Roman World: Divine Sonship in its Social and Political Context* (Oxford: Oxford University Press, 2011), 139–40.

113 Peppard's translation in *The Son of God in the Roman World*, 139.

114 Cf. A child is adopted and registered as a legitimate son in P.Oxy. 9.1206 (ἀπογράψομαι αὐτὸν εἰς ἐμαυτοῦ γνήσιον υἱόν).

115 *Contra* Peppard, *The Son of God in the Roman World*, 139. Dunn, Burke, and Walter holds the same opinion with Peppard. See Dunn, *Romans 1–8*, 460; Trevor J. Burke, *Adopted into God's Family: Exploring a Pauline Metaphor* (Downers Grove: IVP, 2006), 63; James C. Walters, "Paul, Adoption, and Inheritance," in *Paul in the Greco-Roman World: A Handbook* (ed. J. Paul Sampley; Harrisburg: Trinity, 2003), 53.

116 Kyu Seop Kim, "Another Look at Adoption in Romans 8:15 in Light of Romans Social Practices and Legal Rules," *BTB* 44 (2014): 140.

this nuanced expression may imply that adopted sons were not completely treated in the same way as the biological children of adopters. In contrast with biological sons, adopted sons could not participate in a certain form of inheritance, i.e., *bonorum possessio* (the right for a deceased father's property established by a praetor) (*Digest*, 37.4.8.11–2; *Digest*, 37.4.8.12). Thus, the status of adopted sons was lower than biological sons in the Roman legal context.[117] In this context, if some adoptee was addressed as πρωτότοκος of the adopter, it may reflect a certain situation of the adoptive family, and it is doubtful that this title in P.Lips. 28 can be applied to general situations. Furthermore, P.Lips. 28 was written approximately in CE 381, and family practices could be changed in the later Roman period. Thus, Peppard's argument remains unconvincing, and it is unwarranted that πρωτότοκος in Rom 8:29 should be read in the sense of an adopted son.

Instead, it seems that, in Rom 8:29, πρωτότοκος refers to an original legitimate son and the representative of Israel. In the Jewish context (chapters 2 and 3), the title of πρωτότοκος does not convey the sense that Israel was adopted, but Israel is the heir of divine promise. In Jewish literature, the adoptive sonship of Israel is not accentuated, when the title of the firstborn son is employed.[118] Rather, when the title is used, it conveys the sense that Israel is the principal heir of divine promise. We should note that the Jews are not addressed as the firstborn son of God in Paul's letters, and that they are the adoptive sons of God (Rom 9:4). In Rom 8:15, Paul states that the believers were adopted as the sons of God, and it implies how the believers enter the new family of God as the adoptive children. Paul does not mention that Christ was adopted in Rom 8. Instead, Christ is a joint-heir with the believers (Rom 8:17), and it seems that, in Rom 8:17, Paul describes that the believers share in the inheritance of the promise with Christ, the legitimate son and the representative of Israel. Both Jewish and Gentile Christians experience God's mercy as adoptees (Rom 8:15; 9:4). Thus, adoption in Rom 8 and 9 is the metaphor which enables the inclusion of Jews and Gentile Christians alike into the family of God.

In brief, πρωτότοκος in Rom 8:29 refers to the title of Israel in relation to inheritance. In Jewish literature, the firstborn son does not refer to an adopted son, but to the heir of promise (chapter 3). Thus, in Paul's metaphors of adoption and inheritance, Christ as the firstborn son is not an adopted son of God

117 Adopted freedmen were also discriminated in some social relationships (e.g., marriage (*Digest*, 23.2.17, 44; *Digest*, 23.2.32, 44; Gaius, *Inst.* 1.61) and political engagements (*De Viris Illustribus*, 72)).

118 See chapter 3 of this work. Also see our conclusion in chapter 4.

(or the Davidic king adopted by God), but a legitimate son of God and the heir of promise.

4.1.3.4 Is Christ Not yet the Firstborn Son?

Does Rom 8:29b suggest that Christ is not yet the firstborn son? Gieniusz writes, “Christ is not yet the firstborn whose status others will reach in due time but rather he will become such upon their arrival at this status (of brothers).”[119] However, “in order that Christ may be the firstborn son among many brothers” in 8:29b does not imply that Christ is not yet the firstborn son. Instead, Christ is not yet *the firstborn son among many brothers*. Christ is the son of God in Rom 1:2–4 and 8:3. In Rom 4:13, Christ was installed as an heir. So, it can be inferred that, in Paul’s mind, Christ is already the firstborn son. On the other hand, the believers do not yet experience the full adoptive sonship in Rom 8:23: “as we wait eagerly for our adoption as sons, the redemption of our bodies.” Adoption as sons in the future (8:23) is linked with the redemption of our bodies, which was meant as transformation into heavenly bodies (cf. “we will also bear the image of the man of heaven” (1 Cor 15:49)). Thus, the believers are already adoptive sons of God (8:17), but are not yet the sons of God who rule over all creation (8:23; cf. 8:21). Christ dwells in heaven in Rom 8:34, but the believers exist on earth. That is, Christ is already the heavenly firstborn son, but is not yet the firstborn son *among many brothers*. Therefore, it remains for Christ not to become the firstborn son, but to become the firstborn son ‘among many brothers.’

Paul implies that the believers will become the adoptive brothers (with full sonship) of Christ (8:29b) through conformity to His son (8:29a). “Εἰκών” in Rom 8:29 is directly linked with the concept of the son Christology (the image of His son).[120] While εἰκών in Rom 8:29a can be related to Paul’s Damascus experience in terms of its origin, we should also note that εἰκών is a kinship concept and can be linked with the image of Jacob/Israel. In this regard, “conformity to the image of His son” may be related to living as sons of God through union with the son of God.[121] Thus, “εἰκών τοῦ υἱοῦ αὐτοῦ” in Rom 8:29 is a procreative image, and “εἰκών τοῦ υἱοῦ αὐτοῦ” and “ἐν πολλοῖς ἀδελφοῖς” as a kinship concept highlight that the believers became kinsmen of Christ, and have been

119 Gieniusz, *Romans 8:18–30*, 274.

120 For the meaning of “conformed to the image of his son,” see J. Kürzinger, “σύμμορφος τῆς εἰκόνος τοῦ υἱοῦ αὐτοῦ (Rom 8,29),” *BZ* 2 (1958): 294–99; A.R. Leaney, “Conformed to the Image of His Son (Rom 8,29),” *NTS* 10 (1964): 470–79; Jewett, *Romans*, 529. Wilckens notes that the image is not *Abbild*, but *Wesenserscheinung*: “Christus ist das Bild Gottes in dem Gottes Wesen, seine Herrlichkeit, ausstrahlend erscheint,” in Wickens, *An die Römer*, 163.

121 Thüsing, *Per Christum in Deum*, 125. Cf. 2 Cor 4:4.

made the descendants of Abraham.[122] In this vein, Rom 8:29a corresponds with the kinship concepts of the firstborn son and brothers in Rom 8:29b.[123] Therefore, Christ as εἰκών is the prototype 'Son of God' and 'descendant of Abraham,' and Christ as πρωτότοκος is a bearer of the chosen status of Israel as 'Son of God' and 'descendant of Abraham.'

In conclusion, Rom 8:29b does not imply that Christ is not yet the firstborn son, but suggests that Christ is not yet *the firstborn son among many brothers*. Paul presents in Rom 8:29b that the believers have not yet attained full sonship and that, when the believers are fully conformed to the image of "His son" (i.e., experiencing full sonship), Christ will become *the firstborn son among many brothers*.

4.1.3.5 Conclusion

The firstborn son in Rom 8:29 should be interpreted as the title of Israel in respect of chosenness and inheritance as presented in Jewish literature. The firstborn son in Rom 8:29 symbolises the status of Israel as the divine heir and the chosen people, and Rom 8:29b connotes that the divine promise is fulfilled in Christ, the firstborn son. The motif of the firstborn son in Rom 8:29 is linked with the election story of Jacob and Israel in Rom 9:10–18. Christ as πρωτότοκος also corresponds with the heir of the entire world and the seed of the promise in Rom 4:13. Through designating Christ as πρωτότοκος, Paul answers the following question: who is the true heir of the promise? That is, the true heir is Christ the firstborn son, and Christ's brothers (i.e., the Jewish and Gentile believers) will be his joint-heirs through union with Christ. Rom 8:29b demonstrates the fulfilment of the Abrahamic promise concerning the Land and the seeds. In Judaism, the election and the inheritance are two sides of the same coin. The Elect ones receive their inheritance, and enjoy their primacy and centrality over the nations as the firstborn son in the OT and Jewish literature. Therefore, Christ as εἰκών in Rom 8:29a is the archetype 'Son of God' and 'descendant of Abraham,' and πρωτότοκος in Rom 8:29b originated in the self-perception of Israel as the Elect.[124] In addition, the sense of πρωτότοκος as the eldest son in a temporal sense does not fade away in Rom 8:29. The eldest son was a principal heir of the father (see Section 2.2) in the Jewish family, and accordingly, πρωτότοκος in Rom 8:29 has a double force and refers to the status

122 Hodge, *If Sons, then Heirs*, 111.

123 Cf. J.R. Daniel Kirk, *Unlocking Romans: Resurrection and the Justification of God* (Grand Rapids: Eerdmans, 2008), 142–43.

124 As Kaminsky agrees, "Election by definition requires that distinctions be maintained between God's people and those not elected." Joel Kaminsky, *Yet I Loved Jacob: Reclaiming the Biblical Concept of Election* (Nashville: Abingdon, 2007), 154.

of Israel as the heir of God and the eldest brother of his Christian siblings in a temporal sense.

4.2 Colossians

4.2.1 *The Background*

There is a broad consensus among scholars that Paul fights over some false teachers or errorists in Colossians (e.g., Col 2:8–23).[125] As for the false teaching, scholars diverge on Judaism (or Jewish mysticism), Hellenistic philosophy, or Hellenistic-Jewish syncretism.[126] R.E. DeMaris contends that the false teaching stems from a sort of Middle-Platonism, centred on the pursuit of divine knowledge. Yet, he neglects Jewish features of the false teaching concerning circumcision, Sabbath or calendric observances in Colossians.

Alternatively, Clinton Arnold draws out his attention to Jewish and Pagan syncretic folk religion. He mentions that θρησκείᾳ τῶν ἀγγέλων in Col 2:18 possibly reflects the Jewish-syncretic ritual which invokes angels for protection from the personised demonic spirits.[127] However, the author of Colossians does not directly state specific magical practices such as charms and spells.[128] Furthermore, the author of Colossians does not explicitly mention some kind 'fear' which the Colossian believers were experiencing. Thus, it is unclear that the author of Colossians felt some needs to respond to some 'fear' of demonic spirits.

On the other hand, an agreement is emerging among current scholars (particularly in the Anglophone world) that the false teaching in Col 2:8–23 contains some Jewish features,[129] and is probably not influenced only by

---

125 An exception is found in Morna D. Hooker, who argues that there was not false teachers behind the Colossian church. See Morna D. Hooker, "Were There False Teachers in Colossae?" in *From Adam to Christ* (Cambridge: Cambridge University Press, 1990), 121–36.

126 For the interreligious character of the Lycus valley, see Paul N. Anderson, "The Johannine Logos-Hymn: A Cross-Cultural Celebration of God's Creative-Redemptive Work," in *Creation Stories in Dialogue: The Bible, Science, and Folk Traditions, Radboud Prestige Lecture Series by R. Alan Culpepper* (BibInt 139; eds., R. Alan Culpepper and Jan van der Watt; Leiden: Brill, 2016), 236.

127 Clinton E. Arnold, *The Colossian Syncretism: The Interface between Christianity and Folk Belief at Colossae* (Tübingen: Mohr Siebeck, 1995), 90–102.

128 Ian Smith, *Heavenly Perspective*, 32.

129 Thomas Sappington says that the Colossian error "was strongly oriented toward the ascetic-mystical piety of Jewish apocalypticism," in Sappington, *Revelation and Redemption at Colossae* (Sheffield: JSOT press, 1991), 225. Other scholars currently in favor of Jewishness of false teachers in Colossians are James Dunn, *Colossians*, 29–35; N.T. Wright, *Colossians*,

Middle-Platonism, Cynicism[130] or pagan folk-religion. The cultic and ascetic practices depicted in 2:8–23 can be explained in terms of Jewish practices such as circumcision, which is mentioned in 2:11. The phrase Ἰοῦστος, οἱ ὄντες ἐκ περιτομῆς in 4:11 undergirds that the circumcision in 2:11 is related to a Jewish practice. 2:16 and 2:21 refer to purity and food: the food regulations and calendric observance mentioned in 2:16 can be understood as typical Jewish cultic practices,[131] defined according to Jewish purity law, as in Lev 13:45–46; 15:5; and Num 19:11–13, for example. Eating unclean food is also forbidden by Jewish law, as seen in Lev 11:1–23 and Deut 14:3–21, etc.[132] ἀφειδίᾳ σώματος and πλησμονὴν τῆς σαρκός in Col 2:23 may be also concerned with Jewish ascetic practices.

It is also argued that the Colossian errorists are related to Jewish mysticism.[133] Indeed, Colossians is evocative of some Jewish mystic features. Firstly, in 2:18, ταπεινοφροσύνῃ and θρησκείᾳ τῶν ἀγγέλων in 2:18 are reminiscent of Jewish ascetic or mystic practices. One may argue that this phrase should be interpreted as an objective genitive (worshipping the angels). However, the chief problem of this reading is that Paul does not strongly rebuke this practice in the text, which would be expected since worshipping anything other than God would be a serious violation of Jewish monotheism. A reading of the phrase θρησκείᾳ τῶν ἀγγέλων as a subjective genitive is therefore more fitting to the Jewish context;[134] this reading is supported by the usage of θρησκεία as a subjective genitive in *4 Macc* 5:7 (Ιουδαίων θρησκεία; worship performed by the Jews).[135] If it is to be read as a subjective genitive, it must refer to partici-

23–30; Allan Bevere, *Sharing in the Inheritance*, 53–59; Markus Bockmuehl, *Revelation and mystery in ancient Judaism and Pauline Christianity* (Tübingen: Mohr Siebeck, 1990), 179–80; Marianne Thompson, *Colossians & Philemon*, 6–9; Michael Bird, *Colossians*, 15–26; Andrew Bandstra, "Did the Colossian errorists need a mediator?" in *New Dimensions in New Testament Study* (eds., R.N. Longenecker and M.C. Tenney; Grand Rapids: Zondervan, 1974), 329–43;

130 Troy W. Martin, *By Philosophy and Empty Deceit: Colossians as Response to a Cynic Critique* (Sheffield: Sheffield Academic Press, 1996).

131 Cf. Shaye Cohen argues that observing Jewish rituals is directly linked with the identity of Jews, in Cohen, *The Beginnings of Jewishness*, 59.

132 Dunn, *Colossians*, 172.

133 For the definition, e.g., see Rachel Elior, "The Foundations of Early Jewish Mysticism: The Lost Calendar and the Transformed Heavenly Chariot," in *Wege Mystischer Gotteserfahrung: Judentum, Christentum und Islam* (ed. Peter Schäfer; Munich: Oldenbourg, 2006), 3. Yet, Peter Schäfer criticises Elior's definition in Peter Schäfer, *The Origins of Jewish Mysticism* (Tübingen: Mohr Siebeck, 2009), 14–17.

134 Smith, *Heavenly Perspective*, 126; Arnold, 91.

135 F.O. Francis, "Humility and Angelic Worship in Col 2:18," in *Conflict at Colossae: A Problem in the Interpretation of Early Christianity Illustrated by Selected Modern Studies* (eds. F.O. Francis and W.A. Meeks; Missoula: Scholars, 1975), 180.

pation in the angels' worship of God. Participation in angelic worship is often mentioned in the OT and the Jewish literature.[136] For instance, Isaiah 6:1–5, Isaiah ascended to heaven and sees angels worshiping God. In *1 Enoch* 14:8–11, Enoch was taken up to the Heavenly Temple, and receives some divine revelations. If θρησκείᾳ τῶν ἀγγέλων can be read in terms of Jewish mystic tradition, this phrase suggests that some Colossian believers are involved in some Jewish mystic practice, including that of ascending to heaven and participating in the heavenly worship of angels.

Secondly, ἑόρακεν ἐμβατεύων in 2:18 also recalls Jewish mystic practices, As in *1 Enoch* 14:9 and 4Q405, ascending to heaven (entry into heaven) is connected to the Jewish mystic practice concerning divine relation.[137] It is highly likely that ἑόρακεν refers to a visionary practice.[138] Therefore, ἑόρακεν ἐμβατεύων may mean "the things that the person who has received the heavenly vision has seen, in particular the worship performed by the angels."[139]

The identity of the Colossian errorists will be a theme of continuing scholarly debates, and it may be beyond the scope of this work to determine their identity. However, it would be safe to conclude that the false teaching chiefly contains some Jewish mystic or (Hellenistic) Jewish-syncretic features. If so, Col 2:8–23 must be viewed as a response against these Jewish practices which some Colossian believers performed.[140]

4.2.2 *The Theme of the Christ Hymn in Col 1:15–20*

In this section, we will consider the characteristics and themes of the Christ hymn in Colossians. Most scholars regard Colossians 1:15–20 as one unit.[141] The boundaries of 1:15–20 are justified as follows. Firstly, we can find the chiastic—ὅς ἐστιν … πρωτότοκος (1:15, 18b), ὅτι ἐν αὐτῷ … ἐν τοῖς οὐρανοῖς καὶ ἐπὶ τῆς γῆς (1:16, 19–20), and δι' αὐτοῦ (1:16, 20), εἰς αὐτόν (1: 16, 20). Secondly, πᾶς is intensively used (eight times) in 1:15–20. Thirdly, the third person sequence in the Christ hymn is contrasted with the first/second person (we/you) sequence in

136 Smith, *Heavenly Perspective*, 126–27.

137 Cf. Dunn, *Colossians*, 183.

138 Murray Harris, *Colossians & Philemon* (Grand Rapids: Eerdmans, 1991), 121.

139 Smith, *Heavenly Perspective*, 130.

140 Parenetic aspects of Colossians have been pointed out as well as polemic aspects. E.g., Walter Wilson, *The Hope of Glory: Education and Exhortation in the Epistle to the Colossians* (Leiden: Brill, 1997).

141 E.g., Luis Carlos Reyes, "The Structure and Rhetoric of Colossians 1:15–20," *Filologia Neotestamentaria* 7 (1999): 145; Dunn, *The Epistles to Colossians and to Philemon*, 84; Pizzuto, *A Cosmic Leap of Faith*, 110; Wright, "Poetry and Theology," 118; Georg Strecker, *Theology of the New Testament* (trans. Eugene Boring; Louisville: WJK, 2000), 554–55; Ernst Bammel, "Versuch zu Col 1.15–20," *ZNW* (1961): 88–95.

1:12–14 and 1:21–23. Fourthly, the hymnic form is widely acknowledged.[142] A relative clause beginning with "who" commonly introduces the hymns in the NT (Phil 2:6; 1 Tim 3:16; Heb 1:3; 1 Pet 2:22). A sequence of clauses and phrases can easily be understood to match rhythmic units.[143] In addition, elaborate parallelisms are also found, and the Christ hymn contains the literary style of Jewish Psalmody.[144] Therefore, this study will regard Col 1:15–20 as one unit.

Many scholars argue that the Christ hymn in Col 1:15–20 was not written by Paul.[145] Firstly, they find elaborated parallelism and rhythm separated from the context. Secondly, words which Paul uses only infrequently in his undisputed letters appear in the Christ hymn (e.g., πρωτεύων in Col 1:18, εἰρηνοποιήσας in 1:20, ἀρχή in 1:18 instead of ἀπαρχή, θρόνοι in 1:16, κυριότητες in 1:16, ἀποκαταλλάξαι in 1:20). So, in his influential monograph, Eduard Norden postulates that the author of Colossians used a preceding ritual tradition (doxology to God and Christ).[146] Ernst Käsemann argues that this hymn originated in pre-Christian Gnosticism,[147] and Eduard Schweizer writes that the Christ hymn was derived from a Hellenistic Jewish hymn and redacted later as a Christian hymn.[148]

---

142 E.g., Gordley locates the genre of Col 1:15–20 in a type of ancient prose hymn for praise of the divine, which presents a fusion of Jewish and Greco-Roman conventions. See Matthew E. Gordley, *The Colossian Hymn in Context: An Exegesis in Light of Jewish and Greco-Roman Hymnic and Epistolary Conventions* (WUNT II/228; Tübingen: Mohr Siebeck, 2007), 229. Cf. Edsall and Strawbridge doubt the widespread assumption that this passage is a hymn. See Benjamin Edsall and Jennifer R. Strawbridge, "The Songs We Used to Sing? Hymn 'Traditions' and Reception in Pauline Letters," *JSNT* 37 (2015): 290–311.

143 Dunn, *The Epistles to Colossians and to Philemon*, 84.

144 Pizzuto asserts that the Christ hymn should be read in the context of the larger Second Temple Jewish worldview. See V.A. Pizzuto, *A Cosmic Leap of Faith: An Authorial, Structural, and Theological Investigation of the Cosmic Christology in Col 1:15–20* (CBET 41; Leuven: Peeters, 2006), 212–41.

145 In this section, "Paul" refers to the author of Colossians. This study assumes the authenticity of Colossians, but the specific arguments for this are beyond the scope of this study. See A. Feiullet, *Le Christ sagesse de Dieu d'après les épîtres Pauliniennes* (Ebib; Paris: Gabalda, 1966), 246–73; J.F. Balchin, "Colossians 1:15–20: An Early Christian Hymn? The Arguments from Style," *Vox Evangelica* 15 (1985): 65–93; Kim, *The Origin of Paul's Gospel*, 144–47; N.T. Wright, *Colossians & Philemon* (Grand Rapids: Eerdmans, 1986), 31–34; J.D.G. Dunn, *The Epistle to the Colossians and to Philemon*, 35–39; Allan Bevere, *Sharing in the Inheritance: Identity and the Moral Life in Colossians* (JSNTSup 226; Sheffield: Sheffield Academic Press, 2003), 53–59; Moo, *Colossians and Philemon*, 28–41; Michael Bird, *Colossians and Philemon* (NCC; Eugene: Cascade, 2009), 4–9.

146 Eduard Norden, *Agnostos Theos: Untersuchungen zur Formengeschichte religiöser Rede* (Leipzig: Teubner, 1913), 253.

147 Ernst Käsemann, "A Primitive Christian Baptismal Liturgy," 149.

148 Schweizer, *The Letter to the Colossians*, 68.

It is probable that Paul himself could have written the Colossian hymn, while it is also probable that he could have utilised a preceding hymn in his epistle. Some words in the Christ hymn were used in the undisputed Pauline letters. Εἰκών τοῦ θεοῦ in Col 1:15 is found in 2 Cor 4:4 (cf. Rom 8:29). We find another theological use of the verb "καταλλα-" in Rom 5:10. In the undisputed Pauline letters, Ἀρχαί and ἐξουσίαι are employed in a cosmological sense (e.g., Rom 8:38–39). The firstborn son in Col 1:15 and 1:18 is also utilised in Rom 8:29. Secondly, some motifs in Col 1:15–20 fit well within the context of Colossians. For example, the motif of inheritance in Col 1:12–13 continues in 1:15 (the firstborn son as a principal heir of the family). Εἰρηνοποιέω in Col 1:20 foreshadows ἡ εἰρήνη τοῦ Χριστοῦ in 3:15 which means "peace brought by Christ,"[149] and the genitive "τοῦ Χριστοῦ" recalls Christ's crucifixion in Col 1:20. The theme of reconciliation in Col 1:20 recurs in 1:22. The motif of the crucifixion is found in 1:20 and 22. Πλήρωμα in Col 1:19 prefigures the fullness of Christ in 2:9—"ὅτι ἐν αὐτῷ κατοικεῖ πᾶν τὸ πλήρωμα τῆς θεότητος σωματικῶς," and it is applied to the fullness of the saints in 2:10: "ἐστὲ ἐν αὐτῷ πεπληρωμένοι." Thus, Paul could have used the hymn that he himself composed, but could also have utilised a preceding hymn in order to express his own faith in Christ according to his own purpose.[150] What is clear is that Paul employed motifs in the Christ hymn to achieve a theological breakthrough to correct the errors of the Colossian believers.

The Christ hymn in Col 1:15–20 also fits well with the adjacent context. The Christ hymn chimes with the theme of "forgiveness of sins" in Col 1:14 and 1:21–23. The ritual motif in Col 1:19–20 recurs in Col 1:22 and in Col 1:13–14. Reconciliation is accomplished between God and all things in heaven and on earth through the blood of the cross in Col 1:20. God reconciled with the believers in Christ's fleshly body through death (ἐν τῷ σώματι τῆς σαρκὸς αὐτοῦ διὰ τοῦ θανάτου) in Col 1:22a. This reconciliation provides the foundation of the believer's maturity or perfection: "παραστῆσαι ὑμᾶς ἁγίους καὶ ἀμώμους καὶ ἀνεγκλήτους κατενώπιον αὐτοῦ," in 1:22b. So, the Christ hymn matches well with its adjacent context, while Col 1:15–20 may also originate in the pre-Pauline tradition.

Moreover, we need to note "εἰκών" in Col 1:15 and "κτίζω" in 1:16 foreshadow "κατ᾽εἰκόνα τοῦ κτίσαντος αὐτόν" in Col 3:10. The theme of reconciliation in Col 1:19–20 is linked with the exhortation to the unity of the church in Col 3:11: "In that renewal there is no longer Greek and Jew, circumcised and uncircumcised, barbarian, Scythian, slave and free; but Christ is all and

149 Harris, *Colossians*, 165.

150 Kim, *The Origin of Paul's Gospel*, 232.

in all."[151] The theme of the new creation in Col 3:10 is connected to the theme of ethnic unity in the Colossian church in Col 3:11 through the conjunction ὅπου: "in which (ὅπου) there is no longer Greek and Jew, circumcised and uncircumcised, barbarian, Scythian, slave and free; but Christ is all and in all." So, in Col 3:10–11, new creation according to the image of God is directly orientated towards ethnic unity. Furthermore, it seems that the cosmic reconciliation in Col 1:20 serves as an exemplar of unity, and this motif of reconciliation could be linked to the ethnic unity of the Colossian church. Therefore, whilst Paul could utilise the preceding hymnic tradition, it seems that Paul carefully harmonised the thread of Colossians with the contents and the theme of the Colossian hymn and could select and employ some significant motifs of the Christ hymn for the whole letter according to his own purpose.

There is no consensus on the structure of the Christ hymn. Ernst Bammel, Eduard Lohse, Reinhard Deichgräber, J.D.G. Dunn, Ben Witherington and N.T. Wright support the two-strophe structure of the Christ hymn.[152] On the contrary, Otfried Hofius, Paul Beasley-Murray, Ralph Martin, Luis Carlos Reyes, Georg Strecker and Douglas Moo espouse the three-strophe structure.[153] A two-strophe structure has merits since it is the simplest structure which indicates an elaborate chiasm in Col 1:15–20. In favour of the three-strophe structure, some interpreters argue that the second-strophe functions as a hinge and

151 This exhortation arguably originated in the baptismal creed of the Pauline churches. See Gal 3:27–28.

152 See Eduard Lohse, *Colossians and Philemon* (trans. W.R. Poehlmann and R.J. Karris; Hermeneia; Philadelphia: Fortress, 1972), 44–45; N.T. Wright, "Poetry and Theology in Colossians 1.15–20," in *The Climax of the Covenant: Christ and the Law in Pauline Theology* (Minneapolis: Fortress, 1993), 101–4; Bammel, "Versuch zu Col 1.15–20," 88–91; Dunn, *The Epistles to Colossians and to Philemon*, 84–85; Ben Witherington III, *The Letters to Philemon, the Colossians, and the Ephesians: A Socio-Rhetorical Commentary on the Captivity Epistles* (Grand Rapids: Eerdmans, 2007), 129; Reinhard Deichgräber, *Gotteshymnus und Christushymnus in der frühen Christenheit: Untersuchungen zu Form, Sprache und Stil der frühchristlichen Hymnen* (SUNT 5; Göttingen: Vandenhoeck & Ruprecht, 1967), 150.

153 See Otfired Hofius, "'Erstgeborener vor aller Schöpfung'—'Erstgeborener aus den Toten': Erwägungen zu Struktur und Assage des Christushymnus Kol 1,15–20," in *Paulusstudien II* (WUNT I/143; Tübingen: Mohr Siebeck, 2002), 220; Ralph P. Martin, *Reconciliation: A Study of Paul's Theology* (Grand Rapids: Zondervan, 1989), 114; Douglas Moo, *The Letters to the Colossians and to Philemon* (PNTC; Grand Rapids: Eerdmans, 2008), 116; Strecker, *Theology of the New Testament*, 554–55; Reyes, "The Structure and Rhetoric of Colossians 1:15–20," 140–46; Paul Beasley-Murray, "Colossians 1:15–20: An Early Christian Hymn Celebrating the Lordship of Christ," in *Pauline Studies: Essays Presented to F.F. Bruce on His 70th Birthday* (eds. D.A. Hagner and M.J. Murray; Grand Rapids: Eerdmans, 1980), 169–70. Vincent Pizzuto observes a chiastic structure (a-b-c-b'-a') in Col 1:15–20. See Pizzuto, *A Cosmic Leap of Faith*, 144–48.

nexus. The complex chiastic structure of the Colossian hymn can be organised as follows:

v. 15		a	ὅς ἐστιν εἰκὼν τοῦ θεοῦ τοῦ ἀοράτου,
		b	πρωτότοκος πάσης κτίσεως,
v. 16		c	ὅτι ἐν αὐτῷ ἐκτίσθη τὰ πάντα
	A		ἐν τοῖς οὐρανοῖς καὶ ἐπὶ τῆς γῆς,
		e	τὰ ὁρατὰ καὶ τὰ ἀόρατα,
			εἴτε θρόνοι εἴτε κυριότητες
			εἴτε ἀρχαὶ εἴτε ἐξουσίαι·
		d	τὰ πάντα δι’ αὐτοῦ καὶ εἰς αὐτὸν ἔκτισται·
v. 17	B		καὶ αὐτός ἐστιν πρὸ πάντων
	X		καὶ τὰ πάντα ἐν αὐτῷ συνέστηκεν,
v. 18	B’		καὶ αὐτός ἐστιν ἡ κεφαλὴ τοῦ σώματος τῆς ἐκκλησίας·
		a’	ὅς ἐστιν ἀρχή,
		b’	πρωτότοκος ἐκ τῶν νεκρῶν,
			ἵνα γένηται ἐν πᾶσιν αὐτὸς πρωτεύων,
v. 19	A’	c’	ὅτι ἐν αὐτῷ εὐδόκησεν πᾶν τὸ πλήρωμα κατοικῆσαι
v. 20		d’	καὶ δι’ αὐτοῦ ἀποκαταλλάξαι τὰ πάντα εἰς αὐτόν,
			εἰρηνοποιήσας διὰ τοῦ αἵματος τοῦ σταυροῦ αὐτοῦ,
		e’	[δι’ αὐτοῦ] εἴτε τὰ ἐπὶ τῆς γῆς
			εἴτε τὰ ἐν τοῖς οὐρανοῖς.

This double parallel structure consistently shows the complex parallel structure of the Christ-hymn. The large chiastic structure of the Christ hymn is A-B-X-B’-A’. In the large pairs of A-A’ includes the smaller parallel elements (A: a-b-c-d-e-; A’: a’-b’-c’-e’-d’). a and a’ is paired up by “ὅς ἐστιν.” Πρωτότοκος also makes a parallel of b-b’. “ὅτι ἐν αὐτῷ”+ aorist tense verb also make c-c’ pairs in the chiastic form. d-d’ (τὰ πάντα + δι’ αὐτοῦ + εἰς αὐτόν + verb) also explains the mediatorship of Christ in the creation and the new creation. e-e’ explains the contents of πᾶς which is created and reconciled in the Christ hymn. In the A structure, it is probable that the order of d and e in v. 16 was inverted since the author of the Christ hymn eschewed to reiterate the verb, κτίζειν in consecutive sentences.

B (v. 17a)-B’ (v. 18) functions as a bridge in the middle of A-X-A’ and each of B-B’ serves to summarise A (vv. 15–16) and A’ (vv. 18b–20). A (vv. 15–16) elucidates that Christ is supreme over the creation, and B (v. 17a) sums up the contents of A: "καὶ αὐτός ἐστιν πρὸ πάντων." On the other hand, B' encapsulates A' (vv. 18b–20) in that Christ is the head of the church as well as every creature: "καὶ αὐτός ἐστιν ἡ κεφαλὴ τοῦ σώματος τῆς ἐκκλησίας." X (v. 17b: καὶ τὰ πάντα ἐν αὐτῷ συνέστηκεν) is located in the centre of the chiastic structure (A-B-X-B'-A), and X recapitulates the theme of the Christ hymn. The perfect tense (συνέστηκεν) in 1:17b denotes a stative idea—continuing coherence,[154] and it implies that God continues to hold all things in Christ. Reyes also says, "The perfect tense συνέστηκεν seems to be highlighted by being placed between two identical present tenses."[155] So, according to the given structure, it seems that the main theme is related to Christ's office to reign over creation and new creation (1:17).

Some scholars define the reconciliation in Col 1:20 in light of Greco-Roman cosmology as the ordering of the world that was in chaos (Ordnen der in Unordnung geratenen Welt), and link the reconciliation in Col 1:20 to cosmic Lordship (kosmisch-herrscherliche Versöhnung).[156] If so, the Christ hymn should be read in the context of Greco-Roman cosmological speculations. For instance, Eduard Schweizer presumes that belief in the disequilibrium of the cosmos was widely held in the Hellenistic era. One of the main cosmological concerns in the Greco-Roman era was sustainability of the universe, and some people were worried that the conflicts among cosmic elements could result in the catastrophe of the universe.[157] In other words, they believed that the cosmos had a fragile order, and humanity was vulnerable to the possible collapse of the cosmos. Accordingly, the actual peace of the cosmos is established when the cosmos is in unity, and this is the theme of the original Colossian hymn. However, Paul does not explicitly state in Colossians that strife among the cosmic powers existed. Most importantly, "the basic fault line" in Colossians is between God and creation, not between the cosmological elements.[158]

Nonetheless, the cosmological emphasis in the Colossian hymn is remarkable. In this vein, the Christ hymn in Col 1:15–20 has been widely observed

154 Douglas J. Moo, *The Letters to the Colossians and to Philemon* (Grand Rapids: Eerdmans, 2008), 125.

155 Reyes, "Structure," 144.

156 E.g., Hofius, "Erwägungen," 199.

157 Schweizer, *The Letter to the Colossians*, 93–94; likewise, Lohse argues that the cosmos suffered from serious disorder, but was then reconciled by Christ event. Heaven and earth have been restored into the order which was created by God, and this happened through the resurrection and ascent of Christ, as found in Lohse, *Colossians and Philemon*, 59–61.

158 Moo, *The Letters to the Colossians and to Philemon*, 135–36. Also see Allan Bevere, *Sharing in the Inheritance*, 35–46.

to contain features of Wisdom speculations in Hellenistic Jewish literature.[159] Furthermore, the influence of Jewish Wisdom tradition should be noted (e.g. the pre-existent Wisdom of God in Prov 8:22–31, the image of God in *Wis* 7:26, and God who dwells among the people of God or Shekinah theology (*Sir* 24:3–8). Thus, the Christ hymn in Col 1:15–20 and its adjacent context can be considered in the Jewish background (or Hellenistic Jewish background). The Christ hymn does not seem to be an allusion of Prov 8:22–31 in a strict sense, but must be related to the interpretative trajectory of Jewish Wisdom tradition such as *Wis* 7 or *Sir* 24.[160] The cosmological agency of Christ in the Colossian hymn can be explained in the similar context (cf. Philo, *Leg* 1.43; *Conf* 146–147). That is, Christ is the agent of creation, as Wisdom is (e.g., Prov 8:30). So, it seems clear that Christ was identified with Wisdom in the Colossian hymn.[161]

In this context, the Colossian hymn presents two distinct themes: Christ in creation (Col 1:15–17) and Christ in redemption (1:18–20).[162] Εἰκών in Col 1:15, πάσης κτίσεως in 1:15, ἐκτίσθη τὰ πάντα in 1:16, τὰ πάντα δι᾽αὐτοῦ καὶ εἰς αὐτὸν ἔκτισται in 1:16, πρὸ πάντων in 1:17 and ἀρχή in 1:18 clearly show that the Christ hymn is directly related to the theme of creation.[163] In this hymn, we also find the cosmological dimension of the cross and the cosmic mediatorship of Christ. Δι᾽ αὐτοῦ καὶ εἰς αὐτόν in Col 1:16 denotes the intermediate agency of Christ in creation,[164] which may reflect Hellenistic Jewish speculation about

159 E.g., James Dunn, *Christology in the Making: A New Testament Inquiry into the Origins of the Doctrine of the Incarnation*, 2nd ed. (Grand Rapids: Eerdmans, 1996), 187–94; Moo, *The Letters to the Colossians and to Philemon*, 113.

160 Christopher Beetham, *Echoes of Scripture in the Letter of Paul to the Colossians* (BibInt 96; Leiden: Brill, 2008), 113–14.

161 For the theme of the cosmological agency in the Colossian hymn, see Ronald Cox, *By the Same Word: Creation and Salvation in Hellenistic Judaism and Early Christianity* (BZNW 145; Berlin: Walter de Gruyter, 2007), 172–93.

162 The thematic movement from creation to redemption is detected in Jewish psalm tradition. See Gordley, *The Colossian Hymn in Context*, 199. Stettler writes, "Jesus is also nicht nur in der Schöpfung, sondern auch in der Verwirklichung des verheißenen Heils der Erste." See Christian Stettler, *Der Kolosserhymnus: Untersuchungen zu Form, traditionsgeschichtlichen Hintergrund und Aussage von Kol 1,15–20* (WUNT II/131; Tübingen: Mohr Siebeck, 2000), 247.

163 The divine passive ἐκτίσθη in 1:16 indicates that God is the creator. This aorist is replaced by the perfect form ἔκτισται in the end of 1:16, and this perfect form connotes the continuing creating action. See Lohse, *Colossians and Philemon*, 49.

164 The phrases δι᾽αὐτοῦ καὶ εἰς αὐτόν depicts Christ's mediation in creation. E.g., Ernst Käsemann, "A Primitive Christian Baptismal Liturgy," in *Essays on New Testament Themes* (trans. W.J. Montague; London: SCM, 1982), 157. Cf. *BDF* §17; Daniel Wallace, *Greek Grammar Beyond the Basics* (Grand Rapids: Zondervan, 1997), 434. Col 1:15 is connected to Col 1:16 through the conjunction ὅτι (for), and 'for' "introduces the reason for Christ's

Wisdom. The new creation is the restitution of the original creation, and everything created through Christ is restored through Christ's death, and everything is reconciled with God through Christ's crucifixion.[165]

Arguably, a certain mystic and ascetic practice put the faith of the Colossian believers in jeopardy. In this context, Paul presents Christ as the foundation of salvation and the believers' identity. The cosmic rulership of Christ in the Christ hymn may serve as the foundation of salvation which rails against false teachers who agitate the Colossian saints.[166]

In addition, the Christ hymn can be interpreted in terms of the election of Israel.[167] The land of Israel was regarded as the place where Wisdom dwells, and Col 1:19 reflects this idea.[168] The verb in Col 1:19 (εὐδοκέω) is used with the expression of election in Ps 44:3; 147:11; 149:4 and "πλήρωμα" occurs with "κατοικέω" in LXX Ps 68:17; 131:13, 14; Isa 8:18; 49:20. Christ can be regarded as containing all that God is. In this vein, Col 1:19–20 can be interpreted in terms of Temple and Shekinah theology (cf. Col 2:9; and *Sir* 24:3–12), and God is pleased to dwell in Christ,[169] as LXX Ps 67:17 God has been pleased to dwell on Mount Zion."[170] So, we find the notion in Col 1:19–20 that Christ is the temple, which was regarded as the centre of the universe by the Jews. Therefore, the notion of election redefined by means of Christology underlies the Christ hymn.[171]

---

priority over all creation," See Murray, *Colossians*, 44. So, what is stressed in Col 1:15b is the primary status of Christ as the firstborn son. Αὐτός ἐστιν πρὸ πάντων in Col 1:17a and κεφαλή, πρωτεύων and ἀρχή in Col 1:18 which highlights superiority of Christ may support our reading.

165 Stettler, *Kolosserhymnus*, 328–29.

166 Dübbers, *Christologie und Existenz*, 122.

167 Wright, "Poetry and Theology," 118–19.

168 See Wright "Poetry and Theology," 113; Beetham, *Echoes of Scripture in the Letter of Paul to the Colossians*, 143–56.

169 Some scholars find the origin of "πλήρωμα" in Gnosticism or Stoicism, but it is most fitting that this originated in the OT. See O'Brien, *Colossians*, 164. The OT acknowledges that the cosmos is filled with God himself (Jer 23:24, Ps 72:19, Isa 6:3, Ezek 43:5; 44:4).

170 Wright, "Poetry and Theology," 117.

171 The similarities between Col 1:15–20 and Heb 1 have been noticed by some scholars. E.g., Dunn, *Christology in the Making*, 190; L.D. Hurst, *The Epistle to the Hebrews: Its Background of Thought* (SNTSMS 65; Cambridge: Cambridge University Press, 1990), 177. Yet, Hurst maintains that "while the hymn of Colossians is closer to Hebrews than is Paul in Philippians, Colossians and Hebrews cannot be placed into any relationship of literary dependence at this point." Some interpreters note an affinity between the Christ hymn in Phil 2:5–11 and Heb 1 in terms of a literary relationship. See Ernst Lohmeyer, *Kyrios Jesus: Eine Untersuchung zu Phil. 2:5–11* (Heidelberg: C. Winter, 1928), 77; Michel, *Hebräer*, 36; Hofius, *Der Christushymnus Philipper 2,6–11*, 92; Hengel, *Der Sohn Gottes*, 135. However, the Christ hymn in Phil 2:5–11 does not mention the term 'firstborn son,' and so the origin of the firstborn son in Heb 1:6 is unclear in terms of the comparison with Phil 2:5–11.

In brief, the Christ hymn in Col 1:15–20 also specifically elucidates the position of Christ in relation to creation and election. In other words, the Christ hymn elaborates the status and ministry of Christ to the world and the church since the beginning of the world.[172] The hymn can be summarised in terms of comparison (Gegenüberstellung) between Christ and all creation.[173] However, we also find the exemplary function of the Christ hymn,[174] and it seems that what was at stake in the Colossian church was the Colossian saints' soteriological foundation and their identity as the people of God. Arguably, Paul presents Christ as the remedy for the Colossian saint's crisis of faith and identity. Therefore, the author of Colossians encourages the readers to understand their identity as the people of God in Christ (e.g., 1:12), and exhorts ethnic unity through the cosmic exemplar of Christ in the Christ hymn (3:10–11).[175] We will explore the meaning of the beloved son in 1:13 and the firstborn son in the Christ hymn in the following sections.

4.2.3 *The Meaning of the Firstborn Son in Col 1:15 and 1:18*

4.2.3.1 Inheritance Motif and the Beloved Son of God in Col 1:12–14

In this section, we will explore the themes of inheritance and the beloved son in Col 1:12–14.[176] The exodus allusions in Col 1:12–14 are widely acknowledged by scholars.[177] The phrases εἰς τὴν μερίδα τοῦ κλήρου in Col 1:12, ἐρρύσατο…ἐκ in Col 1:13 and ἀπολύτρωσιν in Col 1:14 evokes some expressions in the Pentateuch

172 Stettler, *Der Kolosserhymnus*, 327.

173 Stettler, *Der Kolosserhymnus*, 330.

174 Stephen Fowl rightly observes the exemplary function of the Christ hymn. See Stephen E. Fowl, *The Story of Christ in the Ethics of Paul: An Analysis of the Function of the Hymnic Material in the Pauline Corpus* (JSNTSup 36; Sheffield: Sheffield Academic Press, 1990), 123–54.

175 Zeilinger states that 'body of Christ' concept (Begriff Leib Christi) is a central expression in Colossian soteriology. The concept conveys the sense that the believers partake in the area of Christ's life. Participation in a higher life is a salvific reality of the believers. Christ as new Adam is "Urbild einer neuen Schöpfung." See Franz Zeilinger, *Der Erstgeborene der Schöpfung: Untersuchungen zur Formalstruktur und Theologie des Kolosserbriefes* (Wien: Herder, 1974), 207–8.

176 Col 1:12–14 plays a role as an introduction to the Christ hymn in Col 1:15–20. Some interpreters argue that Col 1:12–20 should be read in the liturgical background. See Norden, *Agnostos Theos*, 253; Günter Bornkamm, *Studien zu Antike und Urchristentum: Gesammelte Aufsätze*, vol. 2 (BEvt 28; Munich: Kaiser, 1959), 188–203; Käsemann, "A Primitive Christian Baptismal Liturgy," 154–55. However, it is doubtful that we should read Col 1:12–20 in the baptismal liturgical context. Rather, Col 1:12–24 should be read as "the closing section of Paul's petitionary prayer report" in terms of ancient epistolography. See Peter T. O'Brien, *Introductory Thanksgivings in the Letters of Paul* (NovTSup 49; Leiden: Brill, 1977), 93.

177 E.g., Gary S. Shogren, "Presently Entering the Kingdom of Christ: The Background and Purpose of Col 1:12–14," *JETS* 31 (1988): 176–77; Pizzuto, *A Cosmic Leap of Faith*, 228; Arnold,

(LXX). Κλῆρος is employed as a word pair with μερίς in the context of partitioning the Promised Land in the LXX: e.g., in LXX Deut 32:9, "the LORD's own portion (μερίς) was his people; Jacob is allotted share (κληρονομίας)"; and in LXX Josh 19:9, "The inheritance (κληρονομία) of the tribe of Simeon formed part of the territory (κλήρου) of Judah; because the portion (μερίς) of the tribe of Judah was too large for them, the tribe of Simeon obtained an inheritance (ἐκληρονόμησαν) within their portion (κλήρου)."[178] In these citations, μερίς is referenced in the context of physical inheritance given to Israel. The verb ἐρρύσατο in Col 1:13 may also reflect the uses of ῥύομαι in LXX Exod 6:6–8; 12:27; 14:30; LXX Judg 6:9; LXX *Wis* 10:15; 19:7–9. The noun ἀπολύτρωσιν in Col 1:14[179] can also be linked with the verb λυτρόω employed in the LXX in order to express God's redemption of Israel from Egypt (LXX Exod 6:6; 15:13; LXX Deut 7:8; 9:26; 15:15; LXX 2 Sam 7:23; LXX Ps 73:2; Isa 63:9, etc.).[180] Thus, Col 1:12–24 should be understood as the allusions of the Second Exodus (or *Eisodus*),[181] and the motif of inheritance is perceivable in this passage.

In some Jewish literature, the motifs of light and glory are used in the context of the story of Israel's inheritance. Brightness is a common motif concerning the eschatological situation of Israel in Jewish literature.[182] For instance, the war of the son of light against the son of darkness is the theme of the War Scroll from Qumran (1QM), where the author of 1QM envisages the annihilation of Belial and his forces and "the establishment of a world-wide holy empire of the Sons of Light centred in Jerusalem with God as king."[183]

As shown in previous chapters, inheritance motifs are broadly used in ancient Jewish literature. We have already explored that Israel receives the

---

The Colossian Syncretism, 288; Beetham, *Echoes of Scripture*, 94–95; Barth and Blanke, *Colossians*, 188; Wright, *The Climax of the Covenant*, 109; Fee, *Pauline Christology*, 296–97.

178 Forman, *Politics of Inheritance*, 220–21.

179 Cf. ἀπολύτρωσις in Rom 3:24; 8:23; 1 Cor 1:30; Eph 1:7, 14; 4:30; Heb 9:15; 11:35; Luke 21:28. For the concept of ἀπολύτρωσις, see David Hill, *Greek Words and Hebrew Meaning: Studies in the Semantics of Soteriological Terms* (SNTSMS 5; Cambridge: Cambridge University Press, 1967), 49–81.

180 Beetham, *Echoes of Scripture*, 82.

181 The phrase εἰς τὴν βασιλείαν τοῦ υἱοῦ τῆς ἀγάπης αὐτοῦ in Col 1:13 may be a messianic allusion (cf. 2 Sam 7:14, 18). See Fee, *Pauline Christology*, 297.

182 E.g., *1 En* 14:20–21; *2 En* 65:10; *Sib.Or.* 5:262.

183 See Marvin A. Sweeney, *Form and Intertextuality in Prophetic and Apocalyptic Literature* (FAT 45; Tübingen: Mohr Siebeck, 2005), 268. Cf. Dan 12:3; Zech 9:10; Matt 13:32; 14:7. Thus, motifs of glory and light are linked with the destiny and status of the chosen ones. Motifs of brightness are also employed in the context of the eschatological salvation of Israel in Isa 55–66. For instance, Isa 58:5; 60:1–2, etc. In these verses, it is implied that Israel will dwell in the light and Israel is also the light itself. Further, light is connected to the glorious status of Israel.

Land of Palestine and the entire world as her inheritance and is addressed as the firstborn son in glory and eternal light in 4Q369 (see 3.6.2). In 4Q462, the period of darkness is over and the period of light has arrived (line 10). Light shines over Jacob and illuminates Zion (line 3). Inheritance is given to the seeds of Jacob (line 7), and God's glory will fill the waters and the earth. The fullness of the kingdom is with him (God) and the light is with them (the seeds of Jacob). This passage also reflects Israel's eschatological expectation of the inheritance. The contents of the inheritance for the Israelites is unclear, but may be related to the glory and the rulership implied in line 7.

The author of 4Q475 illustrates the renewed earth. There will be no more guilty deeds on the earth. All the world will be like Eden and at peace forever (lines 5–6). God will give his beloved son (most probably, Israel) everything as his inheritance (line 7). The inheritance for his beloved son perhaps refers to the entire world. In 4Q462 and 4Q475, the inheritance may be related to the entire world and the rulership over the world (cf. 1Q34 3 ii 1–3), but the specific meaning is unclear. In these texts, the motifs of light, the beloved son and inheritance reminds the readers of the text in Col 1:12–14. So, it can be concluded that the inheritance motif in Col 1:12–14 reflects Jewish eschatological expectations of the inheritance (also see section 1.2.2).

It should be noted that the son of love (τοῦ υἱοῦ τῆς ἀγάπης) is referenced in Col 1:13. This must be the Semitic expression of 'the beloved son.' This phrase perhaps originates in the title of Isaac in Gen 22 (see section 4.1.3), but also we should also perceive that a similar title is also used to address Ephraim (i.e., Israel) in LXX Jer 38:20 (υἱὸς ἀγαπητός; cf. MT Jer 31:20). This title is used in the context of returning to the Promised Land (par. LXX Jer 38:16: ἐπιστρέψουσιν ἐκ γῆς ἐχθρῶν). As shown above, in 4Q475, the beloved son also refers to Israel who inherits the Land. So, it is most probable that the title of the beloved son in Col 1:13 originates in the title of Isaac and Israel as the heir. Moreover, the notion of sharing in the inheritance is mentioned in Col 1:12, and this underpins our interpretation of the context of 1:12–14. Christ is designated as the firstborn son in Col 1:15 and 18 together with the motifs of the beloved son and the inheritance (Col 1:12–14), as the title of the firstborn son in Rom 8:29 is used along with the son and the inheritance (Rom 8:32). We will investigate the meaning of the firstborn son in Col 1:15 and 18 in the next sections.

4.2.3.2 The Meaning of "the Firstborn Son of All Creation" in Col 1:15

It seems clear that the false teachers did not properly understand who Christ was (i.e., the status of Christ over angelic powers) and what Christ fulfilled in his crucifixion and resurrection. In Colossians, Paul elucidates the new identity of the Colossian saints in Christ as a counter-argument against Jewish mystic and syncretic teachings. The Colossian saints cannot ensure their salvation through their Jewish mystic and syncretic practices, but Christ offers the foundation of salvation and identity as the people of God for believers. Perhaps, the false teachers denied that Gentile Christians shared in the inheritance of Israel.[184] The circumcision in Col 2:8–15 recalls the same issue in Gal 2:1–10, 12; 5:1–12; 6:15, and the calendric observance including the Sabbath in Col 2:16 and the food law in Col 2:16 and 2:21–22 also evoke Gal 2:11–18 and 4:10. Colossians deals with different issues (i.e., Jewish mysticism) than does Galatians. However, the observance of the ritual law was also a significant issue in both Colossians and Galatians, and the false teachers may have taught the Colossian believers that the observance of the ritual law was a way of earning their salvation and membership as the people of God. So, in Colossians, one of the primary issues for the Colossian believers were the means of salvation and acquiring the membership of the people of God.[185]

In this context, Paul correct the false teachings on the basis of his Christological discussions in Colossians. The Colossian saints are in Christ (Col 1:2) and mature in Christ (Col 1:28). They have died with Christ and were raised with Christ (Col 2:20 and 3:1). They have been raised up with Christ, who is seated at the right hand of God (Col 3:1). They have clothed themselves with a new man (3:10; cf. 1:15). Clothes indicate an important facet of ancient people's identity. Then, "clothing themselves with the new man according to the image" entails and expresses a new identity for the believers.[186] Peace of Christ should rule in the hearts of the Colossian saints (3:15–16). Furthermore, Paul says, "And whatever you do, in word or deed, do everything in the name of the Lord Jesus." So, Christ constitutes a significant part of the believers' new identity. The new identity of the Colossian saints can be spoken of as identity in Christ. In this vein, the identity of the Colossian believers was "centred in Christ as head of the body to which they belonged, the Christ community assembly."[187] In this context, Christ is designated as the firstborn son in Col 1:15 and 1:18.

Col 1:12–20 signals similar eschatological expectations of Israel in the context of the allusions to the Exodus account (see the previous section), and reflects the Jewish tradition which depicts that Israel receives her inheritance in light and glory. Inheritance in Colossians is associated with the entirety of

---

184 See Bevere, *Sharing in the Inheritance*, 58–59.

185 E.g., Bevere, *Sharing in the Inheritance*, 255; Dübbers, *Christologie und Existenz*, 118.

186 Canavan discusses this dimension in a full detail. See Rosemary Canavan *Clothing the Body of Christ at Colossae: A Visual Construction of Identity* (WUNT II/334; Mohr Siebeck: Tübingen, 2012).

187 Canavan, *Clothing the Body of Christ at Colossae*, 192.

creation and with glory (1:27; 3:4), and this accords well with expectations of inheritance in 1Q34 3 ii 1–3, 4Q171, 4Q369, 4Q462 and 4Q418 9 12, as discussed above (section 4.2.3.1). In Col 1:12, the believers share in the inheritance of the saints in the light. This idea corresponds to the description that Israel as the firstborn son receives her inheritance in the eternal light in Jewish literature. Thus, the given context enables us to conclude that the title of the firstborn son (πρωτότοκος) in Col 1:15 is associated with an heir possessing the Promised Land and primacy over other creatures as in 4Q369 and *PrJos*. Therefore, the similarities between Col 1 and some Jewish documents denote that Col 1 clearly reflects Israel's eschatological inheritance pattern: i.e., Israel as the firstborn son receives her inheritance. So, the firstborn son in Col 1:15 should also be understood as a motif of the eschatological inheritance and as the title of Israel.

Justin's *Dial.* 100.1–2 also offers some clues on the meaning of the firstborn son in Col 1:15 (cf. *Dial.* 125.3). In *Dial.* 100.2, Justin asserts that Christ is known as "the firstborn son of God and the one who is before all creation" (γνόντες αὐτὸν πρωτότοκον μὲν τοῦ θεοῦ καὶ πρὸ πάντων τῶν κτισμάτων). This expression may be an echo of Col 1:15 (particularly, see πρὸ πάντων in Col 1:17), and implies the pre-existence of Christ.[188] Justin simultaneously points out that Christ is both Jacob and Israel in the OT (100.1), and the son of the patriarchs (100.2). In particular, the phrase "the son of the patriarchs (τῶν πατριαρχῶν υἱός)" is juxtaposed with the title "the firstborn son of God." So, in this verse, it seems that the intrinsic sense of the firstborn son as the title of Jacob and Israel does not fade in *Dial.* 100.2. Furthermore, we should note that, in Justin, *Dial.* 75.2–4; 125.5; 130.3, Israel is identified with Christ's name.[189] Thus, Justin's *Dialogue with Trypho* provides some examples of Christ being identified with Israel, and that the title of Israel is bestowed upon Christ.[190]

We have already considered that the angelomorphic Israel (v. 1) is addressed as "the firstborn son of every living being which is given life by God" in *PrJos* A, 3 (section 3.9).[191] *PrJos* A 3 also indicates the creation motif in that every living

188 Susan Wendel, *Scriptural Interpretation and Community Self-Definition in Luke-Acts and the Writings of Justin Martyr* (NovTSup 139; Leiden: Brill, 2011), 105. Cf. For the concept of the pre-existence in the Synoptic Gospels, see Simon J. Gathercole, *The Pre-Existent Son: Recovering the Christologies of Matthew, Mark, and Luke* (Grand Rapids: Eerdmans, 2006).

189 Erwin R. Goodenough, *The Theology of Justin Martyr: An Investigation into the Conceptions of Early Christian Literature and its Hellenistic and Judaistic Influences* (Amsterdam: Philo Press, 1968), 171.

190 Cf. Denise Kimber Buell, *Why This New Race: Ethnic Reasoning in Early Christianity* (New York: Columbia University Press, 2005), 98–102.

191 Cf. Hans Windisch, "Die Göttliche Weisheit der Juden und die paulinische Christologie," in *Neutestamentliche Studie: Georg Heinrici zu seinem 70. Geburtstag dargebracht* (ed. Hans Windisch; Leipzig: Heinrichs, 1914), 225; Jarl E. Fossum, *The Name of God and the Angel of*

thing was created (given life) by God, and the Colossian hymn is also deeply related to the theme of creation. Israel in *PrJos* has a heavenly status and dwells in heaven, and the Colossian hymn also indicates that Christ has a heavenly status (par. Col 1:16, 18). Every living being should be subjugated to Israel/Jacob as the angels should be submitted to Israel/Jacob who is the first minister of God (*PrJos* Frag A, 8). In Col 1:16, all things including the angels were created through and for Christ, and Christ has a primacy over everything (αὐτός ἐστιν πρὸ πάντων) in Col 1:17. As discussed in section 3.9. Jacob in Genesis became an heir who inherited the divine promise instead of his brother Esau (see *PrJos* Frag B). Thus, similar mystical depictions between *PrJos* and Col 1 reveal that the firstborn son in Col 1:15 can be understood as the title of Israel holding the supreme status over all creatures.

The firstborn son in Col 1:15 is modified by πάσης κτίσεως, and this stresses the notion of the firstborn son who has rulership and supremacy over every creature.[192] If we read it as a partitive genitive, it suggests that Christ is a part of every creature. Yet, Col 1:16 distinguishes Christ from all creation. Furthermore, when Israel is designated as πρωτότοκος in Jewish literature, it does not mean that Israel is a being which was first created. Alternatively, this can be objective genitive. If we select this view, the firstborn son implies rulership over creation.[193]

Moreover, the firstborn son of every living being does not indicate a brotherly relationship between Israel and every living being in *PrJos*, and rather, it recounts the rulership of Israel as an heir and the supreme status of Israel among every living being (see section 3.9.2). So, this context does not allow the reader to conclude that, in Col 1:15, Christ belongs to "every creature" or Christ has a brotherly relationship with "every creature." Instead, all things were created for Christ (Col 1:16) and Christ takes possession of every creature as his inheritance.

Inheritance in Col 1:12–20 includes the entire creation which will be restored by God through Christ. Inheritance of the physical land corresponds

---

the Lord: Samaritan and Jewish Concepts of Intermediation and the Origin of Gnosticism (WUNT 1/36; Tübingen: Mohr Siebeck, 1985), 314–18.

192 As Stettler maintains, "Also muss doch ein Genetivus partitivus vorliegen; rein grammatisch gesehen wird der 'Erstgeborene' als ein Teil der Grösse 'alle Geschöpfe' bezeichnet. Aber schon die Formulierung πάσης κτίσεως statt πάσης τῆς κτίσεως lässt vermuten, dass der 'Erstgeborene' hier nicht in eine Reihe von Gleichen eingefügt wird, sondern den Geschöpfen in qualitativem Abstand gegenübersteht." See Stettler, *Der Kolosserhymnus*, 148.

193 Larry Helyer, "Recent Research on Col 1:15–20 (1980–1990)," *GTJ* 12 (1992): 64–65. See also Hofius, "Erstgeborener vor aller Schöpfung," 224.

to the eschatological inheritance pattern (e.g., 1Q34 3 ii 1–3; 4Q418 9 12; 4Q369; *Sir* 44:17–23; *4 Ezra* 6:58–59). Αὐτός ἐστιν πρὸ πάντων in 1:17a denotes that Christ holds a pre-eminent status over all things.[194] In the parallel structure, the modifier πάσης κτίσεως acquires a similar meaning with πρὸ πάντων. Every creature is related to "all things in heaven and on earth were created, things visible and invisible, whether thrones or dominions or rulers or powers—all things have been created through him and for him" in Col 1:16. Accordingly, πάσης κτίσεως highlights the pre-eminent status of Christ over all creation as the firstborn son.

Many scholars link the firstborn son in Col 1:15 with the title of Wisdom in Hellenistic Jewish Wisdom literature as shown in the first chapter. Burney, Beetham, Wright and Fossum regard Col 1:15 as an echo of Prov 8:22, and argue that Col 1:15 reflects the development of the Wisdom tradition in ancient Judaism.[195] Yet, they do not provide any evidence that the expressions in Prov 8:22 were developed into the title of the firstborn son. In Hellenistic Jewish Wisdom literature, it is not evinced that the title of the firstborn son ascribed to Logos originated in Prov 8:22 (see also section 3.14.4), while the cosmological agency of Christ in the Colossian hymn possibly originated in Hellenistic Jewish speculation about Wisdom.[196]

In fact, the reason Philo addresses Logos/Wisdom as the firstborn son was not monolithic, and the meanings and the origins of the firstborn son as the title of Logos/Wisdom were also variegated (see section 3.14.4). Among these potential sources of the firstborn son title, *Conf* 146 indicates certain similarities with the Colossian hymn, while it seems that they (Col 1:15–20 and *Conf* 146) do not directly rely on each other.[197] Logos in *Conf* 145–46 is called εἰκών, ἀρχή and πρωτόγονος, and these designations evoke Christ's titles in Col 1:15–20 (cf. *Leg* 1.43). The mediatorship of Christ in Col 1:15–20 recalls the activities of Logos (or Wisdom) in creation. As we have seen in the previous chapter,

194 The proposition πρό in 1:17 can mean 'before' with temporal force or 'superiority in status.' But as with πρωτότοκος in Col 1:15 and *Sir* 1:4 (προτέρα πάντων ἔκτισται σοφία), this likely means the former, but as for the present tense of the verb and "κεφαλή" in 1:18, we can prefer the latter one. See Lohse, *Colossians*, 51.

195 See section 1.1.1.2. Some scholars view the title of the firstborn son in Col 1:15 as an allusion to the Wisdom tradition. E.g., Beetham, *Echoes of Scripture*, 133–34; Fossum, *The Name of God*, 316; Burney, "Christ as the ΑΡΧΗ of Creation," 173–74; Wright, *The Covenant of the Climax*, 112.

196 For the development of the concept of the wisdom in Early Christianity, see Gabriele Boccaccini, "Finding a Place for the Parables of Enoch within Second Temple Jewish Literature," in *Enoch and the Messiah Son of Man: Revisiting the Book of Parables* (ed. Gabriele Boccaccini; Grand Rapids: Eerdmans, 2007), 278–83.

197 Cox, *By the Same Word*, 174–75.

we already concluded that Hellenistic Jewish speculation about Wisdom in *Conf* 145–46 is combined with the tradition relating to the heavenly status of Israel (section 3.14.4).[198] A similar phenomenon is also detected in Col 1:15–20. It seems clear that the mediatorship of Christ in creation in the Christ hymn was derived from Hellenistic Jewish Speculation about Wisdom.[199] However, we should also bear in mind that Israel is regarded as the centre of creation in Jewish literature (e.g., *Jub* 1–2; *4 Ezra* 6; *PrJos* A). In Jewish literature, the chosen righteous plays a central role in creation and re-creation. For instance, in *the Animal Apocalypse* (*1 En* 90), the righteous community is centred on divine judgement and re-creation of the heaven and earth. In *the Apocalypse of Weeks* (*1 En* 93:10), the "chosen righteous" receives "sevenfold teaching concerning his whole creation." In *Jub* 1:26, the Jews are elected before creation. "Πρωτόγονος παντὸς ζῴου" in *PrJos* A 3 also denotes the primacy and centrality of Israel over all creation. The land of Israel was also regarded as the place where Wisdom dwells. Temple and Shekinah theology is also found in Col 1:19 (cf. *Sir* 24:3–12) and Col 1:19 alludes to LXX Ps 67:17, which mentions that God was pleased to dwell on Mount Zion.[200] So, it is extremely likely that the tradition about Wisdom is combined with the story of heavenly Israel in Col 1:15–20. Therefore, it is most reasonable to conclude that the firstborn son in Col 1:15 originated in the title of Israel, and that the Christ hymn was influenced by the tradition which links the story of heavenly Israel with the concept of Wisdom (or Logos).

We have already concluded that the εἰκών in Rom 8:29 originated in the Jacob–Israel tradition (e.g., Philo, *Conf* 147; *b. Hul.* 91b; *Tg. Ps.-J. Gen* 28:12; *Tg. Neof. Gen* 28:12; *Gen.Rab.* 82:2; *Lam. Rab.* 2:2; *Num. Rab.* 4:1, etc) as well as the Wisdom and Adam tradition.[201] We also observe the same combination of εἰκών and πρωτότοκος in Rom 8:29 and Col 1:15, and this may imply that Rom 8:29 and Col 1:15 are rooted in a similar heavenly Israel tradition concerning εἰκών and πρωτότοκος. The heavenly Israel tradition in Rom 8:29 and

---

198 Cf. Hayward, *Interpretations of the Name Israel*, 201.

199 Cox, *By the Same Word*, 171.

200 Wright, "Poetry and Theology," 117; Stettler, *Der Kolosserhymnus*, 252–59.

201 In Classical Greek, the meaning of εἰκών straddled a variety of spectrum such as 1) likeness and image, whether picture or statue; 2) image in a mirror; 3) living image, representation; and 4) semblance, phantom. H.G. Liddell and R.Scott, *A Greek-English Lexicon* (Oxford: Clarendon, 1996), 485. In the LXX, the meaning of εἰκών ranges from likeness (Gen 1:26; 5:3; Hos 13:2; *Sir* 17:3) to something made in resemblance of something else (*Wis* 2:23; as statue (Ezek 16:17); as painting (Ezek 23:14)). Takamitsu Muraoka, *A Greek-English Lexicon of the Septuagint* (Louvain: Peeters, 2009), 192. On the other hand, εἰκών also refers to a philosophical concept. In Plato, *Timaeus* 29B, εἰκών occurs in relation to cosmological discussion: "It is wholly necessary that the cosmos should be a copy (εἰκόνα) of something."

Col 1:15 is referenced in the context of the inheritance tradition in Rom 8 and Col 1. In Philo, *Conf* 146–147, εἰκών is associated with Logos but simultaneously refers to the one who sees God, i.e., Israel. We detect the cosmic agency of Christ which stemmed from Wisdom tradition in the Colossian hymn, but this Logos/Wisdom tradition is not incompatible with the heavenly Israel tradition in Col 1:15–20. Rather, it seems that Wisdom tradition is combined with the heavenly Israel tradition in Col 1:15–20 just as in *Conf* 146–147. Thus, Rom 8:29 and Col 1:15 indicate that they share a similar tradition about εἰκών and πρωτότοκος in connection with the heavenly Israel and Logos.

It should also be acknowledged that εἰκών τοῦ θεοῦ in Col 1:15 is a procreative image (e.g., Gen 5:1 and 3), and is related to an *Urbild* of Israel and the family of God. Through conformity to the image of God, the believers live as family members of God (Col 3:10–11). This understanding of εἰκών fits well with the adoption image in Col 1:12–13. The believers were transferred into the kingdom of God's beloved son, and share in the inheritance of the saints in the light, and this implies that the Colossians believers became the descendants of Abraham. They could also enjoy privilege and election equal to the Jews (3:11). The image and the firstborn son in Col 1:15 should be considered in this regard. Thus, εἰκών in Col 1:15 is related to becoming members of the kingdom of God's beloved son (Col 1:13). Therefore, Christ as εἰκών represents an archetype of 'children of God,' and πρωτότοκος as the title of Israel signifies the status of Israel as the Elect in primacy and inheritance.

Martin Hengel finds the origin of the divine sonship in its Hellenistic-Jewish usage as messianic figures and pre-existent Wisdom or Metatron in *Sirach*, *Wisdom of Solomon*, *Joseph and Aseneth*, 3 *Enoch* and wisdom traditions. He also makes a claim that three thought patterns are involved with the son of God title in Hellenistic-Jewish usage: pre-existence, mediation at creation and sending into the world.[202] While his overall arguments are persuasive, his view on the sapiential traditional origin of the firstborn son seems problematic at some points.[203] First of all, we do not find any direct connections between the 'son of God' and Wisdom in the evidence which Hengel presents. Indeed, it is doubtful that Wisdom is addressed as son of God in Jewish Wisdom literature. Rather, Wisdom is designated as daughter of God (Philo, *Fug.* 50; *Virt.* 62; *Q.Gen.* 4, 97) or πρωτόγονος (Philo, *Conf.* 146; *Somn* 1.125). In Philo's writings, the term πρωτόγονος is used as a kinship metaphor which indicates the status of Israel. In *Wis* 2:18, those inspired by Wisdom are addressed as "sons of

202 Hengel, *Son of God*, 57.

203 For a similar view, see Klaus Berger, "Zum traditionsgeschichtlichen Hintergrund christologischer Hoheitstitel," *NTS* 17 (1971): 422.

God," but Wisdom is not nominated as a "son of God." So, Wisdom is associated with "son of God," but is not identified with "son of God." Rather, the one who is designated as a "son of God" is Israel, as Hengel notes,[204] and this reflects Jewish usage of "son of God" as the title of Israel (e.g., Exod 4:22; Deut 14:1; Jer 31:9, 20). Therefore, we conclude that Hengel's connection between the title "firstborn" and the Wisdom tradition is not fully persuasive.

J.D.G. Dunn observes that Christ was viewed as personified Wisdom, particularly "the exhaustive embodiment of divine Wisdom" in early Christianity.[205] Christ embodies Wisdom of God, but this does not mean that Christ is pre-existent as Wisdom of God.[206] That is, Wisdom Christology cannot evidence that Christ was identified with God in early Christianity. However, Dunn's view also contains the same problem as Hengel's. Dunn identifies πρωτόγονος in Philonic literature with πρωτότοκος in the LXX and the NT,[207] and he uses this identification in order to define the meaning of πρωτότοκος in Col 1:15 in terms of Jewish (Hellenistic-Jewish) Wisdom speculation. However, Dunn overlooks that both πρωτόγονος and πρωτότοκος were used as titles of Israel in Hellenistic Jewish literature. In Philo, *Conf* 146, the term, πρωτόγονος reflects the tradition about the heavenly Israel (cf. *PrJos* A, 3).[208] In *Conf* 146 and *PrJos*, Jacob and Israel is a sort of boundary figure between heaven and earth, and the title πρωτόγονος is bestowed upon Jacob–Israel (*PrJos*) and Logos–Israel (*Conf* 146). The term πρωτόγονος does not simply refer to the title of Logos in Hellenistic Jewish literature, but also was used as a title for Israel.[209]

Jarl Fossum writes that the Christ hymn "actually seems to bear witness to an Anthropos-Christology," and that the concept of the firstborn son in Col 1:15 and *PrJos* originated in the notion of "the Glory" and "the heavenly Man,"[210] and also insists that the concept of the firstborn son in Col 1:15 is related to the

---

204 Hengel, *Son of God*, 50–51. Cf. Ziener considers the righteous man in *Wis* 2:12–20 as a messianic figure. See Georg Ziener, *Die theologische Begriffssprache im Buche der Weisheit* (BBB 11; Bonn: Peter Hanstein, 1956), 116–18.

205 J.D.G. Dunn, *Christology in the Making: An Inquiry into the Origins of the Doctrine of the Incarnation* (1st edition; London: SCM, 1980; 3rd edition; Grand Rapids: Eerdmans, 2010), 195.

206 Dunn, *Christology in the Making*, 210.

207 Dunn, *Christology in the Making*, 333, n. 110; 189.

208 Hayward, *Interpretations of the Name Israel*, 193.

209 Cf. Christopher R.A. Morray-Jones, "The Body of the Glory: Approaching the New Testament from the Perspective of Shiur Koma Traditions," in *The Mystery of God: Early Jewish Mysticism and the New Testament* (eds. C. Rowland and C.R.A. Morray-Jones; CRINT 12; Leiden: Brill, 2009), 561–62.

210 Jarl E. Fossum, "Colossians 1. 15–18a. in the Light of Jewish Mysticism and Gnosticism," *NTS* 35 (1989): 201.

demiurgic activity.[211] However, we do not find the evidence in ancient Judaism that the concept of the firstborn son is related to the demiurgic activity (see chapter 3). We have already observed the meaning of the firstborn son in *PrJos* in section 3.9.2 and in Philo in section 3.14.3 and 3.14.4, and have concluded that the title of the firstborn son originated in the title of Jacob/Israel. So, contrary to Fossum's view, it is doubtful that the concept of the firstborn son in Col 1:15 is related to the role of a demiurgic figure.

Ronald Cox contends that the firstborn son in Col 1:15 is associated with *Wis* 6:22:[212] "I will tell you what wisdom is and how she came to be, and I will hide no secrets from you, but I will trace her course from the beginning of creation, and make knowledge of her clear, and I will not pass by the truth." However, no linguistic and thematic parallel is found between Col 1:15 and *Wis* 6:22. Ἀρχῆς γενέσεως ἐξιχνιάσω (I will explore from the beginning of creation) in *Wis* 6:22 does not contain any notion of the firstborn son. Thus, this study concludes that the title of the firstborn son in Col 1:15 refers to the title of Israel possessing the central status over all creation and over the nations. The story of Israel is combined with the tradition about Logos in *Conf* 146, so it seems that the Christ hymn in Col 1:15–20 was influenced by this kind of combination of the concepts of Israel and Wisdom (or Logos).

In addition, we should note that the title of the firstborn son in Col 1:15 can be interpreted as a Davidic messianic title. In chapter 3, we did not find the evidence that the term 'firstborn son' was used as a messianic title, it is still probable that early Christians re-interpreted the title of πρωτότοκος in LXX Ps 88:28 as a messianic title. The heavenly status of Christ in Col 1:15 corresponds to the image of a messiah as an exalted heavenly figure in Jewish literature.[213] Therefore, this study does not deny that the title of the firstborn son can refer to a messianic title, while it is also the title of Israel.

In brief, πρωτότοκος πάσης κτίσεως in Col 1:15 symbolises the status of Israel in respect of inheritance and primacy over all creation.[214] In Col 1:15, Christ as

211 Fossum, *The Name of God*, 317.

212 Cox, *By the Same Word*, 171.

213 Chester, *Messiah and Exaltation*, 394–95.

214 Finally, how can we translate πρωτότοκος—the firstborn or the firstborn son? In the previous section, we explored that, when πρωτότοκος is used in the context of inheritance, it should be translated as the firstborn 'son.' When πρωτότοκος refers to Israel in LXX Exod 4:22, πρωτότοκος is juxtaposed with υἱός and this shows that πρωτότοκος in LXX Exod 4:22 is not merely the firstborn, but the firstborn 'son' in parallel with υἱός. We have argued that πρωτότοκος in Col 1:15 refers to the title of Israel as the heir of the promise. So, in this context, πρωτότοκος in Col 1:15 can be translated as the firstborn son.

the firstborn son embodies the status as the chosen possessing the primacy and enjoying the inheritance originally promised to Israel.

4.2.3.3 The Meaning of the Firstborn Son in Col 1:18

Κεφαλή in Col 1:18 refers to the headship of the church, and κεφαλὴ τοῦ σώματος τῆς ἐκκλησίας also implies that Christ is the head of the church (see Gen 1:1; Exod 12:2; Ezek 40:1). The perfect tense (συνέστηκεν) in 1:17b implies that God continues to hold all things in Christ.[215] Reyes also says, "The perfect tense συνέστηκεν seems to be highlighted by being placed between two identical present tenses."[216] Ἵνα γένηται ἐν πᾶσιν αὐτὸς πρωτεύων in Col 1:18b reveals that a supreme status was conferred on Christ. Ἀρχή in Col 1:18 means *Ursprung*,[217] and is paired up with ἀρχαί in Col 1:16 which means authorities or rulers (cosmic or angelic powers), and so, κεφαλή, πρωτεύων and ἀρχή in Col 1:18 highlight the primacy of Christ over the church (1:18a) and over "everything" (1:18c). In this context, the firstborn son in Col 1:18 can also be related to the pre-eminent status and heir of the promise in Col 1:12 and 15. Thus, κεφαλή, ἀρχή and πρωτεύων in Col 1:18 match the concept of πρωτότοκος in Col 1:18 as the pre-eminent status.[218]

Most scholars assume that ἐκ τῶν νεκρῶν highlights the concept of the temporal priority of the firstborn son.[219] It seems clear that πρωτότοκος ἐκ τῶν νεκρῶν is related to Christ's temporal priority in terms of resurrection. However, if the author of the Christ hymn intended to emphasise only the temporal priority of Christ in resurrection, why did he not use πρῶτος or ἀπαρχή (cf. 1 Cor 15:20)? Perhaps, πρωτότοκος ἐκ τῶν νεκρῶν in Col 1:18 has a double force.[220] If we define the firstborn son in 1:18 exclusively in the sense of temporal priority, it does not match the meaning of the firstborn son in 1:15 because most scholars do not conceive that the firstborn son in Col 1:15 refers to the temporal priority over creation. The firstborn son in Col 1:18 is asyndetic, and so it is

215 Moo, *Colossians and Philemon*, 125.

216 Reyes, "Structure," 144.

217 Hofius, "Erstgeborener vor aller Schöpfung," 226. Cf. Philo, *Heres* 172; *Decal* 52. Cf. Stettler, *Der Kolosserhymnus*, 245.

218 C.F.D. Moule, *The Epistles to the Colossians and to Philemon* (The Cambridge Greek Testament Commentary; Cambridge: Cambridge University Press, 1958), 68; Stettler, *Der Kolosserhymnus*, 236.

219 E.g., Deichgräber, *Gotteshymnus*, 153; Harris, *Colossians*, 48; Dunn, *Colossians and Philemon*, 98; Stettler, *Kolosserhymnus*, 242, 247; Moo, *Colossians and Philemon*, 129; Lohse, *Colossians and Philemon*, 56; Marianne Meye Thompson, *Colossians and Philemon* (THNTC; Grand Rapids: Eerdmans, 2005), 32; Schweizer, *Colossians*, 74.

220 Cf. Elisabeth Schüssler Fiorenza, *Priester Für Gott: Studien zum Herrschafts-und Priestermotiv in der Apokalypse* (NTAbh 7; Münster: Aschendorff, 1972), 201.

natural to read this notion in terms of the concept already stated in Col 1:15.[221] We already concluded that the firstborn son in Col 1:15 refers to the title of Israel possessing elected status. If so, it is highly likely that the firstborn son in Col 1:18 conveys the same meaning as the firstborn son in Col 1:15.

The connection between "the firstborn son" and "from the dead" denotes that the concept of the firstborn son is related to resurrection and new creation (cf. Rom 8:29; Heb 1:6; Rev 1:5).[222] In Heb 1:6, the firstborn son ascends into the heavenly realm and this means that Christ as the firstborn son (i.e., an heir of the promise) enters the Promised Land. "The firstborn son from the dead" in Col 1:18 evokes Christ as the firstborn son who was resurrected and entered the heavenly realm (i.e., the Promised Land) in Heb 1:6. As J.D. Levenson states, resurrection was understood by the Jews in terms of the national restoration (e.g., Ezek 37:1–14). So, "the Jewish expectation of a resurrection of the dead is always and inextricably associated with the restoration of the people Israel."[223] Πρωτότοκος ἐκ τῶν νεκρῶν implies this concept. So, the firstborn son is the title of Israel and resurrection is the event of Israel's restoration. Resurrection should not be thought of merely as an individual post-mortem destiny. Rather, resurrection was believed to be the national destiny of Israel. Accordingly, in Col 1:18, it is natural to link the firstborn son denoting the title of Israel to resurrection which means the restoration of the people of God. So, πρωτότοκος ἐκ τῶν νεκρῶν does not lose its meaning as the title of Israel. Christ resurrected as representative of Israel and the resurrection of Christ is the prototype of all Christians' resurrection.[224] As previously discussed, we already concluded that the theme of the Christ hymn is related to creation and election. Resurrection is the destiny of the chosen nation (i.e., the people of God), and Christ is representative of the chosen people (cf. Rom 6:8; 8:28–30). "The firstborn son from the dead" in Col 1:18 reveals that Christ is the chosen son of God and representative of Israel in terms of resurrection. The firstborn son is an heir of divine promise, and the divine promise of restoration of the people of God was accomplished through Christ's resurrection. Therefore, the firstborn son in Col 1:18 should be understood as the title of Israel, and "the firstborn son from the dead" in Col 1:18 signifies that Christ, representative of Israel, initiated the restoration of the people of God.

221 Harris, *Colossians*, 48; Barth and Blanke, *Colossians*, 207.

222 Hofius, "Erstgeborener vor aller Schöpfung," 227; Stettler, *Der Kolosserhymnus*, 236.

223 Jon D. Levenson, *Resurrection and the Restoration of Israel: The Ultimate Victory of the God of Life* (New Haven: Yale University Press, 2006), 164–65.

224 Hofius, "Erstgeborener vor aller Schöpfung," 227; Stettler, *Der Kolosserhymnus*, 242. Cf. Barnabas Lindars, *New Testament Apologetic: The Doctrinal Significance of the Old Testament Quotations* (London: SCM, 1961), 72–74.

In addition, we concluded, in chapter 2.2, that primogeniture existed in the Jewish family, and that the principal heir of the father was not arbitrarily chosen by the father, but was determined by the chronological order. In this perspective, πρωτότοκος in Col 1:18 can refer not only to the title of Israel, but simultaneously to the eldest brother in a temporal sense. In terms of primogeniture, πρωτότοκος is the eldest son of the father. Therefore, it would be natural that πρωτότοκος in Col 1:18 contains a temporal sense.

In summary, the firstborn son in Col 1:18 should be read as the title of Israel, and represents the realisation of the promise made to Israel. "The firstborn son from the dead" presents Christ as the representative of Israel and who initiated the accomplishment of the covenant given to Israel.

4.2.4 *Conclusion*

In this section, we have argued that the firstborn son in Col 1:15 and 1:18 refers to the title of Israel who possesses the promise and the exalted status over all creation. The title of the firstborn son in Col 1:15 and 1:18 has double connotations. In Col 1:15, the firstborn son is related to the title of Israel and Wisdom. In Col 1:18, the firstborn son is associated with the title of Israel and the temporal priority in terms of resurrection. On the other hand, the firstborn son represents the central and chosen position of Israel. It is highly probable that faith and identity of the Colossian believers as the people of God were threatened by the errorists who taught Jewish mystic and ascetic practices. So, Paul needed to respond to the false teaching which taught that the believers could earn their salvation and gain identity as the people of God through Jewish legal and mystic practices. Therefore, the Colossian saints can partake in eschatological inheritance through union with Christ the firstborn son, not through Jewish mystical and ascetic practices. In addition, πρωτότοκος in Col 1:18 contains the sense of temporal priority, since the firstborn son was also the eldest son in terms of Jewish primogeniture.

4.3 Hebrews

4.3.1 *The Letter-Recipients and the Purpose of Hebrews*

This section will consider the purpose of Hebrews. In Heb 6:4–6, 10:25–27 and 12:16–17, the author warns against apostasy. In Heb 5:11-6:8, the author of Hebrews states that the recipients were slow to realise what was fulfilled in Christ.[225] Perhaps, the letter-recipients were at risk of apostasy, or of

225 G.L. Cockerill, *The Epistle to the Hebrews* (NICNT; Grand Rapids: Eerdmans, 2012), 16.

compromising their faith. Heb 10:32-34, 11:1-40 and 12:1-11 indicate that the letter-recipients experienced social marginalisation due to their Christian faith.[226] It seems that the recipients were familiar with the cultic institutions and the Mosaic Law in the OT and that they acknowledged the authority of the OT.[227] The author of Hebrews reassures his audience to hold fast to their faith that the sacrifice of Christ fulfilled the promise given to Abraham and to Moses.

Yet, there has been no consensus regarding the ethnic identity of the recipients. As Attridge observes, the meaning of "those from Italy send you greetings" in Heb 13:24 is unclear, because the preposition ἀπό does not necessarily designate "the place of origin."[228] Two main possibilities about the ethnic background of the recipients are 1) Jewish Christians and 2) a Gentile or mixed congregation.[229] Interpreters in support of the first option mostly assume the relapse theory that Hebrews was written in order to persuade the Jewish Christian recipients not to return to their previous Jewish religion and its cult. The former view could be persuasive, since Hebrews contains sharp warnings against apostasy, and appears to elaborate the superiority of Christianity over the Jewish cultic system.[230]

Other exegetes view the letter-recipients as Gentile believers or as a mixed community.[231] Hans-Friedrich Weiss maintains that it is not reasonable to assume the ethnic identity of the recipients on the basis of discussions on the Jewish cult, since similar discussions on the Jewish cultic Law are found in the Pauline corpus (particularly, Galatians and Colossians), *Barnabas* and

226 Cockerill, *Hebrews*, 17.

227 Paul Ellingworth, *The Epistle to the Hebrews* (NIGTC; Grand Rapids: Eerdmans, 1993), 23.

228 H.W. Attridge, *Hebrews: A Commentary on the Epistle to the Hebrews* (Hermeneia; Minneapolis: Fortress, 1989), 409–10: Cockerill argues that "those from Italy" in Heb 13:24 implies that the author and "his hearers moved in a circle that included people living outside Palestine." See Cockerill, *Hebrews*, 16.

229 Ellingworth supports the theory of the mixed congregation, and argues that "the systematic exclusion" of OT quotations or allusions in Hebrews which negatively mention the Jews or Gentiles implies the mixed congregations. See Ellingworth, *The Epistle to the Hebrews*, 25.

230 Iutisone Salevao, *Legitimation in the Letter to the Hebrews: The Construction and Maintenance of a Symbolic Universe* (JSNTSup 219; Sheffield: Sheffield University Press, 2002), 113. In a similar vein, Salevao argues that the author aims at separating the recipients from Jewish religion. See Salevao, *Legitimation in the Letter to the Hebrews*, 114.

231 E.g., Martin Karrer, *Der Brief an die Hebräer: Kapitel 1,1–5,10* (ÖTK 20/1; Gütersloh: Gütersloher, 2002), 100. Cf. Ernst Käsemann, *The Wandering People of God: An Investigation of the Letter to the Hebrews* (Trans. R.A. Harrisville and I.L. Sandberg; Minneapolis: Augsburg, 1984), 59. He reads the epistle in terms of a Gnostic myth of the redeemed redeemer.

1 Clement (e.g., 41:2) sent to Gentile Christians.[232] Heb 3:12 can be read as a warning against a general falling away from the faith, rather than returning to their Jewish religious faith: "Take care, brothers, lest there be in any of you an evil, unbelieving heart, leading you to fall away from the living God." "Not to fall away from the living God" could be an improper exhortation, if the recipients were Jewish Christians[233] because the Jews were generally not atheists and followed their living God. Moreover, exhortations in Heb 6:1–9 can be regarded as typical *topoi* of *Heidenmissionspredigt*.[234] Heb 2:3b implies that the recipients are second generation Christians: "It was declared at first through the Lord, and it was attested to us by those who heard him." So, Hebrews can be situated at the point where the church was falling into typical religious weariness (Glaubensmüdigkeit) and losing their religious passion.[235] DeSilva states that the title of Hebrews (the Epistle to the Hebrews) was simply derived from the early Christians' conjecture that the recipients would be Jewish Christians.[236] While the ethnic composition of the letter-recipients has been disputed, it is clear that the author of Hebrews proposes that the recipients take a salvation-historical look at their situation, and encourages them to perceive themselves as those who can approach God through the new covenant.[237]

There are some debates on the attitude of Hebrews towards Judaism. Firstly, some scholars assume that the author of Hebrews was not interested in Judaism. Ernst Käsemann writes that the main interest of the author in Hebrews is the comparison between the heavenly and the earthly, in which Judaism merely represents earthly things.[238] Secondly, some scholars maintain that the author of Hebrews exhorts his readers to forsake the Jewish identity, and believe that Hebrews implies specific conflicts between Christianity and Judaism.[239] Thirdly, other interpreters stress Jewish features of Hebrews, and hold that Hebrews does not contain a certain rivalry between two religious systems (i.e., Christianity and Judaism), but the conflicts implied in Hebrews

232 Hans-Friedrich Weiss, *Der Brief an die Hebräer* (KEK 13; Göttingen: Vandenhoeck & Ruprecht, 1991), 71–72.

233 Ellingworth argues that falling back from the living God is tantamount to hardening hearts (3:8, 13, 15) and that rejecting God's final revelation is rejecting God himself in Hebrews. See Ellingworth, *The Epistle to the Hebrews*, 24.

234 Weiss, *Der Brief an die Hebräer*, 71. Also see Karrer, *Der Brief an die Hebräer*, 101.

235 Erich Grässer, *An die Hebräer: 1. Teilband Hebr 1–6* (EKKNT; Zürich: Benziger, 1990), 24.

236 David DeSilva, *Perseverance in Gratitude: A Socio-Rhetorical Commentary on the Epistle "to the Hebrews"* (Grand Rapids: Eerdmans, 2000), 2.

237 DeSilva, *Perseverance in Gratitude*, 5.

238 Ernst Käsemann, *The Wandering People of God: An Investigation of the Letter to the Hebrews* (trans. R. Harrisville and I. Sandberg; Minneapolis: Augsburg, 1984), 59.

239 E.g., Salevao, *Legitimation in the Letter to the Hebrews*.

can be explained in terms of intra-Jewish debates. Some writes the author of Hebrews does not seek to separate Christian identity from Jewish identity.[240]

The debates on this issue are ongoing, but it is most likely that the author of Hebrews confirms that the true access to God is given to the Christian community.[241] The author of Hebrews therefore encourages his readers to stand firm in their Christian faith by highlighting that the true heir of the divine promise is Christ (1:2–3), and that the recipients are the true descendants of Abraham through Christ (2:16; 3:14) and will receive the promised inheritance (12:28). Thus, it is probable that Hebrews was written for the consolidation of the in-group formation through positive evaluations of the Christian community and negative evaluations of Jewish cultic institutions.

While the ethnicity tends to be centred in the debates on the identity of the recipients of Hebrews, we also have to consider the socio-economic background of the letter. The author depicts the socio-economic situation of the original readers in Heb 10:32–36:

> But recall those earlier days when, after you had been enlightened, you endured a hard struggle with sufferings, sometimes being publicly exposed to abuse and persecution, and sometimes being partners with those so treated. For you had compassion for those who were in prison, and you cheerfully accepted the plundering of your possessions, knowing that you yourselves possessed something better and more lasting. Do not, therefore, abandon that confidence of yours; it brings a great reward. For you need endurance, so that when you have done the will of God, you may receive what was promised.
>
> NRSV

From the quotation above, it is clear that the original readers experienced some sort of socio-economical marginalisation and disadvantages due to their Christian faith. In this situation, it seems that the author of Hebrews seeks to shape the identity of his audience as 'other.'[242] The identity of 'otherness' in

240 E.g., Richard B. Hays, "'Here We Have No Lasting City': New Covenantalism in Hebrews," in *The Epistle to the Hebrews and Christian Theology* (eds. Richard Bauckham, et al.; Grand Rapids: Eerdmans, 2009), 151–73.

241 DeSilva, *Perseverance in Gratitude*, 5–6.

242 Benjamin Dunning, "The Intersection of Aline Status and Cultic Discourse in the Epistle to the Hebrews," in *Hebrews: Contemporary Methods—New Insights* (BibInt 75; ed. Gabriella Gelardini; Leiden: Brill. 2005), 186. For outsider status of the letter recipients, see Ole Jakob Filtvedt, *The Identity of God's People and the Paradox of Hebrews* WUNT II/400; Tübingen: Mohr Siebeck, 2015), 240–52.

Hebrews can be viewed in terms of Platonic or Philonic otherworldliness[243] or anti-cultic attitude,[244] yet can also be related to the situation of the original readers, who were socially marginalised as seen above. The author of Hebrews reminds his readers that they do not belong to this present world. The sojourning motifs described in Hebrews can also be linked to the social situation of the original audience. For example, Abraham was a sojourner and serves as an ideal role model to those who are marginalised and separated from the rest of society.[245] Moses is another such figure, as pointed out by Dunning: "Moses is constructed as a hero who chose outsider status" (Heb 11:25–26).[246]

So, the author of Hebrews exhorts his readers to "go outside the camp" (13:13), which implies an encouragement to embrace their socially marginalised reality. 13:13–14 does not simply mean to depart from Judaism,[247] but can be linked to the author's exhortation to follow Christ, who is a representative of outsiders, and to embrace the wilderness experience as outsiders.[248] As Dunning points out, "Therefore, the call to go 'outside the camp' does not simply orient the readers towards an otherworldly city; rather, the concern extends to matters of tangible everyday life."[249] Thus, the author of Hebrews seeks to shape and legitimate the identity of God's people as sojourners and outsiders, and to encourage them in the hardship of their wilderness experience.

4.3.2 *The Meaning of the Firstborn Son in Heb 1:6*

In this section, we will explore the origin and the implications of the firstborn son in Heb 1:6 as follows. In Heb 1:4–5, the author demonstrates "the Son's ontological superiority" over the angels, and in Heb 1:6, he reinforces the substance delineated in the previous two verses.[250] The meaning of ὅταν δὲ πάλιν εἰσαγάγῃ τὸν πρωτότοκον εἰς τὴν οἰκουμένην in Heb 1:6 has been disputed. Does it

243 E.g., James W. Thompson, *The Beginning of Christian Philosophy: The Epistle to the Hebrews* (Washington, DC: The Catholic Biblical Association of America, 1982).

244 E.g., Helmut Koester, "'Outside the Camp': Hebrews 13:9–14," *HTR* 55 (1962): 299–315.

245 Pamela Eisenbaum, *The Jewish Heroes of Christian History: Hebrews 11 in Literary Context* (SBLDS 156; Atlanta: Scholars, 1997), 161.

246 Dunning, "The Intersection of Aline Status," 189.

247 F.F. Bruce, *The Epistle to the Hebrews* (NICNT; Grand Rapids: Eerdmans, 1964), 403.

248 Filtvedt, *The Identity of God's People*, 242. Filtvedt mentions that Heb 13:7–17 subverts the Yom Kippur ritual.

249 Dunning, "The Intersection of Aline Status," 197.

250 David M. Allen, "Who, What, and Why?: The Worship of the Firstborn in Hebrews 1:6," in *Mark, Manuscripts, and Monotheism: Essays in Honor of Larry W. Hurtado* (ed. Chris Keith and Dieter T. Roth; LNTS 528; London: T&T Clark, 2015), 169. Cf. Jody A. Barnard, *The Mysticism of Hebrews: Exploring the Role of Jewish Apocalyptic Mysticism in the Epistle to the Hebrews* (WUNT II/331; Tübingen: Mohr Siebeck, 2012), 252.

refer to the incarnation,[251] the second coming,[252] or the ascension of Christ?[253] This question is directly related to the meanings of πάλιν in 1:6a and οἰκουμένη in 1:6b. Firstly, is the adverb πάλιν connected to the verb εἰσαγάγῃ or to the OT quotation in 1:6? Some argue that πάλιν can be best understood in conjunction with the verb εἰσαγάγῃ.[254] If we accept this view, Heb 1:6a can be understood as "when he again brings the firstborn son into the world."[255] It is, however, more plausible that πάλιν is linked with the OT quotation in Heb 1:6 because πάλιν is often used as an introductory formula of OT quotations in Hebrews:[256] e.g., "For we know the one who said, 'Vengeance is mine, I will repay.' And again (πάλιν), 'The Lord will judge his people'" (Heb 10:30). On the other hand, πάλιν has a temporal sense when it is not used in relation to an OT quotation in Heb 5:12 and 6:1, 6.[257] So, πάλιν functions as a connective which links OT quotations with the given passage.[258] As Andriessen notes, the word order also disagrees with the temporal reading which supports "again brings." If the author of Hebrews intended the temporal sense of πάλιν, he should have written πάλιν δὲ ὅταν, not ὅταν δὲ πάλιν.[259] Further, we can regard the adverb πάλιν as emphasising the adversative conjunction δέ. Thus, πάλιν (again) should be understood as a formula of introduction to the OT quotation in Heb 1:6, and εἰσαγάγῃ cannot mean the second coming.

Does οἰκουμένη in Heb 1:6 refer to the present world, or the heavenly world? Firstly, whilst οἰκουμένη literally refers to the habitable world, οἰκουμένη in Heb 2:5 does not refer to the present world, since μέλλουσαν modifies οἰκουμένη,

---

251 So Attridge, *Hebrews*, 56.

252 So Käsemann, *The Wandering People of God*, 101.

253 In favour of the ascension of Christ, see Ardel Caneday, "The Eschatological World Already Subjected to the Son: The οἰκουμένη of Hebrews 1.6 and The Son's Enthronement," in *Cloud of Witnesses: The Theology of Hebrews in Its Ancient Contexts* (eds. Richard Bauckham, et al.; LNTS 387; London: T&T Clark, 2008), 28–39; O'Brien, *The Letter to the Hebrews*, 69; William Lane, *Hebrews 1–8* (WBC; Dallas: Word, 1991), 27; Vanhoye, "L'οἰκουμένη dans l'épître aux Hébreux," *Bib* 45 (1964): 248–53; Weiss, *Der Brief an die Hebräer*, 162, Cockerill, *Hebrews*, 104; P.C.B. Andriessen, "La Teneur Judéo-Chrétienne de He I 6 et II 14b–III 2," *NovT* 18 (1976): 293–4.

254 So, Käsemann, *The Wandering People of God*, 101.

255 B.F. Westcott, *The Epistle to the Hebrews: The Greek Text with Notes and Essays* (Grand Rapids: Eerdmans, 1950), 21–23.

256 E.g., Heb 1:5; 2:13; 4:5, 7; 10:30.

257 Rhee, "The Role of Chiasm for Understanding Christology in Hebrews 1:1–14," 355.

258 Καὶ πάλιν in Heb 1:5; μὲν… δέ in 1:7–8; δέ in 1:13. See Meier, "Symmetry and Theology," 509; Weiss, *Der Brief an die Hebräer*, 162; Franz Laub, *Bekenntnis und Auslegung: Die paränetische Funktion der Christologie im Hebräerbrief* (BU 15; Regensburg: Pustet, 1980), 59; Larry Helyer, "The Prototokos Title in Hebrews," *StBibTh* 6 (1976): 7–8.

259 Andriessen, "La Teneur Judéo-Chrétienne de He I 6 et II 14b–III 2," 296–7.

and adds a futuristic sense (i.e., the world to come; τὴν οἰκουμένην τὴν μέλλουσαν).[260] Secondly, as O'Brien observes,[261] the added clause "about which we are speaking" in Heb 2:5 implicitly recalls Heb 1:6. Heb 2:5 implies that Heb 1:6 should be read with regard to Heb 2:5, and that Christ ascended to the heavenly divine realm after his death and resurrection. Thirdly, οἰκουμένη was used in the sense of the Promised Land in LXX texts, as Moffitt observes,[262] and is referenced together with the verb εἰσάγω which is used in Exod 3:8, Deut 6:10 and 11:29 in the sense of "bringing in the Promised Land." In this vein, it is highly likely that οἰκουμένη in Heb 1:6 alludes to the usage in LXX texts. These points indicate that the meaning conveyed is not that of "the earthly world." Furthermore, Heb 1:6b cites LXX Deut 32:43, which lies in the context of enter ing the Promised Land (e.g., ἐκκαθαριεῖ κύριος τὴν γῆν τοῦ λαοῦ αὐτοῦ in LXX Deut 32:43 c),[263] and this point underpins that οἰκουμένη in Heb 1:6a should be understood in terms of the story of Israel who enters the Promised Land.[264]

Accordingly, we can conclude that οἰκουμένη in Heb 1:6 alludes to the Promised Land, and that Christ as the firstborn son ascended to the heavenly Promised Land in Heb 1:6. We should note that the connection between the firstborn son and the Promised Land evokes the uses of the firstborn son in relation to the divine promise in Gen 25, Exod 4, *Sir* 36, *4 Ezra*, 4Q369 and 4Q504. It also corresponds to the assembly of the firstborn sons who dwell in the heavenly Zion (i.e., the Promised Land) in Heb 12:23.

In addition, it is unlikely that Heb 1:6 indicates the incarnation. Firstly, we have already concluded that οἰκουμένη refers to the Promised Land, not the earthly world. So, the reading of the incarnation is also inappropriate in this context. Secondly, Hebrews writes that Christ became lower than the angels

---

260 For further analysis of οἰκουμένη as the heavenly world, see Caneday, "The Eschatological World," 34. See also Andriessen, "La Teneur Judéo-Chrétienne de He I 6 et II 14b–III 2," 297.

261 O'Brien, *The Letter to the Hebrews*, 69.

262 Moffitt is correct to observe evidences that οἰκουμένη was used in the sense of the Promised Land in LXX Ps 92:1; 95:10, 96:4, etc. This perhaps reflects that the author of Hebrews was aware of the term οἰκουμένη used in the LXX. See David M. Moffitt, *Atonement and the Logic of Resurrection in the Epistle to the Hebrews* (NovTSup 141; Leiden: Brill, 2011), 69–78. See also his discussions on the Dead Sea Scrolls, *Jubilees*, *4 Ezra*, *LAB*, and *2 Baruch*, in Moffitt, *Atontment*, 81–116. See also Vanhoye, "L'οἰκουμένη," 253; Amy L.B. Peeler, *You Are My Son: The Family of God in the Epistle to the Hebrews* (London: T&T Clark, 2014), 53.

263 For the citation of Deut 32:43 in Heb 1:6, see Susan E. Docherty, *The Use of the Old Testament in Hebrews: A Case Study in Early Jewish Bible Interpretation* (WUNT II/260; Tübingen: Mohr Siebeck, 2009), 133–34.

264 Andriessen, "La Teneur Judéo-Chrétienne de He I 6 et II 14b–III 2," 295.

when the incarnation of Christ is explained in Heb 2:9.[265] However, in the context of Heb 1:6, Christ is exalted over the angels. Thirdly, the author of Hebrews uses κόσμος when he means the earthly world (Heb 4:3; 9:26; 10:5; 11:7; 11:38). Οἰκουμένη in Heb 1:6 refers to "the world to come" in Heb 2:5 in a futuristic sense, and instead, κόσμος is referenced in the context of incarnation in Heb 10:5 ("when Christ came into the world (εἰς τὸν κόσμον)").[266] Fourthly, Heb 1:6 (he brings the firstborn son into the world) is in thematic parallel with Heb 2:10 (in bringing many children to glory), and Heb 2:10 does not appear in the context of the past, but is related to the future of the believers. Fifthly, the verb εἰσαγάγῃ was used in the sense of bringing into the Promised Land in LXX Exod 3:8, LXX Deut 6:10 and 11:29.[267] Therefore, Heb 1:6 depicts that Christ as the firstborn son entered the heavenly realm (i.e., the Promised Land).[268]

The firstborn son in Heb 1:6 can be best understood in terms of the eschatological inheritance pattern (i.e., Israel as the firstborn son receives their inheritance in glory at the climax of history). Firstly, Christ is the radiance of God's glory (ἀπαύγασμα τῆς δόξης; 1:3), and is exalted over angelic powers in Heb 1. Inheritance is a significant motif in Hebrews (e.g., συγκληρονόμος in 11:9; κληρονομέω in 1:4, 14; 6:12, 17; 12:17). Particularly, Heb 1:2 shows that the spectrum of inheritance is all encompassing (cf. Rom 4:13): "in these last days has spoken to us in His Son, whom He appointed heir of all things (κληρονόμον πάντων), through whom also He made the world" (Heb 1:2). Inheriting the entire world was a widespread expectation of the ancient Jews (e.g., *Sir* 36; *4 Ezra* 6:58–59; 1Q34 3 ii 1–3). In Heb 12:28, the believers also inherit the kingdom which cannot be shaken: "Therefore, since we receive a kingdom which cannot be shaken …" The motif of rest (e.g., 3:11, 19; 4:1–13) is related to the theme of entering the Promised Land. Rest is the final destination of believers and recalls the theme of entering the Promised Land (cf. Jos 21:43–45).[269] In Heb 6:12, 17, the believers inherit the promise (κληρονομούντων τὰς ἐπαγγελίας), and in 10:34, the author states, "you yourselves (ἑαυτούς) possessed something better and more lasting." Using the emphatic ἑαυτούς, the author highlights in Heb 10:34 that it is "you" who have an enduring possession. In Heb 11:14, the believers seek the home land (πατρίς), and the home land of the believers is located in heaven (11:16). The promise of inheriting and entering the Land is

265 Caneday, "The Eschatological World," 31.

266 Caneday, "The Eschatological World," 31.

267 Andriessen, "La Teneur Judéo-Chrétienne de He I 6 et II 14b–III 2," 297.

268 Andriessen, "La Teneur Judéo-Chrétienne de He I 6 et II 14b–III 2," 312.

269 Especially, entering the heavenly Zion in 12:22 is tantamount to entering God's rest in 4:9. See Son, *Zion Symbolism in Hebrews*, 144.

fulfilled in Heb 12. Ἐπαγγελία given to Abraham in Heb 7:6 can be linked to the promise concerning his offspring and linked with the promise given to the believers in 4:1 and 6:17. The promise for the believers is connected to the eschatological promise for access to the heavenly holy place (9:15), and inheriting the Promised Land (12:26).[270] In the heavenly Zion symbolism (par. Heb 12:23 and 28), the believers as the assembly of the firstborn sons inherit the kingdom which cannot be shaken.[271] Therefore, it is most reasonable to conclude that the motifs of the Promised Land, glory and the firstborn son in Heb reflect the eschatological expectation relating to inheritance of the people of God. Thus, we conclude that the title of the firstborn son in Heb 1:6 represents the title of Israel as the chosen line and the divine heir.[272]

Heb 1:5–14 is thematically linked with Heb 12:18–24 in several aspects. Firstly, the superiority of the son and of the heavenly Zion is elucidated in 1:5–14 and 12:18–24.[273] Secondly, the images of the heavenly Zion including the image of the assembly of the firstborn sons are contrasted with the Sinai event.[274] Thirdly, the festival celebration of the angels in 12:22 recalls the angels' celebration of Christ exalted to the heavenly realm in 1:6.[275] Fourthly, the assembly of the firstborn sons in 12:23 evokes Christ the firstborn son in 1:6. Therefore, Heb 1:6–14 and 12:18–24 are thematically related to each other, and the designation of Christ as the firstborn son in Heb 1:6 foreshadows the status of the believers in 12:23.[276]

Some scholars argue that the firstborn son in Heb 1:6 should be understood as a guardian or a model of Christian siblings.[277] Heb 12:23, however, does not

---

270 Christian Rose, "Verheißung und Erfülling: Zum Verständnis von ἐπαγγελία im Hebräerbrief," *BZ* 33 (1989): 80.

271 As Käsemann discusses, it is a significant motif throughout the epistle that the wandering people of God enters the Promised Land. See Käsemann, *The Wandering People of God*, 22–24.

272 As for the relationship between 1:2–4 and 1:5–13, see David Wider, *Theozentrik und Bekenntnis: Untersuchungen zur Theologie des Redens Gottes im Hebräer* (Berlin: Walter de Gruyter, 1997), 37. As for the function of Heb 1:4, see Scott D. Mackie, "Confession of the Son of God in the Exordium of Hebrews," *JSNT* 30 (2008): 450.

273 Jipp, "The Son's Entrance into the Heavenly World," 565–66. Cf. Kiwoong Son, *Zion Symbolism in Hebrews: Hebrews 12:18–24 as a Hermeneutical Key to the Epistle* (PBM; Milton Keynes: Paternoster, 2005), 84–87.

274 Jipp, "The Son's Entrance into the Heavenly World," 566.

275 Jipp, "The Son's Entrance into the Heavenly World," 567–68.

276 See further discussions in section 4.3.5. See also Jipp, "The Son's Entrance into the Heavenly World," 569; Caneday, "The Eschatological World," 36; Peeler, *You Are My Son*, 170.

277 E.g., Joshua Jipp, "The Son's Entrance into the Heavenly World," 570; Gray, "Brotherly Love and the High Priest Christology of Hebrews," *JBL* 122 (2003): 336; Caneday, "The Eschatological World," 36.

indicate that the believers are younger siblings of Christ the firstborn son, but rather denotes that *the believers themselves are the firstborn sons*. Accordingly, it is unclear that the title of the firstborn son in Heb 1:6 refers to the role of Christ as the guardian of the believers. It seems clear that Heb 1:6 (εἰσαγάγῃ τὸν πρωτότοκον εἰς τὴν οἰκουμένην) has some thematic and lexical parallels with Heb 2:10 (πολλοὺς υἱοὺς εἰς δόξαν ἀγαγόντα).[278] So, one may assume that ἀρχηγός τῆς σωτηρίας in Heb 2:10 is paralleled with πρωτότοκος in Heb 2:10, and may conclude that πρωτότοκος refers to a sort of ἀρχηγός.[279] However, in Heb 1:6 and 2:10, the one who is syntactically paralleled with πρωτότοκος (the object of εἰσαγάγῃ) is not ἀρχηγός, but πολὺς υἱός (the object of ἀγαγόντα) in Heb 2:10. Thus, it is unclear that the title of πρωτότοκος is related to the leadership of the eldest brother, and it is also doubtful that πρωτότοκος refers to a guardian (see my critique in section 1.1.3).

Rather, it seems that the term πρωτότοκος in Heb 1:6 stresses temporal priority of Christ,[280] and can refer to the eldest son in the family of God. As Peeler observes, the familial theme (i.e., God as Father, Jesus as Son, and the congregation as children of God) is prominent in Hebrews.[281] The parallel between πρωτότοκος and πολὺς υἱός also implies that πρωτότοκος is a son of many sons (see the similar concept in Rom 8:29). In this context, in Heb 1:6, πρωτότοκος may refer to the eldest son of God who entered the heavenly Promised Land (cf. glory in Heb 2:10).[282] As a kinship concept, πρωτότοκος refers to the eldest son in the family (see section 2.2), and so, it seems that πρωτότοκος in Heb 1:6 has a double force as the eldest son in the family of God and as the title of Israel as the heir of the promise.

Some interpreters argue that πρωτότοκος in Heb 1:6 is a messianic title.[283] We have already explored in chapter 3 that we do not find evidence that the firstborn son was used as a messianic title in the OT and Jewish literature. We also do not have evidence that, in extant Second Temple literature, Ps 89

278 Cf. Peeler, *You Are My Son*, 85–88.

279 In LXX Num 13:2b, the leaders among each tribe were sent into the Land of Canaan to assay the land, and they were called as ἀρχηγός. As Moffitt observes, ἀρχηγός can be understood as "the representatives of the entire people" in this context. See Moffitt, *Atonement*, 129. The significance of the motif of ἀρχηγός in Heb 2:10 was recognised by Julius Kösel, in *Der Sohn und die Söhne: Eine exegetische Studie zu Hebräer 2, 5–18* (Breiträge zur Förderung christlicher Theologie VIII, 5–6; Gütersloh: Bertelsmann, 1904), 108. However, it is unconvincing that Kösel argues that Heb 2:1–10 was written as a kind of an ethical statement.

280 E.g., Allen, "Who, What, and Why?" 168.

281 Peeler, *You Are My Son*, 179. E.g., Heb 1:1–4; 2:6–10; 2:11–13; 3:1–6; 7:1–10; 12:12–17.

282 It seems that "all things" in Heb 2:6 refers to the same entity with "all things" in Heb 1:2. See Peeler, *You are My Son*, 70.

283 See section 1.1.1.3.

(LXX Ps 88) is messianically read. Rather, Israel is mentioned as the heir of the entire world (*1 En* 5:7; *4 Ezra* 6:59; *Sir* 44:21; *Jub* 22:14; 32:19; 1Q34+1Q34bis 3 ii 3). In *JosAs* 18:11, 21:4 and 23:11, Joseph is designated as the firstborn son, and this provides an example of an individual who is addressed as the title of Israel (section 3.13). In *JosAs*, Joseph is an ideal model and a representative of Israel, but the firstborn son is not used as a messianic title. In Heb 12:23, the believers are considered to be the assembly of the firstborn sons, which refers to the people of God in the heavenly Zion.[284] The designation of the firstborn son in Heb 1:6 can be related to the mystification of Israel in ancient Judaism.[285] In Philo, *Conf* 146 and *PrJos*, Israel who is designated as the firstborn son is personified as a heavenly figure, or the boundary figure between heaven and earth (section 3.9 and 3.14).[286] Furthermore, the verb used with πρωτότοκος in Heb 1:6 is not τίθημι (cf. LXX Ps 88:28), but εἰσάγειν, and "recalls the formula in Deut 6:10 and 11:29 which refers to Israel's entry into the Promised Land" (e.g., ὅταν εἰσαγάγῃ σε κύριος ὁ θεός σου εἰς τὴν γῆν).[287] So, it would be clear that the term πρωτότοκος in Heb 1:6 refers to the title of Israel as the heir of the promise, and that Christ is a representative of Israel in Heb 1:6.

Nonetheless, it is still probable that the author of Hebrews messianically re-interpreted Ps 89:27, and also understood the firstborn son as a messianic title.[288] Further, the image of the firstborn son who enters the heavenly Promised Land recalls a heavenly exalted figure in ancient Judaism.[289] In section 4.1.2.3, we already considered that the title of 'son of God' can be understood as a messianic title as well as the title of Israel. So, this work does not forsake the probability that the firstborn son in Heb 1:6 contains a messianic

284 For further discussions, see section 4.3.5.

285 Morray-Jones offers further evidences that Jacob–Israel was mystified as a heavenly figure in ancient Jewish, Gnostic and Manichean sources. See Morray-Jones, "The Body of the Glory," 560–68.

286 See section 3.9.2 and 3.14.4. Justin martyr offers some examples that some early Christians identified Israel with Christ's name. E.g., Justin, *Dial.* 75.2–4; 114.2; 125.5; 130.3.

287 Loren T. Stuckenbruck, *Angel Veneration and Christology: A Study in Early Judaism and in the Christology of the Apocalypse of John* (WUNT II/70; Tübingen: Mohr Siebeck, 1995), 120.

288 In particular, "appointing (ἔθηκεν) heir of all things" in Heb 1:2 and "sitting down at the right hand of the Majesty on high" in Heb 1:4 allude to some messianic texts (LXX Ps 2:8 and LXX Ps 109:1). Schenck argues that the worship of πρωτότοκος in Heb 1:6 recalls the veneration towards a royal figure, and falls short of the cultic veneration towards God.

289 Chester, *Messiah and Exaltation*, 62–79.

implication.[290] The title of the firstborn son as a messianic title is compatible with the concept of the firstborn son as the status of Israel.[291]

Charles A. Gieschen asserts the angelomorphic connotations of the 'firstborn son' title in Heb 1:6, and connects the origin and the meaning of πρωτότοκος in Heb 1:6 to the title given to the Angel Israel in *PrJos*.[292] It can be acknowledged that the concept of the firstborn son in Heb 1:6 is referenced in the context of the comparison with the angels and all creation.[293] Moreover, as shown above, it seems clear that the concept of the firstborn son is related to the exalted heavenly status of Christ. It is doubtful, however, that the title of the firstborn should be read as the title given to an angelomorphic figure. Firstly, I believe that Gieschen does not understand that the concept of the firstborn son is used with the concept of οἰκουμένη, which refers to the heavenly Promised Land, as shown above. In this context, the title of πρωτότοκος is linked with the notion of the Promised Land, and should be interpreted as the title of Israel who has access to the Promise as an heir. Secondly, as already discussed in section 3.9.2, the concept of the firstborn son in *PrJos* is not merely the title of the angel, but the title given to Jacob and Israel, and symbolises the heavenly status of Israel who is superior to the angels and all creation. Thus, the concept of the firstborn son in Heb 1:6 is related to the status of heavenly

290 E.g., for priestly messianism in Hebrews, see Eric F. Mason, *"You are a Priest Forever": Second Temple Jewish Messianism and the Priestly Christology of the Epistle to the Hebrews* (STDJ 74; Leiden: Brill, 2008).

291 In addition, the title of the firstborn son in Heb 1:6 may be related to the pre-existence of Christ, even though πάλιν in Heb 1:6 does not seem to mean that Christ returns 'again' to the heavenly realms as discussed above. In *Dial* 100.2, Justin interprets the meaning of the firstborn son in this sense: "γνόντες αὐτὸν πρωτότοκον μὲν τοῦ θεοῦ καὶ πρὸ πάντων τῶν κτισμάτων." The perfect tense in Heb 1:4 signals that Christ already owned the excellent name. So, there is no ground to claim that the context of Heb 1 does not demonstrate that Christ is a divine and pre-existent figure. See Christopher Rowland, *The Open Heaven: A Study of Apocalyptic in Judaism and Early Christianity* (New York: Crossroad, 1982), 113.

292 Charles A. Gieschen, *Angelomorphic Christology: Antecedents and Early Evidence* (AGJU 42; Leiden: Brill, 1998), 298. Cf. Barnard, *The Mysticism of Hebrews*, 163.

293 The reason Christ is contrasted with the angels in Heb 1 is controversial. The motif of Christ's superiority over angels is developed in 1:5–14 and suggests the foundation of the discussion in 2:1–4. The angels were important beings who mediated the Mosaic Law to the Jews in Jewish literature. This idea is also found in Heb 2:2, and the comparison between Christ and angels perhaps demonstrates the priority of the gospel mediated by Christ over the Mosaic Torah through angels. So, the contrast between Christ and angels in 1:5–14 could be comprehended within the argument of Hebrews concerning the contrast between the Old and New covenants. See Craig Koester, *Hebrews: A New Translation with Introduction and Commentary* (New York: Doubleday, 2001), 200; Barnabas Lindars, *The Theology of the Letter to the Hebrews* (Cambridge: Cambridge University Press, 1991), 37–38; Schenck, "A Celebration of the Enthroned Son," 469–85.

Israel (4Q369, *PrJos*, *Conf* 146, *Jub* 2:20, etc.), and does not connote that Christ is a kind of angel, but implies that Christ holds an exalted status in the heavenly Promised Land.

Amy L.B. Peeler correctly highlights the significance of the familial relationship between God and Jesus Christ in Hebrews 1. However, whereas she precisely notes that Christ is the appointed heir of God in the family of God, she does not explore the background of Jewish primogeniture and the traditional background of the firstborn son. In the OT and Jewish literature, the firstborn son as the divine heir is consistently understood as the title of Israel. Peeler states that LXX Ps 88:28 is the only text where "a single person is designated as God's own πρωτότοκος."[294] Yet, in *JosAs* 18:11, 21:4 and 23:11, Joseph (a single person) is also addressed as the firstborn son of God, and the title of the firstborn son originated in the title of Israel in Exod 4:22 (section 3.13.2). In *PrJos* A. 3, Israel as a heavenly figure is designated as the firstborn son (section 3.9.2). In *Sir* 44:23, God acknowledges Jacob as the firstborn son (section 3.8.2.2). The firstborn son in Heb 1:6 is referenced in the context of entering the heavenly Promised Land (οἰκουμένη), and this context recalls the story of Israel in *Eisodus*.[295]

Finally, how can we translate πρωτότοκος—the firstborn or the firstborn son? In section 4.1.2, we explored that, when πρωτότοκος is used in respect of the father and inheritance, it can be understood as the firstborn 'son.' We have argued that πρωτότοκος in Heb 1:6 refers to the title of Israel as the heir of the promise. So, in this context, we conclude that πρωτότοκος can be interpreted as the firstborn son.

Peeler translates πρωτότοκος in Heb 1:6 as "the firstborn," and maintains that "πρωτότοκος is associated with the priestly class" in Numbers.[296] However, I believe that she confuses the cultic definition of πρωτότοκος with the concept relating to inheritance (see section 4.1.3). Furthermore, while the Levites are associated with πρωτότοκος, they are not identified with πρωτότοκος in Numbers (section 2.3.3). Identification differs from association, and it is doubtful that πρωτότοκος can be linked with the status of the Levites in Hebrews.

In conclusion, the firstborn son is referenced in the context of "εἰσαγάγῃ … εἰς τὴν οἰκουμένην" which means entering the Promised Land,[297] and it is evident that the title of the firstborn son in Heb 1:6 refers to the status of Israel

294 Peeler, *You Are My Son*, 52.

295 Cf. Peeler, *You Are My Son*, 53.

296 Peeler, *You are my Son*, 52.

297 Andriessen, "La Teneur Judéo-Chrétienne de He I 6 et II 14b–III 2," 297; Ellingworth, *The Epistle to the Hebrews*, 118.

as the divine heir. Christ enters the heavenly Promised Land (οἰκουμένη; Heb 1:6) and this prefigures the believers as the firstborn sons who dwell in the heavenly Zion (Heb 12:23).

4.3.3 *The Meaning of the Firstborn (τὰ πρωτότοκα) in Heb 11:28*

This section will explore the meaning and implications of the firstborn in Heb 11:28. Hagiology in Heb 11 connects Heb 10:32–39 to 12:1–13, and provides a close unity between these two passages.[298] In this context, after the author describes the persecution, shame, suffering and faith of Moses in Heb 11:23–27, the Exodus event is illustrated in Heb 11:27–29. Moses is depicted as a great and virtuous leader in ancient Jewish literature.[299] However, in Heb 11, Moses is not described as a national hero in respect of his accomplishments for the Israelites. Rather, Moses is portrayed as the person who departed from his previous community (a royal Egyptian family) of which he was a member.[300] In this vein, Eisenbaum argues that the actions of the heroes in Heb 11 are delineated as denationalised performances.[301] In other words, they are not national, but supernational heroes.[302] In particular, Moses is not portrayed as a great leader of the Exodus. Rather, the author places his emphasis on Moses' personal departure from Egypt. So, Hebrews does not regard Moses as the great leader or national hero who led Israel out of Egypt, but as a saint who made wise choices for himself.[303] Moses' heroic leadership of Israel, his intercessory prayer, or his action in the divine revelation is not presented except in Heb 3:16.[304] Therefore, according to Eisenbaum, these portrayals of Moses are considerably different from descriptions of Moses in Jewish literature.[305] Furthermore, the status of heroes in Heb 11 is associated with their faith regardless of their national role. Eisenbaum further contends that the author purports to denationalise the history of Israel. By the same token, the heroes in Heb 11 are viewed as great models of faith without nationalistic connotations.[306] In other words, the heroes

298 Weiss, *Der Brief an die Hebräer*, 553.
299 Eisenbaum, *The Jewish Heroes of Christian History*, 167.
300 Eisenbaum, *The Jewish Heroes of Christian History*, 168, 188.
301 Eisenbaum, *The Jewish Heroes of Christian History*, 184–88.
302 Eisenbaum, *The Jewish Heroes of Christian History*, 225.
303 Eisenbaum, *The Jewish Heroes of Christian History*, 170–1. Cf. Acts 7:38. Philo also depicts Moses an individual sage. See Philo, *Opif* 8; *Mos* 2.192; 2.40; *Her* 214.
304 "Τίνες γὰρ ἀκούσαντες παρεπίκραναν; ἀλλ' οὐ πάντες οἱ ἐξελθόντες ἐξ Αἰγύπτου διὰ Μωϋσέως," in Heb 3:16.
305 Eisenbaum, *The Jewish Heroes of Christian History*, 183. The exception is 11:28 which describes Moses' doing something for his people (sacrificial act). Cf. 11:17–19. Also see Eisenbaum, *The Jewish Heroes of Christian History*, 171.
306 Cf. Cockerill, *Hebrews*, 569; Eisenbaum, *The Jewish Heroes of Christian History*, 167.

in Heb 11 are no longer Jewish heroes, but they are examples of faith for the Gentile believers regardless of their ethnic origins.

Yet, Eisenbaum's arguments require some critiques. In Heb 11:13–16, the author stresses that Abraham was a stranger and Abrahams and his sons did not obtain the Promised Land, and that "they were still in search of their homeland."[307] In Heb 11:22, Joseph also requested to bring his bones out of Egypt to the Promised Land, and this implies that his hope for the Promised Land was not gave up.[308] Moreover, Moses identified himself with Israel in Heb 11:25. Therefore, it is doubtful that the heroes in Hebrews 11 were denationalised, and rather it seems clear that they are depicted as the heroes of Israel.

Secondly, Eisenbaum does not recognise the communal significance of faith in Heb 11, while she emphasises the individual behaviour of each hero.[309] However, Moses identifies himself with the people of God in Heb 11:25. In Heb 11:28–29, the faith of Moses is also identified with that of Israel, and this displays that Hebrews 11 does not focus merely on individual faith. In Heb 11:28, Moses kept the Passover and the sprinkling of the blood by faith. In parallel with Heb 11:28, Heb 11:29 describes how Israel passed through the Red Sea by faith. What is stressed in Heb 11:28–29 is not simply the individual faith of Moses, but also the faith of the people of God. Therefore, it is obvious that the heroes in Heb 11 are non-national (non-ethnic) heroes and that their faith is the main theme of Heb 11. Yet, we do not have to confine the theme of Heb 11 to the individual faith of the heroes.[310] Moses and Israel represent the people of God who have faith in Christ, and the main theme of Heb 11 is the faith of the people of God in the OT. Thus, faith in Heb 11 is a communal concept which is applied to the people of God re-constituted regardless of their ethnic origins, and the heroes in Heb 11 are the examples of faith as the people of God redefined by faith.

Heb 11:28 and 29 articulate the contrasting destinies of Israel and Egypt, particularly the failure of Egypt and the salvation of Israel.[311] The Egyptian firstborn were destroyed, but the firstborn of Israel were untouched. Israel crossed over the Red sea, but the Egyptians were drowned. God acts for Israel who was in faith, and against the Egyptians who was in unbelief. Hebrews does

307 Matthew Thiessen, "Hebrews and the End of the Exodus," *NovT* 49 (2007): 363.

308 Thiessen, "The End of the Exodus," 364.

309 Eisenbaum claims that Moses made "the choice of the opprobrium or reproach of Christ," and that Moses was a Christian martyr, "a martyr pro fide Christi" or an example of Christian endurance in Heb 11. See Eisenbaum, *The Jewish Heroes of Christian History*, 170.

310 Cf. Cockerill, *Hebrews*, 569; Eisenbaum, *The Jewish Heroes of Christian History*, 167.

311 Cockerill observes that the 11:28–9 implies "the preservation of God's own 'by faith' amid such destruction," in Cockerill, *Hebrews*, 580.

not explicitly blame the Egyptians and Egypt,[312] but in Heb 11, the Egyptians are depicted as being destroyed due to their unbelief in contrast to Israel.[313] Κατά of κατεπόθησαν in Heb 11:29 is intensive, which stresses the contrasting destinies of the Israelites and the Egyptians.[314] Heb 11 displays examples of faith, but also provides counterexamples of unbelief (namely, Egypt; cf. Esau in Heb 12). Egypt is presented as the place which enjoys the fleeting pleasures of sin (11:25), which has treasures and wealth (11:26), and which can disquiet Moses (11:27). Accordingly, Egypt implicitly represents the world of unbelief. In this context, the author of Hebrews comforts the members of the community who are in danger of social marginalisation and in conflict with outside groups by highlighting the contrasting destinies of the Israelites and the Egyptians. In particular, Heb 11:28–29 is depicted in the context of the salvation of Israel's firstborn and the destruction of the Egyptian firstborn. Thus, Heb 11 implies that, despite their present sufferings, the community of faith has a status and destiny distinct from outside groups.[315]

What is a proper translation of τὰ πρωτότοκα in Heb 11:28? The firstborn (τὰ πρωτότοκα) is neuter, and it has the comprehensive meaning which refers to both human beings and animals. Furthermore, πρωτότοκα is used in terms of the Passover and its cultic action (sprinkling the blood). So, it seems more reasonable to translate πρωτότοκα as 'the firstborn' in the cultic context.

Exod 11–12 clearly reveals the divergence of destinies of the Israelites and the Egyptians' destinies through the death of the Egyptian firstborn sons and the salvation of the Israelite firstborn. In Exodus, Egypt is "the major 'other' over and against which the unique and distinct identity of Israel is constructed by contrast."[316] The concept of the firstborn in Exod 11–12 is related to the primacy of Israel over the Egyptians and the contrasted destinies of the Israelites and the Egyptians which demonstrate God's favour upon Israel.[317]

The death of the firstborn Egyptians is a recurring motif in the OT and Jewish literature. In Ps 136, the Psalmist recollects God's creation and redemption for Israel. In Ps 136:10–15, God's acts in favour of Israel in the Exodus story are enumerated, and in Ps 136:10–12, the Passover story is mentioned. God's mercy is eternal, and his mercy is given to Israel. In the given text, the destruction of the

312 Cf. 3:16; 8:9; 11:26–27.

313 Furthermore, the relative pronoun ἧς occurs in the context of contrast. See Ellingworth, *The Epistle to the Hebrews*, 620.

314 O'Brien, *The Letter to the Hebrews*, 436; Attridge, *Hebrews*, 344.

315 Cf. Exod 4:22. Also see Marohl, *Faithfulness and the Purpose of Hebrews*, 110.

316 F.V. Greifenhagen, *Egypt on the Pentateuch's Ideological Map: Constructing Biblical Israel's Identity* (JSOTSup 361; Sheffield: Sheffield Academic Press, 2002), 157.

317 See also Ps 76: 51; 105:36.

Firstborn Egyptians is referenced as a significant event in terms of the salvation of Israel. The Israelites should give thanks to the Lord for his destruction of the firstborn Egyptians. Therefore, the plague visited on the Egyptian firstborn is one of the motifs which convey the sense of God's favour upon Israel and the contrasting destiny of Israel and the Gentiles in Ps 136.

In *Wis* 18:5–19, the motif of destruction of the Firstborn Egyptians is more specifically elucidated. In *Wis* 18:5a, one child (i.e., Moses) was saved, when the Egyptians slayed the Jewish infant children. In 18:5b, the author of *Wisdom* states God's punishment to the Egyptians: "you in punishment took away a multitude of their children; and you destroyed them all together by a mighty flood." Thus, the author of *Wisdom* implies that the destruction of the firstborn Egyptians was God's punishment as a consequence of their slaughter of the Jewish children. Grabbe points out four sins committed by the Egyptians in *Wisdom*: 1) killing of infants in the Nile (11:7); 2) Animal worship (11:15); 3) Refusal to recognise God (16:16); and 4) captivity of the Israelites (18:4).[318] The author of *Wisdom* also writes that the Egyptians practised magic in *Wis* 18:13. Jewish ancestors were informed of God's vengeance towards the Egyptians through the prior destruction of the firstborn Egyptians and they offered sacrifice in secret. When the firstborn Egyptians were destroyed, the Egyptian people acknowledged the Jewish people to be God's son in *Wis* 18:13. In *Wis* 18:15–16, God's all powerful word leaped from the heaven, and carried the sharp sword of God's authentic decree and filled all things with death. On the contrary, Jewish people experience death in the desert but God's wrath did not long continue in *Wis* 18:20. In the Hellenistic Jewish midrash on Exod 12 conveyed in *Wis* 18:5–19, the destruction of the firstborn Egyptians is incurred as a consequence of their slaughter of the Jewish children and the destiny of the Egyptians is contrasted with God's favour and forgiveness towards the Jewish people in *Wis* 18:20–25.[319] Thus, it seems that the firstborn Egyptians are representative of all Egyptian children in *Wis* 18:5–19.

Whereas Philo literally explains the destruction of the Egyptian firstborn sons in *Mos* 1.135, Philo also allegorises the Egyptian firstborn in the sense of the dominant elements of blind passion in *Sacr* 134. After the destruction of the Egyptian firstborn, "the sanctification of the elder and precious offspring of Israel who has clear vision of God" follows. The contrast between the status of Israel and that of Egypt suggests that Philo accepts and follows the flow of the Pentateuch. Thus, Philo develops the links between the first fruit (or cultic offering) and the firstborn, and also elaborates the reason for election and

318 Lester L. Grabbe, *Wisdom of Solomon* (GAP 3; Sheffield: Sheffield Academic Press, 1997), 42.

319 Grabbe, *Wisdom of Solomon*, 39–43.

curse in the Pentateuch. In this context, Philo claims the status of Israel by negation to some degree, since Philo accepts the strategy of the Pentateuch to distinguish Israel's status from Egypt's, stressing Israel's superiority over Egypt through the destruction of the Egyptian firstborn and through the sanctification of the Israelite firstborn. In the writings of Philo, the title of firstborn is not ascribed to Gentiles. The title is only for the elected, the Israelites, and the Levites, if the title is attributed to a specific person or people. Philo also employs the title of the firstborn in relation to the privilege of election. Therefore, the firstborn title is not used for the non-Elect, and functions to distinguish the Elect from the non-Elect. We should also note that Logos as the firstborn son refers to the mental part distinct from bodily and sensual part.[320] Accordingly, in Philo, the firstborn son refers to the privileged status of the Elect, Israel, and the Levites, and this point is also depicted in the annihilation of the Egyptian firstborn. Peder Borgen also writes:[321]

> Accordingly, when Philo interprets references to Egypt and Egyptians allegorically to mean the body, passions, moral values, etc., he combines these two aspects of his dualism: Egypt and Egyptian represent the pagans in contrast to the Jewish nation, and at the same time they represent the evil body over and against the Jewish nation which has the heavenly quality of the soul.

We find considerably negative descriptions of Egypt in Philo's writings. While Hebrews describes Egypt as the land of unbelief, Philo illustrates Egypt as the land of the passions. Egypt in Philonic literature is regarded as "the ultimate other." Egypt in Philo is generally depicted negatively. For example, the

320 The body in Philo is negatively described in terms of Platonic dualistic anthropology. Body is mortal, subject to finite world, and the tomb of the soul. Cf. *Spec Leg* 1.107–108; *Somn* 1. 25–26. However, body is also understood as creation as the temple for the rational soul. Cf. *Opif* 137; *Det* 19. However, we need to remember that body is not regarded more highly than the soul. See Sarah J.K. Pearce, *The Land of Body: Studies in Philo's Representation of Egypt* (WUNT 208; Tübingen: Mohr Siebeck, 2007), 87. As well, Israel's suffering in Egypt is demonstrated as binding with "bodily nets" (*Somn* 1.77), and Passover is "the spiritual Pascha," in *Spec Leg* 3.94, 165. See also *Migr* 25. Cf. Pearce, *The Land of Body*, 124. Exodus is interpreted as "the migration of the immortal soul away from the body" (*Spec Leg* 3.172). See Pearce, *The Land of Body*, 103.

321 Borgen, "Philo," 339. Cf. It seems that the author of *Jubilees* did not impose any special meaning upon the firstborn son in *Jub* 48–49. In the case of *LAB* 10:1, the destruction of the firstborn Egyptians is also underplayed in this context, and is only mentioned as one of the ten plagues. However, the underlying intention is unclear since the description of the event in *LAB* is relatively short.

Egyptians are "jealous by nature" (*Flacc* 29), "Irreligious and irrational hedonists" (*Mos* 2.193–96; *Jos* 254; *Flacc* 17, 29) and self-lovers (φίλαυτος; *Cher* 74). Their religion is "Egyptian atheism (*Legat* 163)." "Egypt is to be translated as 'oppressing' (*Q.G.* 4.177)," and this is explained in terms of passions, namely, desire, pleasure, grief and fear. Cf. *Post* 31; *Spec Leg* 3.23–24.). Egypt is also defined as "the mother of every disorder" (*Migr* 25) and "symbol of the body (*Q.G.* 4.177; *Heres* 82)." After all, the Egyptians are those who fail to see God.[322] In first-century Alexandria, ethnicity and social status became more significant than they were during the Ptolemaic period, and it can be argued that Philo wanted to differentiate his Jewish people, who were generally an urban people, from the uncivilised rural people, the lower class Egyptians. So, in Philonic literature, the Egyptians are the ultimate 'others' depicted as inferior to the Jews.[323] Thus, in Exodus 11–12 and several Jewish documents, the story of the deaths of the firstborn son Egyptians accentuate the distinct status of Israel from the Egyptians and the contrasted destinies of the Israelites and the Egyptians.

By the same token, in Hebrews 11, the Egyptian firstborn were destroyed, but the firstborn of Israel were untouched. Israel crossed over the Red sea, but the Egyptians were drowned. God acts for Israel and against the Egyptians. These images show the contrasting destinies of Israel to Egypt. So, Heb 11:28 implies that the community of faith holds a distinct destiny when compared to outside groups, and prefigures the story of Esau in Heb 12:16 surrounding πρωτοτόκια.

4.3.4 *The Meaning of πρωτοτόκια in Heb 12:16*

The theme of Heb 12:13 is developed in 12:14–29, and 12:14–17 functions as an introduction to 12:18–19.[324] Necessity of perseverance is elucidated in 12:1–13, and διό in 12:12 introduces the conclusion of 12:1–11.[325] Heb 12:14–17 exhorts the community in danger of compromising their faith, and repeatedly elucidates a warning against apostasy.[326] Heb 12:14 expresses the requirement of peace and holiness, and the theme of seeing God in 12:14 is connected to the vision of God in Sinai and Zion in 12:18–24.

The present active participle ἐπισκοποῦντες in Heb 12:15 has an imperatival force, and governs the following three sub-clauses (that no one forfeits … that

322 Pearce, *The Land of Body*, 130.

323 Niehoff, *Philo on Jewish Identity and Culture*, 20–22.

324 Lane, *Hebrews 9–13* (WBC; Waco: Word, 1991), 444. As for the structure of 12:14–29, see Lane, *Hebrews 9–13*, 444; Cockerill, *Hebrews*, 632. Contra George Guthrie, *The Structure of Hebrews: A Text-Linguistic Analysis* (NovTSup 73; Leiden: Brill, 1994), 145.

325 Lane, *Hebrews 9–13*, 445.

326 O'Brien, *The Letter to the Hebrews*, 475.

no bitter root grows up ... that no one is apostate or irreligious). Heb 12:15a exhorts the recipients not to be detached from grace, namely, God's saving action in the death of Christ (cf. Heb 2:9; 4:16; 10:29; 12:15, 28; 13:9, 25).[327] Heb 12:15b reflects LXX Deut 29:17b, and ῥίζα πικρίας (root of bitternees) indicates the root which produces poisonous fruits, namely, the stubborn disposition to unbelief.[328] That is, ῥίζα πικρίας in Heb 12:15 symbolises the failure of the covenant people in the story of Israel (par. the story of entering the Promised Land). Esau is often described as a man of sexual immorality in Jewish literature,[329] however, it is more likely that πόρνος in 12:16 signifies Esau's insincerity towards God in a figurative sense. Πόρνος in the LXX is often used in a figurative sense for a person who breaks a covenant with God.[330] Accordingly, the figurative usage of πόρνος fits with the appeal of Heb 12:15 ("no root of bitterness springs up and causes trouble, and through it many become defiled"), and also corresponds to the context of a warning against apostasy.[331] So, πόρνος portrays a negative aspect of Esau whose life was not sincere towards God. Βέβηλος in Heb 12:16 literally means "secular" or "unreligious" and identifies that Esau was absorbed in his own personal desires. It should also be noted that βέβηλος is used as an antonym of ἅγιος in the LXX.[332] Thus, Esau is portrayed as a godless person who forsakes his privilege for momentary satisfactions. In the OT, we find both neutral and negative references to Esau. The neutral references are concerned with exhortations on treating Edomites as Israel's brothers.[333] Yet, the negative references to Esau as the non-Elect are far more frequently found in the OT and Jewish literature.[334] As Dicou states, in the exilic and the post-exilic tradition, "Edom served as Israel's special opponent and the representative of the nations."[335] For instance, in *1 Macc* 5:2,

---

327 Lane, *Hebrews 9–13*, 452.

328 Lane, *Hebrews 9–13*, 453.

329 Cf. *Jub* 25:1, 7–8; 26:23; 35:13–14; Philo *Virt* 208–10; *Q. G.* 4. 201; *Allegorical interpretation* 3.2; *Sobr* 26, *Sacr* 120; Targum *Pseudo-Jonathan* (on Gen 25:27); Gen Rab 63:9, 12. See Attridge, *Hebrews*, 369.

330 E.g., LXX Exod 34:15–17; LXX Deut 31:16. Idolatry was often identified with πορνεία ever since the prophets. E.g., 1QS III–IV.

331 O'Brien, *The Letter to the Hebrews*, 485.

332 LXX Lev 10:10; LXX Ezek 22:26; 44:23.

333 E.g., Deut 23:7.

334 E.g., Obad 1:6–10; Mal 1:2–5; Jer 49:10. For the specific information on the Jacob–Esau tradition in the OT, see Bert Dicou, *Edom, Israel's Brother and Antagonist: The Role of Edom in Biblical Prophecy and Story* (JSOTSup, 169; Sheffield: Sheffield Academic Press, 1994).

335 Dicou, *The Role of Edom*, 199. Yet, we should also note that, while the Edomites represent enemy nations of Israel in the prophetic books, "[t]his does not mean that the universalistic perspective—Israel and the nations living in peace is absent in the prophetic books. See Dicou, *The Role of Edom*, 204.

Esau's descendants are depicted as liars, and in *1 Macc* 5:65, they are the enemy of Israel. In *Jub* 36:9–11, Esau and the Edomites are under the eternal curse.[336] In 1Q18 1–2 1 and 4Q223–224 2 I 49, Esau's inclination is evil from his youth. In 4Q223–224 2 II 6, Esau's ways are violence and wickedness, and Esau is described as untrustworthy. In Philo, *Leg Alleg* 3.88 and 3.195, Esau is depicted to be innately irrational and a slave by nature. In Heb 12, Esau is an anti-hero like Egypt in Heb 11 and the example of apostasy, and, in Heb 12:17, is displayed as an immoral, godless and forsaken son. Thus, Esau exemplifies those who discard heavenly blessings for their earthly satisfactions (12:16–17).[337]

Heb 12:14–17 reflects the sibling rivalry tradition between Esau and Jacob in Gen 25–27. Apostasy is likened to Esau's selling the right of the firstborn son (πρωτοτόκια) in 12:16. The "single" (μιᾶς) in emphatic position highlights Esau's thoughtless action.[338] It should be noted that the motif of inheritance is reiterated in Hebrews[339] and, in Heb 12:23–28, the assembly of the firstborn sons inherit the kingdom which cannot be shaken. So, πρωτοτόκια in Heb 12:16 can be understood in this vein (for the specific discussions, see the following pages). Esau's improper behaviour led to him losing his status as the firstborn son. Heb 12:16 illustrates that apostasy is the action of discarding the rights of the firstborn son (πρωτοτόκια) such as Esau, and implies that the apostates cannot inherit the future promise. Conversely, the believers are those who hold the rights of firstborn sons unlike the apostates who forsake the heirship of the promise.[340]

The term, πρωτοτόκια is a hapax legomenon in the NT. To what, then, does πρωτοτόκια specifically refer? Koester states that πρωτοτόκια in Heb12:16 is the blessing and the right concerning the eternal inheritance, but he does not specifically discuss to which blessing πρωτοτόκια refers.[341] Michel writes that πρωτοτόκια refers merely to the rights of a son.[342] However, in the LXX and Jewish literature, πρωτοτόκια was used in the sense of the privilege of the firstborn son concerning the father's inheritance (see also my discussion on the firstborn son's privilege in section 2.1.3). For example, in LXX Deut 21:17, πρωτοτόκια is the privilege of the firstborn son in inheritance. In Philo, the eldest son (πρεσβύτατος) has priority (πρεσβεία) in inheritance. The son of the

336 Cf. S. Tzoref, "Covenantal Election in 4Q252 and Jubilees' Heavenly Tablets," *DSD* 18 (2011): 87.

337 Thompson, *The Beginning of Christian Philosophy*, 43.

338 Lane, *Hebrews 9–13*, 455.

339 E.g., συγκληρονόμος in Heb 11:9; κληρονομέω in Heb 1:4, 14; 6:12; 12:17.

340 O'Brien, *The Letter to the Hebrews*, 476.

341 Koester, *Hebrews*, 532.

342 Michel, *Hebräer*, 631.

discarded wife should also receive the privilege of the double portion (*Spec Leg* 2.139). Furthermore, the term πρωτοτόκια in Heb 12:16 reflects its uses in LXX Gen 25:32–33; 27:36.[343] In this context, πρωτοτόκια refers to the privilege of the firstborn son as the heir of the patriarchal blessing (section 3.1.2). In this narrative, what was transferred from Esau to Jacob was the covenantal status (e.g., Gen 27:28–29). This motif is recurrent in Jewish literature. In *Jub* 19:26–27, Jacob is addressed as the firstborn son of Abraham, and this reflects that the author of *Jubilees* understands the status of the firstborn son as the heir of the Abrahamic covenant (section 3.5.2.3). In *Sir* 36:16–17, the author invokes God to give the tribes of Jacob their inheritance, and in the context, the inheritance of Israel is related to Israel's status as the firstborn son (section 3.8.2.1). In the context of Hebrews, the motif of inheritance is linked with the new covenant. In Heb 9:15, Christ is the mediator of the new covenant, so that "those who are called may receive the promised eternal inheritance (τὴν ἐπαγγελίαν λάβωσιν οἱ κεκλημένοι τῆς αἰωνίου κληρονομίας)." In Heb 12:24, Jesus Christ is also designated as the mediator of the new covenant, and "we" in Heb 12:28 receives the unshakable kingdom. We should note that in Heb 12:16–17, πρωτοτόκια is juxtaposed with inheritance language ("to inherit the blessing (κληρονομῆσαι τὴν εὐλογίαν)"), and this may imply that πρωτοτόκια does not simply refer to the blessing or the sonship, but specifically, to inheritance of the promise. Inheritance language is used throughout Hebrews (1:2, 14; 6:12, 17; 9:15; 11:7; cf. 12:28; Gal 5:21; 1 Cor 6:9), and plays a significant thematic role in Hebrews.[344] The motif of inheritance is fulfilled in Heb 12:28, when the author states, "We are receiving a kingdom that cannot be shaken."[345] Thus, πρωτοτόκια in Heb 12:16 does not merely refer to the general blessing or sonship, but to inheritance of the promise, particularly, the promise of the Land (cf. Heb 12:26).

This motif of πρωτοτόκια prefigures that the saints who dwell in the heavenly Zion are addressed as the assembly of the firstborn sons in Heb 12:23,[346] and the right of the firstborn son is also linked with Heb 11:29 which recalls that Israel is the firstborn son as distinct from the Egyptians. Thus, Heb 12:16 implies that the firstborn sons in Heb 12:23 are distinct in status and destiny from those who are immoral or fall short of grace such as Esau, and πρωτοτόκια symbolises the covenantal blessing given to the people of God.

343 Attridge, *Hebrews*, 369.

344 Johnson, *Hebrews*, 325.

345 Cf. Moffitt, *Atonement*, 70.

346 So, Attridge, *Hebrews*, 369; Koester, *Hebrews*, 532. However, they do not specifically explore the meaning of πρωτοτόκια in Heb 12:16.

4.3.5 *The Meaning of the Firstborn Son in Heb 12:23*

Many interpreters regard Heb 12:18–24 as the rhetorical climax of the entire epistle.[347] This passage can be structurally understood as "the conclusion of the epistolary part" of Hebrews, which shows the contrasting images between Sinai and Zion.[348] The right of the firstborn son in Heb 12:16 is referenced in comparison with Esau or the apostates who forsook the right of the firstborn son. Heb 12:23 is located in the context of the comparison between Sinai and Zion.

Kiwoong Son notes the significance of the antithesis between Sinai and Zion symbolism in Heb 12:18–24, and argues that the antithesis demonstrates a rhetorical strategy and the conceptual background of the whole epistle.[349] The contrast between the old and the new religious systems forms a core of the epistle through the series of antitheses in Heb 12:18–24. Kiwoong Son maintains that Hebrews manifests the superiority of Christianity and the inferiority of Judaism through the contrasts between the images of the old and the new religious systems.[350] Firstly, Son claims that the contrasts between the Sinai symbols in Heb 12:18–21 and the Zion symbols in 12:22–24 indicate that the divine presence in Zion and the new religious systems are superior to the divine presence in Sinai and the old religious system. The mediation of Christ is also supreme over the mediation of Moses. Burning fire, darkness, gloom, storm and trumpet blast imply the fear of the Sinai community, and depict the images of judgement and punishment for sins of the wilderness community.[351] By contrast, the Zion symbols are focused on three groups, the "myriads of angels in joyful assembly" in Heb 12:22, "the assembly of the firstborn" in 12:23 and "the spirits of righteous men made perfect" in 12:23. The joyful image of "the festal gathering" in 12:22 is contrasted with the "fear" in Sinai symbolism in 12:21. So, the antithesis between joy in Zion and fear in Sinai can be considered as the central theme of this passage.[352]

347 Weiss, *Der Brief an die Hebräer*, 660; Guthrie, *The Structure of Hebrews*, 143; Ellingworth, *The Epistle to the Hebrews*, 669; Lane, *Hebrews 9–13*, 448; Koester, *Hebrews*, 548; Son, *Zion Symbolism in Hebrews*, 78.

348 Son, *Zion Symbolism in Hebrews*, 87.

349 Son, *Zion Symbolism in Hebrews*, 102.

350 Contra Lane, *Hebrews 9–13*, 461; Hugh W. Montefiore, *A Commentary on the Epistle to the Hebrews* (BNTC; London: A&C Clark, 1979), 227.

351 Son, *Zion Symbolism in Hebrews*, 88–90.

352 Son, *Zion Symbolism in Hebrews*, 90–91.

However, Hebrews is not attempt at "pitting Judaism against Christianity."[353] Rather, the Sinai and Zion symbolism shows certain continuity.[354] For instance, the myriads of angels recall the gathering of angels in Deut 33:2. That is, the Zion images in Heb 12 present the same image as the Sinai images in Deut 33. The image of a consuming fire in Heb 12:29 is linked with the image of the mountain on fire (Sinai) in Heb 12:18.[355] Fear also exists in both Sinai (Heb 12:21) and Zion (12:28). So, the images of God as a judge continue in both Sinai and Zion symbolism. Allen observes the Deuteronomic framework of Hebrews, and argues that Hebrews re-presents (not replaces) Deuteronomy.[356] Furthermore, the heroes of faith in Heb 11 are those who were under the old covenant, and this implies that the author of Hebrews does not totally negatively evaluate the old covenant. Therefore, the new covenant embraces the old, and Zion re-presents Sinai.[357]

Nonetheless, we should also note distinct features of Zion from Sinai. The strong adversative conjunction "ἀλλά" in Heb 12:22 introduces the Zion symbols, and sharply contrasts 12:18–21 (the Sinai images) with 12:22–24 (the Zion images). The fearful images of Sinai and the contrasting joyful images of Zion are elaborated in these passages, and the negative images of Sinai are connected to the negative warning against apostasy (cf. 12:25). The positive images of Zion are concerned with the positive exhortation for faith and sincerity (cf. 12:28). Accordingly, the contrasts between Sinai and Zion and the adversative "ἀλλά" in 12:22 denote the clear antithesis between the negative images of Sinai and the positive images of Zion.[358]

---

353 Cockerill, *Hebrews*, 643. Traditionally, interpreters assumed that Hebrews articulates supercessionism. Yet, Hays recently finds "the New Covenantalism" in Hebrews, and observes that the new covenant images in Hebrews are used in respect of the restoration of Israel, not the rejection of Israel. Hays also argues that "the typological strategy of Hebrews" does not disinherit Israel. See Hays, "Here We Have No Lasting City," 162, 167. Cf. Jon D. Levenson, *Sinai and Zion: An Entry into the Jewish Bible* (San Francisco: Harper, 1987).

354 David M. Allen, *Deuteronomy and Exhortation in Hebrews: A Study in Narrative Representation* (WUNT II/238; Tübingen: Mohr Siebeck, 2008), 216.

355 Cf. Heb 10:27: "but a fearful prospect of judgment, and a fury of fire that will consume the adversaries [NRSV]."

356 Allen, *Deuteronomy and Exhortation in Hebrews*, 208.

357 Allen, *Deuteronomy and Exhortation in Hebrews*, 216. We should note that "what replaces the old covenant is a covenant that is also informed and shaped by the old." See Lloyd Kim, *Polemic in the Book of Hebrews: Anti-Judaism, Anti-Semitism, Supersessionism* (PTMSeries 64; Eugene: Pickwick, 2006), 199.

358 For the heavenly sanctuary motifs in Hebrews, see Scott D. Mackie, "Heavenly Sanctuary Mysticism in the Epistle to the Hebrews," *JTS* 62 (2011): 117.

The concept of the firstborn son is juxtaposed with the concept of the heavenly tablet in Heb 12:23 (the assembly of the firstborn who are enrolled in heaven). The heavenly tablet is a common motif which indicates the chosen status of the Jews in the OT and Jewish literature.[359] The images of the heavenly tablet and the firstborn son in 12:23 demonstrate that the notion of the firstborn son is associated with the chosen status of the people of God.

Scholars interpret the meaning of "the assembly of the firstborn sons" in terms of the angels, all the saints including the ones still alive,[360] or the dead saints[361] who dwell in heaven including the OT saints.[362] To whom do the assembly of the firstborn sons in 12:23 refer?

Does, then, the assembly of the firstborn sons refer to those who are already dead? If we consider the usage of firstborn son in 1:6, 11:28 and 12:16, it is not natural to conclude that the firstborn sons are those who are already dead. We should remember that the firstborn son is used as the title of Christ in Heb 1:6. Heb 12:16 depicts that Esau held his right as the firstborn son when he was alive. We do not find any clue that the concept of the firstborn sons in Heb 11:28 is related to those already dead. The second person plural perfect tense verb προσεληλύθατε also clearly shows that the letter-recipients ("you") have already come to Mount Zion, the city of the living God, and the heavenly Jerusalem (i.e., the Promised Land). Therefore, it is more appropriate to regard the firstborn sons in 12:23 as all the saints who dwell in the heavenly Zion regardless of their death or survival.[363]

The firstborn sons do not include the angels. Firstly, ἐκκλησία appears twice in Hebrews (2:12; 12:23) and ἐκκλησία in Heb 2:12 refers to the gatherings of the saints. Ἐκκλησία originally means a civil assembly in Greek society,[364] however, also refers to the assembly of the people of God in LXX texts.[365] In particular, we should note that ἐκκλησία in LXX texts is used in the sense of the

359 E.g., Exod 32:32–33; Ps 139:16; Is 4:3; Dan 12:1; *Jub* 2:20; 19:9; 30:20–22; *1 En* 47:3; 104:1; 108:3; *JosAs* 15:4.

360 Käsemann, *The Wandering People of God*, 50; Montefiore, *A Commentary on the Epistle to the Hebrews*, 231.

361 Bruce, *The Epistle to the Hebrews*, 359.

362 John Scholer, *Proleptic Priests: Priesthood in the Epistle to the Hebrews* (JSNTSup 49; Sheffield: JSOT Press, 1991), 146.

363 "The spirits of the righteous made perfect" (12:23b) may be related to the already dead saints in Jewish literature. E.g., *Jub* 23:30–1; *1 En* 22:9; 102:4; 103:3–4; *2 Bar* 30:2. See Lane, *Hebrews 9–13*, 470. Also, it can refer to all the saints who are dead under both the old and new covenants. See O'Brien, *The Letter to the Hebrews*, 489.

364 J. Roloff, "ἐκκλησία," in *EDNT* vol. 1 (eds. Horst Balz and Gerhard Schneider; Grand Rapids: Eerdmans, 1990), 411.

365 E.g., LXX Deut 4:10; 9:10; 18:16 and so on.

wilderness community in the story of Exodus (e.g, LXX Deut 4:10; 9:10; 18:16; 23:1; 23:2, 4; 31:30). This sense of ἐκκλησία accords well with the story of Israel (or Exodus and *Eisodus*) which underlies Hebrews. We will consider the motif of Exodus in Hebrews below.

Secondly, we have no evidence that the angels are designated as בכר or πρωτότοκος in the OT and Second Temple literature. As we discussed in section 3.9 and 3.14.4, Philo, *Conf.* 146, and *PrJos* indicate some tendency in ancient Judaism that Israel was personified as a kind of angelomorphic figure. Moreover, in second century AD, Clement of Alexandria mentions the phrase "the firstborn princes of the angels" (πρωτόγονοι ἀγγέλων ἄρχοντες) in *Strom.* 5.6.35; 6.16.142–43; *Ecl.* 57.1; *Exc.* 10, but it refers to the Holy Spirit, not to the angels.[366]

Alternatively, we can understand the assembly of the firstborn sons as the people of God. First, we should note that the images of the pilgrimage of Israel to the homeland is used in Hebrews, and the images fit well with the motif of the firstborn son in Heb 12:23.[367] The wandering people of God is a significant motif in Hebrews,[368] and Heb 3:7–4:11 and 11:8–39 indicate the journey of Israel towards the promised rest through the wilderness: "These verses encapsulate the author's re-narration of Israel's history—a narration in which the author has placed both himself and his readers in the wilderness period together with all the generations of God's people who have been awaiting entry into God's promised rest."[369] Heb 11:8–39 renders some images of Israel's pilgrimage to the home land. In Heb 11:8–9, while Abraham was an alien, he received the promise of the Land as Isaac and Jacob did. Heb 11:13–16 deals with people who were in search of their homeland and a better country. Inheritance of the Promised Land is a significant motif throughout Hebrews (1:2, 14; 6:12, 17; 9:15; 11:7; cf. 12:28). In Heb 11:22, Joseph made mention of the Exodus of the Israelites, and requested to bring his bones out of Egypt. In Heb 11:13–16, all who died in faith without having received the promises desired their homeland and a better country (i.e., a heavenly one), and God prepared a city for them. Thus, the motif of the pilgrimage towards the Promised Land is significant in Hebrews.

---

366 This phrase may be related to "the seven eyes of the Lord" (Zech 3:9 and 4:10) and "the seven gifts of the Spirit" (Isa 11:2–3). For the similar concept, see *Herm. Vis.* 3.4.1; *Herm. Sim.* 5.5.3. See Bogdan Gabriel Bucur, *Angelomorphic Pneumatology: Clement of Alexandria and Other Early Christian Witnesses* (VigliaeSup 95; Leiden: Brill, 2009), 174; Amy E. Richter, *Enoch and the Gospel of Matthew* (PTMS 183; Eugene: Pickwick, 2012), 142.

367 William G. Johnson, "The Pilgrimage Motif in the Book of Hebrews," *JBL* 97 (1978): 239–51.

368 Käsemann, *The Wandering People of God*, 240. See also Thiessen, "The End of Exodus," 360–69.

369 Thiessen, "The End of Exodus," 368.

The motif of God's discipline in Heb 12:5–13 can be viewed in terms of Israel's wilderness experience. The wilderness period of Israel is described as a form of God's disciplinary action in the OT and Jewish literature.[370] Besides evidence suggested by Thiessen,[371] we find another evidence of the link between God's discipline and the wilderness experience in 4Q504. In 4Q504 1–2 iii 6 (cf. 4Q504 1–2 v 16), God disciplines Israel as his son and the firstborn son. In particular, in 4Q504 1–2 v 16, Israel is disciplined by God 'in the wilderness,' and so, Israel's wilderness period can be viewed as God's disciplinary action in 4Q504. Likewise, God's discipline in Heb 12:5–13 can be viewed in terms of Israel's wilderness experience. In Heb 12:15, "a root of bitterness" alludes to Deut 29:18 which is one of the warnings given to Israel in the wilderness. Finally, in Heb 12:22, the author declares "But you have come to Mount Zion and the city of the living God, the heavenly Jerusalem."[372] The images of Zion are linked with the pilgrimage images in Hebrews. In this context, the images of pilgrimage to the Promised Land fit well with the motif of the firstborn son. Israel was designated as the firstborn son of God in Exod 4:22. In Jewish literature, the title of the firstborn son is used as the heir of the promise. Therefore, the assembly of the firstborn son in Heb 12:23 can be viewed as the title of Israel and the heir of the promise in the context of the sub-narrative of Exodus.

Secondly, the designation of the believers as the firstborn sons corresponds with the eschatological inheritance pattern (e.g., *Sir* 36:17; 4Q369; *4 Ezra* 6:58).[373] In the similar context, it seems that Heb 12 reflects a similar expectation of eschatological inheritance, and the assembly of the firstborn sons should be understood in terms of Israel's title.[374] That is, the believers are described as a heavenly gathering and inherit the kingdom which cannot be shaken in the midst of angels (cf. *2 Bar* 51:3).

Thirdly, the phrase "the assembly of the firstborn sons" in Heb 12:23 is referenced in the context which elucidates the new covenant. Israel is the firstborn

370 Matthew Thiessen observes this perspective in Deut 8:5; Prov 3:11–12; *Wis* 11:9–10; Philo, *Vit Mos* 1.199. For more details, see Matthew Thiessen, "Hebrews 12.5–13, the Wilderness Period, and Israel's Discipline," *NTS* 55 (2009): 369–73.

371 Matthew Thiessen, "Hebrews 12.5–13," 369–72.

372 Thiessen concludes, "[T]he narrative world in which the author has placed both himself and his readers in Heb 3.7–4.11 and 11.8–40 has been clearly defined as Israel's wilderness period." See Thiessen, "Hebrews 12.5–13," 378. Cf. Allen, *Deuteronomy and Exhortation in Hebrews*, 195.

373 For further information on the eschatological inheritance patterns in Jewish literature, see pages 123–25 in this work.

374 Allen argues that ecclesia recalls the wilderness assembly in Deut 4:10 and the expectation of the inheritance in Deut 32:43. See Allen, *Deuteronomy and Exhortation in Hebrews*, 216.

son according to the old covenant (Exod 4:22). By contrast, the believers are the firstborn sons according to the new covenant (12:24). The death of Christ is the vindication of the saints before God the judge (12:23). The motif of inheritance is employed in Heb 12:28: "we are receiving the kingdom which cannot be shaken." This denotes that the concept of the firstborn son in Heb 12:23 is associated with the divine heirship motif. The firstborn sons are those enrolled in heaven and have the status as the chosen, and they are distinct from those who refuse "the one who is speaking" (i.e. God) in Heb 11:24–25. The firstborn sons appear in joyful Zion and they are distinct from the ones who stay in fearful Sinai. Therefore, regardless of whether the eschatological context in 12:18–24 is Platonic or a Jewish apocalyptic two-age frame, it seems clear that the phrase "the assembly of the firstborn sons" in Heb 12:23 refers to the people of God as the heirs of the divine promise (cf. Heb 12:16).

Fourthly, some early Christian documents espouse our interpretation. In *Protrepticus* chapter 9, Clement of Alexandria alludes to Heb 12:22, and his reading of Heb 12:22–23 is consistent with our interpretation:

> ταῦτ᾽ ἔστι τὰ πρωτότοκα τὰ ἐναπογεγραμμένα ἐν οὐρανοῖς καὶ τοσαύταις μυριάσιν ἀγγέλων συμπανηγυρίζοντα.

While πρωτότοκα in the citation above is neuter, it does not refer merely to the first male offspring of animals or the angels, but to the people of God. Rather, Clement of Alexandria designates the church as the firstborn son (ἡ πρωτότοκος ἐκκλησία) in the previous sentence, which is definitely an allusion to Heb 12:23 (see also μυριάσιν ἀγγέλων in Heb 12:22 and *Protrepticus* chapter 9), and he states, "we are the firstborn sons (πρωτότοκοι δὲ παῖδες ἡμεῖς)" in the next sentence. In this context, πρωτότοκα refers to the church. In *Protrepticus* chapter 9, Clement of Alexandria mentions that the church enters into the kingdom of heaven (εἰς τὴν βασιλείαν τῶν οὐρανῶν), which alludes to Heb 1:6, and God made the church the heir of God. So, Clement of Alexandria understands the assembly of the firstborn sons in Heb 12:23 as the church, and believed that the church inherits the kingdom of heaven as the firstborn sons.[375]

In *the Epistle of Barnabas* 13:5–6, πρωτότοκος also refers to the heir of the promise.[376] In *Barnabas* 13, the author discusses who is the authentic heir

375 Cf. Denise Kimber Buell, *Why This New Race: Ethnic Reasoning in Early Christianity* (New York: Columbia University Press, 2005), 74.

376 William Horbury writes that *Barnabas* could be "assigned, with fair probability, to the very end of the first century." See William Horbury, "Jewish-Christian Relations in Barnabas

of the covenant, and whether or not the Jews are the heir of the covenant. *Barnabas* 13:2–6 describes that the blessing of the firstborn son was transferred to the younger son, and, in *Barnabas* 13:5, the author quotes Joseph's words in Gen 48:18: "Transfer your right hand to the head of Manasseh, for he is my firstborn son." In this citation, the firstborn son does not merely refer to the eldest son of Joseph, but the heir of the covenant. In *Barnabas* 13:6, the author states, "Observe how by these means he [Ephraim] has ordained that this people should be first, and heir of the covenant (τὸν λαὸν τοῦτον εἶναι πρῶτον καὶ τῆς διαθήκης κληρονόμον)."[377] So, the blessing given to the firstborn son is related to being the first and possessing the promise of the covenant. Thus, Ephraim was not the firstborn son in a chronological sense, but took possession of the promise of the covenant given to the firstborn son. In this way, the author of *Barnabas* illustrates how the Gentile believers take part of the blessing of the firstborn son. Likewise, in Hebrews, the link between the covenant and inheritance (9:15; 12:24–27) and between the firstborn son and inheritance (12:23 and 12:28) may signal that "the assembly of the firstborn sons" in 12:23 does not refer to the angels or the bearer of general blessing, but to the heir of the covenant.[378]

It is described in Heb 12:28 that the believers receives the kingdom which cannot be shaken. Do the believers inherit the heavenly world in Heb 12:28 (cf. Heb 11:16)? Is Heb 12:25–29 Platonic or apocalyptic? Does everything include both the earthly and heavenly world? Siker writes that Hebrews tends to spiritualise the promises given to Abraham.[379] Knut Backhaus argues, "Das Verheißungsland, im Sinne des Autor ad Hebraeos verstanden, läßt damit

and Justin Martyr," in *Jews and Christians: The Parting of the Ways A.D. 70 to 135* (ed. J.D.G. Dunn; Tübingen: Mohr Siebeck, 1992), 321. For a similar view, see P. Richardson and M.B. Shukster, "Barnabas, Nerva, and the Yavnean Rabbis," *JTS* 34 (1983): 31–55. However, some other scholars prefer to date it to the period of Hadrian the emperor (CE 117–138). E.g., L.W. Barnard, "The 'Epistle of Barnabas' and Its Contemporary Setting," *ANRW* II, vol. 27/1 (Berlin: Walter de Gruyter, 1993), 173–80; James N. Rhodes, *The Epistle of Barnabas and the Deuteronomic Tradition* (WUNT II/188; Tübingen: Mohr Siebeck, 2004), 75–87. Thus, the date of *Barnabas* is still controversial, but we may safely conclude that *Barnabas* was composed between CE 70 (the destruction of the temple) and the times of Hadrian.

377 The translation taken from Michael W. Holmes, *The Apostolic Fathers: Greek Texts and English Translations* (3rd ed.; Grand Rapids: Baker, 2007), 423.

378 Peeler correctly writes, "Every member of the assembly is given the honourable designation of being the firstborn. This is a reiteration of the sermon's theme that those who follow Jesus are considered children of God (2.10, 12–13, 14; 3.6; 12.5–9)." See Peeler, *You Are My Son*, 170. However, she does not specifically explore the meaning of "the assembly of the firstborn sons" in Heb 12:23.

379 Jeffrey S. Siker, *Disinheriting the Jews: Abraham in Early Christian Controversy* (Louisville: WJK, 1991), 97.

alle irdischen Landverheißungen als heilsgeschichtlichen Anachronismus verstehen."[380] Mackie understands Heb 12:22–24 as the community's entry into the heavenly sanctuary. The motif of the heavenly sanctuary is prominent in Hebrews (e.g., 6:18–20; 7:25).[381] However, in Hebrews, it seems that the expectation of the earthly inheritance is not completely abandoned. In Heb 1:2, Christ inherits everything which seems to include the earthly and heavenly realms.

This issue is related to whether the heavenly Zion is a future-eschatological (temporal) concept or present-eschatological (spatial) concept. The traditional view takes the spatial concept, which demonstrates that the main eschatological structure of Hebrews is the Platonic framework elaborating the transcendent metaphysical world. The traditional view does not deny the Jewish apocalyptic eschatology, but it is relativised by the Platonic cosmology.[382] However, it seems more probable that Jewish apocalyptic two-age eschatology underlies Hebrews. In this vein, Hurst declines the dichotomy between the vertical-spatial eschatology and the horizontal-temporal eschatology.[383] In Jewish apocalyptic literature, the boundary between the heavenly and the early world is blurred.

For example, the author of *the Animal Apocalypse* depicts that the Lord will descend to the earth and will build his throne. In *1 En* 90:15–20, Israel triumphs over her enemies, and the righteous carry out divine judgment on their enemies. In *1 En* 90:20–27, the last judgment is depicted, and 90:28–36 and 90:37–38 respectively delineate the New Jerusalem and the advent of the true Jacob/Israel. The judgment takes place in "the pleasant land" (cf. *1 En* 89:40), which must be identical with the New Jerusalem in *1 En* 90:28–36. *1 En* 90:1–12 reflects historical accounts of the Jews in Palestine who were assimilated with pagan environments and who were in conflict with the Seleucids and other Gentiles. "The pleasant land" in *1 En* 90:20 alludes to Ps 106:24: "Then they despised the pleasant land, having no faith in his promise." In Ps 106:24, the pleasant land refers to the Promised Land in the story of Exodus. We should also

380 Knut Backhaus, "Das Land der Verheißung: Die Heitmat der Glaubenden im Hebräerbrief," *NTS* 47 (2001): 187.

381 Scott D. Mackie, "Ancient Jewish Mystical Motifs in Hebrews' Theology of Access and Entry Exhortations," *NTS* 58 (2011): 88–104.

382 For example, see Thompson, *The Beginning of Christian Philosophy*, 49; Gregory Sterling, "Ontology versus Eschatology: Tensions between the Author and Community in Hebrews," *SPhilo* 13 (2001): 190–211.

383 See L. Hurst, *The Epistle to the Hebrews: Its Background of Thought* (SNTSMS 65; Cambridge, Cambridge University Press, 1990), 13–42. Ellingworth endorses Hurst. See Ellingworth, *The Epistle to the Hebrews*, 408. Cf. Thomson, *The Beginning of Christian Philosophy*, 49.

note that the scene of *1 En* 90:20 resembles Dan 7:9–12 which depicts the last judgement in heaven. So, Olson maintains that the distinction between heaven and earth is blurred in *the Animal Apocalypse*.[384]

Accordingly, as Moffitt argues, "a dichotomy between the spiritual realm and the material ream was neither constitutive of nor necessary for the eschatological hope of at least some Jews of this time period."[385] Therefore, it seems more reasonable that inheritance in Hebrews includes both the earthly and the heavenly realms.

In brief, the mention of "the assembly of the firstborn sons" in Heb 12:23 accords with the Jewish usage of the firstborn son, the sub-narrative of Exodus in Hebrews and the eschatological inheritance expectations of Israel. In the eschatological inheritance expectations, Israel (or the righteous) receives her inheritance, and the author of Hebrews implies that this expectation is fulfilled in the community of the new covenant. Therefore, in Hebrews, the believers hold the status of the firstborn sons who refer to the heir of the promise in status and destiny. Through designations of Christ and the believers as the firstborn son(s), the author of Hebrews implicitly encourages the recipients to understand and to hold fast to their identity as the firstborn sons.

4.3.6 *Conclusion*

We have examined four passages in Hebrews in order to define the meaning of the firstborn son. The title of the firstborn son as an heir of promise was ascribed solely to Israel in the OT and Jewish literature, while the term 'firstborn' in a cultic sense is ascribed to the Egyptians. In the OT and Jewish literature, the notion of the firstborn son symbolises the election of Israel in status and inheritance, and refers to the self-perception of Israel which was distinct in privilege and destiny from the non-Elect. The concept of the firstborn son in Hebrews is defined by comparison with the angels (1:6), the Egyptians (11:28), Esau (12:16) and Sinai symbolism (12:23). Accordingly, the status of the firstborn son in Hebrews surpasses that of Sinai, the Egyptians, Esau, which respectively represent the Jewish cultic institution, the outer society and the apostates. Thus, the concept of the firstborn son in Hebrews implies that the promise given to Israel was realised in the believers' community.

384 Daniel C. Olson, *A New Reading of the Animal Apocalypse of 1 Enoch: 'All Nations Shall Be Blessed* (Leiden: Brill, 2013), 224. Olson also observes that, in Enochic literature, "God descends to a mountaintop to conduct the Last Judgment (*1 En* 1:4; 25:1–6), but God's mountain reaches to heaven (17:2; 18:8)."

385 Moffitt, *Atonement*, 117.

It seems that the notion of the firstborn son in Hebrews implicitly functions to comfort the letter-recipients who faced their present hardship and social marginalisation. In other words, Hebrews implies that the believers are the firstborn sons who outrank everything in heaven and on earth, and that they were called to the eternal inheritance (9:15) and will inherit and enter the Promised Land as the firstborn sons. Therefore, Hebrews implicitly legitimises the status of the letter-recipients of Hebrews through designating Christ and the believers as the firstborn son(s).[386]

4.4 Revelation

4.4.1 *The Background*

The Book of Revelation[387] is a symbolic cosmic discourse which relates a narrative of warfare between God and the power of evil, written in an apocalyptic tone against the backdrop of the persecution and the social marginalisation of Christians.[388] Revelation was written as a circular letter sent to seven churches in Asia Minor, and thus also reflects the specific interests and situations of these churches.[389] The author of Revelation addresses how the believers in the seven churches enter the New Jerusalem by overcoming their afflictions in the cosmic war.[390]

There is no consensus on the social background of Revelation. Thompson doubts that there were widespread persecutions toward Christians under

386 This conclusion corresponds to Mackie's observations: "To the Son's conferral of membership in the family of God, they [the recipients] are exhorted to offer a reciprocative confession of familial mutuality and identification." See Scott D. Mackie, "Confession of the Son of God in Hebrews," *NTS* 53 (2007): 128–29.

387 For the genre of Revelation, see David Hellholm, "The Problem of Apocalyptic Genre and the Apocalypse of John," *Semeia* 36 (1986): 13–64. For the Hellenistic Jewish Apocalytpic genre, see J.J. Collins, "The Genre Apocalypse in Hellenistic Judaism," in *Apocalypticism in the Mediterranean World and the Near East: Proceedings of the International Colloquium on Apocalypticism, Uppsala, August 12–17, 1979* (ed. David Hellholm; Tübingen: Mohr Siebeck, 1983), 531–48.

388 Richard Bauckham, *The Theology of the Book of Revelation* (Cambridge: Cambridge University Press, 1993), 12–17; David A. DeSilva, "The Social Setting of the Revelation to John: Conflicts Within, Fears Without," *WTJ* 54 (1992): 273–302; Elisabeth Schüssler Fiorenza, *The Book of Revelation: Justice and Judgment* (Philadelphia: Fortress, 1985), 6; Thomas B. Slater, *Christ and Community: A Socio-Historical Study of the Christology of Revelation* (JSNTSup 178; Sheffield: Sheffield Academic Press, 1999), 22.

389 David E. Aune, "The Social Matrix of the Apocalypse of John," in *Apocalypticism, Prophecy, and Magic in Early Christianity* (WUNT 1/199; Tübingen: Mohr Siebeck, 2006), 184.

390 Bauckham, *The Theology of the Book of Revelation*, 14.

Domitian.[391] However, the absence of an empire-wide persecution "does not necessarily mean that there was not a limited, regional repression of Christians during this time period."[392] As Yarbro Collins notes, the cause of crisis in Revelation may be not simply political oppressions, but conflicts with the Jews and neighbouring Gentiles and precarious relations between Christian communities and Roman officials.[393]

The majority of scholars date Revelation to the reign of Domitian (CE 81–91);[394] according to Irenaeus, it was written late in his reign (*Adv. Haer.* 5.30.3). Babylon is mentioned six times in Revelation, and clearly refers to the Roman Empire. Yarbro-Collins points out that Babylon is used to symbolise the Roman Empire in Jewish apocalyptic documents (e.g., *4 Ezra* 3:1–2; *2 Bar* 10:1–3; 11:1, etc.) because, just as Babylonia destroyed the Jerusalem temple, so did the Roman army (CE 67–70).[395] Further evidence that Revelation dates to this time includes the reference in Rev 6:6 to limiting the production of grapes, which most likely refers to the Domitian decree (CE 92),[396] and the phrase 'the twelve apostles' used in 21:14, which is not believed to have been used before CE 80.[397] It can therefore be concluded that, while Revelation may reflect some traditions which originated in CE 60–70,[398] it was written in the Domitian era.

We also detect a number of symbols which can be related to Roman imperial worship (e.g., 13:4, 15–16; 14:9–11; 15:2; 16:2; 19:20; 20:4). For instance, the tribulation (2:9–11) and the idol food (2:14; 20) can be linked with some pressure to attend the Roman imperial cult. The king of the beasts force people to worship the beasts, reminding the readers of the imperial cult (13:1–18). In this context, the author of Revelation stresses that the master of the world is not Caesar, but God.

---

391 Leonard K. Thompson, *The Book of Revelation: Apocalypse and Empire* (Oxford: Oxford University Press, 1990), 16–17.

392 Slater, *Christ and Community*, 32.

393 A. Yarbro Collins, *Crisis and Catharsis: The Power of the Apocalypse* (Philadelphia: Westminster, 1984), 84–99.

394 E.g., Yarbro Collins, *Crisis and Catharsis*, 54–83.

395 Adele Yarbro Collins, "Dating the Apocalypse of John," *BR* 26 (1981): 35. Collin Hemer also notes that the situations depicted in Rev 2–3 reflect the Domitian era. Colin J. Hemer, *The Letters to the Seven Churches of Asia in their Local Setting* (Grand Rapids: Eerdmans, 2001), 2–5.

396 Hemer, *The Letters to the Seven Churches*, 158.

397 David Aune, *Revelation 1–5* (WBC 52a; Waco: Word, 1997), 35.

398 Cf. J.C. Wilson, "The Problem of the Domitianic Date of Revelation," *NTS* 39 (1993): 597–605.

4.4.2 *The Meaning of the Firstborn Son in Rev 1:5*

Rev 1:4–6 is a part of the prologue of the book of revelation. The prologue is divided into a foreword (1:1–3), epistolary greeting and doxology (1:4–6) and confession or motto (1:7–8).[399] The greeting and doxology in 1:4–6 reflect a general Hellenistic epistolary convention, but the benediction in Rev 1:5 is similar to Paul's greeting (i.e., grace and peace to you). Three actions of Jesus are delineated in 1:5a–6. Jesus Christ loves "us," set "us" free from sins and made "us" to be a kingdom and priests to his God and Father. In this context, Christ is designated by three Christological titles: ὁ μάρτυς ὁ πιστός; ὁ πρωτότοκος τῶν νεκρῶν; and ὁ ἄρχων τῶν βασιλέων τῆς γῆς.

Some scholars argue that the doxology (1:5–6) may have originated from early Christian baptismal tradition.[400] The firstborn son is the title found in Rom 8:29; Col 1:15, 18; and Heb 1:6, so it was most probably adopted from a preceding tradition. However, the first title (the faithful witness) seems to reflect John's own theology, as it is rarely found in other Christological confessions outside of Revelation (cf. Rev 2:13; 3:14). The rulership of Christ is also a significant motif in Revelation as shown below. So, it is probable that John formed Christological confessions in Rev 1:5a as a unit together utilising a preceding tradition (πρωτότοκος) and John's own motifs (μάρτυς and ἄρχων).[401] Thus, it seems that the author of Revelation drew on the previous tradition as well as his own themes (μάρτυς and ἄρχων) to draw together and develop the Christological confessions in Rev 1:5.

It also seems clear that the three Christological titles were not unintentionally juxtaposed and that the three Christological titles reveal John's own theological interests.[402] The three Christological titles in 1:5a prefigure the life patterns and status of the believers. Christ is the faithful eschatological witness (ὁ μάρτυς ὁ πιστός).[403] Two witnesses in Rev 11:1–14, perhaps, symbolise the church. Two witnesses are killed (Rev 11:3–8), risen and ascend to the heaven (11:11–12). The believers are required to remain faithful (πιστός) and to record and keep the faithful words in Rev 21:5 and 22:7.

---

399 Grant R. Osborne, *Revelation* (BECNT; Grand Rapids: Baker, 2002), 50; Elisabeth Schüssler Fiorenza, *Revelation: Vision of a Just World* (Edinburgh: T&T Clark, 1991), 35.

400 E.g., Akira Satake, *Die Gemeindeordnung in der Johannesapokalypse* (WMANT 21; Neukirchen-Vluyn: Neukirchener Verlag, 1966), 113–14; Schüssler Fiorenza, *Revelation*, 41.

401 Schüssler Fiorenza, *Revelation*, 41.

402 So Caird writes, "The titles of Christ are equally carefully chosen for John's pastoral purpose," in G.B. Caird, *A Commentary on The Revelation of St John the Divine* (BNTC; London: A&C Black, 1966), 16. See also Fiorenza, *Revelation*, 70.

403 Cf. Christ is the faithful and true witness (3:14). "The rider", i.e., Christ is called Faithful and True (Rev 19:11). See also 22:6: "These words are trustworthy and true."

With reference to the ruler of the kings of the earth (Rev 1:5), we find similar designations of Christ as the ruler of all nations (e.g., Rev 15:8; 17:14; 19:16; cf. Rev 2:25–27; cf. 3:21; 5:10; 11:15 21:4).[404] This verse (Rev 2:25–27) evokes the Davidic king in Ps 2:8–10.[405] In Revelation, the rulership is ascribed to God (15:3) and Christ (11:15–18; 12:5; 17:14; 19:16). The believers will also share in the rulership of Christ (e.g., 1:6, 9; 2:26; 3:21; 5:10; 20:4, 6; 22:5).[406] In this vein, Rev 1:5a provides a Christological template for the believers, both in terms of life on earth as faithful witnesses and in terms of their destiny as ruler of kings of the earth.

It seems clear that "ὁ πρωτότοκος τῶν νεκρῶν" in Rev 1:5 is associated with the priority of resurrection.[407] The term πρωτότοκος refers to the eldest son of the father in the LXX and Jewish literature, and accordingly seems to signify temporal priority in terms of resurrection in Rev 1:5. In Rev 1:5, πρωτότοκος is juxtaposed with ὁ ἄρχων τῶν βασιλέων τῆς γῆς, which ostensibly alludes to ὑψηλὸν παρὰ τοῖς βασιλεῦσιν τῆς γῆς in LXX Ps 88:28b. So, it seems that the firstborn son of the dead in Rev 1:5 could refer to a Davidic messianic title,[408] and that early Christians messianically re-interpreted the term πρωτότοκος in LXX Ps 88, and that this notion was reflected in Rev 1:5.[409]

While the term πρωτότοκος in Rev 1:5 is evocative of LXX Ps 88:28b, it can also be viewed as the title of Israel. Firstly, as explored in chapter 3, the term

404 Allusions to Davidic Messiah are widespread in Revelation. E.g., "the Lion of the tribe of Judah, the Root of David, has conquered …" (5:5); and "The root and the descendant of David" (22:16). See also 2:27 and 12:5b.

405 Particularly, Ps 2:9 is also cited in Rev 2:5–6.

406 Rulership of God and Christ is shared with believers in 22:5: "And there will be no more night; they need no light of lamp or sun, for the Lord God will be their light, and they will reign (βασιλεύσουσιν) forever and ever." Cf. Rev 1:9. As Slater writes, "John employed the 'one like a son of man', the slain Lamb and the Divine Warrior Christological images to maintain the unity between Christ and community. Christ gathers an elect community of priest-kings en route to the New Jerusalem," in *Christ and Community*, 245.

407 Cf. Schüssler Fiorenza writes that the priority of resurrection is not a focal point of this expression, as Schüssler Fiorenza notes. Elisabeth Schüssler Fiorenza, *Priester Für Gott: Studien zum Herrschafts-und Priestermotiv in der Apokalypse* (NTAbh 7; Münster: Aschendorff, 1972), 201. However, she does not provide specific evidences.

408 E.g., Schüssler Fiorenza, *Priester Für Gott*, 202; G.K. Beale, *The Book of Revelation* (NIGTC; Grand Rapids: Eerdmans, 1999), 190–91; Brian K. Blount, *Revelation: A Commentary* (NTL; Louisville: WJK, 2009), 35; Robert H. Mounce, *The Book of Revelation* (NICNT; Grand Rapids: Eerdmans, 1998), 48–49.

409 It seems that the portrayal of Jesus in Rev 1:1–20 is in parallel with a messianic figure in *1 Enoch* and *4 Ezra*. See Slater, *Christ and Community*, 106–7. Firstly, Christ in Rev 1:19 is a revealer of mystery as in *1 En* 46:3. Secondly, Christ in Rev 1:13, 16, 18 and 20 rules the universe in *1 En* 62:6–7. Thirdly, Christ as human-like Messiah in Rev 1:7 rides on a cloud (*4 Ezra* 13:3).

'firstborn son' was used as the title of Israel in many cases. The title of the firstborn son refers to the status of Israel in Exod 4:22 and some Jewish literature, and the title of the firstborn son in Rev 1:5 can be interpreted in this context. Revelation can be understood in the context of Israel's story. The teaching of Balaam in Rev 2:14 is reminiscent of the story of Israel in Numbers. In Rev 7:1–8, those who were sealed come out of every tribe of the people of Israel. Two faithful witnesses are killed in the place called Egypt: and their dead bodies will lie in the street of the great city that is spiritually called Sodom and Egypt (11:8). The song of the Lamb is spoken of as the song of Moses (15:3). The curses of seven bowls also allude to curses of Exodus (16:1–21). Therefore, the allusions to the story of Exodus in Revelation lead us to read Revelation in terms of the story of Israel who was rescued from Egypt and entered the Promised Land (particularly, 21:7). In the context of the story of Israel, we can interpret the firstborn son as the title of Israel in the OT and Jewish literature. Βασιλείαν ἱερεῖς (a kingdom, priests) in Rev 1:6 echoes ממלכת כהנים (the kingdom of priests) in Exod 19:6, namely, the title of Israel. In Exod 19:6, the kingdom of priests symbolises the status and privilege of Israel set apart from the nations.[410] Accordingly, "a kingdom, priests" in Rev 1:6 refers to the privileges previously conferred upon Israel in Exod 19:6, and, in Rev 1:6, the status as βασιλείαν ἱερεῖς is granted to the believers.[411] Likewise, the firstborn son in Rev 1:5 also is redolent of the title of Israel possessing the privileged status in Exod 4:22. The concept of the firstborn son in Rev 1:5 shares a similarity with "a kingdom, priests" in Rev 1:6, in that "the firstborn son" and "the kingdom of priests" refer to the

---

410 For the specific meaning of "the kingdom of priests" in Exod 19:6, see Kyu Seop Kim, "The Meaning of מַמְלֶכֶת כֹּהֲנִים in Exod 19:6 Revisited," *JBTR* 35 (2014): 249–67. Cf. William L. Moran, "A Kingdom of Priests," in *The Bible in Current Catholic Thought* (ed. John L. McKenzie; New York: Herder & Herder, 1962), 8–20; Georg Fohrer, "Priesterliches Königtum (Ex 19,6)," in *Studien zur alttestamentlichen Theologie und Geschichte (1949–1966)* (BZAW 115; Berlin: Walter de Gruyter, 1969), 151–52; Cornelis Houtman, *Exodus II, 7:14–19:25* (trans., Sierd Woudstra; Kampen: Kok, 1996), 445; J. B. Bauer, "Könige und Priester, ein heiliges Volk (Ex 19,6)," *BZ* 2 (1958): 283–86; Georg Steins, "Priesterherrschaft, Volk von Priestern oder was sonst? Zur Interpretation von Ex 19, 6," *BZ* 49 (2001): 28–32. For the specific sense of βασίλειον ἱεράτευμα in LXX Exod 19:6, see Arie van der Kooij, "The Promulgation of the Pentateuch in Greek according to the Letter of Aristeas," in *Scripture in Transition: Essays on Septuagint, Hebrew Bible, and Dead Sea Scrolls in Honour of Raija Sollamo* (eds., Anssi Voitila and Jutta Jokiranta; Leiden: Brill, 2008), 189–90; Van der Kooij, "A Kingdom of Priests: Comments on Exodus 19:6," in *The Interpretation of Exodus: Studies in Honour of Cornelis Houtman* (eds., Riemer Roukema et al.; Leuven: Peeters, 2006), 173–75.

411 Cf. Beale, *Revelation*, 193. As for the priest as privilege, see E. Schüssler Fiorenza, *Priester für Gott*, 115–17.

status and privileges of Israel in Exodus. This enables us to conclude that the title 'firstborn son' in Rev 1:5 is associated of the title and the status of Israel.

Secondly, the concept of the firstborn son in Rev 1:5 can be related to the expectation that Israel as the firstborn son would receive her inheritance in some Jewish literature. In Rev 21–22, the believers (i.e., "he who overcomes") receive their inheritance, and partake in the rulership and eternal life with Christ. The motif of inheritance in Rev 21:6–7 is found in the climax of the literary structure of Revelation, i.e., Rev 21:5–8,[412] which expresses the fulfilment of the covenant. It denotes that inheriting eternal life is a part of the accomplishment of the covenant. The believers will receive the inheritance which was formerly promised to the Jews. In Rev 21, the promise of inheritance is given to the believers and this is an intrinsic component of the central message of Revelation. In Rev 21:6–7, the believers' inheritance refers to eternal life (a gift from the spring of the water of life). By contrast, the wicked will experience the second death (21:8). Israel (or the righteous) inherits eternal life in Jewish literature (e.g., 4Q418 69 ii 13–14; *Sib.Or.* 3:45; *1 En* 58:2). Particularly, inheritance in Rev 21:7 recalls *1 En* 58:2–3, where the author depicts that the righteous will enjoy eternal life in glory and light. In Rev 22:19, partaking in the tree of life is described in respect of μέρος, which was used when Israel inherited the Promised Land (LXX Deut 32:9; LXX Jos 19:9). Sharing (μέρος) in the tree of life in Rev 22:19 is paralleled with inheriting eternal life in Rev 21:7. Thus, Revelation reflects the expectation that the people of God will receive their inheritance. In this context, the title of the firstborn son in Rev 1:5 can be linked with the motif of inheritance as Israel's eschatological privilege and inheritance, as presented in Jewish literature.

In Rev 1:5, πρωτότοκος is qualified by τῶν νεκρῶν. This indicates that the title of the firstborn son is linked with the motif of resurrection (ὁ πρωτότοκος τῶν νεκρῶν). As conveyed in Rom 8:29, Col 1:15, 18 and Heb 1:6, it seems that πρωτότοκος contains the sense of 'the eldest son.' So, naturally, πρωτότοκος conveys the sense of 'the first one who resurrected. Two witnesses are resurrected and ascend to heaven (Rev 11:11–12).[413] In Rev 20:6, the motif of the resurrection is used as a significant paradigm of the believers. In this vein, ὁ πρωτότοκος τῶν νεκρῶν foreshadows the resurrection of the believers. So, Christ is the representative of Israel, and initiates the restoration of the people of God. Resurrection

412 David E. Aune, "The Apocalypse of John and the Problem of Genre," in *Apocalypticism, Prophecy, and Magic in Early Christianity* (WUNT 1/199; Tübingen: Mohr Siebeck, 2006), 65.

413 Cf. the exaltation of the lamb that was slaughtered (5:12–13): "Worthy is the Lamb that was slaughtered to receive power and wealth and wisdom and might and honor and glory and blessing!" It is highly likely that the crucifixion and the resurrection are implied in the motif of the exaltation of the lamb that was slaughtered.

was regarded as a national event—i.e., the restoration of Israel (e.g., Ezekiel 37).[414] In this context, ὁ πρωτότοκος τῶν νεκρῶν in Rev 1:5 implies that Christ represents the whole of Israel (or the people of God), and foreshadows that Christ as representative of Israel initiates the realisation of the promise through his resurrection.

In conclusion, the title of the firstborn son in Rev 1:5 should be defined in the sense of the title of Israel as well as a Davidic messianic title. The believers will receive their inheritance as the sons of God (Rev 21:7). So, the concept of the firstborn son in Rev 1:5 is suggestive of the title of Israel in the OT and Jewish literature (par. Exod 4:22), and implies that the promise previously given to Israel is fulfilled in Christ and the believers' community. The firstborn son is linked with the image of resurrection which means the restoration of Israel, and this reveals that Christ is the firstborn son as representative of Israel.

4.5 [Excursus] Luke 2:7[415]

In Luke 2:7, Mary gives birth to her firstborn (ἔτεκεν τὸν υἱὸν αὐτῆς τὸν πρωτότοκον), namely Jesus. It seems that this designation of Jesus as the firstborn functions to prepare the reader for Luke 2:23–24.[416] Yet, some scholars take different interpretations. For instance, Schürmann claims that the firstborn in Luke 2:7 refers to a Davidic messianic figure:[417] "Als erstgeborener Davidide ist das Kind als möglicher messianischer Prätendent charakterisiert."

---

414 Jon D. Levenson, *Resurrection and the Restoration of Israel: The Ultimate Victory of the God of Life* (New Haven: Yale University Press, 2006), 164–65.

415 Many scholars concur that the Lukan birth and infancy narratives are integral to the purpose of Luke-Acts, even though they diverge on the composition of Luke 1–2. For instance, H.H. Oliver, "The Lukan Birth Stories and the Purpose of Luke-Acts," *NTS* 10 (1964): 202–26; W. Barnes Tatum, "The Epoch of Israel: Luke I–II and the Theological Plan of Luke-Acts," *NTS* 13 (1967): 184–95; Raymond E. Brown, *The Birth of The Messiah: A Commentary on the Infancy Narratives in Mathews and Luke* (New York: Doubleday, 1977), 242; René Laurentin, *Structure et Théologie de Luc I–II* (Ebib; Paris: Gabalda, 1964), 191–223; P. Benoit, "L'infance de Jean-Baptiste selon Luc I," *NTS* 3 (1956/57): 169–94; Matthew Thiessen, *Contesting Conversion: Genealogy, Circumcision, and Identity in Ancient Judaism and Christianity* (Oxford: Oxford University, 2011), 114; Heinz Schürmann, *Das Lukasevangelium: Erster Teil* (HTKNT; Freiburg: Herder, 1990), 18.

416 Cf. I. Howard Marshall, *The Gospel of Luke: A Commentary on the Greek Text* (NIGTC; Grand Rapids: Eerdmans, 1978), 106; Darrell L. Bock, *Luke: 1:1–9:50* (BECNT; Grand Rapids: Baker, 1994), 207.

417 Schürmann, *Das Lukasevangelium: Erster Teil*, 104. For a similar opinion, Frederick. W. Danker, *Jesus and the New Age According to St. Luke: A Commentary on the Third Gospel* (Philadelphia: Fortress, 1988), 55; Mark L. Strauss, *The Davidic Messiah in Luke-Acts:*

However, "ἔτεκεν τὸν υἱὸν αὐτῆς τὸν πρωτότοκον" in Luke 2:7 denotes that Jesus is the first male offspring of Mary (αὐτῆς), and this phrase falls into the cultic definition of the firstborn (the first male offspring who opened the mother's womb). So, it is implausible that the firstborn in Luke 2:7 symbolises a messianic figure.

On the other hand, Darrell Bock claims that its use indicates Jesus's primogeniture in terms of the father's inheritance.[418] In its Jewish usage, the firstborn as a principal heir of the family is defined in relation to his father, as discussed in chapter 2.1.[419] However, the term "the firstborn" in Luke 2:7 is used in relation to Mary, Jesus' mother. Further, there is no reference to Jesus' right to possess His father's property in Luke's Gospel. Thus, Bock' view is unconvincing.

The firstborn in Luke 2:7 refers to the first male offspring from his mother's womb. The sentence, ἔτεκεν τὸν υἱὸν αὐτῆς τὸν πρωτότοκον stresses that Jesus was born as Mary's first male offspring in Luke 2:7. In Exod 13:2, the firstborn who opened the womb belongs to the Lord, and should be consecrated to God. The firstborn of all the Israelites should be redeemed in the Tabernacle,[420] and the redemption of the firstborn is performed in Luke 2:23–24. This context enables the readers to conclude that the firstborn in Luke 2:7 is employed in a cultic sense. That is, Jesus is the first male offspring of the mother (Mary) and its reference in Luke 2:7 offers a reason why Joseph and Mary brought Jesus to the Temple (cf. Luke 2:23). There is no evidence that Luke understood πρωτότοκος as a messianic title or as the title of Wisdom. The firstborn in Luke 2:27 is not used as titular, or as the father's heir, but in the cultic sense. So, a proper translation of πρωτότοκος in Luke 2:27 would be "the firstborn" or "the first male offspring" rather than "the firstborn son." It is unclear that the use of πρωτότοκος in Luke 2:27 is related to the tradition of πρωτότοκος in Rom 8:29, Col 1:15, 18, Heb 1:6 and Rev 1:5, since the term πρωτότοκος in Luke 2:7 is not linked with the motif of promise and inheritance reserved for Israel.

Finally, we should also consider the reason why the cultic motifs (Jesus' circumcision and the firstborn) are employed in Luke 2. The circumcision is the sign of the membership of Israel according to the Sinai covenant. As explored in section 2.3.2, the redemption of the firstborn recalls the saving action of God for Israel in Exodus. So, the cultic observances in Luke 2 suggest that Jesus is the member of Israel, and this story is connected to the issue of Israel and

---

The Promise and its Fulfillment in Lukan Christology (JSNTSup 110; Sheffield: Sheffield Academic Press, 1995), 88–89.

418 So, Bock, *Luke*, 207.

419 E.g., Deut 21:15–17.

420 E.g., Num 3:12–13; 18:15–16; Josephus, *Ant* 4.70–71.

the Gentile inclusion in the Gospel of Luke.[421] In other words, the motif of the firstborn in Luke 2 functions to stress Jesus' Jewish identity,[422] and confirms that Jesus is the member of the people of God (also see the conclusion in section 2.3.2). In this context, the motif of the firstborn is implicitly linked with the issue of Israel and God's people in Luke.[423]

---

421 Particularly, note Simeon's praise at the Temple in Luke 2:30–32. The theme of the circumcision reiterates in Acts 15. See also Fearghus Ó Fearghail, *The Introduction to Luke-Acts: A Study of the Role of Lk 1,1–4,44 in the Composition of Luke's Two Volume Work* (AB 126; Rome: Editrice Pontificio Istituto Biblico, 1991), 151.

422 Cf. Thiessen, *Contesting Conversion*, 140–41.

423 So, V. George Shillington, *An Introduction to the Study of Luke-Acts* (London: T&T Clark, 2006), 72–73. For various views on the issue of the people of God in Luke-Acts, see Jacob Jervell, *Luke and the People of God: A New Look at Luke-Acts* (Minneapolis: Augsburg, 1972); Robert Maddox, "Jews, Gentiles and Christians," in *the Purpose of Luke-Acts* (SNTW; Edinburg: T&T Clark, 1982), 31–62; Stephen G. Wilson, *The Gentiles and the Gentile Mission in Luke-Acts* (SNTSMS 23; Cambridge: Cambridge University Press, 1973); Jack T. Sanders, *The Jews in Luke-Acts* (Philadelphia: Fortress, 1987); Robert Brawley, *Luke-Acts and the Jews: Conflict, Apology and Conciliation* (LMS 33; Atlanta: Scholars, 1987).

CHAPTER 5

Conclusion

Our goal in chapter two and three was to analyse the institution of primogeniture in the Greco-Roman family (2.1) and the Jewish family (2.2), to understand the implications of offering the firstborn (2.3), and to trace the meaning of the firstborn son as Jewish ethnic identity (3) in the OT and Jewish literature. The major findings of chapter 2 and 3 can be summarised as follows.

In Greco-Roman society, fathers' inheritance was flexibly distributed to remaining children, and primogeniture was not usually practised. So, primogeniture was a unique institution of inheritance in Jewish society distinct from non-Jewish society.

In the Pentateuch, when it is referenced in respect of his father and inheritance, בכר or πρωτότοκος was a kinship concept which refers to the eldest son in the Jewish family. On the other hand, when it is used in the cultic context, בכר or πρωτότοκος is the first male offspring of the mother. In chapter 2.1, we concluded that, in Greco-Roman society, a deceased father's inheritance was equally distributed to his remaining offspring, and primogeniture was not generally exercised. Yet in chapter 2.2, this study observed that primogeniture was practised in the Jewish family. Contrary to the arguments of Greenspahn, the designations of younger sons as בכר (or πρωτότοκος in LXX texts) in the patriarchal narratives do not indicate that the institution of primogeniture did not exist in the ancient Jewish family. *Rather, the firstborn son (*בכר *or πρωτότοκος) can be defined as the eldest son according to birth rank in terms of his paternal lineage, and as the one who held the birthright (*בכרה*/πρωτοτόκια or πρεσβεία) in the Jewish family. So, the firstborn son was the principal heir of the family and the successor of his father.* Therefore, contrary to many scholars' assumption (see section 2.2.1), the title of the firstborn son can be related to his right relating to primogeniture as well as his privileged status over his younger brothers.

On the basis of this argument, we concluded that, as discussed in chapter 3, ancient authors of the OT and Jewish literature employed the concept of the firstborn son in order to portray the self-perception of Israel, and the unique Jewish institution of primogeniture (chapter 2.2) provides a significant background for 'the title of the firstborn son' in the OT and Jewish literature. It is highly probable that ancient authors envisioned the concept of the family of God, and that in this concept, the firstborn son refers to the title of Israel as a principal heir of God's inheritance in the family of God.

 | DOI:10.1163/9789004394940_006

In the OT, "the firstborn son" refers to the heir of divine promise (chapter 3). As the firstborn son, Israel holds a supreme position over the Gentiles (cf. Gen 27:29) and the right to inherit the Promised Land (cf. Gen 28:4; Jer 31:9–11) or the entire world (cf. Gen 26:4). In Exodus, the concept of the firstborn son implies that Israel is distinct from the Egyptians in terms of primacy and destiny. The title of Israel as the firstborn son (cf. Exod 4:22) has an affinity with the titles "the kingdom of priests" and "the holy nation" in Exod 19:6 which reveal that Israel is privileged and set apart from the nations.

In some Jewish literature, the concept of the firstborn son is developed as stressing the heavenly status of Israel as the exalted figure pre-eminent over all creation and the nations (4Q369; 4Q504; *PrJos*; Philo, *Conf* 145–6; *4 Ezra* 6:59; cf. Philo, *Spec Leg* 2.166). "The firstborn son" in 4Q369, 4Q504, *Sir* 36:17, 44:23, *LAB* 18:6 and *4 Ezra* 6:58 is associated with the concept of the divine heir. In *Post* 62, Philo states that Israel holds primogeniture as the firstborn son. In *PrJos*, *JosAs*, *Jubilees*, *PsSol* 13:9; 18:4, the concept of the firstborn son highlights Israel's primacy over the nations or all creation. Accordingly, in the OT and Jewish literature, the concept of the firstborn son represents the self-perception of Israel as the Elect, and reflects the anticipation of the fulfilment of the divine promise. Thus, Israelites understood themselves as the firstborn son of God, and it means that they perceived themselves as the principal heir of God who had the right of the firstborn son, and who was distinct from other peoples. It should be noted that the title of the firstborn son is often related to the motif of inheritance which refers to the Land of Palestine or the entire world.

Then, does the title of the firstborn son imply that Israel was adopted by God? The OT texts and the Jewish authors generally do not stress the 'adoptive' sonship of Israel, when they employ the title of the firstborn son (e.g., *Jubilees*, 4Q369, 4Q504, *Sir*, *4 Ezra*, *PrJos*, *LAB*, *PssSol*, *JosAs*, *Philo*). Rather, what is highlighted in the title of Israel is that Israel is the principal heir of divine promise has a distinct status from other nations, as discussed above.

Thus, in the OT and Jewish literature, the concept of the firstborn son defines the self-perception of Israel as the heir of the divine promise and the superior one to the Gentiles by comparison with the non-Elect. Thus, the concept of the firstborn son reflects a particularistic notion on the election, and in the OT and Jewish literature, those who are not the firstborn son are identical with the ones who are not in the chosen line.

While the firstborn son refers to the title of Israel, we find the several cases in the OT and Jewish literature that the title of the firstborn son is ascribed to individuals. In the OT and Jewish literature, Jacob (Gen, *Jub* and *Sir* 44:23, etc.), Joseph (*JosAs*) and David (Ps 89:27) are individuals who hold the title of the firstborn son. In *PrJos* and Philo, *Conf* 146, Israel is personalised as an exalted and heavenly figure. So, Christ's title of the firstborn son in the NT can be viewed in terms of the title of the firstborn son which was given to individuals as representative of Israel, i.e., Jacob, Joseph, David and the exalted personalised Israel (*JosAs*, *PrJos* and *Conf* 146).

In contrast to the Christological discussions of the early church (e.g., the Arius-Athanasius debates arguing the humanity-divinity of Jesus), the πρωτότοκος motif in the NT deals with the soteriological implications of the gospel, and in contrast to the setting of ethnic and societal boundaries of the theme in contemporary Jewish writings, the NT developments of the πρωτότοκος motif transcend societal and religious boundaries in extending the gift of inheritance and familial belonging to all who are receptive to it. The title of the firstborn son in the NT is not simply nominal, but indicates his access to the promise of Israel, and is associated with the right of the inheritance (primogeniture) and the special status of Israel. *In the NT, the motif of the firstborn son signals that the promise given to the firstborn son (i.e., Israel) was fulfilled in Christ and his believers' community.*

In contrast to Jewish texts setting up ethnic boundaries, the NT uses of the motif of πρωτότοκος erase ethnic and socio-economic boundaries in the interest of extending an open invitation to the divine family and inheritance through the grace availed in Christ.[1] This point may also be contextually applicable to the interreligious settings of Colossae and Rome, the transcendent thrust of Hebrews, and a push-back against the imperial presence behind Revelation.

In Romans, the concept of the firstborn son is employed in the context of the discussions about the equal relationship between the Jewish and the Gentile believers at the Roman churches. The Jews are no more addressed as the firstborn sons of God in Romans, but rather the Jewish and Gentile believers alike are the adoptive children of God (e.g., οἵτινές εἰσιν Ἰσραηλῖται, ὧν ἡ υἱοθεσία; Rom 9:4). In this situation, Paul implies that the Gentile believers could have access to the benefits of the divine promise in union with Christ, the firstborn son (8:29). The concept of the firstborn son in Rom 8:29 is referenced in the context of Israel's election and inheritance, and should be understood in terms of the self-awareness of Israel, as seen above. The context of Rom 4 and 8 elucidates how the believers became legitimate heirs of the divine promise. In this context, Christ is designated as the firstborn son who is the heir of the divine promise (8:29), and the believers partake in the inheritance reserved for Israel

1 For the concept of grace in Paul's letters, see J.M.G. Barclay, *Paul and the Gift* (Grand Rapids: Eerdmans, 2015).

as joint-heirs through their union with Christ (8:17). Thus, the firstborn son in Rom 8:29 is one of the kinship metaphors relating to the family of God.

By contrast, the author of Colossians accentuates that Christ is prior to all things and is the head of the church. The focus here is placed upon Christ's relationship with all creation and the church. It is highly likely that the faith and identity of the Colossian believers as the people of God were jeopardised by the false teaching in the Colossian church, and is highly probable that, in this situation, Paul needed to defend the supremacy of Christ over all things, and sought to respond to the errorists who taught that people could earn their salvation and gain their identity as the people of God through Jewish legal and mystic practices. In this situation, everything the Colossian believers needed was Christ and their union with him, and so they were exhorted to find their true identity and security in him. Christ is the representative of God's people, is exalted and seated at the right hand of God (3:1), and is designated as the firstborn son of all creation and the firstborn son from the dead. The title of the firstborn son in Col 1:15 indicates the central status given to Israel in creation. Our study in chapter 3 suggests that some Jews believed that they as the firstborn sons held a pre-eminent status over creation. So, Christ as the firstborn son holds primacy in and rulership over creation. In Col 1:18, the firstborn son has a double connotation: 1) temporal priority in terms of resurrection; and 2) the status of Israel. In both references to the firstborn son in Col 1:15 and 18, the intrinsic sense of Israel's status is not eclipsed.

Thus, in Colossians, the title of the firstborn son is associated with the themes of creation and resurrection, and Paul asserts that the Colossian saints can partake in the eschatological inheritance through their union with Christ the firstborn son, not through Jewish mystical and ascetic practices. So, the title of the firstborn son is employed in order to express the primacy and the heirship of Christ as a remedy against the false teaching.

For the original readers of Hebrews, who were marginalised due to their Christian belief, the concept of inheritance is related to more transcendental areas. In contrast to Romans and Colossians, the believers are designated as 'firstborn sons' (rather than as those in union with the firstborn son); this direct designation was possibly caused by the need to justify and solidify the identity and status of believers who were under socio-economic pressure and hardship. It is likely that, in this situation, the author of Hebrews felt a need to clearly define the identity and the status of the believers as the true people of God and the heirs of the divine promise. Accordingly, what is stressed in Hebrews is that the believers have a hope of having a part in the divine promise and the inheritance as 'the firstborn sons.'

In Heb 1:6, the firstborn son as representative of Israel enters the Promised Land. In Heb 12:23, the saints are designated as the firstborn sons. Through designating Christ and his believers as the firstborn son(s), the author of Hebrews implicitly legitimises the status and existence of the believers' community to whom Hebrews was addressed.

We should note the distinct features between the uses of the firstborn son in Romans and Hebrews.[2] Firstly, one of the key differences is that the saints in Heb 12:23 are designated as the assembly of the firstborn sons, while, in Rom 8:29, Christ is nominated as the firstborn son distinct from "many brothers (i.e., the believers)." In Romans, the believers are not "the firstborn sons," but adoptive sons of God (8:15, 22). Therefore, Paul does not ascribe the title of Israel to the believers.

By contrast, in Heb 12:23, the saints themselves are designated as the firstborn sons. As a result, the author of Hebrews may imply that the letter-recipients (i.e., Jewish and Gentile Christians) were the legitimate successors of the Jewish religion. In other words, it seems that Paul's interest was to include the believers in the covenantal privilege of Israel, but Hebrews' interest was to re-construct the identity of the letter-recipients as the firstborn sons.

Secondly, the title of the firstborn son in Rom 8:29 is referenced in the context of election and inheritance. In Romans, designating Christ as the firstborn son implies that, as joint-heirs of Christ, the believers (Jewish and Gentile) can equally participate in the primacy and the inheritance of the firstborn son. So, in Romans, the motif of the firstborn son is used in order to highlight equality between the Jewish and Gentile believers.

Yet, compared to Romans, the firstborn son motif in Hebrews stresses the distinctness and the superiority of the believers' community compared to outside society and the apostates. In Hebrews, the concept of the firstborn son implies that the Christian community enjoys a distinct status from outside society which "the Egyptians" symbolise and from the apostates whom "Esau" signifies. The status of the firstborn son surpasses that of the angels, the Egyptians, Esau and Sinai, which represent outside society, the apostates and the Jewish cultic institutions. These uses of the firstborn son reflect that the author of Hebrews implicitly sought to legitimise the status of the believers' community through comparisons with the Jewish cultic institutions and the outside world. However, in Romans, Paul does not legitimise the status of the

---

2 Yet, as discussed in pages 242–243, we should note a similar logic between Heb 1:6 and Rom 8:29. The firstborn son in Heb 1:6 can be read as the eldest son (see section 4.3.2) (cf. Heb 2:10), and πρωτότοκος in Rom 8:29 is also the eldest son among his many brothers.

believers' communities in Rome in relation to outer society or Judaism, but one of Paul's foci in Romans was equality between Jewish and Gentile Christians.

In Revelation, it seems that the author needed to encourage the believers who lived under the Empire. In this situation, the author designates the believers as a kingdom and priest (βασιλεíαν, ἱερεῖς; a title originally given to Israel) in 1:6. Christ is addressed as the faithful witness and the firstborn son of the dead. It should be noted that the Roman emperor was called *divi fillius* (son of God) in the Roman world. Yet, Christ, a firstborn son, is superior to the *divi fillius*, and furthermore, Christ as the ruler of the kings of the earth, he outweighs the Roman emperor in status. The title 'the firstborn son of the dead' may be influenced by a tradition which was used in Col 1:18; the resurrection was a significant concept in Revelation to the believers under persecution and hardship. Christ is not merely a representative of God's people, but also a faithful witness who were crucified and resurrected.

Accordingly, these variations of the firstborn son tradition in the NT can be understood according to the distinctive situations of each NT book. This indicates that the motif of the firstborn son was contextually developed by each of the early Christian communities.

Notwithstanding the differences, the title of the firstborn son in the NT is used in a very similar way, and can be basically understood as 'the status of Israel as the Elect and the divine heir.' In the NT, the common expressions in the adjacent context can be organised as follows:

	Rom	Col	Heb	Rev
The firstborn son	8:29 (πρωτότοκος)	1:15, 18 (πρωτότοκος)	1:6 (πρωτότοκος)	1:5 (πρωτότοκος)
Inheritance (of the entire world)	4:13; 8:17; 8:32	1:12	1:2; 1:4; 1:6; 12:17	21:7
The image	8:29 (εἰκών)	1:15 (εἰκών)	1:3 (χαρακτήρ)	N/A
Cosmic (angelic) powers	8:38–39	1:16; 2:18	1:4–14; 2:7	5:2; 10:1–11; 15:1–8; 16:11; 17:15; 18:1
Heavenly status of Christ (or Israel)	8:3; 8:34	1:15–20; 3:1, 4	1:6; 10:19; 12:23	4:4; 7:9; 11:12
Glory	8:17, 21, 30	1:11, 27 (cf. "in light" in 1:12)	1:3 (for Christ); 2:10 (for the believers)	5:13; 7:12; 21:11; 21:24; 26

It is notable that πρωτότοκος in the NT is always mentioned along with the concept of inheritance. As shown in the table, it can be inferred that the concept of the firstborn son in the NT originated in a shared tradition or a common Christological confession concerning the concept of inheritance and heavenly status of Christ in early Christianity, and that the shared firstborn son tradition was differently applied to each Christian community according to its different theological and situational needs.

It is highly probable that the heavenly status of Christ as the firstborn son in the NT is rooted in a similar tradition which depicts Israel's heavenly status in Jewish literature. In *PrJos*, 4Q369 and Philo, *Conf* 145–46 (cf. *Jub* 2:20), Israel holds exalted status as the firstborn son, and dwells in heaven. Therefore, in terms of its origin, the concept of the firstborn son is associated with Jewish anticipation of eschatological inheritance. In this vein, the notion of the firstborn son in the NT reveals that this anticipation was fulfilled in Christ and Christ's communities.

In particular, πρωτότοκος is juxtaposed with εἰκών in Rom 8:29 and Col 1:15 (cf. Heb 1:3), and this juxtaposition signals that these verses are based on a similar tradition in respect of the firstborn son. As discussed in section 4.1.3.3, πρωτότοκος and εἰκών are related to the concept of the heavenly Israel, and εἰκών refers to the *Urbild* of the people of God (not simply humankind), and πρωτότοκος signifies the title of Israel.

Therefore, we conclude that early Christians re-interpreted this anticipation, and coined the Christological confession that Christ is the firstborn son. In other words, if the divine promise given to the firstborn son was realised in Christ, it means that the believers can partake in the chosenness and inheritance through union with Christ (Rom 8), or the believers themselves become the firstborn sons (Heb 12). In this vein, it seems that the origin of the confession of Christ as the firstborn son is related to Gentile inclusion in early Christianity. So, the concept of the firstborn son in the OT and Jewish literature symbolises the exclusive privileges given to the Jews, but early Christians overturned the ethnic notion of the firstborn son. Ancient Judaism had both universalistic and particularistic features, but the concept of the firstborn son presents a particularistic vision in ancient Judaism. *Previously, the non-Elect such as Ishmael and Esau could not take part in the promise reserved for the firstborn son. However, in the NT, those who were not originally the firstborn sons (i.e., the forsaken) can now partake in the status and privilege reserved for Israel.* Thus, firstborn son Christology in the NT reflects early Christian re-interpretation of Jewish election theology and the ethnic notion of the firstborn son, and proposes a route for the originally non-Elect to enable them to share in the status and inheritance promised to the firstborn son.

Bibliography

Primary Texts and Translations

Atkinson, Kenneth. *An Intertextual Study of the Psalms of Solomon: Pseudepigrapha.* Lewiston: Edwin Mellen, 2001.

Barnes, Jonathan. *The Complete Works of Aristotle: The Revised Oxford Translation.* Princeton: Princeton University Press, 1984.

Bauckham, Richard, et al. *Old Testament Pseudepigrapha: More Noncanonical Scriptures. Volume 1.* Grand Rapids: Eerdmans, 2013.

Beentjes, Pancratius C. *The Book of Ben Sira in Hebrews: A Text Edition of All Extant Hebrew Manuscripts and a Synopsis of All Parallel Hebrew Ben Sira Texts.* Supplements to Vetus Testamentum 68. Leiden: Brill, 1997.

Birks, Peter, et al. *Justinian's Institutes.* Ithaca: Cornell University Press, 1987.

Charles, R.H. *The Apocrypha and Pseudepigrapha of the Old Testament in English with Introductions and Critical and Explanatory Notes to the Several Books. Volumes 1–2.* Oxford: Clarendon, 1913.

Charlesworth, James H. *The Old Testament Pseudepigrapha, Volumes 1–2.* New York: Doubleday, 1983.

Colson, F.H., et al. *Philo. 10 Volumes and Two Supplementary Volumes.* Loeb Classical Library. Cambridge: Harvard University Press, 1929–1953.

Cooper, John M. *Plato: Complete Works.* Indianapolis: Hackett, 1997.

Delcogliano, Mark and Radde-Gallwitz, Andrew. *St. Basil of Caesarea: Against Eunomius.* Washington: The Catholic University of America Press, 2011.

Elliger, K., et al. (eds.). *Biblica Hebraica Stuttgartensia.* Stuttgart: German Bible Society, 1997.

Falls, Thomas B. *The Writings of Saint Justin Martyr.* The Fathers of the Church. New York: Christian Heritage, 1948.

Feldman, Louis H. *Judean Antiquities Books 1–4.* Flavius Josephus Translation and Commentary. Edited by Steve Mason. Leiden: Brill, 2000.

Freedman, Harry, et al. *Midrash Rabbah. Volumes 1–10.* London: Soncino, 1992.

Guggenheimer, Heinrich W. *The Jerusalem Talmud Fourth Order: Neziqin Tractates Bava Qamma, Bava Mesia, and Bava Batra.* Studia judaica 45. Berlin: Walter de Gruyter, 2008.

Halo, William W. and Lawson, K. (eds.). *The Context of Scripture: Canonical Compositions, Monumental Inscriptions and Archival Documents from the Biblical World.* Volumes 1–3. Leiden: Brill, 2003.

Helmbold, W.C. *Plutarch: Moralia. Volume 6.* Cambridge: Harvard University Press, 1939.

Holmes, Michael W. *The Apostolic Fathers: Greek Texts and English Translations*. Grand Rapids: Baker, 2007.

Jackson, John. *Tacitus: The Annals. Books IV–VI, XI–XII*. Loeb Classical Library. Cambridge: Harvard University Press, 1989.

Jacobson, Howard. *A Commentary on Pseudo-Philo's Liber Antiquitatum Biblicarum: With Latin Text and English Translation. Volume 1*. Arbeiten zur Literatur und Geschichte des hellenistchen Judentums 31; Leiden: Brill, 1996.

James, Montague Rhodes. *The Biblical Antiquities of Philo*. Translations of Early Documents Series 1. New York: KTAV, 1971.

Marcovich, Miraslov (ed.). *Iustini Martyris Dialogus cum Tryphone*. Patristische Texte und Studien 47. Berlin: Walter De Gruyter, 1997.

Martínez, Florentino García and Tigchelaar, Eibert J.C. *The Dead Sea Scrolls: Study Edition*. Grand Rapids: Eerdmans, 1999.

Nestle, E., Aland, B., and Aland, K., et al. (eds.), *Novum Testamentum Graece*. 28th Edition. Stuttgart: German Bible Society, 2012.

Nickelsburg, George W. E. and VanderKam, James C. *1 Enoch: A New Translation Based on the Hermeneia Commentary*. Minneapolis: Fortress Press, 2004.

Page, D.L. *Selected Papyri III*. Loeb Classical Library. Cambridge: Harvard University Press, 1941.

Poste, E. *Institutes of Roman Law by Gaius with a Translation and Commentary*. Oxford: Clarendon, 1904.

Rahlfs, A. (ed.). *Septuaginta, id est Vetus Testamentum graece iuxta LXX interpretes*. Stuttgart: Wurttembergische Bibelanstalt, 1979.

Reinmuth, Eckart (ed.). *Joseph und Aseneth*. Scripta Antiquitatis Posterioris ad Ethcam Religionemque pertinentia 15. Tübingen: Mohr Siebeck, 2009.

Sage, Evan T. *Livy: History of Rome. Volume 12*. Loeb Classical Library. Cambridge: Harvard University Press, 1989.

Vanderkam, James C. *The Book of Jubilees: A Critical Text*. Scriptores Aethiopici Tomus 88. Leuven: Peeters, 1989.

Vermes, Geza. *The Complete Dead Sea Scrolls in English*. London: Penguin, 2004.

Watson, Alan. *The Digest of Justinian. Volumes 1–4*. Philadelphia: University of Pennsylvania Press, 2008.

Yadin, Yigael, et al. *The Documents from the Bar Kokhba Period in the Cave of Letters*. Jerusalem: Israel Exploration Society, 1989.

Secondary Sources

Aasgaard, Reidar. *"My Beloved Brothers and Sisters": Christian Siblingship in Paul*. Library of New Testament Studies 265. London: T&T Clark, 2004.

Abegg, Martin G. "Messianic Hope and 4Q285: A Reassessment." *Journal of Biblical Literature* 113 (1994): 81–91.

Adams, Edward. "Paul's Story of God and Creation: The Story of How God Fulfils His purposes in Creation." Pages 19–43 in *Narrative Dynamics in Paul: A Critical Assessment*. Edited by Bruce W. Longenecker. Louisville: WKJ, 2002.

Aitken, James K. "The Semantics of 'Glory' in Ben Sira: Traces of a Development in Post-Biblical Hebrews?" Pages 1–24 in *Sirach, Scrolls and Sages: Proceedings of a Second International Symposium on the Hebrews of the Dead Sea Scrolls, Ben Sira and the Mishnah, Held at Leiden University, 15–17 December 1997*. Edited by T. Muraoka and J.F. Elwolde. Studies on the Texts of the Desert of Judah 33. Leiden: Brill, 1999.

Aletti, J.-N. *Colossiens 1,15–20: Genre et exégèse du texte Fonction de la thématique sapientielle*. Analecta Biblica 91. Rome: Biblical Institute Press, 1981.

Allen, David M. *Deuteronomy and Exhortation in Hebrews: A Study in Narrative Representation*. Wissenschaftliche Untersuchungen zum Neuen Testament II 238. Tübingen: Mohr Siebeck, 2008.

Allen, David M. "Who, What, and Why?: The Worship of the Firstborn in Hebrews 1:6." Pages 159–175 in *Mark, Manuscripts, and Monotheism: Essays in Honor of Larry W. Hurtado*. Edited by Chris Keith and Dieter T. Roth. Library of New Testament Studies 528. London: T&T Clark, 2015.

Anderson, A.A. *The Book of Psalms: 73–150*. New Century Biblical Commentary. Grand Rapids: Eerdmans, 1980.

Anderson, Bradford A. "The Inversion of the Birth Order and the Title of the Firstborn Son." *Vetus Testamentum* 60 (2010): 655–658.

Anderson, Bradford A. "Election, Brotherhood and Inheritance: A Canonical Reading of the Esau and Edom Traditions." PhD diss., Durham University, 2010.

Anderson, C.P. "Who are the Heirs of the New Age in the Epistle to the Hebrews?" Pages 255–277 in *Apocalyptic and the New Testament: Essays in Honor of J. Louis Martyn*. Journal for the Study of the New Testament Supplement Series 24. Sheffield: Sheffield Academic Press, 1989.

Anderson, Paul N. *The Christology of the Fourth Gospel: Its Unity and Disunity in the Light of John 6*. Wissenschaftliche Untersuchungen zum Neuen Testament II/78. Mohr Siebeck: Tübingen, 1996.

Anderson, Paul N. "The Johannine Logos-Hymn: A Cross-Cultural Celebration of God's Creative-Redemptive Work." Pages 219–242 in *Creation Stories in Dialogue: The Bible, Science, and Folk Traditions, Radboud Prestige Lecture Series by R. Alan Culpepper*. Biblical Interpretation Series 139. Edited by R. Alan Culpepper and Jan van der Watt. Leiden: Brill, 2016.

Andriessen, P.C.B. "La Teneur Judéo-Chrétienne de He I 6 et II 14b–III 2." *Novum Testamentum* 18 (1976): 293–313.

Asheri, David. "Laws of Inheritance, Distribution of Land and Political Constitutions in Ancient Greece." *Historia: Zeitschrift für Alte Geschichte* 12 (1963): 1–21.

Attridge, H. and Strugnell, J. "The Prayer of Enosh." Pages 353–362 in *Qumran Cave 4. VIII: Para-biblical Texts: Part 1. Discoveries in the Judaean Desert XIII*. Oxford: Clarendon Press, 1994.

Attridge, Harold. *The Epistle to the Hebrews: A Commentary on the Epistle to the Hebrews*. Hermeneia: A Critical and Historical Commentary on the Bible. Philadelphia: Fortress, 1989.

Aune, David E. "The Apocalypse of John and the Problem of Genre." *Semeia* 36 (1986): 65–96.

Aune, David E. "The Social Matrix of the Apocalypse of John." Pages 175–189 in *Apocalypticism, Prophecy, and Magic in Early Christianity*. Wissenschaftliche Untersuchungen zum Neuen Testament 199. Tübingen: Mohr Siebeck, 2006.

Backhaus, Knut. "Das Land der Verheißung: Die Heimat der Glaubenden im Hebräerbrief." *New Testament Studies* 47 (2001): 171188.

Bakhos, Carol. *Ishmael on the Border: Rabbinic Portrayals of the First Arab*. Albany: State University of New York Press, 2006.

Balchin, J.F. "Colossians 1:15–20: An Early Christian Hymn? The Arguments from Style." *Vox Evangelica* 15 (1985): 65–93.

Bammel, Ernst. "Versuch zu Col 1.15–20." *Zeitschrift für die neutestamentliche Wissenschaft* (1961): 88–95.

Bandstra, Andrew. "Did the Colossian errorists need a mediator?" Pages 329–343 in *New Dimensions in New Testament Study*. Edited by R.N. Longenecker and M.C. Tenney. Grand Rapids: Zondervan, 1974.

Bannon, Cynthia J. *The Brothers of Romulus: Fraternal Pietas in Roman Law, Literature, and Society*. Princeton: Princeton University Press, 1997.

Barclay, J.M.G. *Jews in the Mediterranean Diaspora: From Alexander to Trajan (323 BCE–117 CE)*. Hellenistic Culture and Society 33. Edinburgh: T&T Clark, 1996.

Barclay, J.M.G. *Colossians and Philemon*. New Testament Guides. Sheffield: Sheffield Academic Press, 1997.

Barclay, J.M.G. "There is Neither Old nor Young? Early Christianity and Ancient Ideologies of Age." *New Testament Studies* 53 (2007): 225–241.

Barclay, J.M.G. "'By the Grace of God I Am What I Am': Grace and Agency in Philo and Paul." Pages 140–157 in *Divine and Human Agency in Paul and His Cultural Environment*. Library of New Testament Studies 335. Edited by J.M.G. Barclay and S.J. Gathercole. London: T&T Clark, 2008.

Barclay, J.M.G. *Paul and the Gift*. Grand Rapids: Eerdmans, 2015.

Barnard, Jody A. *The Mysticism of Hebrews: Exploring the Role of Jewish Apocalyptic Mysticism in the Epistle to the Hebrews*. Wissenschaftliche Untersuchungen zum Neuen Testament II/331. Tübingen: Mohr Siebeck, 2012.

Barth, M. and Blanke, H. *Colossians: A New Translation with Introduction and Commentary*. Anchor Bible. New York: Doubleday, 1995.

Barth, Markus. *The People of God*. Journal for the Study of the New Testament: Supplement Series 5. Sheffield: JSOT Press, 1983.

Bassler, Jouette. *Divine Impartiality: Paul and a Theological Axiom*. Society of Biblical Literature Dissertation Series 59. Chico: Scholars, 1982.

Bauckham, Richard. *The Theology of the Book of Revelation*. Cambridge: Cambridge University Press, 1993.

Bauckham, Richard. *Jesus and the God of Israel: God Crucified and Other Studies on the New Testament Christology of Divine Identity*. Grand Rapids: Eerdmans, 2008.

Baur, F.C. *Paul the Apostle of Jesus Christ: His Life and Work, His Epistles and His Teachings. A Contribution to a Critical History of Primitive Christianity*. Translated by E. Zeller. London: Williams and Norgate, 1873.

Beale, G.K. *The Book of Revelation*. New International Greek Testament Commentary. Grand Rapids: Eerdmans, 1999.

Beasley-Murray, Paul. "Colossians 1:15–20: An Early Christian Hymn Celebrating the Lordship of Christ." Pages 169–82 in *Pauline Studies: Essays Presented to F.F. Bruce on His 70th Birthday.* Edited by D.A. Hagner and M.J. Murray. Grand Rapids: Eerdmans, 1980.

Beentjes, Pancratius C. "Ben Sira 44:19–23—the Patriarchs: Text, Tradition, Theology." Pages 209–228 in *Studies in the Book of Ben Sira*. Edited by G. Xeravits and J. Zsengeller. Supplements to Journal for the Study of Judaism Supplement 127. Leiden: Brill, 2008.

Beetham, Christopher. *Echoes of Scripture in the letter of Paul to the Colossians*. The Biblical Interpretation 96. Leiden: Brill, 2008.

Beker, J. Christiaan. *Paul the Apostle: The Triumph of God in Life and Thought*. Minneapolis: Fortress, 1980.

Bell, Richard. *The Irrevocable Call of God: An Inquiry into Paul's Theology of Israel*. Wissenschaftliche Untersuchungen zum Neuen Testament 184. Tübingen: Mohr Siebeck, 2005.

Bendor, S. *The Social Structure of Ancient Israel: The Institution of the Family (Beit' ab) from the Settlement to the end of the Monarchy*. Jerusalem Biblical Studies 7. Jerusalem: Simor, 1996.

Benoit, P. "L'infance de Jean-Baptiste selon Luc 1." *New Testament Studies* 3 (1956/57): 169–94.

Berger, Peter L. and Luckmann, Thomas. *The Social Construction of Reality: A Treatise in the Sociology of Knowledge*. New York: Anchors, 1966.

Bevere, Allan. *Sharing in the Inheritance: Identity and the Moral Life in Colossians*. Journal for the Study of the New Testament: Supplement Series 226. Sheffield: Sheffield Academic Press, 2003.

Bird, Michael. *Colossians and Philemon*. New Covenant Commentary Series. Eugene: Cascade, 2009.

Birnbaum, Ellen. *The Place of Judaism in Philo's Thought: Israel, Jews, and Proselytes*. Brown Judaic Studies 90. Atlanta: Scholars, 1996.

Blank, Josef. *Paulus und Jesus: Eine theologische Grundlegung*. SANT 18; München: Kösel, 1968.

Blenkinsopp, Joseph. *Isaiah 40–55: A New Translation with Introduction and Commentary*. Anchor Bible. New York: Doubleday, 2002.

Blount, Brian K. *Revelation: A Commentary*. New Testament Library. Louisville: WJK, 2009.

Blum, Erhard. "Das Sog. 'Privilegrecht' in Exod 34,11–26: Ein Fixpunkt der Komposition des Exodusbuches?" Pages 147–166 in *Studies in the Book of Exodus*. Bibliotheca ephemeridum theologicarum lovaniensium. Edited by M. Vervenne. Leuven: Leuven University Press, 1996.

Blum, Erhard. *Die Komposition der Vätergeschichte*. Wissenschftliche Monographien zum Alten und Neuen Testament 57. Neukirchen-Vluyn: Neukirchener Verlag, 1984.

Bock, Darrell L. *Luke: 1:1–9:50*. Baker Exegetical Commentary on the New Testament. Grand Rapids: Baker, 1994.

Bockmuehl, Markus. "Redaction and Ideology in the Rule of the Community." *Revue de Qumran* 18 (1998): 541–560.

Bockmuehl, Markus. *Revelation and Mystery in Ancient Judaism and Pauline Christianity*. Wissenschaftliche Untersuchungen zum Neuen Testament II 36. Tübingen: Mohr Siebeck, 1990.

Bohak, Gideon. *Joseph and Aseneth and the Jewish Temple in Heliopolis*. Society of Biblical Literature Early Judaism and Its Literature 10. Atlanta: Scholars, 1996.

Borgen, Peder. "Philo of Alexandria." Pages 333–342 in *Anchor Bible Dictionary. Volume 5*. New York: Doubleday, 1991.

Borgen, Peder. *Philo of Alexandria: An Exegete for His Time*. Supplements to Novum Testamentum 86. Leiden: Brill, 1997.

Bornkamm, Günter. "The Heresy of Colossians." Pages 123–145 in *Conflict at Colossae*. Edited by F.O. Francis and W.A. Meeks. Society of Biblical Literature: Sources for Biblical Studies 4. Missoula: Scholars, 1973.

Braude, William G. *The Midrash on Psalms*. New Haven: Yale University Press, 1987.

Breytenbach, Cilliers. *Versöhnung: Eine Studie zur paulinischen Soteriologie*. Wissenschftliche Monographien zum Alten und Neuen Testament 60. Düsseldorf: Neukirchener Verlag, 1989.

Brin, Gershon. *Studies in Biblical Law: From the Hebrew Bible to the Dead Sea Scrolls*. Translated by Jonathan Chipman. Journal for the Study of the New Testament: Supplement Series 176. Sheffield: Sheffield Academic Press, 1994.

Brooke, George. "Men and Women as Angels in Joseph and Aseneth." *Journal for the Study of the Pseudepigrapha* 14 (2005): 159–177.

Brown, Raymond E. *The Birth of The Messiah: A Commentary on the Infancy Narratives in Mathews and Luke*. New York: Doubleday, 1977.

Bruce, F.F. "The Colossian Heresy." *Bibliotheca Sacra* 141 (1984): 195–208.

Bubelis, William S. "Inheritance, Priesthoods and Succession in Classical Athens: The Hierophantai of the Eumolpidai." Pages 95–105 in *Families in the Greco-Roman World*. Edited by Ray Laurence, et al. London: Bloomsbury, 2012.

Burchard, Christoph. "The text of *Joseph and Aseneth* reconsidered." *Journal for the Study of the Pseudepigrapha* 14 (2005): 83–96.

Burchard, Christoph. *Untersuchungen zu "Joseph und Aseneth," Überlieferung-Ortsbestimmung*. Wissenschaftliche Untersuchungen zum Neuen Testament 8. Tübingen: Mohr Siebeck, 1965.

Burke, Trevor. "The Characteristics of Paul's Adoptive-Sonship (Huiothesia) Motif." *Irish Biblical Studies* 17 (1995): 62–74.

Burke, Trevor. *Adopted into God's Family: Exploring a Pauline Metaphor*. Downers Grove: IVP, 2006.

Burney, C.F. "Christ as the ΑΡΧΗ of Creation (Prov. viii 22, Col I 15–18, Rev. iii 14.)." *Journal of Theological Studies* 27 (1926): 160–177.

Byrne, Brendan. *Sons of God—Seed of Abraham*. Analecta biblica 83. Rome: Biblical Institute Press, 1979.

Caird, G.B. *A Commentary on The Revelation of St John the Divine*. Black's New Testament Commentaries. London: A&C Black, 1966.

Calabi, Francesca. *God's Acting, Man's Acting: Tradition and Philosophy in Philo of Alexandria*. Studies in Philo of Alexandria 4. Leiden: Brill, 2007.

Campbell, Douglas. "The Story of Jesus in Romans and Galatians." Pages 97–119 in *Narrative Dynamics in Paul: A Critical Assessment*. Edited by Bruce W. Longenecker. Louisville: WKJ, 2002.

Campbell, William S. *Paul and the Creation of Christian Identity*. Library of New Testament Studies 322. London: T&T Clark, 2008.

Canavan, Rosemary. *Clothing the Body of Christ at Colossae: A Visual Construction of Identity*. Wissenschaftliche Untersuchungen zum Neuen Testament II 334. Mohr Siebeck: Tübingen, 2012.

Caneday, Ardel. "The Eschatological World Already Subjected to the Son: The οἰκουμένη of Hebrews 1.6 and The Son's Enthronement." Pages 28–39 in *Cloud of Witnesses: The Theology of Hebrews in Its Ancient Contexts*. Edited by Richard Bauckham, et al. Library of New Testament Studies 387. London: T&T Clark, 2008.

Cassuto, Umberto. *Commentary on Genesis, Part 1*. Jerusalem: Magnes, 1978.

Chae, Daniel Jong-Sang. *Paul as Apostle to the Gentiles: His Apostolic Self-Awareness and its Influence on the Soteriological Argument in Romans*. Paternoster Biblical Monograph. Carlisle: Paternoster, 1997.

Champlin, Edward. *Final Judgments: Duty and Emotion in Roman Wills, 200BC–AD250*. Berkeley: University of California Press, 1991.

Charles, R.H. *The Ascension of Isaiah*. London: Black, 1900.

Charlesworth, James H. and Olson, Dennis T. "Prayers for Festivals." Pages 46–106 in *The Dead Sea Scrolls: Hebrew, Aramaic, and Greek Texts with English Translations: Pseudepigraphic and Non-Masoretic Psalms and Prayers. Volume 4a*. Edited by J.H. Charlesworth, et al. Tübingen: Mohr Siebeck, 1994.

Chazon, Esther. "Words of the Luminaries." Pages 989–990 in *Encyclopedia of the Dead Sea Scrolls*. Edited by Lawrence Schiffman and James VanderKam. Oxford: Oxford University Press, 2000.

Chester, Andrew. *Messiah and Exaltation: Jewish Messianic and Visionary Traditions and New Testament Christology*. Wissenschaftliche Untersuchungen zum Neuen Testament 207. Tübingen: Mohr Siebeck, 2007.

Chestnutt, Randall. *From Death to Life: Conversion in Joseph and Aseneth*. Journal for the Study of the Pseudepigrapha: Supplement Series 16. Sheffield: Sheffield Academic Press, 1995.

Childs, B.S. *Introduction to the Old Testament as Scripture*. Minneapolis: Fortress, 1973.

Childs, B.S. *The Book of Exodus: A Critical, Theological Commentary*. Old Testament Library. Philadelphia: Westminster, 1974.

Choi, Soo Ho. "The Struggle for Family Succession and Inheritance in a Rural Korean Village." *Journal of Anthropological Research* 51 (1995): 329–346.

Clarke, Andrew D. "Jew and Greek, Slave and Free, Male and Female: Paul's Theology of Ethnic, Social and Gender Inclusiveness in Romans 16." Pages 103–125 in *Rome in the Bible and the Early Church*. Edited by Peter Oakes. Carlisle: Paternoster, 2002.

Clarke, Andrew D. "Equality or Mutuality: Paul' Use of 'Brother' Language." Pages 159–163 in *The New Testament in Its First Century Setting: Essays on Context and Background in Honour of B.W. Winter on His 65th Birthday*. Edited by A.D. Clarke and P.J. Williams, et al. Grand Rapids: Eerdmans, 2004.

Clarysse, Willy and Thompson, Dorothy J. *Counting the People in Hellenistic Egypt, Vol. 1: Population Registers*. Cambridge Classical Studies. Cambridge: Cambridge University Press, 2006.

Clarysse, Willy and Thompson, Dorothy J. *Counting People in the Hellenistic Egypt, Volume 2: Historical Studies*. Cambridge Classical Studies. Cambridge: Cambridge University Press, 2006.

Clarysse, Willy. *The Petrie Papyri. Volume 1: The Wills*. Collectanea Hellenistica. Brussels: Koninklijke Academie voor Wetenschappen, 1991.

Clements, Ronald. *Abraham and David: Genesis XV and its Meaning for Israelite Tradition*. London: SCM, 1967.

Clinton, Kevin. "A Family of Eymolpidai and Kerykes Descended from Pericles." *Hesperia: The Journal of the American School of Classical Studies at Athens* 73 (2004): 39–57.

Cockerill, G.L. "Hebrews 1:6: Source and Significance." *Bulletin for Biblical Research* 9 (1999): 51–64.

Cockerill, G.L. *The Epistle to the Hebrews*. New International Greek Testament Commentary. Grand Rapids: Eerdmans, 2012.

Cohen, Anthony P. *The Symbolic Construction of Community*. Key Ideas. London: Routledge, 1989.

Cohen, Shaye J.D. *The Beginning of Jewishness: Boundaries, Varieties, Uncertainties*. Hellenistic Culture and Society 31. Berkley: University of California, 2001.

Colautti, Federico M. *Passover in the Works of Josephus*. Supplements to Journal for the Study of Judaism 75. Leiden: Brill, 2002.

Collins, A. Yarbro. *Crisis and Catharsis: The Power of the Apocalypse*. Philadelphia: Westminster, 1984.

Collins, A. Yarbro and Collins, J.J. *King and Messiah as Son of God: Divine, Human, and Angelic Messianic Figures in Biblical and Related Literature*. Grand Rapids: Eerdmans, 2008.

Collins, J.J. "The Jewish Apocalypses." *Semeia* 14 (1979): 21–59.

Collins, J.J. "The Heavenly Representative: The 'Son of Man' in the Similitudes of Enoch." Pages 111–33 in *Ideal Figures in Ancient Judaism: Profiles and Paradigms*. Edited by G.W.E. Nickelsburg and J.J. Collins. Society of Biblical Literature Septuagint and Cognate Studies 12. Missoula: Scholars, 1980.

Collins, J.J. "The Genre Apocalypse in Hellenistic Judaism." Pages 531–548 in *Apocalypticism in the Mediterranean World and the Near East: Proceedings of the International Colloquium on Apocalypticism, Uppsala, August 12–17, 1979*. Edited by David Helholm. Tübingen: Mohr Siebeck, 1983.

Collins, J.J. *Jewish Wisdom in the Hellenistic Age*. Edinburgh: T&T Clark, 1997.

Collins, J.J. *The Apocalyptic Imagination: An Introduction to Jewish Apocalyptic Literature*. Grand Rapids: Eerdmans, 1998.

Collins, J.J. *Between Athens and Jerusalem: Jewish Identity in the Hellenistic Diaspora*. Grand Rapids, 2000.

Collins, J.J. "Joseph and Aseneth: Jewish or Christian?" *Journal for the Study of the Pseudepigrapha* 14 (2005): 97–112.

Colpe, Carsten. *Die Religionsgeschichtlicheschule: Darstellung und Kritik ihres Bildes vom gnostischen Erlösermythus*. Forschungen zur Religion und Literatur des Alten und Neuen Testaments 78. Göttingen: Vandenhoeck & Ruprecht, 1961.

Cotter, David. *Genesis*. Collegeville Bible Commentary. Collegeville: Liturgical, 2003.

Cox, Cheryl Anne. "Sibling Relationships in Classical Athens: Brother-Sister Ties." *Journal of Family History* 13 (1988): 377–395.

Cox, Ronald R. *By the Same Word: Creation and Salvation in Hellenistic Judaism and Early Christianity*. Beihefte zur Zeitschrift für die neutestamentliche Wissenschaft 145. Berlin: Walter de Gruyter, 2007.

Craigie, Peter C. *The Book of Deuteronomy*. New International Commentary on the Old Testament. Grand Rapids: Eerdmans, 1976.

Cranfield, C.E.B. *The Epistle to the Romans. Volume 1*. International Critical Commentary. Edinburgh: T&T Clark, 1975.

Cromhout, Markus. *Walking in Their Sandals: A Guide to First-Century Israelite Ethnic Identity*. Eugene, OR: Cascade, 2010.

Crook, J.A. "Patria Potestas." *The Classical Quarterly* 17 (1967): 113–122.

Cross, F.M. "Reuben, Firstborn of Jacob." *Zeitschrift für die alttestamentliche Wissenschaft* 100 (1988): 46–65.

Cross, F.M. "A Reconstruction of the Judean Restoration." *Journal of Biblical Literature* 94 (1975): 4–18.

Dahl, Nils A. "Der Erstgeborene Satans und der Vater des Teufels (Polyk, 7,1 und Joh 8.44)." Pages 70–84 in *Apophoreta: Festschrift für Ernst Haenchen*. Edited by Walter Eltester. Beihefte zur Zeitschrift für die neutestamentliche Wissenschaft und die Kunde der älteren Kirche 30; Berlin: Töpelmann, 1964, 70–84.

Dahl, Nils A. *Studies in Paul: Theology for the Early Christian Mission*. Minneapolis: Fortress, 1977.

Daniélou, Jean. *Philo of Alexandria*. Translated by J.G. Colbert. James Clarke & Co, 2014.

Danker, Frederick W. *Jesus and the New Age according to St. Luke: A Commentary on the Third Gospel*. Philadelphia: Fortress, 1988.

Das, A. Andrew. *Solving the Romans Debate*. Minneapolis: Fortress, 2007.

Davies, J.K. *Athenian Propertied Families, 600–300 BC*. Oxford: Oxford University Press, 1971.

Davies, John A. *A Royal Priesthood: Literary and Intertextual Perspectives on an Image of Israel in Exodus 19:6*. Journal for the Study of the Old Testament: Supplement Series 395. London: T&T Clark, 2004.

Davies, P.R. and Chilton, Bruce. "The Aqedah: A Revised Tradition History." *Catholic Biblical Quarterly* 40 (1978): 514–546.

Davies, Philip R. *The Damascus Covenant: An Interpretation of the "Damascus Document"* Journal for the Study of the Old Testament Supplement Series 25. Sheffield: Sheffield Academic Press, 1983.

Davies, W.D. *Paul and Rabbinic Judaism: Some Rabbinic Elements in Pauline Theology*. Philadelphia: Fortress, 1980.

Davila, James R. *Liturgical Works*. Eerdmans Commentaries on the Dead Sea Scrolls. Grand Rapids: Eerdmans, 2001.

De Coulanges, Numa Denis Fustel. *The Ancient City: A Study on the Religion, Laws, and Institutions of Greece and Rome*. Kitchener: Batoche, 2001.

Deichgräber, Reinhard. *Gotteshymnus und Christushymnus in der frühen Christenheit: Untersuchungen zu Form, Sprache und Stil der frühchristlichen Hymnen*. Studien zur Umwelt des Neuen Testaments 5. Göttingen: Vandenhoeck & Ruprecht, 1967.

De Jonge, Marinus. *Christology in Context*. Philadelphia, Westminster, 1988.

De Jonge, Marinus. *God's Final Envoy: Early Christology and Jesus' Own View of His Mission*. Grand Rapids: Eerdmans, 1998.

De Roo, Jacqueline. "Is 4Q525 a Qumran Sectarian Document." Pages 338–367 in *The Scrolls and the Scriptures: Qumran Fifty Years After*. Library of Second Temple Studies 26. Edited by Stanley E. Porter and Craig A. Evans. Sheffield: Sheffield Academic Press, 1997.

De Savignac, Jean. "Note sur le sens du verset VIII 22 des Proverbes." *Vetus Testamentum* 4 (1954): 429–432.

DeSilva, David A. "The Social Setting of the Revelation to John: Conflicts Within, Fears Without." *Westminster Theological Journal* 54 (1992): 273–302.

DeSilva, David A. *Honor, Patronage, Kinship and Purity: Unlocking New Testament Culture*. Downers Glove: IVP, 2000.

DeSilva, David A. *Perseverance in Gratitude: A Socio-Rhetorical Commentary on the Epistle "to the Hebrews."* Grand Rapids: Eerdmans, 2000.

De Vaux, Roland. *Ancient Israel: Its Life and Institutions*. London: Darton, Longman & Todd, 1961.

Dicou, Bert. *Edom, Israel's Brother and Antagonist: The Role of Edom in Biblical Prophecy and Story*. Journal for the Study of the Old Testament 169. Sheffield: Sheffield Academic Press, 1994.

Dillon, John. "The Formal Structure of Philo's Allegorical Exegesis." Pages 77–87 in *Two Treatises of Philo of Alexandria: A Commentary on De gigantibus and Quod Deus sit immutabilis*. Edited by J. Dillon and D. Winston. Brown Judaic Studies 25. Chico: Scholars, 1983.

Dillon, John. *The Middle Platonists: 80 B.C. to A.D. 220*. Cornell University Press: Ithaca, 1996.

Doering, Lutz. *Ancient Jewish Letters and the Beginnings of Christian Epistolography*. Wissenschaftliche Untersuchungen zum Neuen Testament 298. Tübingen: Mohr Siebeck, 2012.

Docherty, Susan. "Joseph and Aseneth Rewritten Bible or Narrative Expansion." *Journal for the Study of Judaism in the Persian, Hellenistic, and Roman Periods* 35 (2004): 27–48.

Donaldson, Terence L. *Judaism and the Gentiles: Jewish Patterns of Universalism (to 135 CE)*. Waco: Baylor University Press, 2007.

Dozeman, Thomas B. *Exodus*. Eerdmans Critical Commentary Series. Grand Rapids: Eerdmans, 2009.

Dübbers, Michael. *Christologie und Existenz im Kolosserbrief: Exegetische und semantische Untersuchungen zur Intention des Kolosserbriefes*. Wissenschaftliche Untersuchungen zum Neuen Testament II 191. Tübingen: Mohr Siebeck, 2005.

Dumbrell, William. "Exodus 4:24–26: A Textual Re-Examination." *Harvard Theological Review* (1972): 285–290.

Dunn, J.D.G. *Romans 1–8*. Word Biblical Commentary. Waco: Word, 1988.

Dunn, J.D.G. *Christology in the Making: A New Testament Inquiry into the Origins of the Doctrine of the Incarnation*. London: SCM, 1989.

Dunn, J.D.G. *The Epistles to the Colossians and to Philemon: A Commentary on the Greek Text*. New International Greek Testament Commentary. Grand Rapids: Eerdmans, 1996.

Dunn, J.D.G. *The Theology of Paul the Apostle*. Grand Rapids: Eerdmans, 1998.

Dunn, J.D.G. *Jesus Remembered*. Grand Rapids: Eerdmans, 2003.

Durham, John. *Exodus*. Word Biblical Commentary. Waco: Word, 1987.

Eaton, John. *Kingship and the Psalms*. London: SCM, 1976.

Eckstein, Hans-Joachim. *Kyrios Jesus: Perspektiven einer christologischen Theologie*. Neukirchen-Vluyn: Neukirchener Verlag, 2011.

Edmondson, Jonathan C. "Family Relations in Roman Lusitania: Social Change in a Roman providence?" Pages 183–229 in *The Roman Family in the Empire: Rome, Italy, and Beyond*. Edited by Michele George. Oxford: Oxford University Press, 2005.

Edsall, Benjamin and Strawbridge, Jennifer R. "The Songs We Used to Sing? Hymn 'Traditions' and Reception in Pauline Letters," *Journal for the Study of the New Testament* 37 (2015): 290–311.

Eisenbaum, Pamela. *The Jewish Heroes of Christian History: Hebrews 11 in Literary Context*. Society of Biblical Literature Dissertation Series 156. Atlanta: Scholars, 1997.

Ellingworth, Paul. *The Epistle to the Hebrews: A Commentary on the Greek Text*. New International Greek Testament Commentary. Grand Rapids: Eerdmans, 1993.

Elliott, Mark Adam. *The Survivors of Israel: A Reconsideration of the Theology of Pre-Christian Judaism*. Grand Rapids: Eerdmans, 2000.

Endo, Masanobu. *Creation and Christology: A Study on the Johannine Prologue in the Light of Early Jewish Creation Accounts*. Wissenschaftliche Untersuchungen zum Neuen Testament II 149. Tübingen: Mohr Siebeck, 2002.

Esler, Philip F. *Conflict and Identity in Romans: The Social Setting of Paul's Letters*. Minneapolis: Fortress, 2003.

Evans, Craig A. "A Note on the 'First-Born Son' of 4Q369." *Dead Sea Discoveries* 2 (1995): 184–201.

Evans, Vyvyan. *How Words Mean: Lexical Concepts, Cognitive Models, and Meaning Construction*. Oxford: Oxford University Press, 2009.

Evans, Vyvyan. "Word Meaning." Pages 917–919 in *The Cambridge Encyclopedia of the Language Sciences*. Edited by Patrick C. Hogan. Cambridge: Cambridge University Press, 2010.

Fearghail, Fearghus Ó. *The Introduction to Luke-Acts: A Study of the Role of Lk 1,1–4,44 in the Composition of Luke's Two Volume Work*. Analecta Biblica 126. Rome: Editrice Pontificio Istituto Biblico, 1991.

Fee, Gordon D. *Pauline Christology: An Exegetical-Theological Study*. Peabody: Henrickson, 2007.

Feiullet, A. *Le Christ sagesse de Dieu d'après les épîtres Pauliniennes*. Études Biblique. Paris: Gabalda, 1966.

Feldman, Louis H. *Josephus's Interpretation of the Bible*. Berkeley: University of California Press, 1998.

Feldman, Louis H. *Flavius Josephus: Judean Antiquities 1–4*. Flavius Josephus: Translation and Commentary. Leiden: Brill, 2000.

Fensham, F.C. "Father and son as Terminology for Treaty and Covenant." Pages 121–135 in *Near Eastern Studies in Honor of William Foxwell Albright*. Edited by H. Goedicke. Baltimore: Johns Hopkins University Press, 1971.

Fillmore, Charles. "Frames and the Semantics of Understanding," *Quaderni di Semantica* 6 (1985): 222–54.

Findeis, H.-J. *Versöhnung- Apostolat- Kirche: Eine exegetisch-theologische und rezeptionsgeschichtliche Studie zu den Versöhnungsaussagen des Neuen Testaments. 2 Kor, Röm, Kol, Eph*. Forschung zur Bibel 40. Würzburg: Echter, 1983.

Fink, Uta. "Textkritische Situation." Pages 33–44 in *Joseph und Aseneth*. Edited by Eckart Reinmuth. Scripta Antiquitatis Posterioris ad Ethicam Religionemque pertinentia 15. Tübingen: Mohr Siebeck, 2009.

Fiorenza, Elisabeth Schüssler. *Priester Für Gott: Studien zum Herrschafts- und Priestermotiv in der Apokalypse*. Neutestamentliche Abhandlungen 7. Münster: Aschendorff, 1972.

Fiorenza, Elisabeth Schüssler. *The Book of Revelation: Justice and Judgment*. Philadelphia: Fortress, 1985.

Fiorenza, Elisabeth Schüssler. *Revelation: Vision of a Just World*. Edinburgh: T&T Clark, 1991.

Fischer, Georg. *Jeremia 26–52*. Herders theologischer Kommentar zum Alten Testament. Freiburg: Herder, 2005.

Fishbane, Michael. "Genesis 25:19–35:22: The Jacob Cycle." Pages 40–62 in *Text and Texture: Close Readings of Selected Biblical Texts*. New York: Schocken Books, 1979.

Fisk, Bruce. *Do You Not Remember: Scripture, Story and Exegesis in the Rewritten Bible of Pseudo-Philo*. Journal for the Study of the Pseudepigrapha: Supplement Series 37. Sheffield: Sheffield Academic Press, 2001.

Fitzmyer, Joseph A. "The Christology of the Epistle to the Romans." Pages 81–90 in *The Future of Christology: Essays in Honor of Leander E. Keck*. Edited by A. Malherbe and W. Meeks. Minneapolis: Fortress, 1993.

Fitzmyer, Joseph A. *Romans*. Anchor Bible. New York: Doubleday, 1993.

Fitzmyer, Joseph A. *The One Who is to Come*. Grand Rapids: Eerdmans, 2007.

Fletcher-Louis, Crispin H.T. *All the Glory of Adam: Liturgical Anthropology in the Dead Sea Scrolls*. Studies on the Texts of the Desert of Judah 42. Leiden: Brill, 2001.

Floyd, Michael. "Psalm LXXXIX: A Prophetic Complaint about the Fulfilment of an Oracle." *Vetus Testamentum* 42 (1992): 442–457.

Fohrer, Georg. "Priesterliches Königtum (Ex 19,6)." Pages 149–153 in *Studien zur alttestamentlichen Theologie und Geschichte (1949–1966)*. Beihefte zur Zeitschrift für die alttestamentliche Wissenschaft 115. Berlin: Walter de Gruyter, 1969.

Fokkelman, J.P. *Narrative Art in Genesis: Specimens of Stylistic and Structural Analysis*. Biblical Seminar 12. Assen: Van Gorcum, 1975.

Fossum, Jarl E. *The Name of God and the Angel of the Lord: Samaritan and Jewish Concepts of Intermediation and the Origin of Gnosticism*. Wissenschaftliche Untersuchungen zum Neuen Testament 36. Tübingen: Mohr Siebeck, 1985.

Fossum, Jarl E. "Colossians 1.15–18a in the Light of Jewish Mysticism and Gnosticism." *New Testament Studies* 35 (1989): 183–201.

Forman, Mark. *The Politics of Inheritance in Romans*. Society of New Testament Studies Monograph Series 148. Cambridge, Cambridge University Press, 2011.

Fowl, Stephen E. *The Story of Christ in the Ethics of Paul: An Analysis of the Function of the Hymnic Material in the Pauline Corpus*. Journal for the Study of the New Testament Studies: Supplement Series 36. Sheffield: Sheffield Academic Press, 1990.

Francis, F.O. "The Background of EMBATEUEIN (Col 2:18) in Legal Papyri and Oracle Inscriptions." Pages 197–207 in *Conflict at Colossae: A Problem in the Interpretation of Early Christianity Illustrated by Selected Modern Studies*. Edited and Translated by F.O. Francis and Wayne A. Meeks. Society of Biblical Literature Sources for Biblical Study 4. Missoula: Scholars, 1975.

Freedman, David N. "The Chronicler's Purpose." *Catholic Biblical Quarterly* 23 (1961): 432–442.

Fretheim, Terence E. *Exodus*. Interpretation: A Bible Commentary for Teaching and Preaching. Louisville: John Knox, 1991.

Fretheim, Terence E. "Which Blessing Does Isaac Give Jacob?" Pages 279–91 in *Jews, Christians and the Theology of the Hebrew Scripture*. Edited by A. Ogden Bellis and J.S. Kaminsky. Society of Biblical Literature Symposium Series 8. Atlanta: SBL, 2000.

Freyne, Sean. "The Herodian Period." Pages 29–43 in *Redemption and Resistance: The Messianic Hopes of Jews and Christians in Antiquity*. Edited by Markus Bockmuehl and James Carleton Paget. London: T&T Clark, 2007.

Frymer-Kenksy, Tikva. "Patriarchal Family Relationships and Near Eastern Law." *Biblical Archeologist* 44 (1981): 209–214.

Gardner, Jane F. "The Adoption of Roman Freedmen." *Phoenix* 43 (1989): 236–257.

Gathercole, Simon J. *The Pre-Existent Son: Recovering the Christologies of Matthew, Mark, and Luke*. Grand Rapids: Eerdmans, 2006.

Gelardini, Gabriella. *Hebrews: Contemporary Methods—New Insights*. Biblical Interpretation Series 75. Leiden: Brill. 2005.

Gerstenberger, Erhard S. *Leviticus: A Commentary*. Old Testament Library. Louisville: WJK, 1996.

Gerstenberger, Erhard S. *Psalms, Part 2 and Lamentations*. Grand Rapids: Eerdmans, 2001.

Gieniusz, Andrzej. *Romans 8:18–30: Suffering Does Not Thwart the Future Glory*. University of South Florida International Studies in Formative Christianity and Judaism 9. Atlanta: Scholars, 1999.

Gieschen, Charles A. *Angelomorphic Christology: Antecedents and Early Evidence*. Arbeiten zur Geschichte des antiken Judentums und des Urchristentums 42. Leiden: Brill, 1998.

Gilders, William. "The Concept of Covenant in Jubilees." Pages 178–192 in *Enoch and the Mosaic Torah: The Evidence of Jubilees*. Edited by Gabriele Boccaccini and Giovanni Ibba. Grand Rapids: Eerdmans, 2009.

Gleason, Randall C. "Angels and the Eschatology of Heb 1–2." *New Testament Studies* 49 (2003): 90107.

Gordley, Matthew E. *The Colossian Hymn in Context: An Exegesis in Light of Jewish and Greco-Roman Hymnic and Epistolary Conventions*. Wissenschaftliche Untersuchungen zum Neuen Testament II 228. Tübingen: Mohr Siebeck, 2007.

Goering, Greg Schmidt. *Wisdom's Root Revealed: Ben Sira and the Election of Israel*. Supplements to the Journal for the Study of Judaism 139. Leiden: Brill, 2009.

Goodenough, Erwin R. *The Theology of Justin Martyr: An Investigation into the Conceptions of Early Christian Literature and its Hellenistic and Judaistic Influences*. Amsterdam: Philo Press, 1968.

Gottwald, Norman K. *The Tribes of Yahweh: A Sociology of the Religion of Liberated Israel, 1250–1050 B.C.E.* Maryknoll: Orbis, 1979.

Grabbe, Lester L. *Wisdom of Solomon*. Guides to the Apocrypha and Pseudepigrapha 3. Sheffield: Sheffield Academic Press, 1997.

Grässer, Erich. *An die Hebräer (Heb 1–6)*. Evangelisch-Katholischer Kommentar zum Neuen Testament 17/1 Zürich: Benziger, 1990.

Gray, Patrick. "Brotherly Love and the High Priest Christology of Hebrews." *Journal of Biblical Literature* 122 (2003): 335–351.

Greenspahn, Frederick E. *When Brothers Dwell Together: The Preeminence of Younger Siblings in the Hebrew Bible*. Oxford: Oxford University Press, 1994.

Greifenhagen, F.V. *Egypt on the Pentateuch's Ideological Map: Constructing Biblical Israel's Identity*. Journal for the Study of the Old Testament: Supplement Series 361. Sheffield: Sheffield Academic Press, 2002.

Grieb, A. Katherine. *The Story of Romans: A Narrative Defense of God's Righteousness*. Louisville: WJK, 2002.

Grossman, Avraham. "From Father to Son: The Inheritance of Spiritual Leadership in Jewish Communities of the Middle Ages." Pages 115–131 in *The Jewish Family:*

Metaphor and Memory. Edited by David Kraemer. Oxford: Oxford University Press, 1989.

Gruen, Erich. *Heritage and Hellenism: The Reinvention of Jewish Tradition*. Hellenistic Culture and Society 30. Berkeley: University of California Press, 1998.

Grundheim, Sigurd. *The Crux of Election: Paul's Critique of the Jewish Confidence in the Election of Israel*. Wissenschaftliche Untersuchungen zum Neuen Testament II 202. Tübingen: Mohr Siebeck, 2005.

Gulf, Friedrich. "'Der Erstgeborene unter vielen Brüdern' (Rom 8,29)." *Geist und Leben* 43 (1970): 465–469.

Gunkel, Herman. *Genesis*. Macon: Mercer University Press, 1997.

Guthrie, George. *The Structure of Hebrews: A Text-Linguistic Analysis*. Supplements to Novum Testament 73. Leiden: Brill, 1994.

Haacker, Klaus. *The Theology of Paul's Letter to the Romans*. Cambridge: Cambridge University Press, 2003.

Hacham, Noah. "Joseph and Aseneth: Loyalty, Traitors, Antiquity and Diasporan Identity." *Journal for the Study of the Pseudepigrapha* 22 (2012): 53–67.

Hahn, Ferdinand. *The Titles of Jesus in Christology: Their History in Early Christianity*. Translated by H. Knight and G. Ogg. London: Lutterworth, 1969.

Hahn, Scott. *Kinship by Covenant: A Canonical Approach to the Fulfillment of God's Saving Promises*. Anchor Yale Bible Reference Library. New Haven: Yale University Press, 2009.

Hall, Jonathan M. *Ethnic Identity in Greek Antiquity*. Cambridge: Cambridge University Press, 1997.

Halliday, M.A.K. *Language as Social Semiotic: The Social Interpretation of Language and Meaning*. London: Edward Arnold, 1978.

Halpern-Amaru, Betsy. "A Note on Isaac as First-born in *Jubilees* and Only Son in 4Q225." *Dead Sea Discoveries* 13 (2006): 127–133.

Hamilton, Victor P. *The Book of Genesis: Chapters 18–50*. New International Commentary on the Old Testament. Grand Rapids: Eerdmans, 1995.

Hannah, Darrell D. *Michale and Christ: Michael Traditions and Angel Christology in Early Christianity*. Wissenschaftliche Untersuchungen zum Neuen Testament II 109. Tübingen: Mohr Siebeck, 1999.

Hanson, K.C. "The Herodians and Mediterranean Kinship. Part III: Economics." *Biblical Theology Bulletin* 20 (1990): 10–21.

Harrington, Daniel J. "Palestinian Adaptations of Biblical Narratives and Prophecies." Pages 239–247 in *Early Judaism and its Modern interpreters*. Edited by R. Kraft and G.W. Nickelsburg. Society of Biblical Literature The Bible and Its Modern Interpreters 2. Atlanta: Scholars, 1986.

Harrington, Daniel J. *Introduction to the Apocrypha*. Grand Rapids: Eerdmans, 1999.

Hartog, Paul. *Polycarp and the New Testament*. Wissenschaftliche Untersuchungen zum Neuen Testament II 134. Tübingen: Mohr Siebeck, 2002.

Hays, Richard B. "'Here We Have No Lasting City': New Covenantalism in Hebrews." Pages 151–173 in *The Epistle to the Hebrews and Christian Theology*. Edited by Richard Bauckham, et al. Grand Rapids: Eerdmans, 2009.

Hayward, C.T.R. *Interpretations of the Name Israel in Ancient Judaism and some Early Christian Writings: From Victorious Athlete to Heavenly Champion*. Oxford: Oxford University, 2005.

Hecht, Richard D. "Philo and Messiah." Pages 139–168 in *Judaisms and their Messiahs at the turn of the Christian Era*. Edited by Jacob Neusner, et al. Cambridge: Cambridge University Press, 1987.

Hellerman, Joseph H. *The Ancient Church as Family*. Minneapolis: Fortress, 2001.

Hellholm, David. "The Problem of Apocalyptic Genre and the Apocalypse of John." *Semeia* 36 (1986): 13–64.

Helyer, Larry R. "The Prototokos Title in Hebrews," *Studia Biblica et Theologica* 6 (1976): 3–28.

Helyer, Larry R. "Arius Revisited: The Firstborn over All Creation (Col 1:15)." *Journal of Evangelical Theological Studies* 31 (1988): 59–67

Helyer, Larry R. "Recent Research on Col 1:15–20 (1980–1990)," *Grace Theological Journal* 12 (1992): 51–67.

Hengel, Martin. *Der Sohn Gottes: Die Entstehung der Christologie und die jüdisch-hellenistische Religionsgeschichte*. Tübingen: Mohr Siebeck, 1975.

Hengel, Martin. *Judentum und Hellenismus: Studien zu ihrer Begegnung unter besonderer Berücksichtigung Palästimas bis zur Mitte des 2. Jahrhunderts v.Chr.* Wissenschaftliche Untersuchungen zum Neuen Testament 10. Tübingen: Mohr Siebeck, 1988.

Hignett, Charles. *A History of the Athenian Constitution to the End of the Fifth Century BC*. Oxford: Oxford University Press, 1952.

Himmelfarb, Martha. *Ascent to Heaven in Jewish and Christian Apocalypses*. Oxford: Oxford University Press, 1993.

Himmelfarb, Martha. *A Kingdom of Priests: Ancestry and Merit in Ancient Judaism*. Jewish Culture and Contexts. Philadelphia: University of Pennsylvania Press, 2006.

Hockel, Alfred. *Christus der Erstgeborene: Zur Geschichte der Exegese von Kol 1,15*. Düsseldorf: Patmos, 1965.

Hodge, Caroline J. *If Sons, Then Heirs: A Study of Kinship and Ethnicity in the Letters of Paul*. Oxford: Oxford University Press, 2007.

Hofius, Otfried. "Erwägungen zur Gestalt und Herkunft des paulinischen Versöhnungsgedankens." *Zeitschrift für Theologie und Kirche* 77 (1980): 186–199.

Hofius, Otfried. *Der Christushymnus Philipper 2, 6–11: Untersuchungen zu Gestalt und Aussage eines urchristlichen Psalms*. Wissenschaftliche Untersuchungen zum Neuen Testament 17. Tübingen: Mohr Siebeck, 1991.

Hofius, Otfried. "'Erstgeborener vor aller Schöpfung'—'Erstgeborener aus den Toten': Erwägungen zu Struktur and Aussage des Christushymnus Kol 1, 15–20." Pages 215–233 in *Paulusstudien II*. Wissenschaftliche Untersuchungen zum Neuen Testament 143; Tübingen: Mohr Siebeck, 2002.

Hogan, Karina Martin. *Theologies in Conflict in 4 Ezra: Wisdom Debate and Apocalyptic Solution*. Supplements to Journal for the Study of Judaism Supplement 130. Leiden: Brill, 2008.

Holladay, William. *Jeremiah 2: A Commentary on the Book of the Prophet Jeremiah Chapters 26–52*. Hermeneia: A Critical and Historical Commentary on the Bible. Philadelphia: Fortress, 1989.

Hooker, Morna D. "'Heirs of Abraham': The Gentiles' Role in Israel's Story: A Response to Bruce W. Longenecker." Pages 85–96 in *Narrative Dynamics in Paul*. Edited by Bruce W. Longenecker. Louisville: WKJ, 2002.

Hopkins, Keith. "The Political Economy of the Roman Empire." Pages 178–204 in *The Dynamic of Ancient Empire: State Power from Assyria and Byzantium*. Edited by Ian Morris and Walter Scheidel. Oxford: Oxford University Press, 2009.

Horbury, William. *Jewish Messianism and the Cult of Christ*. London: SCM, 1998.

Horst, Friedrich. "Das Privilegrecht Jahwes. Rechtsgeschichtliche Untersuchungen zum Deuteronium." Pages 17–154 in *Gottes Recht. Gesammelte Studien zum Recht im Alten Testament*. Theologische Bücherei: Neudrucke und Berichte aus dem 20. 12. München: Chr. Kaiser, 1961.

Houtman, Cornelis. *Exodus. Volume I*. Translated by Sierd Woudstra. Historical Commentary on the Old Testament. Kampen: Kok, 1993.

Houtman, Cornelis. *Exodus. Volume II*. Translated by Sierd Woudstra. Historical Commentary on the Old Testament. Kampen: Kok, 1996.

Huebner, Sabine R. "Household Composition in the Ancient Mediterranean." Pages 73–91 in *A Companion to Families in the Greek and Roman Worlds*. Edited by Beryl Rawson. Chicester: Blackwell, 2011.

Huebner, Sabine R. *The Family in Roman Egypt: A Comparative Approach to Intergenerational Solidarity and Conflict*. Cambridge: Cambridge University Press, 2013.

Huizenga, Leroy A. "The Battle for Isaac: Exploring the Composition and Function of the Aqedah in the Book of Jubilees." *Journal for the Study of the Pseudepigrapha* 13 (2002): 33–59.

Huizenga, Leroy A. *The New Isaac: Tradition and Intertextuality in the Gospel of Matthew*. Supplements to Novum Testaments 131. Leiden: Brill, 2009.

Hultgren, Arland J. *Paul's Letter to the Romans: A Commentary*. Grand Rapids: Eerdmans, 2011.

Hurst, L.D. "The Christology of Hebrews 1 and 2." Pages 151–164 in *The Glory of Christ in the New Testament: Studies in Christology in Memory of George Bradford Caird*. Edited by L.D. Hurst and N.T. Wright. Oxford: Clarendon, 1987.

Hurst, L.D. *The Epistle to the Hebrews: Its Background of Thought*. Society of New Testament Studies Monograph Series 65. Cambridge: Cambridge University Press, 1990.

Hurtado, Larry W. *One God, One Lord: Early Christian Devotion and Ancient Jewish Monotheism*. London: SCM, 1988.

Hurtado, Larry W. *Lord Jesus Christ: Devotion to Jesus in Earliest Christianity*. Grand Rapids: Eerdmans, 2003.

Hurtado, Larry W. "Does Philo Help Explain Christianity?" Pages 73–92 in *Philo und das Neue Testament: Wechselseitige Wahrnehmungen*. Wissenschaftliche Untersuchungen zum Neuen Testament 172. Tübingen: Mohr Siebeck, 2004.

Hyatt, J.P. *Exodus*. New Century Bible Commentary. Grand Rapids: Eerdmans, 1971.

Jacobson, Howard. *A Commentary on Pseudo-Philo's Liber Antiquitatum Biblicarum: With Latin Text and English Translation. Volume 1*. Arbeiten zur Geschichte des antiken Judentums und des Urchristentums 31. Leiden: Brill, 1996.

James, Montague Rhodes. *The Lost Apocrypha of the Old Testament: Their Titles and Fragments*. London: SPCK, 1920.

Japhet, Sara. "The Supposed Common Authorship of Chronicles and Ezra-Nehemiah Investigated Anew." *Vetus Testamentum* 19 (1968): 330–371.

Japhet, Sara. *I&II Chronicles: A Commentary*. Old Testament Library. Philadelphia: WJK, 1993.

Jenkins, Richard. *Rethinking Ethnicity*. London: SAGE, 2008.

Jervell, Jacob. *Imago Dei: Gen. 1.26f im Spätjudentum, in der Gnosis und in den paulinischen Briefen*. Forschungen zur Religion und Literatur des Alten und Neuen Testaments 58. Göttingen: Vandenhoeck & Ruprecht, 1960.

Jervell, Jacob. *Luke and the People of God: A New Look at Luke-Acts*. Minneapolis: Augsburg, 1972.

Jewett, Robert. *Romans*. Hermeneia: A Critical and Historical Commentary on the Bible. Minneapolis: Fortress, 2006.

Jipp, J.W. "The Son's Entrance into the Heavenly World: The Soteriological Necessity of the Scriptural Catena in Hebrews 1.5–14." *New Testament Studies* 56 (2010): 557–575.

Johnson, Aubrey. *Sacral Kingship in Ancient Israel*. Cardiff: University of Wales Press, 1967.

Johnson, L.T. *Hebrews: A Commentary*. New Testament Library. Louisville: WJK, 2006.

Johnson, William G. "The Pilgrimage Motif in the Book of Hebrews." *Journal of Biblical Literature* 97 (1978): 239–251.

Juel, Donald. *Messianic Exegesis: Christological Interpretations of the Old Testament in Early Christianity*. Minneapolis: Fortress, 1988.

Jung, Chang-Wook. *The Original Language of the Lukan Infancy Narrative*. Journal for the Study of the New Testament Supplement Series 267. Sheffield: Sheffield Academic Press, 2004.

Junker, Günther H. "'Children of Promise': Spiritual Paternity and Patriarch Typology in Galatians and Romans." *Bulletin for Biblical Research* 17 (2007): 141–152.

Kaiser, Otto. *Der Gott des Alten Testaments*. Göttingen: Vandenhoeck & Ruprecht, 1993.

Kaminsky, Joel. *Yet I Loved Jacob: Reclaiming the Biblical Concept of Election*. Nashville: Abingdon, 2007.

Kampen, John. *Wisdom Literature*. Eerdmans Commentaries on the Dead Sea Scrolls. Grand Rapids: Eerdmans, 2011.

Karrer, Martin. *Der Brief an die Hebräer: Kapitel 1,1–5,10*. Ökumenischer Taschenbuch-Kommentar 20/1. Gütersloh: Gütersloher, 2002.

Karrer, Martin. *Jesus Christus im Neuen Testament*. Das Neue Testament Deutsch Ergänzungsreihe 11. Göttingen: Vandenhoeck & Ruprecht, 1998.

Käsemann, Ernst. "The Beginnings of Christian Theology." Pages 82–107 in New Testament Questions of Today. Translated by W.J. Montague. London: SCM, 1969.

Käsemann, Ernst. "'The Righteousness of God' in Paul." Pages 168–82 in *New Testament Questions of Today*. Translated by W.J. Montague. London: SCM, 1969.

Käsemann, Ernst. *An die Römer*. Handbuch zum Alten Testament. Tübingen: Mohr Siebeck, 1973.

Käsemann, Ernst. "A Primitive Christian Baptismal Liturgy." Pages 149–168 in *Essays on New Testament Themes*. Translated by W.J. Montague. London: SCM, 1982.

Käsemann, Ernst. *The Wandering People of God: An Investigation of the Letter to the Hebrews*. Translated by Roy A. Harrisville and Irving L. Sandberg. Minneapolis: Augsburg, 1984.

Keesmaat, Sylvia. *Paul and His Story: (Re)Interpreting the Exodus Tradition*. Journal for the Study of the New Testament: Supplement Series 181. Sheffield: Sheffield Academic Press, 1999.

Kegler, J. "Prophetengestalten im Deuteronomistischen Geschichtswerk und in den Chronikbüchern. Ein Beitrag zur Kompositions- und Redaktionsgeschichte der Chronikbücher." *Zeitschrift für die alttestamentliche Wissenschaft* 105 (1993): 481–497.

Kehl, Nikolaus. *Der Christushymnus im Kolosserbrief: Eine motivgeschichtliche Untersuchung zu Kol 1,12–20*. Stuttgarter biblische Monographien 1. Stuttgart: Katholisches Bibelwerk, 1967.

Keown, G., Scalise, P., and Smothers, T. *Jeremiah 26–52*. Word Biblical Commentary. Waco: Word, 1995.

Kim, Kyu Seop. "Another Look at Adoption in Romans 8:15 in Light of Roman Social Practices and Legal Rules." *Biblical Theology Bulletin* 44 (2014): 133–143.

Kim, Kyu Seop. "The Meaning of 'כֹּהֲנִים מַמְלֶכֶת' in Exodus 19:6 Revisited." *Journal of Biblical Text Research* 35 (2014): 249–267.

Kim, Kyu Seop. "Reframing Paul's Sibling Language in Light of Jewish Epistolary Forms of Address." *HTS Teologiese Studies/Theological Studies* 71 (2015): 1–8.

Kim, Lloyd. *Polemic in the Book of Hebrews: Anti-Judaism, Anti-Semitism, Supersessionism*. Princeton Theological Monograph Series. Eugene: Pickwick, 2006.

Kim, Seyoon. *The Origin of Paul's Gospel*. Wissenschaftliche Untersuchungen zum Neuen Testament II 4. Tübingen: Mohr Siebeck, 1984.

Kim, Seyoon. *Paul and the New Perspective: Second Thoughts on the Origin of Paul's Gospel*. Grand Rapids: Eerdmans, 2001.

Kirk, Daniel. *Unlocking Romans: Resurrection and the Justification of God*. Grand Rapids: Eerdmans, 2008.

Kiuchi, N. *Leviticus*. Apollos Old Testament Commentary 3. Nottingham: Apollos, 2007.

Knierim, R.P. and Coats, G.W. *Numbers*. The Forms of Old Testament Literature 4. Grand Rapids: Eerdmans, 2005.

Knibb, M. "The Teacher of Righteousness—A Messianic Title?" Pages 51–65 in *A Tribute to Geza Vermes: Essays on Jewish and Christian Literature and History*. Edited by P.R. Davies and R.T. White. Journal for the Study of the Old Testament Supplement Series 100. Sheffield: Sheffield Academic Press, 1990.

Knoppers, Gary N. "The Preferential Status of the Eldest Son Revoked?" Pages 115–126 in *Rethinking the Foundations: Historiography in the Ancient World and in the Bible, Essays in Honour of John Van Seters*. Edited by S.L. McKenzie, et al. Beihefte zur Zeitschrift für die alttestamentliche Wissenschaft 294. Berlin: Walter de Gruyter, 2000.

Koch, Klaus. *The Rediscovery of Apocalyptic*. Translated by M. Kohl. Studies in Biblical Theology 22. Naperville: Allenson, 1972.

Koch, Klaus. "Königspsalmen und ihr ritueller Hintergrund; Erwägungen zu Ps 89,20–38 und Ps 20 und ihren Vorstufen." Pages 9–52 in *The Book of Psalms: Composition and Reception*. Supplements to Vetus Testamentum 99. Edited by Peter Flint and Patrick Miller. Leiden: Brill, 2005.

Kösel, Julius. *Der Sohn und die Söhne: Eine exegetische Studie zu Hebräer 2, 5–18*. Breiträge zur Förderung christlicher Theologie VIII, 5–6. Gütersloh: C. Bertelsmann, 1904.

Kosmala, H. "The Bloody Husband." *Vetus Testamentum* 12 (1962): 14–28.

Kraemer, Ross. *When Aseneth Met Joseph: A Late Antique Tale of the Biblical Patriarch and His Egyptian Wife, Reconsidered*. New York: Oxford University Press, 1998.

Kramer, Werner. *Christos Kyrios Gottessohn*. Abhandlungen zur Theologie des Alten und Neuen Testaments 44, Zürich: Zwingli, 1963.

Kugel, James. "4Q369 'Prayer of Enosh' and Ancient Biblical Interpretation." *Dead Sea Discoveries* 5 (1998): 119–148.

Kümmel, W.G. *Introduction to the New Testament*. Translated by H.C. Kee. Nashville: Abingdon, 1975.

Lakoff, George and Johnson, Mark. "The Metaphor Structure of the Human Conceptual System." *Cognitive Science* 4 (1980): 195–208.

Lakoff, George and Johnson, Mark. *Metaphors We Live By*. Chicago: The University of Chicago Press, 1980.

Lampe, Peter. *Christians at Rome in the First Two Centuries: From Paul to Valentinus*. London: T&T Clark, 2003.

Lane, William. *Hebrews 1–8*. Word Biblical Commentary. Dallas: Word, 1991.

Laub, Franz. *Bekenntnis und Auslegung: Die paränetische Funktion der Christologie im Hebräerbrief*. Biblische Untersuchungen 15. Regensburg: Pustet, 1980.

Laurentin, René. *Structure et Théologie de Luc I–II*. Études bibliques. Paris: Gabalda, 1964.

Le Page, R.B. and Tabouret-Keller, A. *Acts of Identity: Creole-Based Approaches to Language and Ethnicity*. Cambridge: Cambridge University Press, 1985.

Lee, Aquila H.I. *From Messiah to Preexistent Son: Jesus' Self-Consciousness and Early Christian Exegesis of Messianic Psalms*. Wissenschaftliche Untersuchungen zum Neuen Testament II 192. Tübingen: Mohr Siebeck, 2005.

Lee, W. *Punishment and Forgiveness in Israel's Migratory Campaign*. Grand Rapids: Eerdmans, 2003.

Leonhardt, Jutta. *Jewish Worship in Philo of Alexandria*. Texts and Studies in Ancient Judaism 84. Tübingen: Mohr Siebeck, 2001.

Leonhardt-Balzer, Jutta. "Creation, the Logos and the Foundation of a City: A Few Comments on *Opif* 15–25." Pages 323–344 in *Philo und das Neue Testament: Wechselseitige Wahrnehmungen*. Edited by Roland Deines and Karl-Wilhelm Niebuhr. *Philo und das Neue Testament: Wechselseitige Wahrnehmungen*. Wissenschaftliche Untersuchungen zum Neuen Testament 172. Tübingen: Mohr Siebeck, 2004.

Leonhardt-Balzer, Jutta. "Der Logos und die Schöpfung: Streiflichter bei Philo (Op 20–25) und im Johannesprolog (Joh 1,1–18)." Pages 295–319 in *Kontexte des Johannesevangeliums: Das vierte Evangelium in religions- und traditionsgeschichtlicher Perspektive*. Edited by Jörg Frey and Udo Schnelle. Wissenschaftliche Untersuchungen zum Neuen Testament 175. Tübingen: Mohr Siebeck, 2004.

Leonhardt-Balzer, Jutta. "Jewish Worship and Universal Identity in Philo of Alexandria." Pages 29–54 in *Jewish Identity in the Greco-Roman World*. Arbeiten zur Geschichte des antiken Judentums und des Urchristentums 71. Edited by Jörg Frey, Daniel Schwartz, and S. Gripentrog. Leiden: Brill, 2007.

Leonhardt-Balzer, Jutta. "Israel and the Community in Paul (Rom 9–11) and the Rule Texts from Qumran." Pages 277–294 in *The Dead Sea Scrolls and Pauline Literature*. Edited by J.-S. Rey. Studies on the Texts of the Desert of Judah 102. Leiden: Brill, 2014.

Levenson, Jon D. *Sinai and Zion: An Entry into the Jewish Bible*. San Francisco: Harper, 1987.

Levenson, Jon D. *The Death and Resurrection of the Beloved Son: The Transformation of Child Sacrifice in Judaism and Christianity*. New Haven: Yale University Press, 1993.

Levenson, Jon D. *Resurrection and the Restoration of Israel: The Ultimate Victory of the God of Life*. New Haven: Yale University Press, 2006.

Levison, John R. *Portraits of Adam in Early Judaism: From Sirach to 2 Baruch*. Journal for the Study of the Pseudepigrapha 1. Sheffield: Sheffield Academic Press, 1988.

Levey, S.H. *The Messiah: An Aramaic Interpretation: the Messianic Exegesis of the Targum*. Cincinnati: Hebrew Union College, 1974.

Levine, Baruch. "Firstborn." Pages 44–46 in *Encyclopaedia Judaica, vol. 7*. Edited by Fred Skolnik and Michael Berenbaum. Detroit: Thomson, 2007.

Lied, Liv Ingeborg. *The Other Lands of Israel: Imaginations of the Land in 2 Baruch*. Supplements to Journal for the Study of Judaism 129. Leiden: Brill, 2008.

Lightfoot, J.B. *Saint Paul's Epistles to the Colossians and to Philemon*. Grand Rapids: Zondervan, 1959.

Lim, Timothy H. *Pesharim*. Companion to the Qumran Scrolls 3. Sheffield: Sheffield Academic Press, 2002.

Lincoln, Andrew T. *Ephesians*. Word Biblical Commentary. Waco: Word, 1990.

Lincoln, Andrew T. "The Stories of Predecessors and Inheritors in Galatians and Romans." Pages 172–203 in *Narrative Dynamics in Paul*. Edited by B.W. Longenecker. Louisville: WJK, 2002.

Lindars, Barnabas. *New Testament Apologetic: The Doctrinal Significance of the Old Testament Quotations*. London: SCM, 1961.

Lindsay, Hugh. *Adoption in the Roman World*. Cambridge: Cambridge University Press, 2009.

Lohse, Eduard. *Colossians and Philemon*. Hermeneia: A Critical and Historical Commentary on the Bible. Minneapolis: Fortress, 1972.

Long, A.A. "Philo on Stoic Physics." Pages 121–140 in *Studies in Philo of Alexandria: Philo of Alexandria and Post-Aristotelian Philosophy*. Edited by Francesca Alesse. Studies in Philo of Alexandria 5. Leiden: Brill, 2008.

Longenecker, Bruce W. *Eschatology and the Covenant: A Comparison of 4 Ezra and Romans 1–11*. Journal for the Study of the New Testament: Supplement Series 57. Sheffield: Sheffield Academic Press, 1991.

Longenecker, Bruce W. *2 Esdras*. Guides to the Apocrypha and Pseudepigrapha 1. Sheffield: Sheffield Academic Press, 1995.

Longenecker, Bruce W. "Sharing in Their Spiritual Blessings?: The Stories of Israel in Galatians and Romans." Pages 58–84 in *Narrative Dynamics in Paul: A Critical Assessment*. Edited by B.W. Longenecker. Louisville: WJK, 2002.

Longenecker, Bruce W. *Remember the Poor: Paul, Poverty, and the Greco-Roman World.* Grand Rapids: Eerdmans, 2010.

Lundbom, Jack R. *Jeremiah: A New Translation with Introduction and Commentary, Vol. 2*. Anchor Bible. New York: Doubleday, 2004.

Lundbom, Jack R. *Deuteronomy: A Commentary*. Grand Rapids: Eerdmans, 2013.

Lust, J. "And I Shall Hang Him on a Lofty Mountain: Ezek 17:22–23 and Messianism in the Septuagint." Pages 231–250 in *IX Congress of the International Organization for Septuagint and Cognate Studies: Cambridge 1995*. Edited by B.A. Taylor; Atlanta: Scholars, 1997.

Luz, Ulrich. *Das Geschichtsverständnis des Paulus*. Beiträge zur evangelischen Theologie 49. München: Kaiser, 1968.

Lyall, Francis. "Legal Metaphors in the Epistles." *Tyndale Bulletin* 32 (1981): 81–95.

MacDowell, D.M. *The Law in Classical Athens*. Ithaca: Cornell University Press, 1978.

Mackie, Scott D. "Confession of the Son of God in Hebrews." *New Testament Studies* 53 (2007): 114–129.

Mackie, Scott D. *Eschatology and Exhortation in the Epistle to the Hebrews in the Epistle to the Hebrews*. Wissenschaftliche Untersuchungen zum Neuen Testament II 223. Tübingen: Mohr Siebeck, 2007.

Mackie, Scott D. "Confession of the Son of God in the Exordium of Hebrews." *Journal for the Study of the New Testament* 30 (2008): 437–453.

Mackie, Scott D. "Ancient Jewish Mystical Motifs in Hebrews' Theology of Access and Entry Exhortations." *New Testament Studies* 58 (2011): 88–104.

Mackie, Scott D. "Heavenly Sanctuary Mysticism in the Epistle to the Hebrews," *Journal of Theological Studies* 62 (2011): 78–117.

Makiello, Phoebe. "Abraham and The Nations in the Works of Philo of Alexandria." Pages 139–161 in *Abraham, the nations, and the Hagarites: Jewish, Christian, and Islamic Perspectives on Kinship with Abraham*. Edited by M. Goodman, G. van Kooten, J. van Ruiten. Themes in Biblical Narrative 13. Leiden: Brill, 2010.

Marschall, J.T. "Prayer of Joseph." Page 362 in *Dictionary of the Bible*, Volume 2. Edited by J.R. Hastings. New York: Scribner, 1888.

Marshall, I. Howard. *The Origins of New Testament Christology*. Leicester: IVP, 1976.

Marshall, I. Howard. *The Gospel of Luke: A Commentary on the Greek Text*. New International Greek Testament Series. Grand Rapids: Eerdmans, 1978.

Martin, Dale B. "The Construction of the Ancient Family: Methodological Considerations." *Journal of Roman Studies* 86 (1996): 40–60.

Martínez, F.G. and Tigchelaar, E.J.C. tr., *The Dead Sea Scrolls Study Edition*. Leiden: Brill, 1999.

Mason, Eric F. *"You are a Priest Forever": Second Temple Jewish Messianism and the Priestly Christology of the Epistle to the Hebrews*. Studies on the Texts of the Desert of Judah 74. Leiden: Brill, 2008.

Mason, Steve. "'For I Am Not Ashamed of the Gospel' (Rom. 1.16): The Gospel and the First Readers of Romans." Pages 254–287 in *Gospel in Rome: Studies on Corinthians, Galatians, and Romans for Richard N. Longenecker*. Edited by L.A. Jervis and P. Richardson. Journal for the Study of the New Testament: Supplement Series 108. Sheffield: JSOT Press, 1995.

Mason, Steve. "Jews, Judaeans, Judaizing, Judaism: Problems of Categorization in Ancient History." *Journal for the Study of Judaism* 38 (2007): 457–512.

Marttila, Marko. *Foreign Nations in the Wisdom of Ben Sira: A Jewish Sage Between Opposition and Assimilation*. Deuteronomical and Cognate Literature Studies 13. Berlin: Walter de Gruyter, 2012.

Mattila, Sharon Lea. "Wisdom, Sense Perception, Nature, and Philo's Gender Gradient." *Harvard Theological Review* 89 (1996): 103–129.

Mattila, Sharon Lea. "Ben Sira and the Stoics: A Reexamination of the Evidence." *Journal of Biblical Literature* 119 (2000): 473–501.

Mayordomo, Moises. *Argumentiert Paulus logisch?: Eine Analyse vor dem Hintergrund antiker Logik*. Wissenschaftliche Untersuchungen zum Neuen Testament 188. Tübingen: Mohr Siebeck, 2005.

McDonough, Sean M. *Christ as Creator: Origins of a New Testament Doctrine*. Oxford: Oxford University Press, 2009.

Meier, John. "Symmetry and Theology in the Old Testament Citations of Heb 1:5–14." *Biblica* 66 (1985): 504–533.

Mendels, Doron. *The Land of Israel as a Political Concept in Hasmonean Literature*. Texts and Studies in Ancient Judaism 15. Tübingen: Mohr Siebeck, 1987.

Mendelsohn, I. "On the Preferential Status of the Eldest Son." *Bulletin of the American Schools of Oriental Research* 156 (1959): 38–40.

Merklein, H. "Zur Tradition und Komposition von Eph 2,14–18." *Biblische Zeitschrift* 17 (1973): 79–102.

Meyers, Carol. *Exodus*. New Cambridge Bible Commentary. Cambridge: Cambridge University Press, 2005.

Michaelis, Wilhelm. "πρωτότοκος." Pages 871–881 in *Theological Dictionary on the New Testament, vol. 6*. Edited by Gerhard Friedrich. Translated by Geoffrey Bromiley. Grand Rapids, Eerdmans, 1968.

Michel, Otto. *Der Brief an die Römer*. Kritisch-exegetischer Kommentar über das Neue Testament 4. Göttingen: Vandenhoeck & Ruprecht, 1957.

Milgrom, Jacob. *Numbers*. The JPS Torah Commentary. Philadelphia: Jewish Publication Society, 1990.

Milgrom, Jacob. *Leviticus 1–16*. Anchor Bible. New York: Doubleday, 1991.

Mitchell, Matthew. "Genre Disputes and Communal Accusatory Laments: Reflections on the Genre of Psalm LXXXIX." *Vetus Testamentum* 55 (2005): 511–527.

Moberly, R.W.L. *At the mountain of God: Story and Theology in Exodus 32–34*. Journal for the Study of the Old Testament: Supplement Series 22. Sheffield: JSOT Press, 1983.

Moffitt, David M. *Atonement and the Logic of Resurrection in the Epistle to the Hebrews*. Supplements to Novum Testamentum 141. Leiden: Brill, 2011.

Montefiore, Hugh W. *A Commentary on the Epistle to the Hebrews*. Black's New Testament Commentaries. London: A&C Clark, 1979.

Moo, Douglas. *The Epistle to the Romans*. New International Commentary on the New Testament. Grand Rapids: Eerdmans, 1996.

Moo, Douglas. *The Letters to the Colossians and to Philemon*. Pillar New Testament Commentary. Grand Rapids: Eerdmans, 2008.

Moo, Jonathan A. *Creation, Nature and Hope in 4 Ezra*. Forschungen zur Religion und Literatur des Alten und Neuen Testaments 237. Göttingen: Vandenhoeck & Ruprecht, 2011.

Moran, William L. "A Kingdom of Priests." Pages 7–20 in *The Bible in Current Catholic Thought*. Edited by John L. McKenzie. New York: Herder & Herder, 1962.

Morray-Jones, Christopher R.A. "The Body Of The Glory: Approaching The New Testament From The Perspective Of Shiur Koma Traditions." Pages 501–610 in *The Mystery of God: Early Jewish Mysticism and the New Testament*. Edited by C. Rowland and C.R.A. Morray-Jones. Compendia Rerum Iudaicarum Ad Novum Testamentum 12. Leiden: Brill, 2009.

Moss, Charlene McAfee. *The Zechariah Tradition and the Gospel of Matthew*. Beihefte zur Zeitschrift für die neutestamentliche Wissenschaft 156. Berlin: Walter de Gruyter, 2008.

Moule, C.F.D. *The Epistles to the Colossians and to Philemon*. Cambridge Greek Testament Commentaries. Cambridge: Cambridge University Press, 1958.

Moule, C.F.D. *The Origin of Christology*. Cambridge: Cambridge University Press, 1977.

Mounce, Robert H. *The Book of Revelation*. New International Commentary on the New Testament. Grand Rapids: Eerdmans, 1998.

Mowinckel, Sigmund. *The Two Sources of the Predeuteronomic Primeval History (JE) in Gen. 1–11*. Oslo: I Kommisjon Hos Jacob Dybwad, 1937.

Moxnes, Halvor. *Theology in Conflict: Studies in Paul's Understanding of God in Romans*. Supplements to Novum Testamentum 53. Leiden: Brill, 1980.

Müller, Ulrich B. "'Sohn Gottes': ein messianischer Hoheitstitel Jesu." *Zeitschrift für die neutestamentliche Wissenschaft* 87 (1996): 1–32.

Murphy, Frederick J. *The Structure of Meaning of Second Baruch*. Atlant: Scholars, 1985.

Murphy, Frederick J. "Sapiential Elements in the Syriac Apocalypse of Baruch," *Jewish Quarterly Review* 76 (1986): 311–327.

Murphy, Frederick J. *Pseudo-Philo: Rewriting the Bible*. Oxford: Oxford University Press, 1993.

Nickelsburg, George W.E. *Jewish Literature between the Bible and the Mishnah: A Historical and Literary Introduction*. Minneapolis: Fortress, 1981.

Nickelsburg, George W.E. *1 Enoch: A Commentary on the Book of 1 Enoch*. Hermeneia. Minneapolis: Fortress Press, 2001.

Niehoff, Maren. *Philo on Jewish Identity and Culture*. Texts and Studies in Ancient Judaism 86. Tübingen: Mohr Siebeck, 2001.

Nohfink, N. "Der junge Jeremia als Propagandist and Poet. Zum Grundstock von Jer 30–31." Pages 351–368 in *Le Livre De Jérémie: Le Prophète et Son Milieu les Oracles et leur Transmission*. Bibliotheca ephemeridum theologicarum lovaniensium 54. Leuven: Leuven University Press, 1981.

Norden, Eduard. *Agnostos Theos: Untersuchungen zur Formengeschichte religiöser Rede*. Leipzig: Teubner, 1913.

Noth, Martin. *Überlieferungsgeschichtliche Studien*. Darmstadt: Wissenschaftliche Buchgesellschaft, 1943.

Noth, Martin. *Exodus: A Commentary*. Translated by John Bowden. Old Testament Library. London: SCM, 1962.

Novak, David. *The Election of Israel: The Idea of the Chosen People*. Cambridge: Cambridge University Press, 1995.

O'Brien, Peter. *Colossians and Philemon*. Word Biblical Commentary. Waco: Word, 1981.

O'Brien, Peter. *The Letter to the Ephesians*. Pillar New Testament Commentary. Grand Rapids: Eerdmans, 1999.

O'Brien, Peter. *The Letter to the Hebrews*. Pillar New Testament Commentary. Grand Rapids: Eerdmans, 2010.

Oakes, Peter. *Reading Romans in Pompeii: Paul's Letter at Ground Level*. London: SPCK, 2009.

Oegema, Gerbern S. *Der Gesalbte und sein Volk: Untersuchungen zum Konzeptualisierungsprozeß der messianischen Erwartungen von den Makkabäern bis Bar Koziba*. Schriften des Institutum Judaicum Delitzschianum 2. Göttingen: Vandenhoeck & Ruprecht, 1994.

Oeming, Manfred. *Das wahre Israel: die "genealogische Vorhalle" 1 Chronik 1–9*. Beiträge zur Wissenschaft vom Alten und Neuen Testament 128. Stuttgart: Kohlhammer, 1990.

Oliver, H.H. "The Lukan Birth Stories and the Purpose of Luke-Acts." *New Testament Studies* 10 (1964): 202–26.

Olyan, Saul M. *Rites and Rank: Hierarchy in Biblical Representations of Cult*. Princeton: Princeton University Press, 2000.

Osborne, Grant R. *Revelation*. Baker Exegetical Commentary on the New Testament. Grand Rapids: Baker, 2002.

Oudshoorn, Jacobine G. *The Relationship between Roman and Local Law in the Babatha and Salome Komaise Archives: General Analysis and Three Case Studies on Law of*

Succession, Guardianship and Marriage. Studies on the Texts of the Desert of Judah 69. Leiden: Brill, 2007.

Overfield, P.D. "Pleroma: A Study in Content and Context." *New Testament Studies* 25 (1979): 384–396.

Parker, Julie Faith. *Valuable and Vulnerable: Children in the Hebrew Bible, Especially Elisha Cycle*. Providence: Brown University Press, 2013.

Parke-Taylor, Geoffrey H. *The Formation of the Book of Jeremiah: Doublets and Recurring Phrases*. Society of Biblical Literature Monograph Series 51. Atlanta: SBL, 2000.

Paulsen, Henning. *Überlieferung und Auslegung in Römer 8*. Wissenschaftliche Monographien zum Alten und Neuen Testament 43. Neukirchen-Vluyn: Neukirchener Verlag, 1974.

Pearce, Sarah. "Jerusalem as 'Mother City' in the Writings of Philo of Alexandria." Pages 19–36 in *Negotiating Diaspora: Jewish Strategies in the Roman Empire*. Edited by John Barclay. Journal for the Study of the Pseudepigrapha: Supplement Series 45. London: T&T Clark, 2004.

Pearce, Sarah. *The Land of the Body: Studies in Philo's Representation of Egypt*. Wissenschaftliche Untersuchungen zum Neuen Testament 208. Tübingen: Mohr Siebeck, 2007.

Peeler, Amy L.B. *You Are My Son: The Family of God in the Epistle to the Hebrews*. London: T&T Clark, 2014.

Peppard, Michael. *The Son of God in the Roman World: Divine Sonship in Its Social and Political Context*. Oxford: Oxford University Press, 2011.

Pesch, Rudolf. *Römerbrief*. Die Neue Echter Bibel; Stuttgart: Echter, 1985.

Philonenko, Marc. *"Joseph et Aséneth": Introduction, texte critique, traduction, et notes*. Studia postbiblica 10. Leiden: Brill, 1968.

Pizzuto, V.A. *A Cosmic Leap of Faith: An Authorial, Structural, and Theological Investigation of the Cosmic Christology in Col 1:15–20*. Contributions to Biblical Exegesis and Theology 41. Leuven: Peeters, 2006.

Pomeroy, Sarah B. "Some Greek Families: Production and Reproduction." Pages 155–163 in *The Jewish Family in Antiquity*. Edited by Shaye J.D. Cohen. Brown Judaic Studies 289. Atlanta: Scholars, 1993.

Pomeroy, Sarah B. *Families in Classical and Hellenistic Greece: Representations and Realities*. Oxford: Clarendon, 1997.

Porter, Stanley E. Καταλλάσσω *in Ancient Greek Literature, with reference to Pauline Writings*. Estudios de filologia neotestamentaria 5. Cordoba: Ediciones el Almendro, 1994.

Pouchelle, Patrick. "Prayers for Being Disciplined: Notes on ΠΑΙΔΕΥΩ and ΠΑΙΔΕΙΑ in the Psalms of Solomon." Pages 115–32 in *The Psalms of Solomon: Language, History, Theology* Edited by Eberhard Bons and Patrick Pouchelle. Early Judaism and its Literature 40. Atlanta: SBL press, 2015.

Pressler, Carolyn. *The View of Women Found in the Deuteronomic Family Laws*. Beihefte zur Zeitschrift für die alttestamentliche Wissenschaft 216. Berlin: Walter de Gruyter, 1993.

Propp, William. "That Bloody Bridegroom (Exodus IV 24–26)." *Vetus Testamentum* 43 (1993): 495–518.

Propp, William. *Exodus 1–18: A New Translation with Introduction and commentary*. Anchor Bible. New York: Doubleday, 1999.

Puech, Émile. "The Collection of Beatitudes in Hebrew and in Greek (4Q525 1–4 and Mt 5, 3–12)." Pages 353–368 in *Early Christianity in Context: Monuments and Documents*. Edited by F. Manns and E. Alliata. Jerusalem: Franciscan Publishing House, 1993.

Reed, Annette Yoshiko. "The Textual Identity, Literary History, and Social Setting of 1 Enoch: Reflections on George Nickelsburg's Commentary on 1 Enoch 1–36; 81–108." *Archive für Religionsgeschichite* 5 (2002): 279–296.

Reeves, John C. "The feast of the First Fruits of Wine and the Ancient Canaanite Calendar." *Vetus Testamentum* 42 (1992): 350–361.

Rendsburg, Gary A. *The Redaction of Genesis*. Winona Lake: Eisenbrauns, 1986.

Reyes, Luis Carlos. "The Structure and Rhetoric of Colossians 1:15–20." *Filologia Neotestamentaria* 7 (1999): 139–154.

Rhee, Victor S. "The Role of Chiasm for Understanding Christology in Hebrews 1:1–14." *Journal of Biblical Literature* 131 (2012): 341–362.

Robinson, Bernard. "Zipporah to the Rescue: A Contextual Study of Exodus IV 24–26." *Vetus Testamentum* 36 (1986): 447–461.

Roloff, J. "ἐκκλησία." Pages 410–415 in *Exegetical Dictionary of the New Testament Volume 1*. Edited by Horst Balz and Gerhard Schneider. Grand Rapids: Eerdmans, 1990.

Rose, Christian. "Verheißung und Erfülling: Zum Verständnis von ἐπαγγελία im Hebräerbrief." *Biblische Zeitschrift* 33 (1989): 60–80.

Rubin, Nissan. *Time and Life Cycle in Talmud and Midrash: Socio-Anthropological Perspectives*. Boston: Academic Studies Press, 2008.

Runia, David T. "The Structure of Philo's Allegorical Treatises: A Review of Two Recent Studies and Some Additional Comments." *Vigiliae Christianae* 38 (1984): 209–256.

Runia, David T. *Philo of Alexandria and the Timaeus of Plato*. Philosophia Antiqua. Leiden: Brill, 1986.

Russell, D.S. Divine Disclosure: An Introduction to Jewish Apocalyptic. Minneapolis: Fortress, 1992.

Salevao, Iutisone. *Legitimation in the Letter to the Hebrews: The Construction and Maintenance of a Symbolic Universe*. Journal for the Study of the New Testament: Supplement Series 219. Sheffield: Sheffield University Press, 2002.

Saller, Richard P. *Patriarchy, Property and death in the Roman Family*. Cambridge Studies in Population, Economy and Society in Past Time. Cambridge: Cambridge University Press, 1994.

Saller, R.P. and Shaw, B.D. "Tombstones and Roman Family relations in the Principate: Civilians, Soldiers and Slaves." *Journal of Roman Studies* 74 (1984): 124–156.

Sandmel, Samuel. *Philo's Place in Judaism: A Study of Conception of Abraham in Jewish Literature*. New York: KTAV, 1971.

Sänger, Erich. "Bekehrung und Exodus: Zum jüdischen Traditionshintergrund von 'Joseph und Aseneth'." *Journal for the Study of Judaism* 10 (1979): 11–36.

Sappington, Thomas. *Revelation and Redemption at Colossae*. Journal for the Study of the New Testament: Supplement Series 53. Sheffield: JSOT Press, 1991.

Sarna, Nahum. *Exodus: The Traditional Hebrew Text with the New JPS Translation*. The JPS Torah Commentary. Philadelphia: JPS, 1991.

Sarna, Nahum. "Psalm 89: A Study in Inner Biblical Exegesis." Pages 377–394 in *Studies in Biblical Interpretation*. New York: JPS, 2000.

Satake, Akira. *Die Gemeindeordnung in der Johannesapokalypse*. Wissenschaftliche Monographien zum Alten und Neuen Testament 21. Neukirchen-Vluyn: Neukirchener Verlag, 1966.

Schäfer, Klaus. *Gemeinde als 'Bruderschaft,': ein Beitrag zum Kirchenverständnis des Paulus*. Europäische Hochschulschriften 23. Frankfurt am Main: Peter Lang, 1989.

Schäfer, Peter. *The Origins of Jewish Mysticism*. Tübingen: Mohr Siebeck, 2009.

Schaller, Berndt. "Philon von Alexandreia und das 'Heilige Land'." Pages 172–187 in *Das Land Israel in biblischer Zeit: Jerusalem-Symposium 1981 der Hebräischen Universität und der Georg-August-Universität*. Göttinger Theologische Arbeiten 25. Edited by Georg Strecker. Göttingen: Vandenhoeck & Ruprecht, 1983.

Schaper, Joachim. *Eschatology in the Greek Psalter*. Wissenschaftliche Untersuchungen zum Neuen Testament II 76. Tübingen: Mohr Siebeck, 1995.

Schenker, Adrian. "The Inheritance Contract in Greco-Egyptian Law and διαθήκη in the Septuagint." *Journal of Biblical Text Research* 7 (2000): 36–49.

Schlier, Heinrich. *Der Römerbrief*. Herders theologische Kommentar zum Neuen Testament 6. Freiburg: Herder, 1977.

Schmidt, Hans Wilhelm. *Der Brief des Paulus an die Römer*. Theologischer Handkommentar zum Neuen Testament 6. Berlin: Evangelische Verlagsanstalt Berlin, 1972.

Schmitz, Winfried. *Haus und Familie im antiken Griechenland*. Enzyklopädie der griechisch-römischen Antike 1. München: Oldenbourg, 2007.

Schofield, Alison. "Exile." Pages 615–616 in *The Eerdmans Dictionary of Early Judaism*. Edited by J.J. Collins and Daniel C. Harlow. Grand Rapids: Eerdmans, 2010.

Scholer, John. *Proleptic Priests: Priesthood in the Epistle to the Hebrews*. Journal for the Study of the New Testament: Supplement Series 49. Sheffield: JSOT Press, 1991.

Schürmann, Heinz. *Das Lukasevangelium: Erster Teil.* Herders Theologischer Kommentar zum Neuen Testament. Freiburg: Herder, 1990.

Schwartz, Daniel R. "'Judeans' or 'Jew'? How Should We Translate Ioudaios in Josephus?" Pages 3–28 in *Jewish Identity in the Greco-Roman World.* Edited by Jörg Frey, et al. Arbeiten zur Geschichte des antiken Judentums und des Urchristentums 71. Leiden: Brill, 2007.

Schwartz, Seth. *Were the Jews a Mediterranean Society?: Reciprocity and Solidarity in Ancient Judaism.* Princeton: Princeton University Press, 2010.

Schweizer, Eduard. *Colossians.* Translated by Andrew Chester. London: SPCK, 1982.

Scott, James M. *Adoption as Sons of God: An Exegetical Investigation into the Background of YIOTHESIA in the Pauline Corpus.* Wissenschaftliche Untersuchungen zum Neuen Testament II 48. Tübingen: Mohr Siebeck, 1992.

Scott, James M. "Covenant." Pages 491–494 in *The Eerdmans Dictionary of Early Judaism.* Edited by John J. Collins and Daniel C. Harlow. Grand Rapids: Eerdmans, 2010.

Scott, R.B.Y. "A Kingdom of Priests (Exodus xix 6)." *Old Testament Studies* 8 (1950): 213–219.

Sechrest, Love L. *A Former Jew: Paul and the Dialectics of Race.* Library of New Testament Studies 410. London: T&T Clark, 2009.

Segal, Michael. *The Book of Jubilees: Rewritten Bible, Redaction, Ideology and Theology.* Supplements to Journal for the Study of Judaism 117. Leiden: Brill, 2007.

Seitz, Gottfried. *Redaktionsgeschichtliche Studien zum Deuteronomium.* Beiträge zur Wissenschaft vom Alten und Neuen Testament 93. Stuttgart: Kohlhammer, 1971.

Severino, Bussino. *The Greek Additions in the Book of Ben Sira.* Translated by Michael Tait. Analecta Biblica 203. Rome: Gregorian & Biblical, 2013.

Shillington, V. George. *An Introduction to the Study of Luke-Acts.* London: T&T Clark, 2006.

Siker, Jeffrey S. *Disinheriting the Jews: Abraham in Early Christian Controversy.* Louisville: WJK, 1991.

Silva, Moisés. *Biblical Words and their Meaning: An Introduction to Lexical Semantics.* Grand Rapids: Zondervan, 1983.

Skehan, P. and Di Lella, A. *The Wisdom of Ben Sira.* Anchor Bible. New York: Doubleday, 1987.

Skinner, John. *A Critical and Exegetical Commentary on Genesis.* International Critical Commentary. New York: Charles Scribner's Sons, 1910.

Slater, Thomas B. *Christ and Community: A Socio-Historical Study of the Christology of Revelation.* Journal for the Study of the New Testament: Supplement Series 178. Sheffield: Sheffield Academic Press, 1999.

Smith, Ian K. *Heavenly Perspective: A Study of the Apostle Paul's Response to a Jewish Mystical Movement at Colossae.* Library of New Testament Studies 326. London: T&T Clark, 2006.

Smith, Jonathan Z. "The Prayer of Joseph." Pages 253–294 in *Religions in Antiquity: Essays in Memory of Erwin Ramsdell Goodenough.* Edited by Jacob Neusner. Studies in the History of Religions 14. Leiden: Brill, 1970.

Son, Kiwoong. *Zion Symbolism in Hebrews: Hebrews 12:18–24 as a Hermeneutical Key to the Epistle*. Paternoster Biblical Monograph. Milton Keynes: Paternoster, 2005.

Sprinkle, Joe M. *'The Book of Covenant': A Literary Approach*. Journal for the Study of the Old Testament: Supplement Series 174. Sheffield: JSOT Press, 1994.

Stein, Edmund. "Zur apokryphen Schrift 'Gebet Josephs.'" *Monatsschrift für Geschichte und Wissenschaft des Judentums* 81 (1937): 280–286.

Steins, Georg. "Priesterherrschaft, Volk von Priestern oder was sonst? Zur Interpretation von Ex 19, 6." *Biblische Zeitschrift* 49 (2001): 20–36.

Stendahl, Krister. "The Apostle Paul and the Introspective Conscience of the West." Pages 78–96 in *Paul Among Jews and Gentiles*. Philadelphia: Fortress, 1976.

Sterling, Gregory. "Ontology versus Eschatology: Tensions between the Author and Community in Hebrews." *The Studia Philonica Annual* 13 (2001): 190–211.

Stettler, Christian. *Der Kolosserhymnus: Untersuchungen zu Form, traditionsgeschichtlichem Hintergrund und Aussage von Kol 1,15–20*. Wissenschaftliche Untersuchungen zum Neuen Testament II 131. Tübingen: Mohr Siebeck, 2000.

Still, Todd D. "Eschatology in Colossians: How Realized Is It?" *NTS* 50 (2004): 125–138.

Stone, M.E. "Apocalyptic Literature." Pages 383–394 in *Jewish Writings of the Second Temple Period: Apocrypha, Pseudepigrapha, Qumran, Sectarian Writings, Philo, Josephus.* Edited by M.E. Stone. Philadelphia: Fortress, 1984.

Stone, M.E. *Fourth Ezra: A Commentary on the Book of Fourth Ezra.* Hermeneia: A Critical and Historical Commentary on the Bible. Minneapolis: Fortress, 1990.

Stone, Michael and Henze, Matthias. *4 Ezra and 2 Baruch: Translations, Introductions, and Notes*. Minneapolis: Fortress, 2013.

Strecker, Georg. *Theology of the New Testament*. Edited by Friedrich W. Horn. Translated by M. Eugene Boring. Louisville: WJK, 2000.

Streeter, B.H. *The Four Gospels: A Study of Origin, The Manuscript Tradition, Sources, Authorship & Dates*. London: MacMillan, 1924.

Strobel, August. *Der Brief an die Hebräer*. Das Neue Testament Deutsch 9/2. Vandenhoeck & Ruprecht: Göttingen, 1991.

Strugnell, John. "Notes en marge du volume V des Discoveries in the Judaean Desert of Jordan." *Revue de Qumran* (1969–71): 163–276.

Stuckenbruck, Loren T. *Angel Veneration and Christology: A Study in Early Judaism and in the Christology of the Apocalypse of John*. Wissenschaftliche Untersuchungen zum Neuen Testament II 70. Tübingen: Mohr Siebeck, 1995.

Stuckenbruck, Loren T. "Messianic Ideas in the Apocalyptic and Related Literature of Early Judaism." Pages 90–113 in *The Messiahs in the Old and New Testaments.* Edited by Stanley E. Porter. Grand Rapids: Eerdmans, 2007.

Stuhlmacher, Peter. *Biblische Theologie des Neuen Testament. Band 2*. Göttingen: Vandenhoeck & Ruprecht, 1997.

Stuhlmacher, Peter. *Der Brief an die Römer*. Das Neue Testament Deutsch 6. Göttingen: Vandenhoeck & Ruprecht 1998.

Sutton, Dana F. "The Theatrical Families of Athens." *American Journal of Philology* 108 (1987): 9–26.

Syren, Roger. *The Forsaken Firstborn: A Study of a Recurrent Motif in the Patriarchal Narratives*. Journal for the Study of the Old Testament: Supplement Series 133. Sheffield: Sheffield Academic Press, 1992.

Syren, Roger. "Ishmael and Esau in the Book of Jubilees and Targum Pseudo-Jonathan." Pages 310–315 in *The Aramaic Bible: Targums in their Historical Context*. Edited by D.R.G. Beattie and M.J. McNamara. Journal for the Study of the Old Testament: Supplement Series 166. Sheffield: Sheffield Academic Press, 1994.

Tacoma, L.E. *Fragile Hierarchies: The Urban Elites of Third Century Roman Egypt*. Supplements to Mnemosyne 271. Leiden: Brill, 2006.

Tajfel, Henri. "Social Categorization, Social Identity and Social Comparison." Pages 61–76 in *Differentiation between Social Groups: Studies in the Social Psychology of Intergroup Relations*. Edited by Henri Tajfel. London: Academic, 1978.

Talbert, Charles H. *Ephesians and Colossians*. Paideia Commentaries on the New Testament. Grand Rapids: Baker, 2007.

Tate, M. *Psalms 51–100*. Word Biblical Commentary. Waco: Word, 1991.

Tatum, W. Barnes. "The Epoch of Israel: Luke I–II and the Theological Plan of Luke-Acts." *New Testament Studies* 13 (1967): 184–95.

Terrien, Samuel L. *The Psalms: Strophic Structure and Theological Commentary*. Eerdmans Critical Commentary Series. Grand Rapids: Eerdmans, 2003.

Theobald, Michael. *Römerbrief: Kapitel 1–11*. Stuttgarter Kleiner Kommentar Neues Testament 6/1. Stuttgart: Katholisches Bibelwerk, 1992.

Thielman, Frank. "The Story of Israel and the Theology of Romans 5–8." Pages 169–195 in *Pauline Theology Volume III: Romans*. Edited by David M. Hay and E. Elizabeth Johnson. Minneapolis: Fortress, 1995.

Thiessen, Matthew. "Hebrews and the End of the Exodus." *Novum Testamentum* 49 (2007): 353–369.

Thiessen, Matthew. "Hebrews 12.5–13, the Wilderness Period, and Israel's Discipline." *New Testament Studies* 55 (2009): 366379.

Thiessen, Matthew. *Contesting Conversion: Genealogy, Circumcision, and Identity in Ancient Judaism and Christianity*. Oxford: Oxford University, 2011.

Thompson, M.M. *The Promise of the Father: Jesus and God in the New Testament*. Louisville: WJK, 2000.

Thompson, M.M. *Colossians & Philemon*. The Two Horizons New Testament Commentary. Grand Rapids: Eerdmans, 2005.

Thompson, James W. *The Beginning of Christian Philosophy: The Epistle to the Hebrews*. Washington, DC: The Catholic Biblical Association of America, 1982.

Thompson, Leonard K. *The Book of Revelation: Apocalypse and Empire*. Oxford: Oxford University Press, 1990.

Thüsing, Wilhelm. *Per Christum in Deum: Studien zum Verhältnis von Christozentrik und Theozentrik in den paulinischen Hauptbriefen*. Neutestamentliche Abhandlungen 1. Münster: Aschendorff, 1965.

Tobin, Thomas. "Logos." Pages 350–351 in *Anchor Bible Dictionary. Volume 4*. New York: Doubleday, 1991.

Tobin, Thomas. *Paul's Rhetoric in the Contexts: The Argument of Romans*. Grand Rapids: Baker, 2005.

Trebilco, Paul. *Self-Designations and Group Identity in the New Testament*. Cambridge: Cambridge University Press, 2012.

Tromp, Johannes. *The Assumption of Moses: A Critical Edition with Commentary*. Leiden: Brill, 1993.

Tzoref, S. "Covenantal Election in 4Q252 and Jubilees' Heavenly Tablets." *Dead Sea Discoveries* 18 (2011): 74–89.

Van der Horst, Pieter W. *Philo's Flaccus: The First Pogrom*. Philo of Alexandria Commentary Series. Leiden: Brill, 2003.

Van Kooten, George H. *Cosmic Christology in Paul and the Pauline School: Colossians and Ephesians in the Context of Graeco-Roman Cosmology, with a New Synopsis of the Greek Texts*. Wissenschaftliche Untersuchungen zum Neuen Testament II 171. Tübingen: Mohr Siebeck, 2003.

Van Ruiten, J.T.A.G.M. *Primaeval History Interpreted: The Rewriting of Genesis 1–11 in the Book of Jubilees*. Supplements to Journal for the Study of Judaism 66. Leiden: Brill, 2000.

Van Seters, John. *Prologue to History: The Yahwist as Historian in Genesis*. Louisville: WJK, 1992.

VanderKam, James. "The Origins and Purposes of the Book of Jubilees. Pages 3–24 in *Studies in the Book of Jubilees*. Edited by M. Albani, et al. Texts and Studies in Ancient Judaism 65. Tübingen: Mohr Siebeck, 1997.

VanderKam, James. *The Book of Jubilees*. Guides to the Apocrypha and Pseudepigrapha 9. Sheffield: Sheffield Academic Press, 2001.

Vanhoye, Albert. "L'οἰκουμένη dans l'épître aux Hébreux," *Biblica* 45 (1964): 248–253

Vanni, Ugo. "Liturgical Dialogue as a Literary Form in the Book of Revelation." *New Testament Studies* 37 (1991): 348–372.

Veijola, Timo. *Verheißung in der Krise: Studien zur Literatur und Theologie der Exilszeit anhand des 89. Psalms*. Annales Academiae scientiarum fennicae B 220. Helsinki: Suomalainen Tiedeakatemia, 1982.

Veijola, Timo. *Deuteronomium: Kapitel 1,1–16,17*. Das Alte Testament Deutsch 8/1. Göttingen: Vandenhoeck & Ruprecht, 2004.

Vellanickal, Matthew. *The Divine Sonship of Christians in the Johannine Writings.* Analecta Biblica. Rome: Pontifical Biblical Institute, 1977.

Vermes, Geza. "Redemption and Genesis xxii." Pages 193–227 in *Scripture and Tradition in Judaism.* Studia post biblica 4. Leiden: Brill, 1961.

Vermes, Geza. "New Light on the Sacrifice of Isaac from 4Q225." *Journal of Jewish Studies* 30 (1979): 140–146.

Von Allmen, Daniel. *La famille de Dieu: la symbolique familiale dans le paulinisme.* Orbis biblicus et orientalis. Göttingen: Vandenhoeck & Ruprecht, 1981.

Von der Osten-Sacken, P. *Römer 8 als Beispiel paulinischer Soteriologie.* Forschungen zur Religion und Literatur des Alten und Neuen Testaments 112. Göttingen: Vandenhoeck & Ruprecht, 1975.

Von Rad, Gerhard. *Genesis: A Commentary.* Translated by John H. Marks. Old Testament Library. London: SCM, 1961.

Vrolijk, Paul. *Jacob's Wealth: An Examination into the Nature and Role of Material Possession in the Jacob-Cycle.* Supplements to Vetus Testamentum 146. Leiden: Brill, 2011.

Wagner, Ross. "The Christ, Servant of Jew and Gentile: A Fresh Approach to Romans 15:8–9." *Journal of Biblical Literature* 116 (1997): 473–485.

Walker Jr., William O. "Romans 8:29–30 as a Non-Pauline Interpolation." *Journal for the Study of Paul and His Letters* 2 (2012): 27–40.

Wallace, Daniel. *Greek Grammar beyond the Basics: An Exegetical Syntax of the New Testament.* Grand Rapids: Zondervan, 1997.

Wallace, David R. *Election of the Lesser Son: Paul's Lament-Midrash in Romans 9–11.* Minneapolis: Fortress, 2014.

Walton, Kevin. *Thou Traveller Unknown: The Presence and Absence of God in the Jacob Narrative.* Paternoster Biblical Monograph. Carlisle: Paternoster, 2003.

Ward, James. "The Literary Form and Liturgical Background of Psalm LXXXIX." *Vetus Testamentum* 11 (1961): 321–339.

Watson, Francis. *Paul, Judaism and the Gentiles: Beyond the New Perspective.* Grand Rapids: Eerdmans, 2007.

Watson, Paul. "A Note on the 'Double Portion' of Deuteronomy 21:17 and 2 Kings 2:9." *Restoration Quarterly* 9 (1965): 70–75.

Weinfeld, Moshe. *The Promise of the Land: The Inheritance of the Land of Canaan by the Israelites.* Taubman Lectures in Jewish Studies. Berkeley: University of California Press, 1993.

Weisberg, Dvora E. *Levirate Marriage and the Family in Ancient Judaism.* Waltham: Brandeis University Press, 2009.

Weiss, Hans-Friedrich. *Der Brief an die Hebräer.* Kritisch-exegetischer Kommentar über das Neue Testament 13. Göttingen: Vandenhoeck & Ruprecht, 1991.

Wellhausen, Julius. *Prolegomena to the History of Ancient Israel.* Edinburgh: Adam and Charles Black, 1885.

Wendel, Susan. *Scriptural Interpretation and Community Self-Definition in Luke-Acts and the Writings of Justin Martyr.* Supplements to Novum Testamentum 139. Leiden: Brill, 2011.

Wenham, Gordon J. *Genesis 1–15.* Word Biblical Commentary. Waco: Word, 1987.

Westbrook, Raymond. *Property and the Family in Biblical Law.* Journal for the Study of the Old Testament: Supplement Series 113. Sheffield: Sheffield Academic, 1991.

Westcott, B.F. *The Epistle to the Hebrews: The Greek Text with Notes and Essays.* Grand Rapids: Eerdmans, 1950.

Westerholm, Stephen. "Paul's Anthropological 'Pessimism' in Its Jewish Context." Pages 71–98 in *Divine and Human Agency in Paul and His Cultural Environment.* Edited by John M.G. Barclay and Simon Gathercole. Library of New Testament Studies 335. London: T&T Clark, 2006.

Westerholm, Stephen. *Justification Reconsidered: Rethinking a Pauline Theme.* Grand Rapids: Eerdmans, 2013.

Westermann, Claus. *Genesis: Kapitel 1–11.* Biblischer Kommentar, Altes Testament 1/1. Neukrichen-Vluyn: Neukirchener Verlag, 1974.

Westermann, Claus. *Die Verheißungen an die Vater: Studien zur Vätergeschichte.* Forschungen zur Religion und Literatur des Alten und Neuen Testaments 116. Göttingen: Vandenhoeck & Ruprecht, 1976.

White, Joel. *Die Erstlingsgabe im Neuen Testament.* Texte und Arbeiten zum neutestamentlichen Zeitalter 45. Tübingen: Francke, 2007.

Wider, David. *Theozentrik und Bekenntnis: Untersuchungen zur Theologie des Redens Gottes im Hebräerbrief.* Beihefte zur Zeitschrift für die neutestamentliche Wissenschaft 87. Berlin: Walter de Gruyter, 1997.

Wiefel, Wolfgang. "The Jewish Community in Ancient Rome and the Origins of Roman Christianity." Pages 85–101 in *The Romans Debate.* Edited by K.P. Donfried. Peabody: Hendrickson, 1991.

Wilckens, Ulrich. *Der Brief an die Römer. Band 2.* Evangelisch-Katholischer Kommentar zum Neuen Testament 6/2. Zürich: Benziger, 1980.

Wilhelmi, G. "Der Versöhner-Hymnus in Eph. 2:14ff." *Zeitschrift für die neutestamentliche Wissenschaft* 78 (1987): 145–152.

Williamson, H.G.M. *Israel in the Books of Chronicles.* Cambridge: University Press, 1977.

Williamson, Ronald. *Philo and the Epistle to the Hebrews.* Arbeiten zur Literatur und Geschichte des hellenistchen Judentums 4. Leiden: Brill, 1970.

Williamson, Ronald. *Jews in the Hellenistic World: Philo.* Cambridge: Cambridge University Press, 1989.

Wilson, Gerald. "The Use of Royal Psalms At the 'Seams' of the Hebrew Psalter." *Journal for the Study of the Old Testament* 11 (1986): 85–94.

Wilson, Stephen G. *The Gentiles and the Gentile Mission in Luke-Acts*. Society of the New Testament Studies Monograph Series 23. Cambridge: Cambridge University Press, 1973.

Wilson, Walter T. *The Hope of Glory: Education and Exhortation in the Epistle to the Colossians*. Supplements to Novum Testamentum 88. Leiden: Brill, 1997.

Wilson, Walter T. *On Virtues: Introduction, Translation and Commentary*. Philo of Alexandria Commentary Series. Leiden: Brill, 2011.

Windisch, Hans. "Die Göttliche Weisheit der Juden und die paulinische Christologie." Pages 220–234 in *Neutestamentliche Studie: Georg Heinrici zu seinem 70. Geburtstag dargebracht*. Edited by Hans Windisch. Leipzig: Heinrichs, 1914.

Winston, David. *The Wisdom of Solomon: A New Translation with Introduction and Commentary*. Anchor Bible. New York: Doubleday, 1979.

Witherington III, Ben. *The Lettres to Philemon, the Colossians, and the Ephesians: A Socio-Rhetorical Commentary on the Captivity Epistles*. Grand Rapids: Eerdmans, 2007.

Wolff, Christian. *Der zweite Brief des Paulus an die Korinther*. Theologisches Handkommentar zum Neuen Testament 8. Berlin: Evangelische Verlagsanstalt, 1989.

Wright, N.T. *Colossians & Philemon*. Tyndale New Testament Commentaries. Grand Rapids: Eerdmans, 1986.

Wright, N.T. *The Climax of the Covenant: Christ and the Law in Pauline Theology*. Minneapolis: Fortress, 1993.

Wright, N.T. "Romans and the Theology of Paul." Pages 30–67 in *Pauline Theology, Vol. 3*. Edited by D.M. Hay and E.E. Johnson. Minneapolis: Fortress, 1995.

Wright, N.T. *Paul and the Faithfulness of God*. London: SPCK, 2014.

Wyschograd, Michael. *The Body of Faith: Judaism as Corporeal Election*. New York: Seabury, 1983.

Xeravits, Geza. *King, Priest, Prophet: Positive Eschatological Protagonists of the Qumran Library*. Studies on the Texts of the Desert of Judah 47. Leiden: Brill, 2002.

Yamauchi, Edwin M. *Pre-Christian Gnosticism: A Survey of the Proposed Evidences*. London: Tyndale, 1973.

Zeilinger, Franz. *Der Erstgeborene der Schöpfung: Untersuchungen zur Formalstruktur und Theologie des Kolosserbriefes*. Wien: Herder, 1974.

Zimmerli, Walter. "Erstgeborenene und Leviten: Ein Beitrag zur exilisch-nachexilischen Theologie." Pages 459–469 in *Near Eastern Studies in Honor of W.F. Albright*. Edited by H. Goedicke. Baltimore: Johns Hopkins University Press, 1971.

Index of Biblical Texts

Index of Modern Authors

Index of Ancient Sources

Deuterocanonical Works and Septuagint

Dead Sea Scrolls and Related Texts

Ancient Jewish Writers

Mishnah, Talmud and Related Literature

Papyri

Printed in the United States
By Bookmasters